America's Greatest Game

Foreword by Pete Rozelle

Introduction by John Wiebusch

Text by:

Ray Didinger

Mickey Herskowitz

Kevin Lamb

Bill McGrane

Phil Musick

Shelby Strother

SIMON AND SCHUSTER

New York

London

Toronto

Sydney

Tokyo

Singapore

by Merv Corning

The Super Bowl: *Cele*

ating a Quarter-Century of

XXV

SIMON AND SCHUSTER
Simon & Schuster Building
Rockefeller Center
1230 Avenue of the Americas
New York, New York 10020

Copyright © 1990 by National Football League Properties, Inc., New York and Los Angeles

Vice President and Creative Director David Boss • *General Manager* Bill Barron • *Editor-in-Chief* John Wiebusch • *Art Director* Cliff Wynne • *Managing Editor* Chuck Garrity, Sr. • *Associate Editors* Jane Alexander, Phil Barber, John Fawaz, Jim Gigliotti, Jim Perry • *Director of Manufacturing* Dick Falk • *Manager Print Services* Tina Dahl • *Associate Art Director* Barbara Hager • *Typesetting* Brian Davids, Sandy Gordon, Rick Jermain, Rick Wadholm.

Text printed by Quad/Graphics, Pewaukee, WI.

Jacket printed by Ringier America, Olathe, KS.
Binding by Ringier America, New Berlin, WI.

Film preparation by American Color, Santa Ana, CA.

Paper by Champion International, Stamford, CT. Text stock, Courtland ®
Gloss 80-pound; jacket stock, Kromekote ® 2000 1S Cover /.006.

1   3   5   7   9   10   8   6   4   2

Library of Congress Cataloguing in Publication Data

ISBN: 0-671-72798-2

Contents

Super Bowl XXV theme art on pages 2-3 by Merv Corning

Foreword

Truly the Biggest Game

By Pete Rozelle

A few years ago, I was having dinner with Bill Granholm, a wonderful man who worked with me for decades—first with the Los Angeles Rams and then in the NFL offices. The owners had just had a rather stormy session about the future site of some Super Bowl or other. It seemed as if everything connected with the game had assumed monumental proportions.

I remember Granny picking up his cocktail, shaking his head, and saying, "Do you believe this? Do you believe this has gotten so big?"

I said "No" then and I'll say it again now. Except today it's even bigger. The stakes are even higher. For Super Bowl XXV, ABC is getting $850,000 for one 30-second commercial! I don't care what kind of financial numbers you're used to, that's a staggering amount.

CBS and NBC both televised the first AFL-NFL World Championship Game (it wasn't called the Super Bowl then). CBS charged $85,000 a *minute* for commercials, and NBC $75,000.

Assuming ABC sells out all commercial spots for XXV—which seems like a safe assumption because every game so far has—the total likely will be somewhere around $43 million.

The reason it sells out is that there is no game, no event, no show that annually reaches a larger audience than the Super Bowl. Maybe three out of four Americans, plus millions more elsewhere, are watching.

No, I never thought it would get this big. I never thought it *could* get this big, mostly because...well, I guess because it never occurred to us back in the 1960s.

Of course, we knew that a matchup of the champions of the National Football League and the American Football League would be a big game. We knew—or I guess we *hoped*—that the public would be eager to see such a square-off.

But then we got our comeuppance in the first Super Bowl when there were roughly 32,000 empty seats in the Los Angeles Coliseum. We're talking about almost 35 percent of the seats in a 94,000-seat stadium! Nine years before, in 1958, when I was general manager of the Los Angeles Rams, we averaged nearly 85,000 per game and had crowds of more than 100,000 for our games against the Baltimore Colts and Chicago Bears. (The Coliseum had a seating capacity of 102,000 in the 1950s.)

Fortunately, those were the last empty seats

we have had for a Super Bowl. It's the most coveted ticket for any event in America.

After that first game, I remember we had a meeting to discuss the possible reasons why we hadn't sold out. A lot of people thought it was the price of the tickets. We had the tickets scaled at $12, $10, and $6. It's all relative, I know, but for the last five years, most game tickets have been priced at $100 or more. Some people resell them for 10, 20, even 30 times face value...and they get it.

So we got a dose of reality in that first game. We worked hard—we had tried everything—to sell seats. It was difficult to explain.

Two weeks before game I, both the AFL Championship Game in Buffalo and the NFL Championship Game in Dallas had sold out. Both the visiting teams—the Kansas City Chiefs of the AFL and the Green Bay Packers of the NFL—had won that day, setting up a game between the best teams from each league.

We couldn't have asked for a more attractive matchup, or more superstars on two teams, or two more colorful coaches—Hank Stram, the Chiefs' bantam rooster, and Vince Lombardi, the Packers' strongman.

In all my 29 years as Commissioner, except for George Halas, I was never closer to a head coach than I was to Vince Lombardi. I know it's a cliche to say that someone is a real man, but it must have been invented for Vince Lombardi. He was so strong, so powerful, so intelligent.

After the Packers outlasted the Cowboys 34-27 in the NFL Championship Game on New Year's Day two weeks before Super Bowl I, I gave Vince a call in Green Bay. He was adamant about wanting to stay in Green Bay, to practice there until the Friday or Saturday before the Super Bowl, and then fly out. I told him he couldn't do that, that he *had* to spend the seven days or so before the game in southern California. I thought it would help sell tickets.

The Packers spent the six days before the game in Santa Barbara, and I have to say that I never saw Vince Lombardi more anxious than he was that week. The man had won four NFL championships to that point, his teams had played in five title games and countless other big games...and I *know* he never felt the pressure like that.

Vince knew that not only did his own ownership expect him to win, but there were 13 other NFL owners who had the same kind of emotional investment.

I was pleased that it was a close game for more than a half. I think we all feared that it might be a one-sided blowout. I was very happy with the 35-10 result.

I honestly can say that there are only three Super Bowls in which I was rooting—silently, of course—for a team. I wanted the Packers to win in both Super Bowls I and II because my NFL loyalties still were strong...and I wanted the Steelers to win in Super Bowl IX for the sake of the finest, most decent man I ever knew apart from my own father, Art Rooney.

Super Bowl II between the Packers and the Oakland Raiders was played in Miami (we played three games there in four years—II, III, and V), and Vince told me before the game that it would be his last as Packers' head coach.

I guess the reality of that decision never sunk in with me because I remember being just as surprised—maybe disappointed—as everyone else when he announced his decision a few weeks after the game.

The biggest stories before Super Bowl II were the rumors that he was going to quit. He never told the team directly, although he came close to breaking down in one pregame meeting, so I think they suspected it very strongly.

Like the first game, it was fairly close for a half, but the Packers came on strong in the third quarter just as they had in January, 1967, and won 33-14.

Then came the one that I like to call the Magic Game. Game III between the Jets and the Colts not only put the Super Bowl on the map, it made it a permanent part of the American sports and entertainment consciousness.

The funny thing was that even though we had sold out game II in Miami fairly easily, we didn't sell out game III until just a few minutes before game time.

Of course, that was the game when Joe Namath went to a dinner a few days before, and, in a speech, "guaranteed" a victory over the heavily favored Baltimore team.

Even for those radical days, Joe was a pretty radical guy—one of the first players to wear his hair long, the first to wear white shoes. He was flamboyant, anti-establishment, a character.

I really did not care who won the game, but I was hoping against hope that we would have a close game. The Packers had won the first games by 25 and 19 points, and the Colts were favored by 18.

After Namath and the Jets prevailed 16-7, the NFL owners were very upset, of course. It was crushing for the old-line club people. But I was secretly pleased because I realized that this shocking turn of events was going to do nothing but help pro football.

It didn't take a brain surgeon to figure out that the Jets' victory was going to mushroom interest in our game. At that point, the merger that would be implemented after the next season was all set. By winning, the Jets proved the AFL teams belonged. Of course, as you might suspect, I never attempted to sell that logic to Carroll Rosenbloom, then the Colts' owner!

Super Bowl IV in January, 1970, at New Orleans, was the last game between the two leagues. In the 1970 season, the merger would be officially completed with realignment into two conferences.

The Vikings looked like the best team in football, but a lot of insiders said not to underestimate Hank Stram's Chiefs, who were big, fast, and talented. I thought Minnesota would win, but again, all I really wanted was a close game. Shows you what I know. It wasn't really a close game—and it was the Chiefs who won, 23-7.

For the first two years, the game officially had that unwieldly handle, the AFL-NFL World Championship Game. That was my idea. I guess coming up with catchy names wasn't something I was very good at.

Some of the press were calling it the Super Bowl from the start, but I never liked the name. To me, "super" was a corny cliche word that we used during my school days at Compton High in California in the 1940s.

The actual source of "Super" in the Super Bowl name had originated a few years before with the daughter of Lamar Hunt, the Chiefs owner. At that time, a popular, faddish children's toy was something called a "Super Ball," which bounced dramatically higher than a regular rubber ball. Lamar's daughter had one of

those balls, and he liked the name—the twist of "Super Ball" to "Super Bowl"—and he urged that we adopt it. Thankfully we did, and game III was the first official Super Bowl.

I'm the first to admit that I was mistaken about the name of the game. Remarkably, "super" takes on a totally different connotation when it is applied to this event. I think the name has played a big part in the game's success.

For me, there was great sadness going into Super Bowl V. In September, just before the start of the 1970 season, Vince Lombardi died after a devastating battle with cancer. Vince was 13 years older than me, but it was like losing a brother. I miss him to this day. Fittingly, the Super Bowl Trophy—that magnificent creation of the Tiffany Company—officially was renamed the Vince Lombardi Trophy before Super Bowl VI.

Coming from a public relations background, one of my great pleasures in pro football was dealing with the media. This was especially true at the Super Bowl, particularly at the early games.

Nowadays, thousands of media people from around the world cover the game, and the closest the commissioner gets to these people is at the giant Friday noon press conference where there's a bank of TV cameras, hundreds of still photographers, and many hundreds of press, radio, and TV representatives. But in those first few years, my contacts with the media were pretty special.

I remember sitting around shooting the breeze with six, seven, eight writers at a time. It seemed to be less serious then, more fun. The game was serious, of course, but that didn't prevent us from kidding around. I have great memories of early sessions with John Steadman from Baltimore, Bob Oates from Los Angeles, Mo Siegel from Washington, Larry Felser from Buffalo, and others.

A lot of things were different then than they are today. In the early years, we had no Super Bowl Site Committee the way we do now. We basically just went with our instincts—and usually that meant Los Angeles, Miami, or New Orleans. The only deviation from those cities the first 15 years was in game VIII, when we played in Rice Stadium at Houston.

The only time I can recall having some reservations about the game site was when we went back to Los Angeles in game VII. Honestly, it took some courage to go back to my hometown after all the empty seats in game I, but I guess by that time we had more confidence in the game as a major event. This time we sold out the Coliseum, the major attraction being whether the Miami Dolphins could complete a perfect 17-0 season (they did).

We always have had a function of some kind for the media, and for all the people from the clubs and the league the Friday night before the game, but this didn't have the significance in the early years that it did later. In fact, before Super Bowl I, I think our "party" was nothing more than cold cuts at the Statler Hilton.

To borrow the trademark phrase of the late Ed Sullivan, I think the first *really big show* we had was at Super Bowl VII in January, 1973. A couple years before, the city of Long Beach had purchased the storied ocean liner, the *Queen Mary*, and had turned it into a major tourist attraction. We used the ship as our party site.

We have had some wonderful Friday night parties over the years, including some great ones in New Orleans, a party city on its own. If I had to pick a personal favorite, however, it would be the one we had before Super Bowl XXI in Los Angeles at Universal City. Being on the Universal lot in a movie studio environment was very exciting for many of the visitors.

I'm a real sucker for pageantry. I always liked balloons and balloon releases. In the early years, we also had a lot of pigeon or dove releases. I liked those, too. The fly-overs that we initiated at Super Bowl VI in New Orleans and made part of all other outdoor Super Bowls starting with Super Bowl XVIII in Tampa— also were a big thrill.

I always was involved in our plans for pregame and halftime festivities because it seemed important to me that we make the entire *event* very special. But I usually let other people pick the person or people who would do the National Anthem. The one time I insisted on an anthem person was at game XXII when I wanted Herb Alpert to do a "pure" horn version.

Three games in New Orleans—IX, XV, and XX—stand out to me for different reasons.

Game IX was the Steelers' first appearance in an NFL Championship Game of any kind after more than four decades of frustration. I am not ashamed to admit that I had tears of joy in my eyes when I presented the trophy to Art Rooney that January, 1975, day. No man ever deserved it more. Of course, I didn't realize at the time that he was going to get greedy and win three more (X, XIII, and XIV)!

On the morning of January 25, 1981, the day of game XV, I remember waking up in my room at the Hyatt-Regency in New Orleans and seeing a big yellow ribbon our people had put up around the Superdome with bows above the exits. If you remember, people had been wearing yellow ribbons in support of the hostages in Iran, and those hostages were released in Tehran just a few days before Super Sunday.

Game XX between the Bears and the Patriots was memorable for a lot of reasons, most of them generated by the very colorful Bears. The sadness was that George Halas was not there to see this great victory; my good friend and an NFL founder had died two years before.

I recall my daughter Anne Marie coming back from an evening in the French Quarter wearing a "ROZELLE" headband. Late in the 1985 regular season, I had to order Bears quarterback Jim McMahon to stop wearing commercial headbands, and he reacted to this by wearing a headband with my name on it in the playoffs. Versions of that headband were big sellers in the city the week before the game.

One of the toughest trophy presentations I had to make was to Al Davis after the Raiders' 38-9 rout of Washington in Super Bowl XVIII in January, 1984. We had been enmeshed in a court battle with Al over the Raiders' move to Los Ángeles in 1982. As I was leaving the room, Raiders guard Mickey Marvin tapped me on the shoulder and said, "Not everyone here hates you." That eased the pressure.

All in all, it's been a great ride—from Super Bowl I through my last game as Commissioner in XXIII to now. I wish I could literally release some balloons and doves at this point, and maybe even arrange for a fly-over for everyone reading this. You'll have to use your imagination, however. Or better, like me, keep dreaming Super Bowl dreams.

Introduction

The Great American Time Out

By John Wiebusch

In a perfect world, the streets are free of traffic. Crime ceases. People are happy. There is no wait for the Matterhorn ride at Disneyland.

In a perfect world, it is Super Sunday and America is watching the Super Bowl.

Some people are not watching, of course. You probably know some of them. But not many of them. Even people who do not watch football during the entire season watch the Super Bowl. People may not go to church all year but they go on Christmas Day.

There are Super Bowl parties everywhere. (Does anyone watch the Super Bowl alone?) Even the television ratings analysts admit their already phenomenal numbers for the Super Bowl aren't accurate. Like the usual ratings, they measure number of sets and assign an average number of viewers to each set. But there is no *average number of viewers* for a Super Bowl. The traditional measuring stick says somewhere between 130 and 150 million Americans watch a Super Bowl. In fact, the real numbers might be as many as 40 million more than that.

Nine of the top ten highest-rated television shows of all time are Super Bowls. The only intruder is the last episode of "M*A*S*H". Seventeen of the top twenty highest-rated television shows of all time are Super Bowls. The only other intruders are a couple parts of the "Roots" miniseries. All of the last 20 Super Bowls are among the top 25 shows of all time. (You really *do* know someone who doesn't watch the Super Bowl, huh?)

Madison Avenue knows the power of the Super Bowl. Dozens of major new products have been introduced to America on Super Sunday. Hundreds of eventually familiar commercial

Vince Lombardi's Packers won the first two Super Bowls. The trophy later was renamed in his honor.

themes have made debuts that day. Billions of dollars have been spent making those commercials and then purchasing the air time to run them. *USA Today* runs an annual viewers' rating poll of the Super Bowl's *commercials*. People who were at the game watch video tapes of the game, and not necessarily to rewatch the game. Often it's to see the commercials they missed.

And so far we've been talking only about the area from Atlanta to Anchorage, from Kauai to Kansas, from Maine to Montana (the state, not the super quarterback). Like it or loathe it, global homogenization is alive and well in our times. There are McDonald's franchises in London and Tokyo, in Milan and Mexico City. And the telecast of the Super Bowl is the biggest game in those towns, too. They watch the game in China, in Australia, in Germany, in Venezuela.

For between three and four hours on Sunday afternoon, Sunday evening, or even Monday morning, more than 1 billion people make neither love nor war (unless it is over the relative merits or demerits of the teams they are watching). It is global warming in the best sense.

I watched the first four Super Bowls on television. My first one in person was V. XXV will be my XXIst. I have seen the Steelers and the 49ers win four games. I have seen the Broncos and Vikings each lose four games. I have seen derring-do and I have seen frustration. In the yin and yang of emotions, I have seen a lot of smiles and a lot of tears. A few of them were mine.

There is no place on earth I would rather have been for those 21 afternoons...for those 21 Saturdays and 21 Fridays and, yes, for those 21 Super *Weeks*.

Super Bowl V seems to have been played in a time and place far, far away...and in fact it was.

I was working on a book about Vince Lombardi when I went to Miami in January, 1971. The great coach had died of intestinal cancer in September, 1970.

I was to stay at the press hotel, the Americana, while I interviewed owners and other club executives who were staying at the Kenilworth Hotel next door.

I looked around as the desk clerk searched for my registration confirmation. The lobby of the Americana looked like a fifties period piece gone old very ungracefully. Then there seemed to be, uh, a problem. The clerk could find no registration confirmation...but would I care to share a room for $22.50 a night? By happy coincidence, I was put in a room with an old friend, Maury White of the *Des Moines Register*. We had a view of the parking lot. And to reveal a 21-year-old secret, Maury's snores bear a remarkable resemblance to the sounds bull elephants make when they are calling in their herd.

The people with whom I wanted to talk all were less than 100 yards away, and my friend Jim Finks, then the Vikings' general manager, took me from cabaña to cabaña to introduce me to George Halas, Art Rooney, Wellington Mara, Art Modell, Carroll Rosenbloom, and other owners.

My first Super Bowl—my first Super Week

—took place in a tiny universe. The teams—the Cowboys and the Colts—were only short rides away. Otherwise, everyone who was anyone connected with the game, the league, and attendant groups was headquartered along one small strip of sand. There were no outward signs of pressure. It was only a game, or so it seemed. There was an NFL party—the Commissioner's Party, it was then called—but it was modest in scope; I have been to Fourth of July parties since then that were bigger. I sat in the main press box for the game, and I knew almost everyone.

In this tale of two cities, take two giant decade-sized steps forward...to New Orleans and Super Bowl XXIV.

This time I shared a room with my wife, and we had a panoramic view of both the Mississippi and the French Quarter. The room cost $185 a night.

The NFL hadn't just invaded New Orleans, it had occupied it. You couldn't find a room anywhere. The kindness of strangers was a distant memory. This was Serious Stuff.

The only owners I saw all week were on the other side of security-guarded ropes at the Friday-night Commissioner's Party, which included 3,000 or so of his most intimate friends in the New Orleans Convention Center. There were tables and tables (and more tables) of fabulous food. There were bands playing Dixieland and Cajun rock and Zydeco in every corner of the place.

There may have been only one game in town, but there definitely was more than one party. Does *every night* sound like a full dance card? By midweek, reporters were interviewing reporters, and broadcasters were covering reporters interviewing reporters. *National Enquirer*-type rumors became historical facts within minutes. The air was charged with manic energy.

I sat with 500 people in the second auxiliary press box (there were 1,000 people in the main press box and 500 more in the first auxiliary press box), just behind a writer who was covering the game for a newspaper in Milan, and just in front of two men who were producing a documentary on the game for a Tokyo television station. Only the man from Milan spoke English. I hardly knew anyone.

Then and now…a study in contrasts. And this is not to knock the "now." Hardly. Bigger may not be better in many things, but in the Super Bowl it seems to magnify the experience. Of course, the experience is not the only thing being magnified; so are our wallets. My combined expenses for Super Bowl V were about the same as one night in a hotel for Super Bowl XXIV.

I have seen—or will have seen—21 Super Bowls in person, but I am a relative newcomer amid a group of Super Visionaries.

Pete Rozelle, the man who conceived this game, watched its birth, nurtured it through its infancy, then guided it through its adolescence and into full-fledged adulthood, has seen every one of them.

So have other people in the NFL office—Bill Granholm and Don Weiss.

So have a modest number of club people, including Jim Finks, now of the Saints; Art Modell of the Browns; Wellington and Tim Mara of the Giants; Bill Bidwill of the Cardinals; Lamar Hunt of the Chiefs; Tex Schramm, now of the World League of American Football but mostly of the Cowboys; Al Davis and Al LoCasale of the Raiders; Paul and Mike Brown of the Bengals; Dan Rooney of the Steelers; Ralph Wilson of the Bills; Virginia and Ed McCaskey of the Bears.

And so have a hardy collection of media survivors. More than 3,000 people may cover the Super Bowl these days, but only 20 have been there for all 24 games.

The Super Bowl XXIV Club (there really *is* a club and it meets annually, as the Roman numerals inflate) includes 13 writers and seven photographers.

The 13 writers: Dick Connor, Art Daley, Mel Durslag, Larry Felser, Jerry Green, Jerry Izenberg, Dave Klein, Will McDonough, Norm Miller, Bob Oates, Ed Pope, Cooper Rollow, and John Steadman.

The seven photographers: John Biever, Vernon Biever, David Boss, Walter Iooss, Jr., Mickey Palmer, Dick Raphael, and Tony Tomsic.

Most of them no doubt would like me to write that they started as children (and a couple of them practically did). You talk about memoirs!

You talk about photo histories! This group could show and tell you a thing or two…and more.

Take Dave Boss, for example. It was Boss who hired me away from the *Los Angeles Times* with the initial lure of the Vince Lombardi book I mentioned earlier.

Boss and pro football go back together a lot longer than just 25 Super Bowls. In 1958, 26-year-old Boss approached 32-year-old Pete Rozelle, who was in his second year as general manager of the Rams, with a novel idea to produce the club's game programs. A visionary even then, Rozelle liked the idea. In 1966, Boss was in his second year as the Creative Director for NFL Properties. Of course, by that time, Rozelle was in his seventh year as Commissioner of the National Football League. Pete asked Dave to produce the first AFL-NFL World Championship Game program (and with only a month's notice). Dave delivered, and he has been helping to do that ever since. I have been the program's editor since Super Bowl VI.

A complete set of Super Bowl game programs costs more than $3,000…if you can *find* a complete set (I don't even have one myself, but of course Boss does; he also has complete sets of media pins, photographer's credentials, game tickets, and game patches—the latter are sewn on a jacket he wears only during Super Bowls).

Boss has been roaming Super sidelines with his camera since the first game in the Los Angeles Coliseum on January 15, 1967. The evolution of the equipment he carries is a metaphor for the evolution of the event. For game I, he had a hand-held single-reflex camera with a 135mm lens. He had a half-dozen or so rolls of black-and-white film and a few rolls of color in his pocket. For game XXIV, he carried a state-of-the-art motor-driven camera with a 300mm lens, all mounted on a monopod, and a second auto-focus camera with a 35-135mm zoom lens. He also had a bag with other lenses and dozens of rolls of high-speed film, most of it color.

Pete Rozelle retired as Commissioner in the fall of 1989 after 29 exceptional years on the job. Meanwhile, Dave Boss endures.

"Talk about up close and personal," he says.

"It doesn't get any better than that. I mean, I was down there to photograph Bart Starr and Joe Namath…to see Lynn Swann and Jerry Rice make those incredible catches…to be there when Terry Bradshaw and Joe Montana came through in the clutch—as you knew they would."

He pauses and then speaks for all of us, even a latecomer who has seen 21 games: "It's been a special privilege."

There is an astonishing symmetry to the all-time "standings" of the Super Bowl.

Six teams—the Steelers, the 49ers, the Packers, the Bears, the Giants, and the Jets—have played in the game a combined 13 times. The six teams are 13-0.

Six teams—the Raiders, the Redskins, the Colts, the Chiefs, the Cowboys, and the Dolphins—have played in the game 22 times. The six teams are 11-11.

Six teams—the Vikings, the Broncos, the Bengals, the Rams, the Patriots, and the Eagles—have played in the game 13 times. The six teams are 0-13.

Go figure!

There are the extreme Haves—the Steelers and the 49ers each have won four times (Pittsburgh by a combined 103-73, San Francisco by a combined 139-63)…and the extreme Have-Nots—the Vikings and the Broncos each have lost four times (Minnesota by a combined 34-95, Denver by a combined 50-163).

The Vikings and the Broncos could point out that it is better to have warred and lost than not to have warred at all. The fact that 18 teams have monopolized the Super Bowl means that 10 teams have been there only as spectators (for the record, the Little 10 include proud old franchises such as the Browns, Lions, and Cardinals, plus the Oilers, Bills, Chargers, Saints, Falcons, Seahawks, and Buccaneers).

The closest Super Bowl was V. The Colts' margin of victory over the Cowboys was the three points that came on Jim O'Brien's field goal with five seconds left to play.

Three other games (X and XIII, both the Steelers over the Cowboys, and XXIII, the 49ers over the Bengals) were decided by four points.

One game was settled by five points, (the 49ers over the Bengals in XVI), one by seven points (the Dolphins over the Redskins in VII), and one by nine points (the Jets over the Colts in III).

The winning teams in the Super Bowl have scored 705 points (an average of 29.4), the losing teams 304 points (12.7). Thus, the average margin is 16.7.

Obviously, a few landslide games have resulted in that seeming imbalance. There have been seven games with margins of more than 20 points. In ascending order: the Cowboys over the Dolphins by 21 in VI, the 49ers over the Dolphins by 22 in XIX, the Packers over the Chiefs by 25 in I, the Raiders over the Redskins by 29 in XVIII, the Redskins over the Broncos by 32 in XXII, the Bears over the Patriots by 36 in XX, and the 49ers over the Broncos by 45 in XXIV.

Three cities (or areas) have combined to host the game a total of 19 times.

New Orleans has seven (IV, VI, IX, XII, XV, XX, and XXIV).

Miami has six (II, III, V, X, XIII, and XXIII).

Los Angeles-Pasadena also has six (I, VII, XI, XIV, XVII, and XXI).

With XXV, Tampa will have two (also XVIII), while four other cities have had it once—Houston (VIII), Detroit (XVI), San Francisco (XIX), and San Diego (XXII). Upcoming first-time host cities include Minneapolis (XXVI), Phoenix (XXVII), and Atlanta (XXVIII).

Enduring above all are the people, the doers of the deeds, the Supermen (many of whom are featured in the photographic portfolio that begins on page 20).

The balloting for the all-time Super Bowl team that took place throughout the 1990 season included the names of five quarterbacks (pick one):

☐ Terry Bradshaw
☐ Joe Montana
☐ Joe Namath
☐ Bart Starr
☐ Roger Staubach

No losers there. Four of them are in the Pro Football Hall of Fame, and the fifth (Montana) will join them five years (and not a minute later) after he leaves the game. In fact, the five quarterbacks are a combined 13-2 in the Super Bowl (the only losses being Staubach's pair of four-point setbacks to Bradshaw).

The five men have won a combined *nine* Super Bowl most valuable player awards. Namath and Staubach won one each, Starr and Bradshaw two each, and Montana (in a class by himself) three.

In fact, a good case might be made for Montana having *four* MVP awards. In Super Bowl XXIII, when wide receiver Jerry Rice was given the honor for catching 11 passes for 215 yards and one touchdown, all Montana did was complete 23 of 36 passes for 357 yards and two touchdowns, and direct a 92-yard drive in the final minutes that ended when he threw the winning 10-yard touchdown pass to John Taylor with 34 seconds left to play.

Of course, to be fair, a good case could be made *against* Montana's MVP award in Super Bowl XVI. Montana passed for just 157 yards that day (he had 331, 357, and 297 in his other three Super Bowls). In truth, the XVI MVP award might have gone to either linebacker Dan Bunz, who made two epic stops in a goal-line stand that held off the Bengals (26-21), or linebacker Jack Reynolds, a defensive leader all day.

Ten head coaches never lost a Super Bowl. Going a combined 17-0 were the Steelers' Chuck Noll (4-0), the 49ers' Bill Walsh (3-0), the Packers' Vince Lombardi and the Raiders' Tom Flores (both 2-0), and the Jets' Weeb Ewbank, the Colts' Don McCafferty, the Raiders' John Madden, the Bears' Mike Ditka, the Giants' Bill Parcells, and the 49ers' George Seifert (all 1-0).

Here's to the winners...but here's also to the losers, men who sadly wear pro football's scarlet letter.

The Vikings lost four Super Bowls—three with Fran Tarkenton at quarterback, one with Joe Kapp at quarterback, and all four with Bud Grant as head coach. In the four games, Minnesota scored a total of five touchdowns.

The Broncos also lost four Super Bowls, first in XII, then in XXI, XXII, and XXIV. John Elway was the quarterback and Dan Reeves the head coach in the latter three games, in which the losing margins were 19, 32, and 45 points.

Even coaches Don Shula and Tom Landry had to take a lot of bitter with the sweet. Shula won back-to-back Super Bowls with the Dolphins in VII and VIII (the former being the finale to a perfect 17-0 season), but he also lost four Super Bowls—III with the Colts, and VI, XVII, and XIX with Miami. Landry directed Cowboys' victories in VI and XII, but lost games V, X, and XIII.

Time magazine has called the Super Bowl "The Great American Time Out."

Norman Vincent Peale said, "If Jesus were alive today, He would be at the Super Bowl."

Pete Rozelle said, "The Super Bowl is like the last chapter in a hair-raising mystery. No one would dare think of missing it."

Of course, the Super Bowl is more than just a mystery. It also is parts comedy and drama, courage and absolution, hearts and flowers and macho swagger.

It is Miami kicker Garo Yepremian giving the game some slapstick in VII by attempting to pass, only to have the ball squirt out of his hands and result in Washington's lone touchdown.

It is Joe Montana driving the 49ers 92 yards in 11 plays to destiny in the closing minutes of XXIII.

It is Joe Montana with the football, period ...arguably the all-time grace-under-big-game-pressure player. In four Super Bowl victories, he has completed 83 passes in 122 attempts (a .680 percentage) for 1,142 yards and 11 touchdowns (with *no* interceptions). His quarterback rating in the biggest game is 127.8.

It is the Jets' Al Atkinson hollering at the team's trainer in III to wrap his separated shoulder so he can get back into the game.

It is the Steelers' Dwight White getting out of a hospital bed (he had been suffering from pleurisy) in IX not only to play in the game, but to *dominate*.

It is the Rams' Jack Youngblood playing XIV on a fractured leg.

It is Doug Williams getting another chance in the 1987 postseason...suffering a knee injury in the first quarter of XXII...then re-entering the game in the second quarter to ignite the most incredible fireworks display (35 points) in the history of the game.

It is the Raiders' Jim Plunkett coming back from pro football's scrap heap to lead his team to victories in XV and XVIII.

It is the Cowboys' Bob Lilly launching his helmet into orbit in the frustrating final moments of V...then emerging a champion a year later in VI.

It is the Packers' 34-year-old Max McGee carousing all night before I because he didn't think he would play, then *having* to play and responding with two crucial touchdown catches.

It is the Giants' Jim Burt hoisting his son onto his shoulder as the seconds ticked off in XXI ...and repeating the act three years later in XXIV when he was with the 49ers.

It is a locker room without a dry eye as Joe Greene hands the Lombardi Trophy for IX to Steelers owner Art Rooney, saying, "This one's for you, Chief."

It is Joe Namath guaranteeing a victory a few days before III, then delivering.

It is the Bears' "Super Bowl Shuffle"—the video they made earlier—shaking the Superdome at halftime of Chicago's rout in XX.

It is the Vikings' Joe Kapp swaggering onto the field at the start of IV, but needing to be helped off later.

It is Fred (The Hammer) Williamson being assisted from the field in I after playing the poundee not the pounder.

Images are endless. The Super Bowl is...

The Steelers' Lynn Swann soaring like Baryshnikov in X, XIII, and XIV...The Steelers' John Stallworth making like Lynn Swann in XIII and XIV...Colorful nicknames such as the Purple People Eaters, Doomsday I, Doomsday II, Killer Bees, No Name Defense, Orange Crush, and the Hogs...Joe Namath's long hair and sideburns and Johnny Unitas's flattop, a study in contrasting styles in III...The Colts' unaffected rookie, Jim O'Brien, touching the sky after delivering a game-winning field goal in the last minute of V...The French Quarter on any night (or day) during seven Super Weeks in New Orleans...The halftime shows in which there seemed to be more people on the field than in the stands.

Ray Didinger, whose mastery lights up four

of the 24 game stories that follow, once wrote:

"Super Bowl is hype and hope, elation and disappointment. It is June Taylor and Jim Taylor....It clears out our streets and fills our family rooms and pulls us together like moon walks and royal weddings have yet to do. Even when it came at the end of a tattered, strike-shortened season, the Super Bowl had us on our feet, cheering and forgiving all the Sundays that had dawned so empty.

"Super Bowl is ritual and legend, the toy we never outgrew, the dame we never leave behind. Let the sociologists argue about the symbolism. Let your mother-in-law worry about the pot roast. When it's fourth-and-goal and Bradshaw is asking for quiet and I'm leaning forward in my chair hollering, 'Give it to Franco!,' I know where I'm supposed to be.

I'm right there beside you, Ray.

We all are.

The right arm of Joe Montana has set eight Super Bowl passing records and won four games.

Supermen

The Super Bowl saga began with Bart Starr, who directed the Packers to victories in Super Bowls I and II and was named most valuable player in both games. It was the culmination of a great career for Starr, who led Green Bay to five NFL cham-pionships in the 1960s. Three future Pro Football Hall of Fame members are shown here—Starr, fullback Jim Taylor (31), and tackle Forrest Gregg (75). In all, eight members of this team, plus head coach Vince Lombardi, are in the Hall.

No player ever shocked more people before a Super Bowl than Joe Namath, who guaranteed the Jets' victory over the Baltimore Colts, who were favored by 18 points in game III. Astonishingly, his actions spoke as loud as his words.

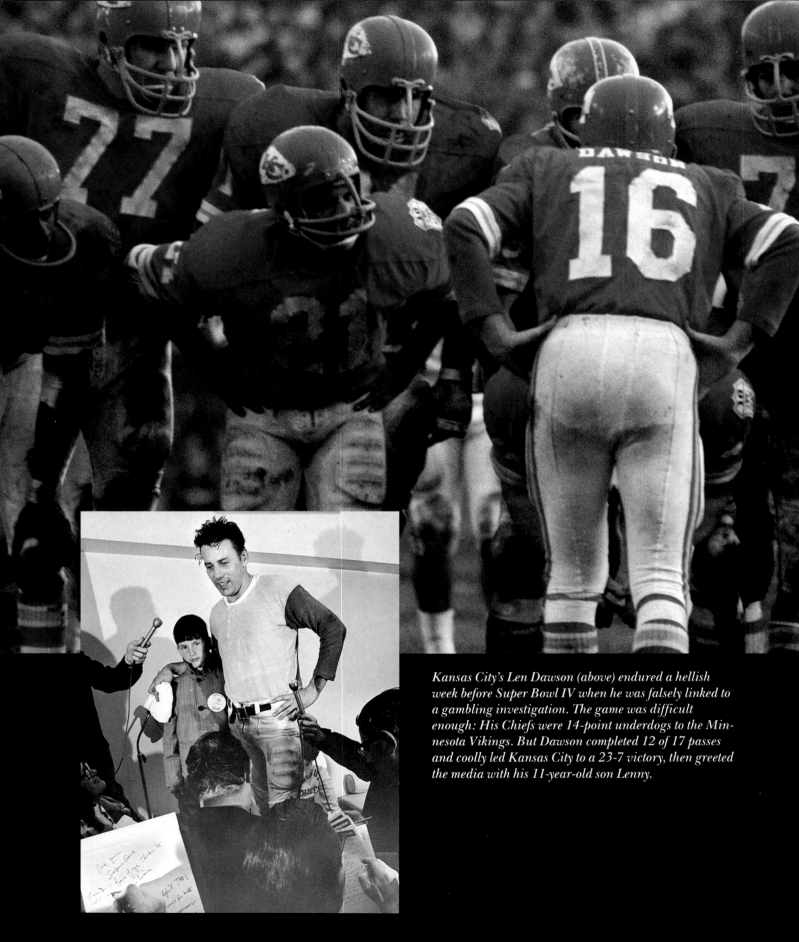

Kansas City's Len Dawson (above) endured a hellish week before Super Bowl IV when he was falsely linked to a gambling investigation. The game was difficult enough: His Chiefs were 14-point underdogs to the Minnesota Vikings. But Dawson completed 12 of 17 passes and coolly led Kansas City to a 23-7 victory, then greeted the media with his 11-year-old son Lenny.

After 24 Super Bowls, Dallas linebacker Chuck Howley is the only player from a losing team to be named most valuable player. Although the Cowboys lost Super Bowl V to Baltimore 16-13, Howley intercepted two passes, including one in the end zone to stop a Colts' drive.

In four appearances, Dallas's Roger Staubach (opposite) led the Cowboys to two Super Bowl victories and almost rallied them to victory in the other two. In all, Staubach threw eight touchdown passes and was most valuable player in Super Bowl VI.

The Cowboys' defense overpowered Denver and Craig Morton (7) in Super Bowl XII, and two of its members, end Harvey Martin (79) and tackle Randy White (54), were named co-most valuable players.

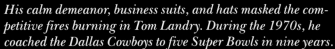

His calm demeanor, business suits, and hats masked the competitive fires burning in Tom Landry. During the 1970s, he coached the Dallas Cowboys to five Super Bowls in nine years.

25

His last name—Csonka—always sounded as if it should belong to a fullback, and Larry Csonka was perfect for the position—big, strong, and quick. He helped lead Miami to three successive Super Bowls, including victories in games VII and VIII, when he rushed for 112 and 145 yards.

Thanks in no small part to safety Jake Scott, the 1972 Dolphins became the only unbeaten, untied team in NFL history, clinching their 17-0 record with a victory in Super Bowl VII. Scott intercepted two passes, returning one of them 55 yards out of the end zone (above) to kill a Washington drive.

Just like Muhammad Ali, Pittsburgh wide receiver Lynn Swann could float like a butterfly and sting like a bee. The graceful Swann averaged nearly 23 yards on 16 catches i Super Bowls X, XIII, and XIV, scoring three touchdowns.

No other NFL team has accomplished what the Pittsburgh Steelers did in the 1970s—winning four Super Bowls in six years, including two in a row twice. They won the first two with a dominant defense and the last two with Terry Bradshaw and the offense (left) scoring 35 and 31 points.

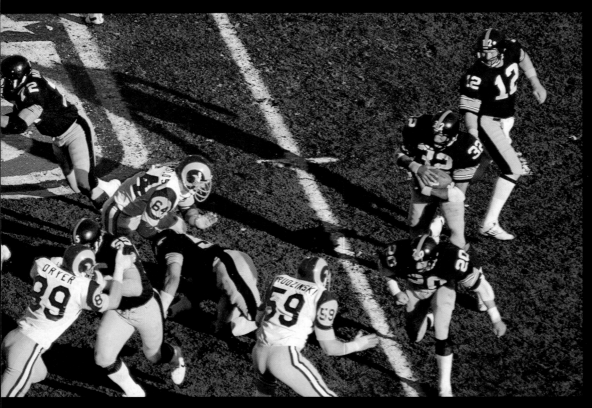

Few quarterbacks ever had stronger arms than Pittsburgh's Terry Bradshaw (opposite), who threw nine touchdown passes in leading the Steelers to four Super Bowl victories. He was named the MVP in both XIII and XIV when he passed for 318 and 309 yards.

Pittsburgh's dominance depended on a combination of fierce defense, quick-strike passing, and a powerful running game. The running attack was centered around Franco Harris (32, above), who holds Super Bowl career records for rushing yards (354) and touchdowns (4).

Through four Super Bowl victories, the Pittsburgh Steelers' brain trust included head coach Chuck Noll (rear, left), owner Art Rooney, Sr. (front, right), and Art Sr.'s sons, Dan (front, left) and Art, Jr.

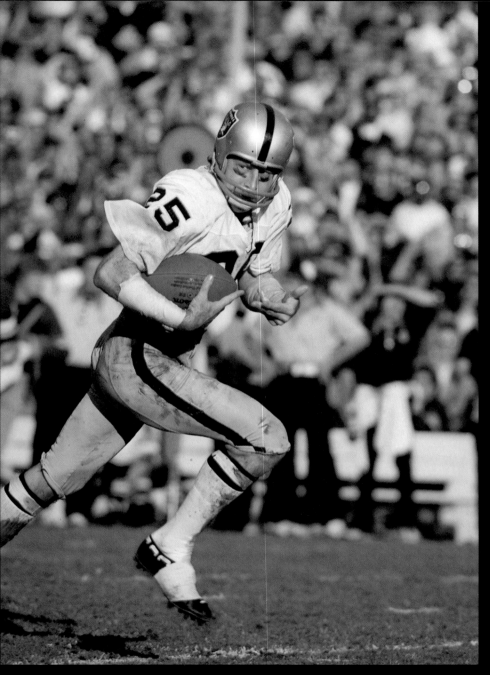

To some he's mysterious, but there's no denying he's a winner. Under the leadership of Al Davis (right), the Oakland-Los Angeles Raiders have gone to four Super Bowls and won three (XI, XV, and XVIII).

Benched, released, and written off more times than he cares to remember, Jim Plunkett kept coming back. And back. He led the Raiders to two Super Bowl victories and was named the MVP in game XV when he passed for three touchdowns.

In Super Bowl XI, Oakland wide receiver Fred Biletnikoff (above) caught four passes—and three of them set up touchdowns that others scored from two yards or less. The Raiders won, and Biletnikoff was named MVP.

Super Bowl XVIII was considered an even game, but the
Raiders shocked the Redskins 38-9. A big reason was
Marcus Allen, who ran for a Super Bowl-record 191
yards and scored twice, once on a dazzling 74-yard run.

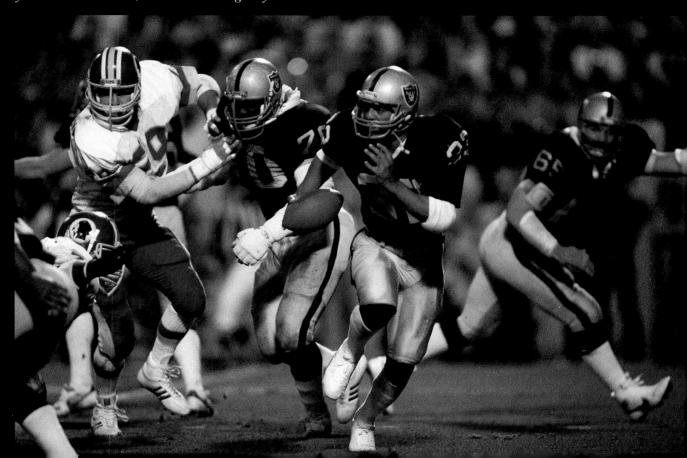

Super Bowl XXI forever will be linked with the name Phil Simms. The 31-year-old Giants quarterback had the most accurate game in NFL playoff history to lead New York past Denver 39-20. Simms completed 22 of 25 passes for 268 yards and three touchdowns and was 10 for 10 in the second half.

Richard Dent (left) never has met a quarterback he didn't dislike. Or a running back. In Super Bowl XX, he had 1 1/2 sacks, three other tackles (one for a loss), two forced fumbles, and a deflection, and set up 10 points as the Bears won 46-10. He also was named the most valuable player.

It was the ultimate in 15-minute football—Super Bowl, regular season, any NFL game ever. With his team trailing Denver 10-0 in the second quarter of Super Bowl XXII, Washington's Doug Williams (left) bombed the Broncos with four touchdown passes and 228 yards passing as the Redskins scored an incredible 35 points and went on to win 42-10. In all, he passed for a Super Bowl record 340 yards.

Off the field, he was a bit eccentric, but that never slowed him down when he carried a football. Washington's John Riggins helped lead the Redskins to two successive Super Bowls, setting records with 38 carries and 166 yards in Super Bowl XVII, a 27-17 victory over Miami.

If the team of the '80s was San Francisco, the wide receiver of the '80s was Jerry Rice (above). In the 49ers' back-to-back victories in Super Bowls XXIII and XXIV, Rice caught a total of 18 passes for four touchdowns. His 215 receiving yards in the first game are an all-time Super Bowl record.

When Bill Walsh took over the 49ers, they were coming off a 2-14 season. In his third year, he won a Super Bowl. Then he won two more. Those three Super Bowl victories (XVI, XIX, and XXIII) added up to these three trophies won during his 10-year career.

Joe Montana (opposite) has had many opportunities to signal touchdown for the 49ers. In leading his team to four Super Bowl victories, he has thrown a record 11 touchdown passes and no interceptions. He also is the only player to be chosen MVP three times.

The years go by...and the legend of Vince Lombardi seems to grow even bigger. Lombardi, who died of cancer in 1970 at 57, coached the Packers to five NFL titles and victories in the first two Super Bowls. It is fitting that the game's trophy carries his name.

I

Green Bay 35, Kansas City 10

3 **26** **6**
TUNNEL   R O W   SEAT

World Championship Game

AFL-NFL

SUNDAY JANUARY 15, 1967
LOS ANGELES MEMORIAL COLISEUM

 KICKOFF ONE O'CLOCK PM
Reserved Seat **$10.00**
This ticket cannot be refunded

AFL-NFL WORLD CHAMPIONSHIP GAME
LOS ANGELES MEMORIAL COLISEUM $10.00
SUNDAY JANUARY 15, 1967 / KICKOFF ONE PM

TUNNEL   R O W   SEAT
3   **26**   **6**

Vital Statistics

Starting Lineups

Kansas City (AFL)	Offense	Green Bay (NFL)
Chris Burford	WR	Carroll Dale
Jim Tyrer	LT	Bob Skoronski
Ed Budde	LG	Fuzzy Thurston
Wayne Frazier	C	Bill Curry
Curt Merz	RG	Jerry Kramer
Dave Hill	RT	Forrest Gregg
Fred Arbanas	TE	Marv Fleming
Otis Taylor	WR	Boyd Dowler
Len Dawson	QB	Bart Starr
Mike Garrett	RB	Elijah Pitts
Curtis McClinton	RB	Jim Taylor
	Defense	
Jerry Mays	LE	Willie Davis
Andy Rice	LT	Ron Kostelnik
Buck Buchanan	RT	Henry Jordan
Chuck Hurston	RE	Lionel Aldridge
Bobby Bell	LLB	Dave Robinson
Sherrill Headrick	MLB	Ray Nitschke
E.J. Holub	RLB	Lee Roy Caffey
Fred Williamson	LCB	Herb Adderley
Willie Mitchell	RCB	Bob Jeter
Bobby Hunt	SS	Tom Brown
Johnny Robinson	FS	Willie Wood

Substitutions

Kansas City-Offense: K-Mike Mercer. P-Jerrel Wilson. WR-Frank Pitts, Reg Carolan. LINE-Tony DiMidio, Dennis Biodrowski, Jon Gilliam, Al Reynolds. RB-Bert Coan, Gene Thomas. QB-Pete Beathard. Defense: LINE-Aaron Brown. LB-Walt Corey, Smokey Stover, Bud Abell. DB-Emmitt Thomas, Fletcher Smith, Bobby Ply.
Green Bay-Offense: K/P-Don Chandler. P/RB-Donny Anderson. WR-Max McGee, Bob Long, Bill Anderson, Red Mack. LINE-Steve Wright, Gale Gillingham, Ken Bowman. QB-Zeke Bratkowski. RB-Jim Grabowski, Phil Vandersea. Defense: LINE-Bob Brown, Jim Weatherwax. LB-Tommy Crutcher. DB-Doug Hart, Dave Hathcock. DNP-RB-Paul Hornung.

Officials

Referee-Norm Schachter (NFL). Umpire-George Young (AFL). Head Linesman-Bernie Ulman (NFL). Back Judge-Jack Reader (AFL). Field Judge-Mike Lisetski (NFL). Line Judge-Al Sabato (AFL).

Scoring

Kansas City	0	10	0	0 — 10	
Green Bay	7	7	14	7 — 35	

GB-McGee 37 pass from Starr (Chandler kick)
KC-McClinton 7 pass from Dawson (Mercer kick)
GB-Taylor 14 run (Chandler kick)
KC-FG Mercer 31
GB-Pitts 5 run (Chandler kick)
GB-McGee 13 pass from Starr (Chandler kick)
GB-Pitts 1 run (Chandler kick)
Attendance-61,946

FINAL TEAM STATISTICS

	Chiefs	Packers
TOTAL FIRST DOWNS	17	21
Rushing	4	10
Passing	12	11
Penalty	1	0
TOTAL NET YARDAGE	239	361
Total Offensive Plays	57	61
Average Gain per Offensive Play	4.2	5.9
NET YARDS RUSHING	72	133
Total Rushing Plays	19	34
Average Gain per Rushing Play	3.8	3.9
NET YARDS PASSING	167	228
Pass Att.-Comp.-Int.	32-17-1	24-16-1
Sacks-Yards Lost	6-61	3-22
Gross Yards Passing	228	250
Avg. Gain per Pass (Incl. Sacks)	4.4	8.4
PUNTS-YARDS	7-317	4-173
Average Distance	45.3	43.3
Had Blocked	0	0
TOTAL RETURN YARDAGE	149	138
Kickoff Returns-Yards	6-130	3-65
Punt Returns-Yards	3-19	4-23
Interception Returns-Yards	1-0	1-50
TOTAL TURNOVERS	1	1
Fumbles-Lost	1-0	1-0
Had Intercepted	1	1
PENALTIES-YARDS	4-26	4-40
TOTAL POINTS SCORED	10	35
Touchdowns Rushing	0	3
Touchdowns Passing	1	2
Touchdowns Returns	0	0
Extra Points	1	5
Field Goals-Attempts	1-2	0-0
Safeties	0	0
THIRD DOWN EFFICIENCY	3/13	11/15
FOURTH DOWN EFFICIENCY	0/0	0/0
TIME OF POSSESSION	28:35	31:25

INDIVIDUAL STATISTICS

RUSHING

Kansas City	No.	Yds.	Avg.	Long	TD
Garrett	6	17	2.8	9	0
McClinton	6	16	2.7	6	0
Dawson	3	24	8.0	15	0
Coan	3	1	0.3	3	0
Beathard	1	14	14.0	14	0

Green Bay	No.	Yds.	Avg.	Long	TD
Taylor	17	56	3.3	14t	1
Pitts	11	45	4.1	12	2
D. Anderson	4	30	7.5	13	0
Grabowski	2	2	1.0	2	0

PASSING

Kansas City	Att.	Comp.	Yds.	Long	TD	Int.
Dawson	27	16	211	31	1	1
Beathard	5	1	17	17	0	0

Green Bay	Att.	Comp.	Yds.	Long	TD	Int.
Starr	23	16	250	37t	2	1
Bratkowski	1	0	0	0	0	0

RECEIVING

Kansas City	No.	Yds.	Long	TD
Burford	4	67	27	0
Taylor	4	57	31	0
Garrett	3	28	17	0
McClinton	2	34	27	1
Arbanas	2	30	18	0
Carolan	1	7	7	0
Coan	1	5	5	0

Green Bay	No.	Yds.	Long	TD
McGee	7	138	37t	2
Dale	4	59	25	0
Pitts	2	32	22	0
Fleming	2	22	11	0
Taylor	1	-1	-1	0

INTERCEPTIONS

Kansas City	No.	Yds.	Long	TD
Mitchell	1	0	0	0

Green Bay	No.	Yds.	Long	TD
Wood	1	50	50	0

PUNTING

Kansas City	No.	Yds.	Avg.	TB	Long
Wilson	7	317	45.3	1	61

Green Bay	No.	Yds.	Avg.	TB	Long
Chandler	3	130	43.3	0	50
D. Anderson	1	43	43.0	0	43

PUNT RETURNS

Kansas City	No.	FC	Yds.	Long	TD
Garrett	2	0	17	9	0
E. Thomas	1	0	2	2	0

Green Bay	No.	FC	Yds.	Long	TD
D. Anderson	3	0	25	15	0
Wood	1	1	-2	-2	0

KICKOFF RETURNS

Kansas City	No.	Yds.	Long	TD
Coan	4	87	31	0
Garrett	2	43	23	0

Green Bay	No.	Yds.	Long	TD
Adderley	2	40	20	0
D. Anderson	1	25	25	0

FUMBLES

Kansas City	No.	Own Rec.	Opp. Rec.
McClinton	1	1	0

Green Bay	No.	Own Rec.	Opp. Rec.
Grabowski	1	0	0
Skoronski	0	1	0

KICKING

Kansas City	XP-A	FG-A	FG Made	FG Missed
Mercer	1-1	1-2	31	40

Green Bay	XP-A	FG-A	FG Made	FG Missed
Chandler	5-5	0-0	--	--

BRYAN ROBLEY

PLAY-BY-PLAY

Green Bay won the coin toss and elected to receive.

FIRST QUARTER

Smith kick to GB 5, Adderley 20 return (Bell).

Green Bay (15:00)

GB 25	1-10	Taylor 4 run right (Rice).
GB 29	2-6	Pitts 5 run left (Robinson).
GB 34	3-1	Taylor 3 run left tackle (Mitchell).
GB 37	1-10	Starr pass to McGee incomplete.
GB 37	2-10	Starr sacked, loss of 10 (Buchanan).
GB 27	3-20	Starr sacked, loss of 5 (Mays, Bell).
GB 22	4-25	Chandler 50 punt, Garrett 9 return.

Kansas City (11:55)

KC 37	1-10	Dawson pass to Burford incomplete.
KC 37	2-10	Garrett 4 draw up middle (Kostelnik).
KC 41	3-6	Dawson 11 pass to Burford (Jeter).
GB 48	1-10	Garrett 1 run left (Jordan).
GB 47	2-9	KC penalized 5 for delay of game.
KC 48	2-14	Dawson pass to Burford incomplete.
KC 48	3-14	Dawson pass to Taylor incomplete.
KC 48	4-14	Wilson 47 punt, D. Anderson 15 return.

Green Bay (9:10)

GB 20	1-10	Pitts 3 run right end (Williams, Hunt).
GB 23	2-7	Starr 11 pass to Fleming middle (Hunt, Bell).
GB 34	1-10	Starr 22 pass to Pitts.
KC 44	1-10	Taylor sweep left, loss of 5 (Holub).
KC 49	2-15	Starr 12 pass to Dale (Williamson).
KC 37	3-3	Starr 37 pass to McGee middle (one-handed catch at KC 23), touchdown (6:04). Chandler kicked extra point.

Green Bay scoring drive: 80 yards, 6 plays, 3:06.

Green Bay 7, Kansas City 0

Chandler kick to KC 1, Garrett 23 return. KC penalized 11 for holding (DiMidio).

Kansas City (5:54)

KC 13	1-10	Dawson 7 run evading pass rush (Nitschke).
KC 20	2-3	Dawson 3 pass to Garrett (Jordan).
KC 23	1-10	Dawson pass to Burford incomplete. Play nullified and GB penalized 5 for pass interference (Jeter). Automatic first down.
KC 28	1-10	McClinton 4 run up middle (Kostelnik).
KC 32	2-6	Dawson 18 pass to Arbanas (Caffey).
50	1-10	Garrett 9 run left (Caffey).
GB 41	2-1	Dawson 2 run evading pass rush (Nitschke).
GB 39	1-10	Garrett sweep right, loss of 1 (Robinson).
GB 40	2-11	Dawson pass to Burford incomplete.
GB 40	3-11	Dawson 7 pass to Carolan (Nitschke).
GB 33	4-4	Mercer's 40-yard field goal attempt was wide right, no good.

Green Bay (:34)

GB 20	1-10	Taylor 3 run right (Buchanan).

END OF FIRST QUARTER:

Green Bay 7, Kansas City 0

SECOND QUARTER

GB 23	2-7	Starr pass to McGee incomplete.
GB 23	3-7	Starr pass to Dale juggled, incomplete.
GB 23	4-7	Chandler 45 punt, E. Thomas 2 return (Wood).

Kansas City (14:24)

KC 34	1-10	Dawson pass to Garrett (Wood).
GB 49	1-10	Coan 3 run up middle (Aldridge).
GB 46	2-7	McClinton 6 run up middle (Aldridge).
GB 40	3-1	Coan 2 run left (Caffey).
GB 38	1-10	Dawson 31 pass to Taylor deep right (Brown).
GB 7	1-goal	Dawson 7 pass to McClinton left end zone, touchdown (10:40). Mercer kicked extra point.

Kansas City scoring drive: 66 yards, 6 plays, 3:44.

Green Bay 7, Kansas City 7

Smith kick to GB 2, D. Anderson 25 return (Corey).

Green Bay (10:40)

GB 27	1-10	Pitts 6 run left (Rice).
GB 33	2-4	Taylor 3 run left end (Hurston).
GB 36	3-1	Starr 64 pass to Dale deep, touchdown. Play nullified and GB penalized 5 for illegal procedure. Penalty marked off incorrectly-ball placed at GB 32.
GB 32	3-5	Starr 10 pass to McGee (Robinson). KC-first time out.

GB 42	1-10	Starr pass to Dale incomplete.
GB 42	2-10	Starr pass to Pitts incomplete.
GB 42	3-10	Starr 15 pass to Dale (Robinson).
KC 43	1-10	Taylor 3 run around left end (Mitchell).
KC 40	2-7	Pitts 2 run right (Rice).
KC 38	3-5	Starr 11 pass to Fleming (Robinson).
KC 27	1-10	Taylor 3 run up middle (Buchanan).
KC 24	2-7	Pitts draw up middle, no gain (Rice).
KC 24	3-7	Starr 10 pass to Pitts (Holub).
KC 14	1-10	Taylor 14 run around left end, touchdown (4:37). Chandler kicked extra point.

Green Bay scoring drive: 73 yards, 13 plays, 6:03.

Green Bay 14, Kansas City 7

Chandler kick to KC 6, Garrett 20 return (Hathcock).

Kansas City (4:37)

KC 26	1-10	Dawson sacked, loss of 8 (Aldridge, Jordan).
KC 18	2-18	Dawson 12 pass to Arbanas (Nitschke).
KC 30	3-6	Dawson 11 pass to Taylor (Adderley).
KC 41	1-10	Dawson 27 pass to Burford. KC declined holding against GB (Robinson).
GB 32	1-10	Garrett 2 run up middle (Nitschke).
GB 30	2-8	McClinton run left, loss of 2, recovered own fumble.
GB 32	3-10	Dawson 8 pass to Garrett middle (Robinson). KC-second time out (:58).
GB 24	4-2	Mercer, 31-yard field goal (:54).

Kansas City scoring drive: 50 yards, 7 plays, 3:43.

Green Bay 14, Kansas City 10

Smith kick to GB 6, Adderley 20 return (Mays, Stover).

Green Bay (:54)

GB 26	1-10	Pitts 7 run around right end (Bell).

END OF SECOND QUARTER:

Green Bay 14, Kansas City 10

THIRD QUARTER

Chandler kick to KC 13, Coan 16 return (Mack).

Kansas City (15:00)

KC 29	1-10	Dawson 15 run evading pass rush (Robinson).
KC 44	1-10	McClinton 3 run up middle (Kostelnik).
KC 47	2-7	Garrett 2 run up middle (Aldridge).
KC 49	3-5	Dawson pass to Arbanas intercepted at GB 45, Wood 50 return (Garrett).

Green Bay (12:42)

KC 5	1-goal	Pitts 5 run over left tackle, touchdown (12:33). Chandler kicked extra point.

Green Bay scoring drive: 5 yards, 1 play, :09.

Green Bay 21, Kansas City 10

Chandler kick to 1 yard into end zone, Coan 31 return (Weatherwax).

Kansas City (12:33)

KC 30	1-10	Dawson pass to Taylor underthrown.
KC 30	2-10	Dawson 11 pass to Taylor (Adderley).
KC 41	1-10	McClinton 4 run up middle (Aldridge).
KC 45	2-6	Dawson 5 pass to Coan (Wood, Jeter).
50	3-1	Coan run left, loss of 4 (Caffey).
KC 46	4-5	Wilson 29 punt downed at GB 25.

Green Bay (10:00)

GB 25	1-10	Pitts 12 run right tackle (Williamson).
GB 37	1-10	Starr sacked, loss of 7 (Holub).
GB 30	2-17	Starr 14 pass to McGee (Mitchell).
GB 44	3-3	Taylor 2 run around left end (Headrick, Hurston).
GB 46	4-1	Chandler 35 punt, Garrett 8 return (Curry).

Kansas City (7:08)

KC 27	1-10	Dawson pass to Burford incomplete.
KC 27	2-10	Dawson sacked, loss of 14 (Caffey, Davis).
KC 2	4-35	Wilson 43 punt, D. Anderson 4 return. GB penalized 15 for clipping.

Green Bay (6:16)

GB 44	1-10	Pitts sweep left, loss of 2 (Holub).
GB 42	2-12	Starr 11 pass to McGee (Mitchell).
KC 47	3-1	Taylor 4 run left tackle (Headrick).
KC 43	1-10	Starr pass to McGee incomplete.
KC 43	2-10	Starr pass to Taylor, loss of 1 (Bell).
KC 44	3-11	Starr 16 pass to McGee (Hunt, Bell).
KC 28	1-10	Taylor 3 run right (Buchanan).
KC 25	2-7	Taylor 4 draw left (Robinson).

KC 21	3-3	Taylor 8 run around left end (Bell).
KC 13	1-10	Starr 13 pass to McGee middle end zone (juggling catch), touchdown (:51). Chandler kicked extra point.

Green Bay scoring drive: 56 yards, 10 plays, 5:25.

Green Bay 28, Kansas City 10

Chandler kick to KC 2, Coan 15 return (Hathcock).

Kansas City (:51)

KC 17	1-10	McClinton 1 run up middle (Jordan).

END OF THIRD QUARTER:

Green Bay 28, Kansas City 10

FOURTH QUARTER

KC 18	2-9	Dawson pass almost intercepted (Wood).
KC 18	3-9	Dawson pass to Taylor incomplete.
KC 18	4-9	Wilson 41 punt, D. Anderson 6 return (Ply).

Green Bay (14:26)

GB 47	1-10	Taylor 3 run left (Buchanan).
50	2-7	Starr pass to McGee deep intercepted at KC 11, Mitchell no return.

Kansas City (13:19)

KC 11	1-10	Dawson 27 pass to McClinton (diving catch).
KC 38	1-10	Dawson 4 pass to Taylor (Adderley).
KC 42	2-6	Dawson 12 pass to Burford (Jeter).
GB 46	1-10	Dawson pass to Taylor end zone incomplete. Play nullified and KC penalized 5 for illegal procedure.
KC 49	1-15	Dawson sacked, loss of 10 (Davis).
KC 39	2-25	Dawson pass to Taylor broken up (Adderley).
KC 39	3-25	Dawson pass to Garrett broken up (Brown).
KC 39	4-25	Wilson 61 punt into end zone, touchback.

Green Bay (10:48)

GB 20	1-10	Starr 25 pass to Dale (Mitchell).
GB 45	1-10	Starr 37 pass to McGee deep middle (Mitchell).
KC 18	1-10	Taylor run up middle, no gain (Mays).
KC 18	2-10	Starr 7 pass to Dale (Mitchell).
KC 11	3-3	Pitts 6 run right tackle (Robinson).
KC 5	1-goal	Taylor 3 run left (Headrick).
KC 2	2-goal	Taylor 1 run around left end (Robinson).
KC 1	3-goal	Pitts 1 run left, touchdown (6:35). Chandler kicked extra point.

Green Bay scoring drive: 80 yards, 8 plays, 4:13.

Green Bay 35, Kansas City 10

Chandler kick to goal line, Coan 25 return (Mack).

Kansas City (6:35)

KC 25	1-10	Beathard 17 pass to Burford (Jeter).
KC 42	1-10	Beathard 14 run evading pass rush (Nitschke).
GB 44	1-10	Beathard pass to Garrett incomplete.
GB 44	2-10	KC penalized 5 for illegal procedure.
GB 49	2-15	Beathard sacked, loss of 11 (Brown).
KC 40	3-26	Beathard pass to Burford broken up (Jeter).
KC 40	4-26	Wilson 42 punt, Wood fair catch.

Green Bay (4:23)

GB 18	1-10	D. Anderson 13 run around left end (Holub)
GB 31	1-10	Grabowski run, no gain (Holub), fumbled, Skoronski recovered for GB at GB 31.
GB 31	2-10	D. Anderson 3 run around right end (Williamson).
GB 34	3-4	Bratkowski pass to Dale deep incomplete.
GB 34	4-7	D. Anderson 43 punt downed at KC 23.

Kansas City (2:14)

KC 23	1-10	Beathard pass to Taylor deep incomplete.
KC 23	2-10	Beathard sacked, loss of 7 (Nitschke).
KC 16	3-17	Beathard pass overthrown.
KC 16	4-17	Wilson 54 punt, Wood return, loss of 2. GB penalized 15 for clipping.

Green Bay (1:12)

GB 13	1-10	Grabowski 2 run up middle (Buchanan).
GB 15	2-8	D. Anderson 10 run around right end (Mays).
GB 25	1-10	D. Anderson 4 run left end (Holub).

FINAL SCORE:

Green Bay 35, Kansas City 10

FINAL RECORDS:

Green Bay 14-2, Kansas City 12-3-1

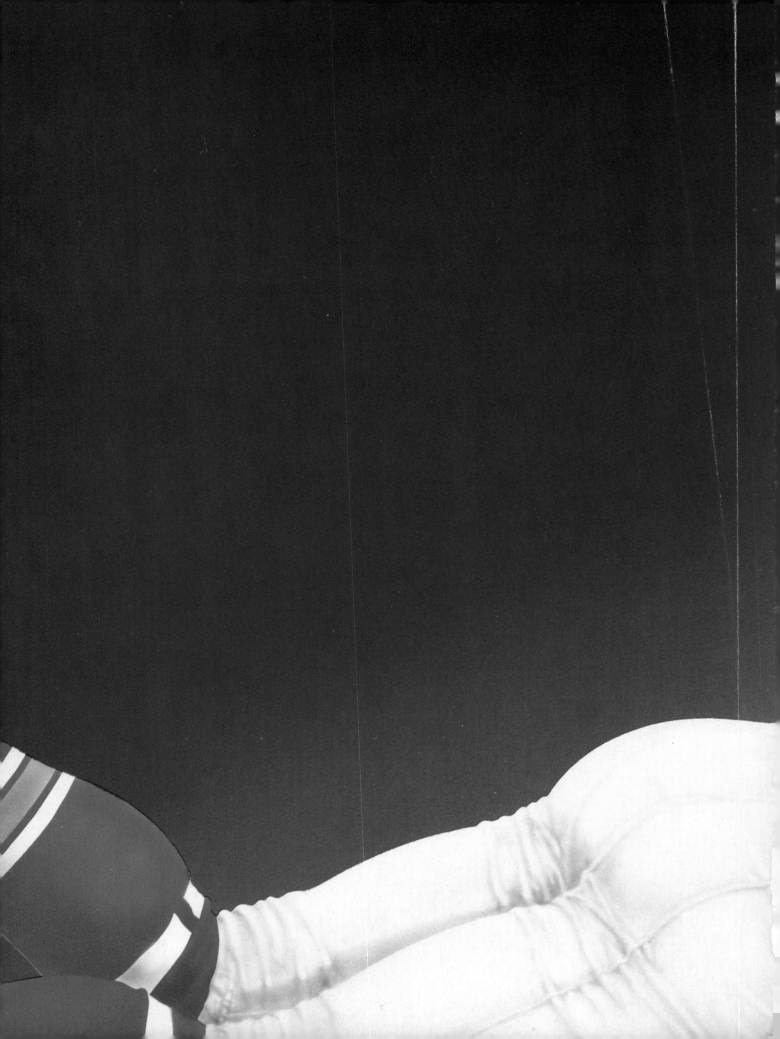

They can play a hundred of them, and probably will, and no Super Bowl ever will equal the emotion and nervousness of the first one.

The notice was short, the staging uncertain, and nobody knew quite what to expect. Oh, the predictions that Green Bay would demolish the Kansas City Chiefs were universal, but there was absolutely no realistic way to compare the teams.

Subsequent games would be played for the best of reasons: to settle the pro football championship of the galaxy. But the first one was as close as the series would ever get to a holy war.

There were so many vendettas working there barely was room for the teams. It was not only the National Football League against the American Football League, but all their children against each other: CBS versus NBC, Ford versus Chrysler. Even the writers who covered the respective leagues huddled in their own corners. This was no time to be neutral.

As a result, no coach ever again is likely to feel the weight that Green Bay's Vince Lombardi carried on January 15, 1967. You don't preach greatness, as Lombardi did, and lose to the champion of a league you have laughed at for seven years.

The two leagues had fought for players, fans, and television dollars, but had not yet met on the field; their champions had not even scouted each other. With final approval of the recently negotiated merger delayed by political and legal wrangles, arrangements for the game had to be completed in 26 days.

There was little of the media circus that would characterize the event a quarter of a century later. Ticket prices—$6, $10, and $12—would be viewed as stiff, and of the 94,000 seats in the spacious Los Angeles Coliseum, a third would go unsold.

The betting line was no surprise: the Packers by 14 points. Each team would use its own league ball on offense, and the AFL's two-point conversion rule was scrapped.

There was no stampede for press credentials: 338 were issued to writers, slightly more to radio and television stations and photographers. The two TV networks shared the same pictures, with their own announcers.

Instead of hype, the game offered fear and loathing and a sweeping curiosity.

Instead of a catchy name with a Roman numeral, it was called the AFL-NFL World Championship Game.

A unity party during the week brought together the rival ownerships in an uneasy truce, a huge wedding cake symbolizing the fusion of the old and the new. The wife of one AFL owner startled the guests by grabbing the microphone to give a short but rousing speech for Kansas City. She concluded it with a stirring cheer: "Go, Chiefs, go!"

NFL owners exchanged significant glances, and they left the party with a nervous feeling. "My God," they wondered, "what if we lose?"

Kansas City revealed no sense of dread at facing the Packers, who had dominated the NFL in the 1960s. Especially vocal was Fred Williamson, a cornerback with acting ambitions who boasted a black belt in karate. He possessed a secret weapon he called "The Hammer," a hard forearm chop across the helmet. He claimed he would drop it on the Packers' receivers.

Green Bay's mood was even harder to gauge. Lombardi would not allow the Packers to be complacent. But age had crept up on some of them—Jim Taylor was 31, Max McGee 34, and the Golden Boy, Paul Hornung, 31—and changes were coming.

On both sides, public words were not consistent with private thought or action. Lombardi kept dropping hints to the press that his team had already proved whatever it needed to prove—beating Dallas 34-27 in an exciting NFL Championship Game.

Yet years later, Fuzzy Thurston says, "He called us together before we left for Los Angeles and told us this was going to be the most important game we had ever played. He told us we were representing the whole league. He read a few telegrams. I remember one was from George Halas [Chicago Bears owner], another from Wellington Mara [New York Giants owner]. They all said pretty much the same thing: 'Go out there and show those clowns who's boss.'"

Super Bowl I was televised by two networks—CBS, which covered the NFL, and NBC, which covered the AFL. Two of the color commentators—Paul Christman (left, NBC) and Frank Gifford (CBS)—met on the field.

On the field before the kickoff, Frank Gifford, then an announcer with CBS, imposed on an old friendship and got Lombardi to agree to an interview. When Lombardi was the Giants' offensive coach in the 1950s, Gifford helped make his run-to-daylight offense click. "During the five minutes or so we talked," Gifford says, "he held onto my arm and he was shaking like a leaf. It was incredible."

Lombardi was not alone. For all their bravado, Chiefs linebacker E.J. Holub confides, the Chiefs were scared to death. "Guys in the tunnel were throwing up and wetting their pants," he says.

It was not just another game. Whether it would be a contest or an execution remained to be seen.

A thin layer of Cali-

fornia's finest smog drifted high above the Coliseum for this first meeting of the teams from opposing planets. The game began on a wary note, particularly on the part of Green Bay, which eyed the Chiefs with the uneasiness of a dog pawing at the first porcupine it ever had seen.

For 30 minutes the Chiefs played on nearly even terms against the Packers, who were representing a league that had a 40-year head start when the AFL began in 1960.

At halftime, Green Bay led by a fragile 14-10.

The fateful play of the first half was the third one, when Boyd Dowler, leading an end sweep by Taylor, separated his shoulder trying to block Johnny Robinson, the Chiefs' free safety. Dowler, Green Bay's best receiver, was finished for the day. Max McGee, who had said he would retire after the game, replaced him.

Cool, calm, and collected Bart Starr, who led the Packers to five NFL titles, passed for 250 yards and two touchdowns in Super Bowl I and was named the game's most valuable player. He completed 16 of 23 attempts.

McGee, an 11-year veteran, had not expected to see action. He was so certain he would be resting that he defied the team curfew the night before the game. He didn't get caught that time but he had a losing history of cat-and-mouse combat with the coach.

McGee was notorious among the Packers for sneaking out after curfew, in search of bright lights and pretty companions.

One time, Lombardi caught and fined McGee twice within a few days. Then came a third infraction. "MAX!" Lombardi roared at a team meeting, "that will cost you five-hundred dollars." That was real money in a time when $25,000 a year would make an all-pro tackle very happy.

Lombardi was shaking with anger. He seemed to be fighting a losing battle, and he didn't like to lose at anything. "Max, if I catch you again"—the coach had turned from red to purple—"the fine will be ONE THOUSAND DOLLARS." The room grew silent and Lombardi stopped shaking. "Max," he said, softly. "If you find anything worth a thousand for sneaking out, call me and I'll go with you."

For the first championship game, Lombardi had raised the ante to $5,000, an indication of how seriously he took the game. McGee's room was checked at 11 o'clock Saturday night, but moments later he was out of there. He returned, by his own admission late, at 7:30 the morning of the game, an indication of how seriously he took his prospects of playing.

During the entire 1966 season, he had caught only four passes for 91 yards. "I knew I wouldn't play unless Dowler got hurt," he says.

Which is exactly what happened. Disbelieving, his head aching, McGee entered the game.

Bart Starr never missed a beat. The Green Bay quarterback finished off a six-play, 80-yard drive by connecting with McGee for the last 37. The pass was behind him, but McGee caught it one-handed, reeled it in, then outran Williamson to the end zone. The Packers led 7-0.

Kansas City, unveiling its "moving pocket" to skeptical NFL fans, surged 66 yards in six plays and tied the score in the second quarter. With his blockers in motion, Chiefs quarterback Len Dawson could throw on the run, creating problems for the defense. He completed three suc-

cessive passes on the drive, including one of 31 yards to Otis Taylor. The next was a seven-yard pass to fullback Curtis McClinton for the touchdown.

Starr, who was to lead the Packers to five NFL titles and two Super Bowl victories in the 1960s, was playing at his peak, however. On the third play of the next series, he fired a 64-yard touchdown pass to Carroll Dale. It was wiped out by an illegal procedure call, but Starr shrugged off the misfortune and got another touchdown anyway, driving the Packers 73 yards for a 14-7 lead.

It was third-and-7 on the Chiefs' 24 when the quarterback threw 10 yards to running back Elijah Pitts for a first down. Starr then sent Taylor around left end for 14 yards and the score.

Starr kept his drives going with third-down hook passes over the middle. The hook pass is one of the oldest pass patterns in football. What it requires of a receiver is courage and sure hands.

To win, Stram believed the Chiefs had to stop the Packers' running game, and he stacked

Len Dawson and the Chiefs trailed the Packers just 14-10 at halftime, but Dawson threw an interception on the first series of the third quarter—to Willie Wood—and it helped break open the game for Green Bay.

I

Fullback Jim Taylor put the Packers ahead 14-7 in the second quarter by running 14 yards around left end for a touchdown. Bart Starr completed four passes on the 73-yard drive to set up the touchdown.

his linebackers, usually with two of them in the middle and frequently blitzing. This strategy took the linebackers out of the passing lanes, and Starr capitalized on it on third down.

But Green Bay scored no more points in the quarter, and, just before halftime, Mike Mercer kicked a 31-yard field goal. The Chiefs went to their locker room trailing by just four points, 14-10. "What I remember best," says Jim Ken-

Kansas City's Mike Mercer trimmed the lead to 14-10 at halftime with a 31-yard field goal, despite the effort of cornerback Bob Jeter (21) to block it. The field goal came with 54 seconds left in the half.

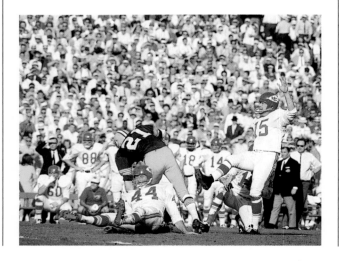

sil, Commissioner Pete Rozelle's number-one aide, "is how surprised some of the writers were at the half. And how tense they were."

Buddy Young, an NFL man and a one-time breakaway runner who was working for the league, said flatly: "Old age and heat will get the Packers in the second half."

The Chiefs were exuberant. Stram says, "I honestly thought we would come back and win it. We felt we were doing the things we had to do, and doing them well. We were only four

The Coliseum had 32,000 empty seats, many visible on Willie Wood's 50-yard interception return.

points behind at halftime. We were confident that we could get that back and more."

In the Green Bay locker room, Lombardi was all business. "All right, defense," he said, with a loud clap of his hands, "we've looked at them for a half. We know what they're trying to do. Let's take control of the game, defense. Let's get more pressure on Dawson and create some opportunities for the offense."

"The coach was *concerned*," is the way Packers defensive end Willie Davis puts it. "But we also knew we couldn't stand Lombardi if we didn't

48

win. That was always a motivation for us."

Max McGee's juggling 13-yard touchdown catch in the third quarter boosted Green Bay's lead to 28-10.

In the second half, Lombardi reluctantly ordered the blitz—a tactic the Green Bay coach always had scorned as "the weapon of weaklings." The Packers referred to it as the red dog.

The Chiefs' failure to react immediately to the tactical change and pick up the blitz was what doomed them. On the fourth play of the third quarter, the Packers brought two linebackers, Lee Roy Caffey and Dave Robinson, and rushed Dawson into a turning-point mistake.

The Chiefs were facing third-and-5. The chart that Kansas City had prepared on the Packers' tendencies said that Lombardi authorized a blitz on third-and-5 "about three times in two years."

Taken by surprise, Dawson was hit as he released the ball and he threw a desperation flutterball in the general direction of tight end Fred Arbanas. But free safety Willie Wood got there first, made the interception, and picked

his way 50 yards to the Kansas City 5, where Chiefs running back Mike Garrett, like Wood a former USC star, caught him from behind.

On first down, Pitts sliced through the flus-

Guard Fuzzy Thurston (left) relaxed with McGee on the sideline as the Packers' defense throttled the Chiefs. McGee, who replaced the injured Boyd Dowler, caught seven passes for 138 yards and two touchdowns.

tered Chiefs and into the end zone. The Packers had stretched their lead to 21-10.

"You don't like to think that one play can make that much of a difference," Hank Stram says, "but in this case it did. The interception changed the personality of our attack. Play action and rolls were the things we did best. But when we got behind we had to deviate from our game plan and we got into trouble."

The Kansas City offense totaled 12 yards in the third quarter, while the Packers scored twice and put the game away. On a 56-yard advance, Starr hit McGee three times—for 11, 16, and 13 yards. McGee juggled the last one before hauling it in one-handed in the end zone.

For the day, McGee, the man who wasn't supposed to play, caught seven passes for 138 yards and two touchdowns.

In the fourth quarter, with Green Bay's re-

McGee already had scored twice when he caught a 37-yard pass from Starr in the fourth quarter and ran to the Chiefs' 18 to set up the Packers' final touchdown. Cornerback Willie Mitchell made the tackle.

serves on the field, Williamson came up to meet a running play. Guard Gale Gillingham, was leading the sweep for rookie Donny Anderson and missed Williamson, but Anderson ran right over him, his knee catching Williamson's helmet. Anderson tumbled over him. Williamson was knocked unconscious on the play, then suffered a broken arm when teammate Sherrill Headrick fell on him.

Just before he was carried off the field, Fuzzy Thurston stood over Williamson's motionless form, not saying a word, but humming softly the tune "If I Had a Hammer...."

When reporters asked Lombardi later why it took the Packers so long to unload on Williamson, he quipped, "That was the first time he got close to a play."

There was a touch of whimsy to the Packers' final points, which came in the fourth quarter following an 80-yard drive. In one of the week's nicer moments, Jerry Mays, the Kansas City defensive end, had told the press how much he admired Green Bay tackle Forrest Gregg. Mays had followed him at Southern Methodist.

Two eventual Hall of Fame members collaborated on this short sweep to the Chiefs' 1-yard line, which set up Green Bay's final touchdown. Tackle Forrest Gregg pulled and blocked, and fullback Jim Taylor carried the ball.

On the first play after Taylor's run, Elijah Pitts ran one yard for the game's final touchdown behind the blocking of tight end Marv Fleming (81). Pitts rushed for 45 yards on 11 carries and scored twice.

With the Packers at the 1-yard line, Starr called a play for Pitts. As both lines settled into their stances, Jerry Kramer turned to Gregg and said, "I'll get number fifty-eight [defensive end Andy Rice] and you take care of the guy whose hero you are." They did.

Pitts tumbled in from the 1, and Don

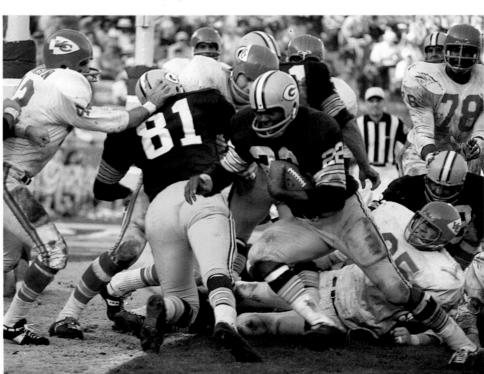

Chandler kicked his fifth extra point. And so the first World Championship Game was over: Green Bay 35, Kansas City 10.

One of the enduring impressions of the game was that the Packers had exploited Kansas City's weakness on the corners for easy yardage. Years later, Stram continues to defend Williamson and Willie Mitchell. Game films showed that they were in nearly hopeless circumstances, going one-on-one against receivers cutting to the middle, making difficult catches on many balls.

"It took exceptional timing between Starr and his receivers," Stram says. "It also took great pass blocking and they got it. We had a variety of coverages, but they were able to isolate our corner men one-on-one."

Dawson blames himself for Wood's interception, and, by extension, the loss itself. "I gave them seven points," he says, "and then we had to play catch up. I should have thrown it away. We sent five receivers downfield and they blitzed. The pressure bothered me. I didn't have any zing on the pass."

There are ways to neutralize a blitzing linebacker. The Chiefs had done it all year by using a quick pass over the middle to a running back. But in the confusion created by Green Bay, the Chiefs called it only once in the second half, and then Curtis McClinton stumbled.

Starr completed 16 of 23 passes for 250 yards, and wore down the Chiefs with one well chosen play after another. In the second half, he completed 8 of his 10 pass attempts for 122 yards.

For his heady performance, Starr was voted the game's most valuable player.

In the dressing room, Commissioner Rozelle presented Lombardi with a trophy designed by Tiffany, a silver football on a pyramid-shaped pedestal that four years later would be named after the Green Bay coach. The trophy sat on a bench alongside him as Lombardi stroked a leather football, like a man petting a puppy.

"The game ball," he said, proudly. "The players gave it to me. It's the NFL ball. It catches better and kicks a little better than the AFL ball."

This was, of course, a sly gibe at the constant questions about how the two leagues differed.

Then Lombardi put it more bluntly: "Dallas is a better team. Kansas City is a good team, but they don't even rate with the top teams in our division. There. That's what you wanted me to say, isn't it?"

The next morning, Lombardi walked into a meeting of National Football League owners and general managers, and they rose as a group to give him a standing ovation.

The ovation offered a small insight into the relief the NFL powers were feeling after the first confrontation.

There was a melancholy footnote to the Packers' victory: Paul Hornung was the only player not to take part in it. Hornung had pinched a nerve in his neck at midseason and hadn't played in six weeks. Still, Lombardi was criticized for failing to call on him. Lombardi said he felt that a token appearance would have been degrading to the running back he once described as "one of the greatest I have ever seen inside the twenty-yard line."

Hornung remembers it differently today. "Actually," he says, "Vince left it up to me. Before the game, he asked me to stay at his side, in case he needed me early. But Pitts did a fine job, and late in the game when he asked me if I wanted to go in, I said no. I didn't see any point in it. Knowing what I learned later, what one lick to my neck could have done, I'm glad I didn't."

The aftermath of the game was bittersweet. Outside of the Packers, it wasn't generally known that Jim Taylor, the great fullback, had played out his option in 1966, and that Lombardi had gone most of the season without talking to him.

Lombardi left Hornung unprotected in the expansion draft that winter, and New Orleans claimed him. But Taylor had elected on his own to return to Louisiana, where he played his college football and still made his home.

When Green Bay held a testimonial dinner for the former touchdown twins, Lombardi was unable to attend. He sent a telegram praising Hornung, but referred to Taylor only indirectly with a quote from Cicero on loyalty.

Meanwhile, Max McGee decided not to retire after all. He announced he would be back for the 1967 season.

II

Green Bay 33, Oakland 14

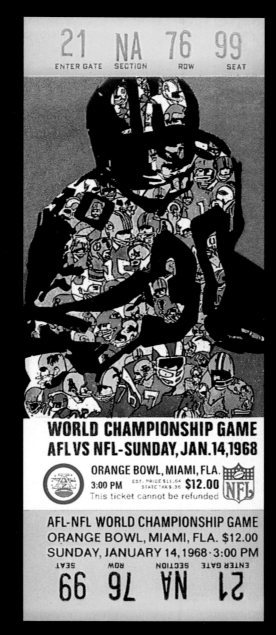

1968

GREEN BAY 33
OAKLAND 14

Vital Statistics

Starting Lineups

Green Bay (NFL)	Offense	Oakland (AFL)
Boyd Dowler	WR	Bill Miller
Bob Skoronski	LT	Bob Svihus
Gale Gillingham	LG	Gene Upshaw
Ken Bowman	C	Jim Otto
Jerry Kramer	RG	Wayne Hawkins
Forrest Gregg	RT	Harry Schuh
Marv Fleming	TE	Billy Cannon
Carroll Dale	WR	Fred Biletnikoff
Bart Starr	QB	Daryle Lamonica
Donny Anderson	RB	Pete Banaszak
Ben Wilson	RB	Hewritt Dixon
	Defense	
Willie Davis	LE	Issac Lassiter
Ron Kostelnik	LT	Dan Birdwell
Henry Jordan	RT	Tom Keating
Lionel Aldridge	RE	Ben Davidson
Dave Robinson	LLB	Bill Laskey
Ray Nitschke	MLB	Dan Conners
Lee Roy Caffey	RLB	Gus Otto
Herb Adderley	LCB	Kent McCloughan
Bobby Jeter	RCB	Willie Brown
Tom Brown	SS	Warren Powers
Willie Wood	FS	Howie Williams

Substitutions

Green Bay-Offense: K-Don Chandler. WR-Bob Long, Max McGee, Dick Capp. LINE-Fuzzy Thurston, Bob Hyland. QB-Zeke Bratkowski. RB-Travis Williams, Chuck Mercein. Defense: LINE-Bob Brown, Jim Weatherwax. LB-Tommy Crutcher, Jim Flanigan. DB-John Rowser, Doug Hart. DNP: RB-Jim Grabowski. QB-Don Horn. T-Steve Wright.
Oakland-Offense: K-George Blanda. P-Mike Eischeid. WR-Warren Wells, Dave Kocourek, Ken Herock. LINE-Bob Kruse, Jim Harvey, Dan Archer. RB-Larry Todd, Roger Hagberg. Defense: LINE-Carleton Oates, Richard Sligh. LB-John Williamson, Bill Budness, Duane Benson. DB-Dave Grayson, Rodger Bird. DNP: WR-Rod Sherman.

Officials

Referee-Jack Vest (AFL). Umpire-Ralph Morcroft (NFL). Head Linesman-Tony Veteri (AFL). Back Judge-Stan Javie (NFL). Field Judge-Bob Baur (AFL). Line Judge-Bruce Alford (NFL).

Scoring

Green Bay	3	13	10	7 —	33
Oakland	0	7	0	7 —	14

GB-FG Chandler 39
GB-FG Chandler 20
GB-Dowler 62 pass from Starr (Chandler kick)
Oak-Miller 23 pass from Lamonica (Blanda kick)
GB-FG Chandler 43
GB-Anderson 2 run (Chandler kick)
GB-FG Chandler 31
GB-Adderley 60 interception return (Chandler kick)
Oak-Miller 23 pass from Lamonica (Blanda kick)
Attendance-75,546

FINAL TEAM STATISTICS

	Packers	Raiders
TOTAL FIRST DOWNS	19	16
Rushing	11	5
Passing	7	10
Penalty	1	1
TOTAL NET YARDAGE	322	293
Total Offensive Plays	69	57
Average Gain per Offensive Play	4.7	5.1
NET YARDS RUSHING	160	107
Total Rushing Plays	41	20
Average Gain per Rushing Play	3.9	5.4
NET YARDS PASSING	162	186
Pass Att.-Comp.-Int.	24-13-0	34-15-1
Sacks-Yards Lost	4-40	3-22
Gross Yards Passing	202	208
Avg. Gain per Pass (Incl. Sacks)	5.8	5.0
PUNTS-YARDS	6-234	6-264
Average Distance	39.0	44.0
Had Blocked	0	0
TOTAL RETURN YARDAGE	144	139
Kickoff Returns-Yards	3-49	7-127
Punt Returns-Yards	5-35	5-12
Interception Returns-Yards	1-60	0-0
TOTAL TURNOVERS	0	3
Fumbles-Lost	0-0	3-2
Had Intercepted	0	1
PENALTIES-YARDS	1-12	4-31
TOTAL POINTS SCORED	33	14
Touchdowns Rushing	1	0
Touchdowns Passing	1	2
Touchdowns Returns	1	0
Extra Points	3	2
Field Goals-Attempts	4-4	0-1
Safeties	0	0
THIRD DOWN EFFICIENCY	5/16	3/11
FOURTH DOWN EFFICIENCY	1/1	0/0
TIME OF POSSESSION	35:38	24:22

INDIVIDUAL STATISTICS

RUSHING

Green Bay	No.	Yds.	Avg.	Long	TD
Wilson	17	62	3.6	13	0
Anderson	14	48	3.4	8	1
Williams	8	36	4.5	18	0
Starr	1	14	14.0	14	0
Mercein	1	0	0.0	0	0

Oakland	No.	Yds.	Avg.	Long	TD
Dixon	12	54	4.5	14	0
Banaszak	6	16	2.7	5	0
Todd	2	37	18.5	32	0

PASSING

Green Bay	Att.	Comp.	Yds.	Long	TD	Int.
Starr	24	13	202	62t	1	0

Oakland	Att.	Comp.	Yds.	Long	TD	Int.
Lamonica	34	15	208	41	2	1

RECEIVING

Green Bay	No.	Yds.	Long	TD
Dale	4	43	17	0
Fleming	4	35	11	0
Dowler	2	71	62t	1
Anderson	2	18	12	0
McGee	1	35	35	0

Oakland	No.	Yds.	Long	TD
Miller	5	84	23t	2
Banaszak	4	69	41	0
Cannon	2	25	15	0
Biletnikoff	2	10	6	0
Wells	1	17	17	0
Dixon	1	3	3	0

INTERCEPTIONS

Green Bay	No.	Yds.	Long	TD
Adderley	1	60	60t	1

Oakland	No.	Yds.	Long	TD
None				

PUNTING

Green Bay	No.	Yds.	Avg.	TB	Long
Anderson	6	234	39.0	1	48

Oakland	No.	Yds.	Avg.	TB	Long
Eischeid	6	264	44.0	0	55

PUNT RETURNS

Green Bay	No.	FC	Yds.	Long	TD
Wood	5	0	35	31	0

Oakland	No.	FC	Yds.	Long	TD
Bird	2	1	12	12	0

KICKOFF RETURNS

Green Bay	No.	Yds.	Long	TD
Adderley	1	24	24	0
Williams	1	18	18	0
Crutcher	1	7	7	0

Oakland	No.	Yds.	Long	TD
Todd	3	63	23	0
*Grayson	2	61	25	0
Hawkins	1	3	3	0
*Kocourek	1	0	0	0

*Kocourek lateraled to Grayson, who returned 11 yards.

FUMBLES

Green Bay	No.	Own Rec.	Opp. Rec.
Capp	0	0	1
Robinson	0	0	1

Oakland	No.	Own Rec.	Opp. Rec.
Bird	1	0	0
Banaszak	1	0	0
Wells	1	0	0
Williamson	0	1	0

KICKING

Green Bay	XP-A	FG-A	FG Made	FG Missed
Chandler	3-3	4-4	39,20,43,31	--

Oakland	XP-A	FG-A	FG Made	FG Missed
Blanda	2-2	0-1	--	47

PLAY-BY-PLAY

Oakland won the coin toss and elected to receive.

FIRST QUARTER

Chandler kick to O 5, Todd 23 return (Crutcher).

Oakland (15:00)

O 28	1-10	Dixon run left, no gain (Nitschke).
O 28	2-10	Lamonica pass to Biletnikoff incomplete.
O 28	3-10	Lamonica pass to Dixon underthrown, incomplete.
O 28	4-10	Eischeid 38 punt, Wood no return.

Green Bay (13:44)

GB 34	1-10	Anderson 5 run right (Keating).
GB 39	2-5	Wilson 3 sweep left (Brown).
GB 42	3-2	Anderson 4 run left tackle (Davidson).
GB 46	1-10	Starr 9 pass to Dale right (McCloughan).
O 45	2-1	Wilson 1 sweep right (Conners).
O 44	1-10	Wilson run right tackle, no gain (Lassiter). Play nullified and Oak. penalized 5 for offsides.
O 39	1-5	Starr 8 pass to Fleming left (Powers).
O 31	1-10	Starr pass to Dale overthrown, incomplete.
O 31	2-10	Anderson run right, loss of 1 (Birdwell).
O 32	3-11	Starr rushed, pass to Fleming incomplete.
O 32	4-11	Chandler, 39-yard field goal (9:53).

Green Bay scoring drive: 34 yards, 9 plays, 3:51.

Green Bay 3, Oakland 0

Chandler kick to O 14, Kocourek lateraled to Grayson, Grayson 11 return.

Oakland (9:53)

O 25	1-10	Banaszak 4 sweep left (Jeter).
O 29	2-6	Lamonica 9 pass to Miller (Robinson).
O 38	2-6	Dixon 4 run right (Brown).
O 42	2-6	Dixon sweep left, no gain (Caffey). Play nullified and Oak. penalized 16 for clipping.
O 26	2-22	Lamonica pass to Miller incomplete. Play nullified and GB penalized 12 for pass interference (Nitschke). Automatic first down.
O 38	1-10	Dixon 3 run right tackle (Nitschke).
O 41	2-7	Lamonica 13 pass to Miller (Brown).
GB 46	1-10	Dixon sweep left, loss of 2 (Aldridge).
GB 48	2-12	Lamonica pass to Banaszak broken up (Wood).
GB 48	3-12	Lamonica pass to Dixon overthrown, incomplete.
GB 48	4-12	Eischeid 45 punt out of bounds at GB 3.

Green Bay (5:32)

GB 3	1-10	Wilson 7 run right (Conners).
GB 10	2-3	Anderson 4 run left (Davidson).
GB 14	1-10	Starr 17 pass to Dale left (Brown).
GB 31	1-10	Wilson 5 run left tackle (Davidson).
GB 36	2-5	Anderson 5 run right (Brown).
GB 41	1-10	Starr pass to Fleming broken up (Powers).
GB 41	2-10	Starr 14 run evading pass rush.
O 45	1-10	Wilson 6 run up middle (Birdwell).
O 39	2-4	Anderson 3 run right tackle (Lassiter).
O 36	3-1	Anderson run left, no gain (Conners).
O 36	4-1	Wilson 5 run around left end (Williams).

END OF FIRST QUARTER:

Green Bay 3, Oakland 0

SECOND QUARTER

O 31	1-10	Starr 6 pass to Anderson (G. Otto).
O 25	2-4	Wilson 12 run left tackle (Brown).
O 13	1-10	Starr pass to Anderson dropped, incomplete.
O 13	2-10	Starr sacked, loss of 11 (Keating, Birdwell).
O 24	3-21	Starr 11 pass to Fleming (Bird).
O 13	4-18	Chandler, 20-yard field goal (11:52).

Green Bay scoring drive: 80 yards, 16 plays, 8:40.

Green Bay 6, Oakland 0

Chandler kick to O 2, Grayson 25 return (Crutcher).

Oakland (11:52)

O 27	1-10	Banaszak 1 run right end (Brown).
O 28	2-9	Lamonica pass to Biletnikoff dropped, incomplete.
O 28	3-9	Lamonica sacked, loss of 9 (Davis).
O 19	4-18	Eischeid 47 punt, Wood 4 return.

Green Bay (11:01)

| GB 38 | 1-10 | Starr 62 pass to Dowler middle (caught at O 44), touchdown (10:50). Chandler kicked extra point. |

Green Bay scoring drive: 62 yards, 1 play, :11.

Green Bay 13, Oakland 0

Chandler kick to goal line, Todd 22 return (Hyland).

Oakland (10:50)

| O 22 | 1-10 | Banaszak 5 run right tackle (Davis). |

O 27	2-5	Banaszak 4 run up middle (Davis).
O 31	3-1	Dixon 9 run left tackle (Davis).
O 40	1-10	Lamonica 4 pass to Biletnikoff (Adderley).
O 44	2-6	Lamonica 16 pass to Miller middle (Wood).
GB 40	1-10	Lamonica pass to Dixon dropped, incomplete.
GB 40	2-10	Lamonica 15 pass to Banaszak left sideline.
GB 25	1-10	Banaszak 2 run left tackle (Kostelnik).
GB 23	2-8	Lamonica 23 pass to Miller right sideline (at GB 5), touchdown (6:15). Blanda kicked extra point.

Oakland scoring drive: 78 yards, 9 plays, 4:35.

Green Bay 13, Oakland 7

Eischeid kick to GB 8, Crutcher 7 return (Benson).

Green Bay (6:15)

GB 15	1-10	Wilson run left, loss of 1 (Conners).
GB 14	2-11	Starr sacked, loss of 8 (Keating).
GB 6	3-19	Wilson 1 run left end (Keating).
GB 7	4-18	Anderson 45 punt, Bird 12 return.

Oakland (4:22)

GB 40	1-10	Banaszak run right end, no gain (Nitschke).
GB 40	2-10	Dixon 1 run left tackle (Jordan).
GB 39	3-9	Lamonica pass to Dixon overthrown, incomplete.
GB 39	4-9	Blanda's 47-yard field-goal attempt was short, fielded at GB 2, Wood 6 return (Kocourek).

Green Bay (2:20)

GB 8	1-10	Williams 2 run right (Conners).
GB 10	2-8	Williams 5 run left tackle (Williams).
GB 15	3-3	Williams 2 run right tackle (Conners).
GB 17	4-1	Anderson 8 run, Bird fair catch, fumbled, Kapp recovered for GB at O 45 (:23).
O 45	1-10	Starr pass to McGee broken up (Williams).
O 45	2-10	Starr pass to Dowler incomplete. (:12)
O 45	3-10	Starr 9 pass to Dowler right sideline.
O 36	4-1	Chandler, 43-yard field goal (:01).

Green Bay scoring drive: 9 yards, 3 plays, :22.

Chandler kick to O 47, Hawkins 3 return (Brown).

END OF SECOND QUARTER:

Green Bay 16, Oakland 7

THIRD QUARTER

Eischeid kick to GB 9, Williams 18 return (Benson).

Green Bay (15:00)

GB 27	1-10	Wilson 2 run left (Conners).
GB 29	2-8	Starr 7 pass to Fleming (Bird).
GB 36	3-1	Wilson run left tackle, no gain (Brown).
GB 36	4-1	Anderson 32 punt, Wells fair catch, fumbled, Williamson recovered for Oak. at O 32.

Oakland (12:07)

O 32	1-10	Dixon 14 run left tackle (Brown).
O 46	1-10	Dixon run left end, loss of 2 (Jeter).
O 44	2-12	Lamonica pass to Cannon broken up (Jeter).
O 44	3-12	Lamonica pass to Banaszak broken up (Brown).
O 44	4-12	Eischeid 38 punt, Wood no return (Kruse).

Green Bay (10:35)

GB 18	1-10	Wilson 13 draw up middle (Williams).
GB 31	1-10	Anderson 8 sweep left (Davidson).
GB 39	2-2	Wilson 1 run right tackle (Conners).
GB 40	3-1	Starr 35 pass to McGee deep middle (Bird).
O 25	1-10	Starr pass to Dowler overthrown, incomplete.
O 25	2-10	Wilson 1 draw up middle (Davidson).
O 24	3-9	Starr 11 pass to Dale (McCloughan).
O 13	1-10	Starr pass to Anderson overthrown, incomplete.
O 13	2-10	Starr rollout right, 12 pass to Anderson middle (G. Otto).
O 1	1-goal	Anderson run left, loss of 1 (Davidson).
O 2	2-goal	Anderson 2 run right tackle, touchdown (5:54). Chandler kicked extra point.

Green Bay scoring drive: 82 yards, 11 plays, 4:41.

Green Bay 23, Oakland 7

Chandler kick into end zone, touchback.

Oakland (5:54)

O 20	1-10	Lamonica pass to Miller overthrown.
O 20	2-10	Lamonica screen to Banaszak, no gain (Robinson).
O 20	3-10	Lamonica pass to Banaszak overthrown.
O 20	4-10	Eischeid 41 punt, Wood no return (Williams).

Green Bay (4:49)

| GB 39 | 1-10 | Starr pass to Dale incomplete. Play nullified and Oak. penalized 5 for holding. Automatic first down. |
| GB 44 | 1-10 | Starr 6 pass to Dale (Brown). |

50	2-4	Anderson 6 run right tackle (Birdwell).
O 44	1-10	Anderson 5 run right end (McCloughan).
O 39	2-5	Starr pass to Dale broken up (Brown).
O 39	3-5	Starr 9 pass to Fleming (Bird).
O 30	1-10	Wilson 3 run right tackle (Laskey).
O 27	2-7	Anderson 4 run right (Davidson).
O 23	3-3	Wilson run right, loss of 1 (Birdwell).
O 24	4-4	Chandler, 31-yard field goal (:02).

Green Bay scoring drive: 37 yards, 8 plays, 4:47.

Chandler kick to O 15, Grayson 25 return (Wood).

END OF THIRD QUARTER:

Green Bay 26, Oakland 7

FOURTH QUARTER

| O 40 | 1-10 | Lamonica 13 pass to Banaszak right, fumbled, recovered by GB at GB 47, Robinson 16 return (Schuh). |

Green Bay (14:25)

O 37	1-10	Starr sacked, loss of 11 (Davidson).
O 48	2-21	Williams run right, no gain. Play nullified and Oak. penalized 5 for offsides.
O 43	2-16	Starr pass to Fleming underthrown.
O 43	3-16	Starr pass to Williams incomplete.
O 43	4-16	Anderson 27 punt downed at O 16.

Oakland (13:25)

O 16	1-10	Lamonica pass to Cannon dropped, incomplete.
O 16	2-10	Lamonica 15 pass to Cannon (Brown).
O 31	3-5	Dixon 15 run right tackle (Adderley).
O 46	1-10	Dixon 2 sweep left (Caffey).
O 48	2-8	Lamonica pass to Dixon dropped, incomplete.
O 48	3-8	Lamonica pass to Biletnikoff right intercepted at GB 40, Adderley 60 return, touchdown (11:03). Chandler kicked extra point.

Green Bay 33, Oakland 7

Chandler kick to O 8, Todd 18 return (Brown).

Oakland (11:03)

O 26	1-10	Dixon 8 run right (Nitschke).
O 34	2-2	Dixon 2 run left (Brown).
O 36	1-10	Lamonica 41 pass to Banaszak deep left (Adderley).
GB 23	1-10	Lamonica 23 pass to Miller deep middle, touchdown (9:13). Blanda kicked extra point.

Oakland scoring drive: 74 yards, 4 plays, 1:50.

Green Bay 33, Oakland 14

Eischeid kick to GB 2, Adderley 24 return (Archer).

Green Bay (9:13)

GB 26	1-10	Williams run left tackle, no gain (Davidson).
GB 26	2-10	Williams 3 run right tackle (Birdwell).
GB 29	3-7	Wilson 4 run up middle (Davidson).
GB 33	4-3	Anderson 46 punt, Bird fair catch.

Oakland (7:01)

O 21	1-10	Todd 5 run left (Jordan).
O 26	2-5	Lamonica pass batted down (Nitschke).
O 26	3-5	Lamonica 10 pass to Cannon (Caffey).
O 36	1-10	Lamonica 6 pass to Biletnikoff (Adderley).
O 42	2-4	Lamonica pass to Todd underthrown.
O 42	3-4	Lamonica pass to Cannon broken up (Robinson).
O 42	4-4	Eischeid 55 punt, Wood 31 return (Archer).

Green Bay (4:34)

GB 34	1-10	Williams 5 run right tackle (Conners).
GB 39	2-5	Anderson 4 run left tackle (Davidson).
GB 43	3-1	Williams 18 run left tackle (Bird).
O 39	1-10	Williams 1 run left end (G. Otto).
		Two-Minute Warning.
O 38	2-9	Mercein run left, no gain (Keating).
O 38	3-9	Bratkowski sacked, loss of 10 (Keating).
O 48	4-19	Anderson 48 punt into end zone, touchback.

Oakland (1:07)

O 20	1-10	Lamonica sacked, loss of 9 (Davis).
O 11	2-19	Todd 32 run around right end (Davis).
O 43	1-10	Lamonica 3 pass to Dixon (Caffey).
O 46	2-7	Lamonica pass to Dixon broken up (Davis).
O 46	3-7	Lamonica 17 pass to Wells (Wood).
GB 37	1-10	Lamonica sacked, loss of 4 (Davis).
GB 41	2-14	Lamonica pass to Wells underthrown, incomplete.

FINAL SCORE:

Green Bay 33, Oakland 14

FINAL RECORDS:

Green Bay 12-4-1, Oakland 14-2

The time was so long ago, the Super Bowl trappings so new and nearly innocent, that it was possible to hear a rumor and actually have it come true.

This one was a beauty: Vince Lombardi would retire as head coach of the Green Bay Packers after the game.

Weeks before the Packers were to defend their world title against the Oakland Raiders, there had been a gathering sense of a circle closing, of sweeping changes to come, of new armies assembling.

By itself, Lombardi's farewell as the Packers' coach would have given the game significance. Two other forces added yet more texture. Miami, a new American Football League city, was wild about hosting the teams. The Orange Bowl would draw a festive full house of 75,546, permanently putting to rest the question of empty seats at a Super Bowl.

And then there was Oakland's Al Davis, who had risen in a remarkably short time to rival Lombardi as a charismatic figure, and had seen what the Super Bowl would become. Davis entertained the press every morning, usually in the lobby of his team's hotel at Boca Raton. The con man in him would carry on about how fortunate his little ragamuffins were to be playing the majestic Packers. But then his cockiness would surface, and he would describe how the Raiders planned to stuff the Packers' legendary power sweep.

One morning, Davis sensed he was losing his audience. The writers' eyes seemed to be fixed on the winding staircase above and behind him. His head swiveled, and he spotted a shapely lady in a bikini slowly ascending the stairs.

"This is the SUPER BOWL!" bellowed Davis. "You guys are DISGUSTING."

Lombardi was the man with the eternal flame, but those who followed the career of Davis doubted that anyone would ever again put together such a parlay.

Davis had been fired as an assistant coach at USC in 1959 after a kind of tong war erupted among recruiters on the Pacific Coast. Sid Gill-

man quickly hired him to coach the receivers for the new AFL Los Angeles Chargers in 1960 as part of a four-man staff. Six years later, Davis had (1) taken the head coaching job at Oakland in 1963, and turned the team around; (2) moved to New York as commissioner of the American Football League in 1966, lobbing the grenades that led to the pro football merger; and (3) returned to the Raiders with stock in the club as managing general partner.

After Davis stepped down as coach, the Silver and Black—Al had picked the colors and shaped their image—continued to win under John Rauch, a head coach who was as dull as dishwater. Davis was the only part-owner in pro football who helped prepare the game plan.

"Al Davis," Esther Gillman, Sid's wife, would recall many years later, "was a darling, just a cute kid." In the matter of finding an angle, cute kid Al had few peers.

The Raiders had won 13 games with Daryle Lamonica at quarterback in 1967, but their best-known player was Ben Davidson, a 6-foot 7-inch defensive end with a handlebar mustache.

Davis loved the role of the 14-point longshot, the poor little lambs who had lost their way. He thought his team could take on the Packers physically. His worst scenario was for the Packers to hit the field believing they were playing their last game under Vince Lombardi.

No one ever accused Lombardi of cuteness. You didn't stand for the things he did, or win the way the Packers had, and take the clever way out. They were coming off their historic victory over Dallas in the Ice Bowl, in which they faced third down on the Cowboys' 1-yard line trailing by three points with 16 seconds to play. Lombardi disdained the field goal that could have sent the game into overtime. Instead, Jerry Kramer, the right guard, kicked out Dallas tackle Jethro Pugh, and Bart Starr punched the ball across for the winning touchdown. The field was frozen slick, the wind-chill factor was measured at an incredible 46 below.

The play made a hero out of Kramer, and it didn't hurt Starr any, either. Lombardi's legend simply grew.

The day the teams arrived in Miami, Ray Nitschke, the Packers' middle linebacker, was

Super Bowl II was the last game Vince Lombardi ever coached for the Packers. He led them to five NFL titles (1959-1967).

observed to be limping. A few of his toes, he said, were being treated for frostbite.

But, elsewhere, Lombardi was assuring the press that "only the Dallas players had been hobbled by the cold." Whereupon, Nitschke stopped limping. It was a natural enough mistake, seeing as how Nitschke's toes had turned purple and his toenails had fallen off.

Of course, this was the Green Bay tradition under Lombardi, the Throw-Away-Your-Crutch-and-Walk School of Coaching. During practice one season, a high wind had knocked over a 25-foot metal tower, pinning Nitschke beneath it. Running to the scene, Lombardi bent down to get a peek. Then he straightened up and assured his anxious players, "It's okay. It's Nitschke. Get back to work."

There was not much more anyone needed to know about the Green Bay Packers on the morning of January 14, 1968. Whatever had gone into the compactor over the previous decade, the Lombardi mystique had been cast in iron. For at least the last month of the season, the players had been hearing that Lombardi would step aside as coach, remaining as the team's general manager. Now they looked for clues in his demeanor the week of the game.

"He was relaxed and cheerful," Starr says. "He even broke a longstanding rule and allowed our wives to accompany us on the trip."

On Thursday morning before the game, Lombardi broke the news to his team—or tried to. He reviewed the 1967 season, and the injuries they had overcome (including the loss of Starr for most of four games). He said it was easier to build a championship team than to maintain one, and now the Packers had won three consecutive NFL titles (five in seven years) and were going to their second Super Bowl in a row.

"I want to tell you," he said, and then his voice cracked, a strange and moving experience for the players who thought they knew this unbending, driven man, "...how very proud I am...of all of you." He looked quickly around the room, wanting to say more, but the words wouldn't come. He

In a colorful showdown before the game began, two giant figures on floats—depicting a Packer and a Raider—squared off at midfield in Miami's Orange Bowl and puffed smoke at each other.

cleared his throat and said, gruffly, "Defense down the hall. Okay, break it up."

He walked out ahead of the players, and in that room there were no longer any secrets. Vince Lombardi would coach his team for the last time Sunday.

"We had lumps in our throats," says Bart Starr, who never really enjoyed being known as Lombardi's push-button quarterback.

There was virtually no mouthing off between the teams. The press, rather than the Packers, had been slighting the Oakland linebackers, and one of them, Dan Conners, took it upon himself to strike back. "They psyche a lot of teams out," he said, "but we won't try to finesse them. That's where Kansas City went wrong. We'll just stick our noses in there. That's our game. Seek and destroy."

He laughed and

added, "That sounds as corny as 'run to daylight.'" The reference was to the philosophy of Green Bay's offense; it was even the title of Lombardi's autobiography. You half expected a lightning bolt to crash down and reduce Conners to the size and consistency of a smoked oyster.

The Packers' scouting report encouraged them to work on the Raiders' linebackers, especially Bill Laskey and Gus Otto on the outside. The game plan encouraged Starr to throw short to Travis Williams and Donny Anderson flaring out of the backfield.

There was a suspicion among serious bettors that the Raiders were not nearly as strong as they would be in two or three seasons. Their hopes for an upset rested on a surprising offensive plan: Davis and Rauch had convinced themselves that tackle Harry Schuh could block end Willie Davis and rookie guard Gene Upshaw would handle tackle Henry Jordan. They wanted to run directly at them with fullback Hewritt Dixon and low-slung Pete Banaszak.

Lamonica owned one of the strongest arms in

Don Chandler had a busy day for Green Bay, kicking four field goals (without a miss) and three extra points. Chandler's Super Bowl record of four field goals has been equaled once, but never broken.

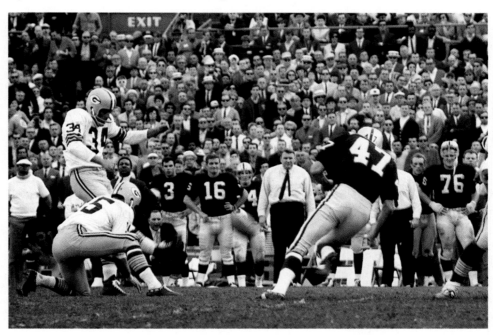

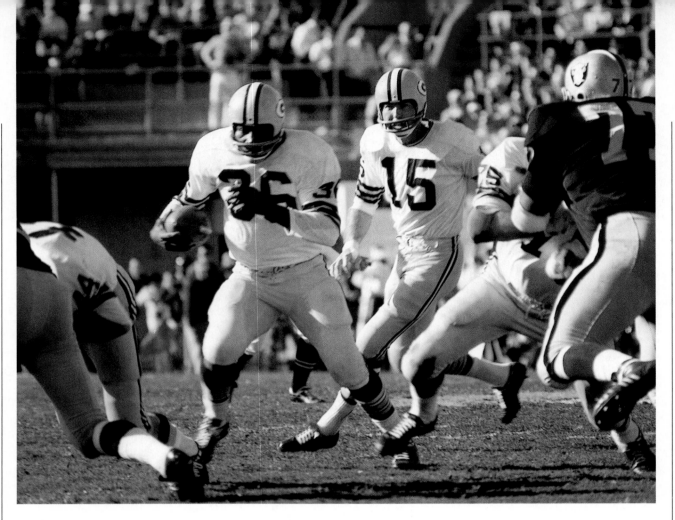

the AFL, but the Raiders hadn't yet acquired the fleet receivers for the long game Davis loved.

The writers were falling asleep during one press conference when the irascible Jimmy Cannon barked at Rauch: "Okay, I'm holding a gun to your head and you've got to answer the question. The question is, what do you do more, run or pass? Remember, there's a gun to your head. Now what do you say?"

Rauch gave him an impassive look: "I'd say we try to balance our offense."

In one voice, the writers cried out, "BANG!!"

The Raiders respected the reach of Packers wide receivers Boyd Dowler (6-5) and Carroll Dale (6-2), but thought their young corner-backs, Willie Brown and Kent McCloughan, could stay with them. As they left the locker room for the pregame introductions, Rauch stopped briefly alongside McCloughan and gave him a reminder: "If it's man-for-man, play Dowler tight. He's all yours."

To set the spiritual tone for the occasion, two 30-foot-high mannequins, a Packer and a Raider, met at midfield in the Orange Bowl. Clouds

Green Bay's 230-pound Ben Wilson was the game's leading rusher, grinding out 62 yards on 17 carries. Bart Starr (15), who handed Wilson the ball, won most valuable player honors for the second time.

of smoke curled from three-foot high nostrils.

By the end of the day, only one of the teams would still look larger than life.

On the first series of the game, Nitschke stopped a Raiders' sweep cold, Lamonica threw incomplete twice, and Oakland punted. The Packers held the ball for 27 snaps on their first two possessions, each ending with a field goal by Don Chandler inside the 40-yard line.

Green Bay settled for the second one, from 20 yards, after defensive tackles Tom Keating and Dan Birdwell flattened Starr for a long loss. If Oakland had won, Keating might have been the day's most dramatic story. He played the entire game with a strained Achilles tendon, the kind of injury that causes a player to miss anywhere from a week to a month.

Whatever the Packers were feeling, they played with the controlled fury Lombardi admired. But every once in a while, Vince liked to

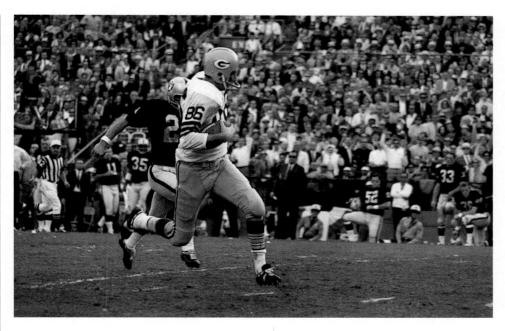

Leading just 6-0 in the second quarter, Starr shocked the Raiders on first-and-10 by throwing a 62-yard touchdown pass to Boyd Dowler. The Packers added a field goal later in the quarter and led 16-7 at halftime.

let his skirts fly, and now came the moment: Leading 6-0 in the second quarter, Starr, on first down, faked a handoff to Williams, who darted into the secondary as a decoy.

Then Starr looked for a receiver. Boyd Dowler had cut straight upfield, past Kent McCloughan, and found himself so open it looked as if he had come out early for practice.

Dowler pulled in Starr's pass at the Oakland 44 without slowing down, completing a 62-yard touchdown play. On the Oakland sideline, Rauch screamed, "Where the hell did everybody go?"

Later, Howie Williams, the Raiders' free safety and a former Packer, tried to explain: "We were in man-for-man. I thought Kent would stay with Dowler, but he released him for me."

"It was a screw-up," McCloughan added. "The way the coverage was supposed to go, if it's a play fake I go for the back and Howie goes for the receiver."

Trailing 13-0, the Raiders could have panicked. Instead, they put together a precise, 78-yard drive, with Banaszak and Dixon running hard inside and Lamonica passing for first downs to Bill Miller and Banaszak.

From the Packers' 23, Miller slipped behind safety Tom Brown, and Lamonica got rid of the ball just as Willie Davis slammed into him. Miller made the catch at the 5 and scrambled into the end zone.

Ageless George Blanda kicked the extra point that cut Green Bay's advantage to 13-7. For the first time, the game seemed to have a temperature.

Twice before the half, the Raiders wasted choice field position. Blanda missed the only field goal he attempted, a 47-yard try.

With 23 seconds left in the half, Donny Anderson's punt was fumbled by Rodger Bird, who had called for a fair catch. Dick Capp, promoted that week from Green Bay's taxi squad, recovered at the Oakland 45.

All of Vince Lombardi's Packers teams played fierce defense, and his two Super Bowl winners allowed only 10 and 14 points. Middle linebacker Ray Nitschke wrestled Oakland's Hewritt Dixon down on this carry.

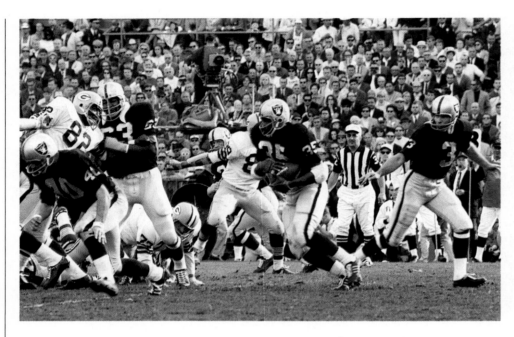

Hewritt Dixon was the Raiders' leading rusher, picking up 54 yards on a dozen carries. Quarterback Daryle Lamonica (3) threw a pair of touchdown passes to wide receiver Bill Miller, one in each half.

On third down, Starr's nine-yard pass to Dowler moved the ball to the 36. Chandler checked in to kick his third field goal, a 43-yard effort into a stiff wind with one second on the clock, and Green Bay led 16-7.

The first half was an echo of the year before, when Green Bay had to perspire to earn a modest lead over the Chiefs. The Raiders had enjoyed a brief, shining moment in the sun, and the difference so far was three field goals, no disgrace in that. The Raiders had troubled the Packers with a slot formation that isolated Miller on the strong safety.

But it was not by accident that the Packers had become known as the mechanical men of the NFL. They didn't lose the ball on a fumble or a pass interception all day, and only once did they draw a penalty.

Jerry Kramer described how Lombardi instilled such discipline. Once, after Kramer had jumped offside, Lombardi railed at him: "The concentration span of a college student is fifteen to twenty minutes. A high school student, ten to fifteen minutes. A kid in grammar school, maybe one minute. Now where the hell

does that leave you?"

For the second year in a row, the game got out of hand in the third quarter. The Packers turned in a stainless effort on offense. They mounted one of their irresistibly tedious drives, trudging 82 yards in 11 plays and taking 4:41 off the clock. The key maneuver was a 35-yard pass to Max McGee, who was back for one more curtain call.

McGee's only catch came under ideal Bart Starr conditions—third down and a yard from his own 40. McGee caught the ball behind Bird, and finally was dragged down at the 25. As in Super Bowl I, McGee entered the game only because of an injury to Dowler.

Starr's short passes kept the drive moving, and Donny Anderson lunged across for the last two yards. Chandler converted. Before the quarter had ended, Chandler had kicked his

George Blanda, the leading scorer in NFL history, had a chance to trim a 13-7 Packers lead to 13-10 in the second quarter, but missed this 47-yard field goal attempt. Blanda played pro football for 26 years.

The Packers blew the game open, taking a 33-7 lead early in the fourth quarter when cornerback Herb Adderley cut in front of Fred Biletnikoff and returned an interception 60 yards for a touchdown.

fourth field goal, from 31 yards. The ball clipped the crossbar and flopped over.

The Packers led 26-7 and, with 13 minutes left in the game, Starr sat down. He had jammed the thumb on his throwing hand when Davidson fell on him; 275 pounds is a lot of weight to land on a thumb.

Zeke Bratkowski relieved Starr on the next offensive series, coming on as a sort of night watchman asked to lock up the store. Only once did ol' Zeke try to pass, and then Keating and Birdwell dumped him for a 10-yard loss.

There was little left to analyze. In the middle of the fourth quarter, the fans began to boo the Packers every time they broke from the huddle. A partial explanation was that Miami was part of The Other League. Some booed out of sympathy for the underdog Raiders; some simply were booing class.

Whatever, no one could deny that they had seen two great teams in action—the Green Bay offense and the Green Bay defense.

The Raiders made only three mistakes, but two were costly: the fumbled punt, and a fourth-quarter interception by the splendid Herb Adderley, who cut in front of receiver Fred Biletnikoff and streaked 60 yards to a touchdown, stretching the Packers' lead to 33-7.

"I never saw Adderley," said Lamonica, apologizing for a mistake he called "the big one." Of course, this attitude seemed to assume that the Raiders at that point had a realistic chance at overcoming a 19-point deficit.

The Raiders, it ought to be noted, never did simply withdraw from the argument. They scored their second touchdown on a 23-yard pass from Lamonica to Miller, set up by a 41-yard pass to Banaszak.

Blanda added the extra point and that is how it ended—33-14, Green Bay. The win was worth $15,000 to each Packer. The loser's share was $7,500.

The true measure for the Raiders was whether the gap had been closed between the leagues. It was hard to tell. Dixon ran tough. Lamonica kept his poise. Rookie guard Gene Upshaw more than held his own against all-pro Henry Jordan. And Bill Miller was the game's leading receiver, with five catches for 84 yards and two touchdowns.

Keating, who harassed the Raiders' coaches into starting him, refused to let the team doctors inject his heel with pain killer. "I was afraid I might tear it," he said, "and not even know it."

"Maybe," mused center Jim Otto, the man with double zero on his back, "we should have run right at 'em. One reason our sweeps didn't work was because we could pull only one guard. The other [Upshaw] had to stay back and take care of Jordan, who was so fast."

While the Packers did not badly whip the Raiders on paper—their edge in total offense was just 29 yards—they won with the kind of football that had made them what they were. They had won on Starr's direction, Chandler's kicking, and the faultless execution Lombardi demanded. They had the ball three times in the third quarter, held it for all but two and a half minutes, and scored a touchdown and a field goal.

Ben Wilson, a surprise starter at fullback, led Green Bay in rushing with 62 yards on 17 carries. Wilson lost a contact lens on the sideline late in the fourth quarter and spent the rest of the game on his hands and knees by the Packers' bench, crawling to daylight.

Starr completed 13 of 24 passes for 202 yards, and ran once, spinning out of Davidson's arms and scrambling for 14 yards.

Starr was chosen the Super Bowl's most valuable player for the second consecutive year, but an interesting case could have been made for Don Chandler. It wasn't so much that Chandler's leg accounted for 15 of his team's points—one more than Oakland—but rather what he meant to the legend of Lombardi.

In 1956, as a punter fresh from the College All-Star Game, Chandler reported to the New York Giants' camp in Vermont. He and another rookie, linebacker Sam Huff, decided to quit the first week.

"We were homesick," recalled Chandler. "Sam had a sore knee. He was a hillbilly from West Virginia, and I was a country boy from Oklahoma. We figured we could make more money teaching school."

They went to turn in their playbooks, and found Lombardi, then an offensive assistant, napping in the room he shared with Jim Lee Howell, the head coach. Huff raised his voice and said, "Coach, we've decided to quit." Chandler was standing behind him in the doorway, peering over his shoulder.

Lombardi flew into a rage and Chandler ran out of the room. Huff couldn't turn quickly enough because of his knee. Chandler kept going, all the way to the airport, and Lombardi went after him. "He talked us into staying," Chandler says. "I finished my career playing for him in Green Bay and so did Sam, in Washington."

As the seconds ran off the clock in Super Bowl II, Jerry Kramer and Forrest Gregg hoisted Lombardi to their shoulders. "One more time, Coach," said Kramer.

"This," said Lombardi, with that jack-o'-lantern smile, "is the best way to leave a football field."

There was retirement talk in the Green Bay locker room: Don Chandler and Max McGee were giving it up. No word was heard from Lombardi, but it would not be long in coming. He was said to be tired, and upset by a national magazine article that painted him as a cruel and sadistic figure. "I'm going to have to give Vince Lombardi a good, hard look," he said.

That look had intimidated many a man. And, of course, it had inspired the Packers to win more than 75 percent of their games and five NFL championships in his last seven years in the league's smallest city.

On the field, Lombardi was, in the clearest sense of the word, a tyrant. But he punished himself as well as his players, and he instilled in them the idea that winning is a habit that can be developed and sustained.

In 1959, he had inherited a team that had won exactly 1 of its previous 15 games. "The harder you work," he told them, "the harder it is to surrender."

His long-time assistant, Phil Bengtson, succeeded him as the Packers' head coach in 1968.

Lombardi became the full-time general manager, but it was nearly impossible to picture him behind a desk. Vince Lombardi, signing expense accounts and dictating letters? Who would he snarl at, the receptionist?

He lasted a year as general manager in Green Bay. One of his heroes was General George Patton, who had led his tanks with ivory-handled pistols strapped to his side. Running the operation from headquarters wasn't Lombardi's game, either.

The next year Lombardi moved to Washington to take on another challenge, rebuilding the Redskins, the only job in his fiery lifetime that Vincent Thomas Lombardi didn't finish. He died of cancer in September, 1970, at age 57, before the start of his second season.

Few public men ever succeed as well at defining a goal, and then fulfilling it. That is why, all these years later, when you think of Lombardi you think of the Packers, and the Super Bowl, and the trophy that he accepted twice and that now carries his name.

III

N.Y. Jets 16, Baltimore 7

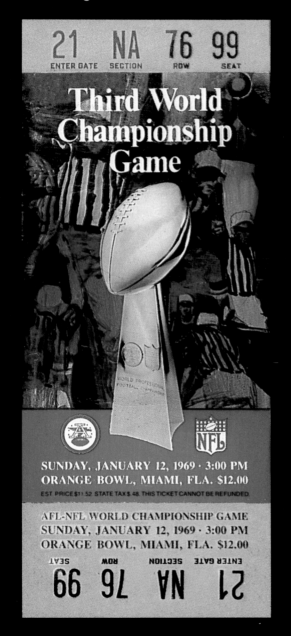

Vital Statistics

Starting Lineups

New York Jets (AFL)	Offense	Baltimore (NFL)
George Sauer	WR	Jimmy Orr
Winston Hill	LT	Bob Vogel
Bob Talamini	LG	Glenn Ressler
John Schmitt	C	Bill Curry
Randy Rasmussen	RG	Dan Sullivan
Dave Herman	RT	Sam Ball
Pete Lammons	TE	John Mackey
Don Maynard	WR	Willie Richardson
Joe Namath	QB	Earl Morrall
Emerson Boozer	RB	Tom Matte
Matt Snell	RB	Jerry Hill
	Defense	
Gerry Philbin	LE	Bubba Smith
Paul Rochester	LT	Billy Ray Smith
John Elliott	RT	Fred Miller
Verlon Biggs	RE	Ordell Braase
Ralph Baker	LLB	Mike Curtis
Al Atkinson	MLB	Dennis Gaubatz
Larry Grantham	RLB	Don Shinnick
Johnny Sample	LCB	Bob Boyd
Randy Beverly	RCB	Lenny Lyles
Jim Hudson	SS	Jerry Logan
Bill Baird	FS	Rick Volk

Substitutions

New York Jets-Offense: K-Jim Turner. P-Curly Johnson. WR-Bake Turner, Bill Rademacher, Mark Smolinski. LINE-Jeff Richardson, Paul Crane, Sam Walton. QB-Babe Parilli. RB-Bill Mathis. Defense: LINE-Steve Thompson. LB-John Neidert, Carl McAdams. DB-Earl Christy, Jim Richards, Mike D'Amato, John Dockery, Cornell Gordon.
Baltimore-Offense: K/DE-Lou Michaels. P-David Lee. WR-Ray Perkins, Alex Hawkins, TE-Tom Mitchell. LINE-John Williams, Cornelius Johnson, Dick Szymanski. QB-John Unitas. RB-Tim Brown, Preston Pearson, Terry Cole. Defense: LINE-Roy Hilton. LB-Sid Williams, Ron Porter. DB-Charles Stukes, Ocie Austin. DNP: QB-Jim Ward.

Officials

Referee-Tom Bell (NFL). Umpire-Walt Parker (AFL). Head Linesman-George Murphy (NFL). Field Judge-Joe Gonzalez (NFL). Back Judge-Jack Reader (AFL). Line Judge-Cal Lepore (AFL).

Scoring

New York	0	7	6	3 —	16
Baltimore	0	0	0	7 —	7

NY-Snell 4 run (Turner kick)
NY-FG Turner 32
NY-FG Turner 30
NY-FG Turner 9
Balt-Hill 1 run (Michaels kick)
Attendance-75,377

FINAL TEAM STATISTICS

	Jets	Colts
TOTAL FIRST DOWNS	21	18
Rushing	10	7
Passing	10	9
Penalty	1	2
TOTAL NET YARDAGE	337	324
Total Offensive Plays	74	64
Average Gain per Offensive Play	4.6	5.1
NET YARDS RUSHING	142	143
Total Rushing Plays	43	23
Average Gain per Rushing Play	3.3	6.2
NET YARDS PASSING	195	181
Pass Att.-Comp.-Int.	29-17-0	41-17-4
Sacks-Yards Lost	2-11	0-0
Gross Yards Passing	206	181
Avg. Gain per Pass (Incl. Sacks)	6.3	4.4
PUNTS-YARDS	4-155	3-133
Average Distance	38.8	44.3
Had Blocked	0	0
TOTAL RETURN YARDAGE	34	139
Kickoff Returns-Yards	1-25	4-105
Punt Returns-Yards	1-0	4-34
Interception Returns-Yards	4-9	0-0
TOTAL TURNOVERS	1	5
Fumbles-Lost	1-1	1-1
Had Intercepted	0	4
PENALTIES-YARDS	5-28	3-23
TOTAL POINTS SCORED	16	7
Touchdowns Rushing	1	1
Touchdowns Passing	0	0
Touchdowns Returns	0	0
Extra Points	1	1
Field Goals-Attempts	3-5	0-2
Safeties	0	0
THIRD DOWN EFFICIENCY	9/18	4/12
FOURTH DOWN EFFICIENCY	0/0	1/2
TIME OF POSSESSION	36:25	23:35

INDIVIDUAL STATISTICS

RUSHING

New York	No.	Yds.	Avg.	Long	TD
Snell	30	121	4.0	12	1
Boozer	10	19	1.9	8	0
Mathis	3	2	0.7	1	0

Baltimore	No.	Yds.	Avg.	Long	TD
Matte	11	116	10.5	58	0
Hill	9	29	3.2	12	1
Morrall	2	-2	-1.0	0	0
Unitas	1	0	0.0	0	0

PASSING

New York	Att.	Comp.	Yds.	Long	TD	Int.
Namath	28	17	206	39	0	0
Parilli	1	0	0	0	0	0

Baltimore	Att.	Comp.	Yds.	Long	TD	Int.
Morrall	17	6	71	30	0	3
Unitas	24	11	110	21	0	1

RECEIVING

New York	No.	Yds.	Long	TD
Sauer	8	133	39	0
Snell	4	40	14	0
Mathis	3	20	13	0
Lammons	2	13	11	0

Baltimore	No.	Yds.	Long	TD
Richardson	6	58	21	0
Orr	3	42	17	0
Mackey	3	35	19	0
Matte	2	30	30	0
Hill	2	1	1	0
Mitchell	1	15	15	0

INTERCEPTIONS

New York	No.	Yds.	Long	TD
Beverly	2	0	0	0
Hudson	1	9	9	0
Sample	1	0	0	0

Baltimore	No.	Yds.	Long	TD
None				

PUNTING

New York	No.	Yds.	Avg.	TB	Long
Johnson	4	155	38.8	0	39

Baltimore	No.	Yds.	Avg.	TB	Long
Lee	3	133	44.3	0	51

PUNT RETURNS

New York	No.	FC	Yds.	Long	TD
Baird	1	1	0	0	0

Baltimore	No.	FC	Yds.	Long	TD
Brown	4	0	34	21	0

KICKOFF RETURNS

New York	No.	Yds.	Long	TD
Christy	1	25	25	0

Baltimore	No.	Yds.	Long	TD
Pearson	2	59	33	0
Brown	2	46	25	0

FUMBLES

New York	No.	Own Rec.	Opp. Rec.
Sauer	1	0	0
Baker	0	0	1

Baltimore	No.	Own Rec.	Opp. Rec.
Matte	1	0	0
Porter	0	0	1

KICKING

New York	XP-A	FG-A	FG Made	FG Missed
Turner	1-1	3-5	32,30,9	41,42

Baltimore	XP-A	FG-A	FG Made	FG Missed
Michaels	1-1	0-2	--	27,46

PLAY-BY-PLAY

New York won the coin toss and elected to receive.

FIRST QUARTER

Michaels kick 2 yards into end zone, Christy 25 return (Hawkins).

New York (15:00)

NY 23	1-10	Snell 3 run left tackle (Shinnick).
NY 26	2-7	Snell 9 run left tackle (Volk).
NY 35	1-10	Boozer run right end, loss of 4 (Shinnick).
NY 31	2-14	Namath 9 pass to Snell (Boyd).
NY 40	3-5	Snell draw up middle, loss of 2 (Miller).
NY 38	4-7	Johnson 44 punt to B 18. Play nullified and Balt. penalized 5 for offsides.
NY 43	4-2	Johnson 39 punt, Brown 9 return (McAdams).

Baltimore (10:55)

B 27	1-10	Morrall 19 pass to Mackey (Elliott).
B 46	1-10	Matte 10 sweep right (Baker).
NY 44	1-10	Hill 7 sweep left (Hudson).
NY 37	2-3	Matte 1 run left (Elliott).
NY 36	3-2	Hill 5 run right tackle (Baird).
NY 31	1-10	Hill run right, loss of 3 (Philbin).
NY 34	2-13	Morrall pass to Orr underthrown, incomplete.
NY 34	3-13	Morrall 15 pass to Mitchell (Baird).
NY 19	1-10	Morrall pass to Richardson dropped.
NY 19	2-10	Morrall pass to Mitchell overthrown, incomplete.
NY 19	3-10	Morrall run evading rush, no gain (Atkinson).
NY 19	4-10	Michaels's 27-yard field goal attempt was wide right, no good.

New York (5:33)

NY 20	1-10	Namath pass to Snell dropped.
NY 20	2-10	Namath 2 pass to Lammons (Lyles).
NY 22	3-8	Namath 13 pass to Mathis (Gaubatz).
NY 35	1-10	Namath pass to Maynard overthrown, incomplete.
NY 35	2-10	Namath 6 pass to Sauer (Lyles).
NY 41	3-4	Namath pass to Sauer overthrown, incomplete.
NY 41	4-4	Johnson 38 punt, Brown 21 return (Snell).

Baltimore (3:05)

B 42	1-10	Morrall pass to Mackey dropped, incomplete.
B 42	2-10	Hill 3 run up middle (Elliott).
B 45	3-7	Morrall pass to Richardson broken up (Sample).
B 45	4-7	Lee 51 punt downed at NY 4.

New York (1:58)

NY 4	1-10	Snell 4 run right tackle (Shinnick).
NY 8	2-6	Snell 5 draw up middle (Gaubatz).
NY 13	3-1	Namath 3 pass to Sauer left (Lyles), fumbled, Porter recovered for Balt. at NY 12.

Baltimore (:14)

| NY 12 | 1-10 | Hill run left tackle, loss of 1 (Philbin). |

END OF FIRST QUARTER:
Baltimore 0, New York 0

SECOND QUARTER

| NY 13 | 2-11 | Matte 7 sweep left (Beverly). |
| NY 6 | 3-4 | Morrall pass to Mitchell off his shoulder pad and intercepted in end zone, Beverly no return, touchback. |

New York (14:09)

NY 20	1-10	Snell 1 run left tackle (Braase).
NY 21	2-9	Snell 7 run left tackle (Shinnick).
NY 28	3-2	Snell 6 run left end (Lyles).
NY 34	1-10	Snell 12 draw up middle (Baird).
NY 46	1-10	Namath pass to Sauer broken up (Shinnick).
NY 46	2-10	Namath 6 pass to Mathis (Bubba Smith).
B 48	3-4	Namath 14 pass to Sauer (Lyles).
B 34	1-10	Namath 11 pass to Sauer (Volk).
B 23	1-10	Boozer 2 run right (Shinnick).
B 21	2-8	Namath 12 pass to Snell (Gaubatz).
B 9	1-goal	Snell 5 run right tackle (B.R. Smith).
B 4	2-goal	Snell 4 run over left tackle, touchdown (9:03). J. Turner kicked extra point.

New York scoring drive: 80 yards, 12 plays, 5:06.
New York 7, Baltimore 0

Johnson kick to B 2, Pearson 26 return (Richards).

Baltimore (9:03)

B 28	1-10	Morrall pass to Richardson overthrown.
B 28	2-10	Morrall 30 pass to Matte (Hudson).
NY 42	1-10	Hill 4 run right tackle (Atkinson).
NY 38	2-6	Matte run right, no gain (Biggs).
NY 38	3-6	Morrall pass to Mackey broken up (Sample).
NY 38	4-6	Michaels's 46-yard field goal attempt was no good.

New York (6:37)

NY 20	1-10	Boozer 1 run right (Logan).
NY 21	2-9	Namath 35 pass to Sauer (Lyles).
B 44	1-10	Snell 9 run left (Gaubatz).
B 35	2-1	Snell 3 run up middle (Shinnick).
B 32	1-10	Namath pass to Maynard overthrown.
B 32	2-10	Namath pass to B. Turner underthrown.
B 32	3-10	Namath sacked, loss of 2 (Gaubatz).

| B 34 | 4-12 | J. Turner's 41-yard field goal attempt was no good. |

Baltimore (4:13)

B 20	1-10	Morrall 6 pass to Richardson (Sample).
B 26	2-4	Matte 58 run around right end (Baird).
NY 16	1-10	Hill 1 run left tackle (Atkinson, Hudson).
NY 15	2-9	Morrall pass to Richardson intercepted at NY 2, Sample no return. Two-Minute Warning.

New York (2:00)

NY 2	1-10	Snell 2 run left (Shinnick).
NY 4	2-8	Snell 3 run left tackle (Miller).
NY 7	3-5	Snell draw left, no gain (Bubba Smith).
NY 7	4-5	Johnson 32 punt, Brown fair catch. Play nullified by offsetting penalties, illegal procedure against NY and roughing the kicker against Balt.
NY 7	4-5	Johnson 39 punt, Brown 4 return (Neidert).

Baltimore (:43)

| NY 42 | 1-10 | Morrall 1 pass to Hill (Crane). |
| NY 41 | 2-9 | Matte lateraled back to Morrall, Morrall pass to Hill middle intercepted at NY 12, Hudson 9 return to NY 21 as time expired. |

END OF SECOND QUARTER:
New York 7, Baltimore 0

THIRD QUARTER

Johnson kick to goal line, Brown 25 return (Smolinski).

Baltimore (15:00)

| B 25 | 1-10 | Matte 8 run, fumbled, Baker rec. for NY at B 33. |

New York (14:25)

B 33	1-10	Boozer 8 run left (Volk).
B 25	2-2	Snell 4 run right (Bubba Smith).
B 21	1-10	Boozer 2 run left (Curtis).
B 19	2-8	Namath 5 pass to Snell (Curtis).
B 14	3-3	Snell 3 run right (Gaubatz).
B 11	1-10	Boozer run left end, loss of 5 (Lyles).
B 16	2-15	Namath sacked, loss of 9 (Bubba Smith).
B 25	3-24	Namath pass to Lammons broken up (Logan).
B 25	4-24	J. Turner, 32-yard field goal (10:08).

New York scoring drive: 8 yards, 8 plays, 4:17.
New York 10, Baltimore 0

Johnson kick to B 5, Brown 21 return (D'Amato).

Baltimore (10:08)

B 26	1-10	Morrall pass to Mackey overthrown.
B 26	2-10	Morrall pass to Hill, no gain (Grantham).
B 26	3-10	Morrall run evading rush, loss of 2 (McAdams).
B 24	4-12	Lee 44 punt, Baird no return (S. Williams).

New York (8:04)

NY 32	1-10	Namath 1 pass to Mathis (Curtis).
NY 33	2-9	Namath 14 pass to Sauer (Volk).
NY 47	1-10	Namath pass to Maynard overthrown.
NY 47	2-10	Boozer 4 run left (B.R. Smith).
B 49	3-6	Namath 11 pass to Lammons (Logan).
B 38	1-10	Namath pass to Maynard overthrown.
B 38	2-10	Namath 14 pass to Sauer (Volk).
B 24	1-10	Mathis 1 draw up middle (Shinnick).
B 23	2-9	Namath pass to Maynard incomplete. Namath hurt.
B 23	3-9	Parilli pass to Sauer underthrown, incomplete.
B 23	4-9	J. Turner, 30-yard field goal (3:58).

New York scoring drive: 45 yards, 10 plays, 4:06.
New York 13, Baltimore 0

Johnson kick hit goalposts, touchback.

Baltimore (3:58)

B 20	1-10	Matte 5 sweep right (Baker).
B 25	2-5	Unitas pass to Matte, no gain (Grantham).
B 25	3-5	Unitas pass to Orr dropped, incomplete.
B 25	4-5	Lee 38 punt, Baird fair catch.

New York (2:24)

NY 37	1-10	Snell 3 run left (B.R. Smith).
NY 40	2-7	Namath pass to Sauer overthrown.
NY 40	3-7	Namath 11 pass to Sauer (Lyles).
B 49	1-10	Namath 39 pass to Sauer (Lyles).
B 10	1-goal	Snell 4 run right tackle (Gaubatz).

END OF THIRD QUARTER:
New York 13, Baltimore 0

FOURTH QUARTER

B 6	2-goal	Snell 3 run left tackle. Play nullified and Balt. penalized 3 (half the distance) for offsides.
B 3	2-goal	Snell run left, no gain (Volk).
B 3	3-goal	Mathis 1 run left (Gaubatz).
B 2	4-goal	J. Turner, 9-yard field goal (13:26).

New York scoring drive: 61 yards, 7 plays, 3:58.
New York 16, Baltimore 0

Johnson kick to 6 yards into end zone, Pearson 33 return (Richards).

Baltimore (13:26)

B 27	1-10	Unitas 5 pass to Mackey (Grantham).
B 32	2-5	Matte 7 sweep right (Baker).
B 39	1-10	Unitas 5 pass to Richardson (Sample).
B 44	2-5	Matte 19 run left (Hudson).
NY 37	1-10	Hill 12 run right tackle (Baird).
NY 25	1-10	Unitas pass to Richardson overthrown.
NY 25	2-10	Unitas pass to Orr deep intercepted in end zone, Beverly no return, touchback.

New York (11:06)

NY 20	1-10	Boozer 2 draw up middle (Miller).
NY 22	2-8	Snell 2 run left (Porter).
NY 24	3-6	Boozer 7 sweep left (Gaubatz).
NY 31	1-10	Snell 10 run left (Curtis). Balt. penalized 15 for personal foul.
B 44	1-10	Snell 7 run up middle (Bubba Smith).
B 37	2-3	Boozer 2 run right tackle (B.R. Smith).
B 35	3-1	Mathis run left tackle, no gain (Michaels).
B 35	4-1	J. Turner's 42-yard field goal attempt was no good.

Baltimore (6:34)

B 20	1-10	Unitas pass to Mackey broken up (Grantham).
B 20	2-10	Unitas pass to Richardson overthrown.
B 20	3-10	Unitas pass to Mackey overthrown.
B 20	4-10	Unitas 17 pass to Orr (Beverly).
B 37	1-10	Unitas pass to Richardson overthrown.
B 37	2-10	Unitas pass to Hill underthrown.
B 37	3-10	Unitas 11 pass to Mackey (Baird). NY penalized 15 for personal foul.
NY 37	1-10	Matte 1 run left (Biggs).
NY 36	2-9	Unitas 21 pass to Richardson (Sample).
NY 15	1-10	Unitas pass to Matte overthrown.
NY 15	2-10	Unitas 11 pass to Orr (Beverly). NY penalized 2 (half the distance) for a personal foul.
NY 2	1-goal	Matte run left, no gain. Play nullified and NY penalized 1 (half the distance) for offsides.
NY 1	1-goal	Unitas keeper middle, no gain (Biggs).
NY 1	2-goal	Matte run right, no gain (Atkinson).
NY 1	3-goal	Hill 1 run over left tackle, touchdown (3:19). Michaels kicked extra point.

Baltimore scoring drive: 80 yards, 14 plays, 3:15.
New York 16, Baltimore 7

Michaels onside kick recovered by Mitchell for Balt. at NY 44.

Baltimore (3:14)

NY 44	1-10	Unitas 6 pass to Richardson (Sample).
NY 38	2-4	Unitas 14 pass to Orr (Beverly).
NY 24	1-10	Unitas 5 pass to Richardson (out of bounds).
NY 19	2-5	Unitas pass to Richardson broken up (Sample).
NY 19	3-5	Unitas pass to Orr underthrown.
NY 19	4-5	Unitas pass to Orr overthrown.

New York (2:21)

NY 20	1-10	Snell 1 run right (Bubba Smith). Balt.-first time out.
NY 21	2-9	Snell 6 run right (Logan). Two-Minute Warning.
NY 27	3-3	Snell 4 run left (Gaubatz). Balt.-second time out (1:54).
NY 31	1-10	Snell 2 run right tackle (Boyd).
NY 33	2-8	NY penalized 5 for delay of game.
NY 28	2-13	Snell 1 run right (B.R. Smith).
NY 29	3-12	NY penalized 5 for delay of game.
NY 24	3-17	Snell 3 sweep left (Austin). Balt.-third time out (:15).
NY 27	4-14	Johnson 39 punt, Brown no return, out of bounds.

Baltimore (:08)

| B 34 | 1-10 | Unitas pass to Richardson incomplete. |
| B 34 | 2-10 | Unitas 15 pass to Richardson (Sample). |

FINAL SCORE:
New York 16, Baltimore 7
FINAL RECORDS:
New York 13-3, Baltimore 15-2

69

It Came With a Guarantee

It was shortly after the oddsmakers announced the Baltimore Colts were "at least 18-point favorites" to beat the New York Jets in Super Bowl III that a man from New York claimed he had proof to the contrary.

Jonathan Booth said the Jets were clearly superior because, "The transiting Jupiter is sextile the natal Mars and Pluto is trine the midheaven."

Booth, a professional astrologer, said he had compiled celestial charts on both the Colts and Jets. He said there was no doubt about it—New York would win the game. But would he guarantee victory? Would he put his money where his mouth was? Booth, who confessed he had never seen a football game before, said, "Of course not. Astrology is an inexact science. I assume football to be much more unpredictable. Only a fool would guarantee such a thing."

Joe Namath, who cared somewhat about heavenly bodies but didn't know a thing about being a celestial scientist, smiled when the check-in clerk at the Galt Ocean Mile Hotel told him his room might be a good-luck charm. The clerk said that Vince Lombardi had slept there the year before, for Super Bowl II. Namath nodded politely, still smiling, and asked if room 534, the Governor's Suite, had an ice bucket.

"I guess I should have seen it as an omen," Namath says now. "I know when we went to practice that week, we used the New York Yankees' spring-training facility. Someone told me that the locker I was assigned was the same one Mickey Mantle always used. Looking back, maybe I was being blessed by the gods of fortune. At the time, though, I wasn't worried about luck. I knew we were talented enough to win the football game."

Lombardi and Mantle would have to agree. Greatness is not a twist of fate. Opportunity is. Maybe that's why the large gold ring Namath wears on special occasions is so unique. Something other than the three glittering diamonds on it, something besides the two words engraved into it—Pride and Execution—brings forth a churning feeling for him and all who wear it. All of the New York Jets who were on that team, who were there January 12, 1969, in Miami's Orange Bowl, say their Super Bowl ring is more special than any other—because it represented the most important Super Bowl game ever played.

And, after all, it did come with a certain guarantee…

In the Age of Aquarius, sociological turmoil was everywhere. The Vietnam conflict was in full stride. Apollo 8 astronauts had just returned from circling the moon, setting the stage for Neil Armstrong's famous footprints and small steps and giant leaps six months later. Richard Nixon was working on his presidential inauguration speech.

And the Colts were playing the Jets in Super Bowl III.

The sharp contrast between the two teams was a perfect metaphor for the times. The Colts symbolized the Establishment. They were the National Football League's solid citizens, the spitting image of a grand old game. The Jets were the Rebels With a Cause, the ones who would dare scribble outside the lines of the game's ancient blueprint. They were instigators, agitators, innovators, flag bearers of the rogue American Football League.

The Colts were personified by their quarterback, Earl Morrall, who sported crewcut hair and black hightop shoes and danced to the beat of a different oboe. For the Jets, Joe Namath wore his hair long and his shoes low-cut and white, and always liked the sweet music of a good time—no matter who was playing.

But when the two opposites collided, when the AFL-NFL planets aligned into the same orbit, would there be any drama? The NFL's Green Bay Packers had steamrolled to victory in the first two Super Bowls. This time it seemed like an even more forgone conclusion. NBC, which would telecast the game, worried privately about a ratings disaster.

The Colts had been overpowering teams for the last two months of the NFL season. They came to Miami with a 15-1 record. They'd won 10 games in a row, including four shutouts. In those 10 games, opponents had scored only seven touchdowns. In the NFL Championship Game, Baltimore had humbled Cleveland 34-0.

"We won so easily," says Morrall, who had

The Colts squandered five scoring opportunities in the first half. Late in the second quarter, Tom Matte escaped on a Super Bowl-record 58-yard run to the Jets' 16-yard line, but then Earl Morrall threw an interception.

been voted the NFL's most valuable player that season, after replacing the injured Johnny Unitas. Many people thought the Colts were one of the best teams of all time. The Twelfth of January could be the Twelfth of Never for the New York Jets.

"I thought we would win handily," Morrall says. "We'd only lost twice in our last thirty games. I'm still not sure what happened that day at the Orange Bowl, however; it's still hard to account for. I still feel we had a fine team. But the Jets were just better. They certainly showed the merger was the right thing to do."

The winds of change also gusted across football fields in 1969. It already had been decided that the NFL would welcome the AFL under its umbrella. But the idea of merging with what many considered to be a "Mickey Mouse league" brought shrieks of dissent from NFL fans. The AFL needed a final validation ticket and it didn't look as if the Jets could get it punched against the Colts.

"We barely got into the Super Bowl," Weeb Ewbank says. "The AFC Championship Game with the Raiders was a classic. You have to marvel that we had the ability to regenerate for the Super Bowl."

Ewbank was the Jets' head coach. Today he is constantly reminded of that season. He has two artificial hips that are everlasting reminders of that season.

"Both times I got hurt celebrating," he says. "Once while getting a victory ride, the other time I got thrown in the shower. Somebody saw me crying and asked me if they were tears of joy. I said 'Heck no—tears of pain.' But what is it now? More than twenty years? It was worth it. It was definitely worth it."

The Jets came to Florida a week early in January, 1969. Ewbank felt quality practice time was necessary, and winter had frozen New York. The Jets had been forced to prepare for the AFC Championship Game in an armory.

New York's Matt Snell scored the only touchdown of the first half on a four-yard run, which culminated a 12-play, 80-yard drive. Shell also was the game's leading rusher with 121 yards on 30 carries.

At first, Ewbank's early arrival decision seemed questionable. His team of roustabouts—Namath was only the most visible and notorious of the Jets' well-stocked gang of carousers—would have a field day, not to mention several noteworthy nights, in Fort Lauderdale.

Meanwhile, Colts head coach Don Shula didn't like being the heavy favorite. At least not publicly. But he did feel confident his team would win the game.

Jets kicker Jim Turner applauded one of his three field goals, all kicked in the second half.

"When we studied films on the Jets," Shula says, "we felt we'd be able to control both lines of scrimmage. Sure, we felt confident. You don't think any other way before a game."

Ewbank and Shula went way back. When Ewbank was an assistant coach at Cleveland, he recommended that the Browns draft Shula, who played at John Carroll, a local college. In 1963, when Ewbank was fired as coach of the Baltimore Colts, he was replaced by Shula.

Ewbank knew the Colts were in a tough spot as prohibitive favorites. He knew Shula would have the tougher job getting his team prepared to win a game almost everyone figured could be won simply by showing up. He knew it would be more difficult for the Colts to match the spirit he could see building within his team.

"If only Joe would keep his mouth shut," Ewbank told reporters the day after the Jets showed up in Fort Lauderdale.

After beating the Raiders to earn the right to play the Colts, Namath dropped the first of his many bombshells. Namath said there were at least four quarterbacks in the AFL better than Earl Morrall.

"Including me," Namath said with a grin. Namath had bypassed the NFL to join the Jets and turn the AFL into a viable league.

At first Shula erupted with anger over Namath's statement. "I don't know how Namath can rap Earl," Shula said. "After all, Earl is number one in the NFL. He's thrown all those touchdown passes, he's thrown for a great percentage without dinky flare passes. He's the player of the year. He's had a great season for us and we're proud of him. Anyone who doesn't give him the credit he deserves is wrong."

Colts receiver Jimmy Orr was asked during a radio interview if he knew any of the Jets. Orr smiled and said, "Don Maynard...he and I were roommates at the Blue-Gray game 'bout ten years ago or so. Good guy, but know what I remember most about him? He used Mexican dimes as quarters for the pay phone."

At the Jets' hotel, Maynard limped from his room and headed for the lounge. He had pulled his left hamstring in the AFL title game. He knew that if the game were played that day, he wouldn't be able to participate.

Maynard, who was voted into the Pro Football Hall of Fame in 1987, looks back on it all with sustained satisfaction now.

"There were a bunch of us who'd been cut loose from the NFL," Maynard says. "The AFL was like the scrap heap. It was real easy to get fired up to play any team from the NFL."

As a rookie, Maynard had been the return man on the opening kickoff for the New York Giants against the Baltimore Colts in the 1958 NFL Championship Game that was called The Greatest Game Ever Played. But the Giants cut him after the season.

"I kept a little bitterness in me," he says. "Who wouldn't? I knew I could play. Ten years later, by golly, I had this chance to show them [the NFL]. And I could hardly walk."

At the same time Maynard was hurting, Weeb Ewbank was coming to an important conclusion. "They're slow," he told his assistants as they looked at films of the Baltimore secondary. "If we can't pass on these guys we ought to get out of the business.

"And they don't have any breakaway runners. They're tough and big but they don't have any real speed people. We can play tighter on their receivers."

Ewbank kept studying the Baltimore secondary, and how it rotated toward Colts cornerback Bobby Boyd. "I think they're trying to protect him," Ewbank said. "I think he's slow."

And then Ewbank said, "We can beat these guys. We're going to win this game."

Johnny Sample also had a personal vendetta against the NFL in general and the Colts in particular. Sample had been cut by the Colts. He also had been on the 1958 championship team.

"I was almost in a frenzy by the time the game arrived," Sample says now. "I held a private grudge against the Colts. I remember that week that Willie Richardson, one of their receivers, said something about how the difference between them and us was that they were used to working against NFL defenses. I was really ready for that game. All of us were."

Most of the Baltimore players were loose and relaxed. They talked among themselves how the big game was just another game, the last one on their way into the record book.

Five years earlier, the Jets' Winston Hill had been a rookie offensive tackle with the Colts. He hadn't made it out of training camp. In Miami, he told reporters he'd blocked the experience out of his mind. But he really hadn't.

"Ordell Braase kept making me look bad in practice," Hill says now. "Coach Shula called me into his office and told me only one rookie tackle was gonna make the team. I knew Bob Vogel was their first-round draft pick and he'd been doing good, too. But it was Braase who was my undoing. I remember when I found out he'd been to war. I thought they were talking about Vietnam. But the man had been in the Korean War."

Braase, in a perfect irony, would be the defensive end Hill would have to block in Super Bowl III.

Dave Herman also squirmed with anticipation. Herman's man for the big game would be Bubba Smith, the huge Colts defensive end. Herman was a guard by trade but Ewbank had switched him to tackle during the season. Smith, 6 feet 7, 275 pounds, was considered the NFL's best pass rusher.

"But I knew all about ol' Bubba before that," Herman says now. "When I was a senior at Michigan State, he was a freshman. He came to campus with a lot of publicity."

Smith remembers his college classmate a lit-

With gimpy Don Maynard serving as a decoy, George Sauer, his Jets teammate, plagued the Colts all day with a game-leading eight catches for 133 yards. Cornerback Lenny Lyles wrapped up Sauer after this catch.

tle differently. "He was always yelling at underclassmen," Smith says. "And I don't like people yelling at me."

In Miami, Smith didn't talk about his ankle that was badly sprained, hideously swollen. What he didn't know was how ineffective he would be against Herman in the Super Bowl.

Ewbank formalized his game plan three days before kickoff.

The coach said, "We can't be fancy. We have to be very basic to win. We must be able to run the ball or we're sunk. This probably will not be a pretty game to watch. Or much fun to play. In the first two Super Bowls, the AFL team lost its poise. There was always one big play—a turnover or something—that caused the game's complexion to change drastically. We must keep our poise. And we must execute."

Maynard rested his leg during Jets practices, which were closed to the public. The prognosis was bad. Maynard might be able to go full speed for a few plays, but his hamstring still was too tender to rely on. But the Colts didn't know this. The last time they saw Don Maynard, he was catching two touchdown passes against the Raiders in the AFL title game.

Ewbank thought about a decoy. If the Colts paid attention to Maynard, his other wide receiver, George Sauer, might have a big game.

Twenty Jets were veterans of knee operations, including the entire starting backfield of Namath, Matt Snell, and Emerson Boozer.

Namath had his knee aspirated twice in the week before the game. Snell also had fluid siphoned from his knee.

Shula says he never underestimated Boozer and Snell as running backs, "but one thing we found out was how good [they] were as blockers. Boozer, especially. Each was excellent at picking up the blitz."

Everything was in place for the Jets. They even joked about being overconfident.

"You could sense it more and more," Sample said. "We could see they weren't supermen. We had answers for everything they did. We knew we were going to win."

Someone finally said it out loud. Namath went to an awards banquet in Miami Springs and stood at a podium and said, "We're going to win this game. I guarantee it."

Nobody guarantees victory in sports. It breaks unwritten rules. It is a sporting sacrilege and only someone like Muhammad Ali dared such nonsense. But Namath did it, and newspapers bannered his boast.

Then something strange happened. The game became something bigger. The merger had been voted into existence two years earlier. But Namath's statement brought everything to the surface. The young turks of the AFL were kicking in their stalls, demanding respect, even "guaranteeing" they would beat the best the NFL had to offer.

Herman loved hearing what Namath said, saying 20 years later that "Joe had this way of instilling confidence in us. When he started talking, he was only saying things we wanted to believe. Then after a while, we did."

It was raining on Sunday morning. Shula went to a nearby Catholic Church. He had slept well. He was confident his team would win.

At the Colts' pregame meal, Shula said, "Everything we've accomplished all year is riding on this game. We can't wait for the Jets to lose it. We've got to go out and win it for ourselves."

In the dressing room at the Orange Bowl, Ewbank thought about what he would say to his team. "I could feel their emotion and I liked it," Ewbank says now. "They were ready. I just decided to go along with them."

Ewbank gathered his team and, with a straight face, said, "After we win, don't pick me up and ruin my other hip. I'll walk, okay?"

Their reaction was a rousing cheer.

The rain had stopped but the wind was building. It would affect both kicking and passing.

Unitas, nursing his sore elbow, noticed it and talked with Morrall about it. A 10-time Pro Bowl selection, Unitas did not figure to take off his parka all day. Morrall said he didn't think the wind would bother him as much as it would Namath and the Jets.

The Jets won the toss and started with the ball. On the second play from scrimmage, Snell took a handoff and ran to his left. The play, called 19-Straight, would be called 16 more times in the game.

On this attempt, Colts safety Rick Volk closed to make the tackle. But he was knocked groggy. Two plays into the game and the Jets had proven one point: The Colts were mortal.

The first time the Colts had the ball, they acted as if the pregame odds were conservative. A pass to tight end John Mackey gained 19 yards. Tom Matte picked up another first down on a sweep. Three more runs and a 15-yard pass gained two more first downs. Suddenly the Colts were at the Jets' 19-yard line.

On the next play, Willie Richardson broke free when safety Jim Hudson fell down. Morrall's pass was perfect...but Richardson dropped it.

Tom Mitchell, a reserve tight end, got just as open as Richardson. Morrall overthrew him.

"Who knows what the final score might have been if we'd hit either pass," Morrall says.

Defensive end Gerry Philbin then chased Morrall from the pocket and nailed him for no gain. The Colts went for a field goal, but kicker Lou Michaels botched a 27-yard attempt.

The Jets took over on their 20 and on third down, Namath found reserve halfback Bill Mathis for 13 yards and a first down at the 35.

The next down produced one of the most important incomplete passes in pro football history. Maynard ran a straight fly pattern and blew by Boyd. Safety Jerry Logan was there to pick him up, but Maynard also got behind Logan. The pass from Namath was just long.

"It was an important play," Namath says.

"Poise, poise," Ewbank screamed. These were the mistakes he feared, the ones that had doomed both Kansas City and Oakland in the first two Super Bowls.

Two running plays moved the Colts to the 6-yard line. Morrall dropped back, saw Mitchell, and threw. But the ball caromed off Mitchell's shoulder and bounced high in the air. Cornerback Randy Beverly made a rolling interception in the end zone.

"That was the game in a nutshell," Matte says. "We were a great team during the sea-

Sore elbow and all, Johnny Unitas relieved Earl Morrall and directed Baltimore's only scoring drive.

Swaggering quarterback Joe Namath "guaranteed" a Jets' victory, then had the poise to pull it off. He completed 17 of 28 passes for 206 yards, didn't throw an interception, and was voted most valuable player.

"Maynard was open. He got behind their bomb-proof secondary. He put the fear of God in them for the rest of the game. It was a real show of courage, going all out like that. Because of that one play, they had to keep their double coverage. That opened things up for George Sauer."

Sauer was guarded on his side by Lenny Lyles, who had been weakened by tonsillitis all week (another of the well-kept secrets of Super Bowl III). The Jets' receiver wound up catching eight passes for 133 yards in the game.

Two minutes later, after an exchange of punts, Sauer took a short pass, was hit, and fumbled. The Colts recovered at the Jets' 12.

son because we did not make mistakes. But that day we threw four interceptions. I fumbled once. We had a chance to have twenty-seven points in the first half. It was right there. We didn't get any."

The Jets defied their stereotyped image, marching 80 methodical yards on 12 plays to a touchdown. Snell scored on a four-yard run around left end. It was the first time in Super Bowl history that the AFL held a lead.

The Jets' winning head coach, Weeb Ewbank, also coached the Colts' 1958-59 NFL champions.

Even when the error-prone Colts did something good, the Jets found a way to turn it into a negative. Matte broke loose on a Super-Bowl-record 58-yard run before he was pulled down from behind by several Jets, including the snarling Sample, who arrived knees first and maybe a split-second late.

"You're a dirty player," Matte snapped.

"You ain't nothing," Sample said. "Getting caught like this. You shoulda scored."

Matte lost his composure. Several Colts started screaming at the Jets. Two plays later, from the Jets' 15, Morrall's pass was intercepted by Sample. When Sample left the field, he waved at Matte.

Near the end of the first half, the crowd was quiet when the Colts got the ball with less than a minute left before intermission. It already felt like an upset.

Before the game some experts had said the Jets' only chance to win was with gadget plays and gimmicks, but it was the Colts who now were reduced to trick plays. Matte took a pitch and headed to his right, stopped, threw the ball back to Morrall.

Safety Bill Baird went for the fake run. Beverly was responsible for Orr short. Baird had the Colts receiver if he went deep.

"I was flying toward the line of scrimmage,"

Baird says today. "I was ready to make a big tackle on Matte."

Orr was 15 yards from everyone. All Morrall had to do was throw the ball. All Orr had to do was catch it. The game would be tied.

"I never saw him," Morrall says.

Shula explained afterward that the play was designed for Orr. He was the first option, the first look. Orr realized Morrall didn't see him and began waving his arms.

"It's hard to believe still—being that wide open," Orr says. "It was a perfect play...I thought."

Morrall did see fullback Jerry Hill, who also was open. But Hudson recovered, stepping in front of Hill to intercept.

Trailing 7-0, Shula thought about making a quarterback change at halftime. Morrall was off. Shula had Unitas, and the veteran had told him he could play if he were needed. Three touchdown chances had been ruined by interceptions. Michaels had missed two field goals.

"I decided to give Morrall one more series," Shula says. "I owed him that. Besides, we were only behind 7-0. It was still anyone's game."

On the first play from scrimmage in the third quarter, Matte fumbled and the Jets' Ralph Baker recovered.

"It wasn't Earl's fault," Shula says, "but when they got a field goal and made it 10-0, we became seriously in trouble."

Jim Turner's 32-

Coming off the field in the gathering darkness, Namath signaled that the upstart Jets were number one.

yard field goal put a sense of desperation into the Colts. It turned into frustration as the Jets, steady, conservative, and efficient, played ball-control. Baltimore ran just seven offensive plays all quarter, gaining a total of 11 yards.

Morrall left the game ignobly. His last official entry in Super Bowl III shows that he rushed for a two-yard loss. After the punt, the Jets were in their huddle when a roar went up. On the Colts' sideline, number 19 was warming up.

"I'd seen him [Unitas] do so many great things," Ewbank says. "Just watching him warm up—I got scared."

Another field goal by Turner made it 13-0, and a large slice of time had been consumed.

On his first series at quarterback, the old magician had nothing up his sleeve but a sore elbow. Unitas could not move the Colts, and they had to punt. Then, 94 seconds into the fourth quarter, Turner kicked another field goal for a 16-0 lead.

Braase was gone from the game, unable to bend over with a stiff back. Linebacker Don Shinnick also was hurt for the Colts. Volk had returned from his first-quarter collision, but he still was suffering from a mild concussion that would hospitalize him that night.

Unitas finally started finding holes in the Jets' defense. At the New York 25, Orr broke free in the Jets' end zone. Unitas's pass was badly underthrown...and Beverly intercepted.

"My elbow was tricky. Sometimes I could throw it hard and get away with it. Other times I had nothing," Unitas says now. "That was one of my nothing throws."

The Jets then used up almost five minutes before Turner came on to try another field goal. This time he missed.

"We were figuring two touchdowns and a field goal," Bubba Smith says. "There was still time. We felt we still could do it."

But after three straight incompletions, Unitas looked weary. Then something clicked and it was almost as if Johnny U had entered a time warp.

On fourth down he hit Orr for 17 yards and a first down to the Colts' 37. He hit Mackey for 11 yards, Richardson for 21, Orr for 11, and, with the help of three penalties, the Colts had the ball, first-and-goal on the Jets' 1.

"We needed to score quick," Shula says, "and we couldn't. I think we wasted at least a minute of time. That looks insignificant in hindsight. But it was a big factor."

It took the Colts three downs before Jerry Hill finally squeezed into the end zone. The shutout of the Baltimore Colts, a team that had been called one of the best of all time, had lasted 56 minutes 41 seconds. It took three Jets penalties, three tries from 36 inches away, and a desperation pass on fourth down to score.

Unitas remembers how important the ensuing onside kick was. "If we recovered it, we still had a chance," he says.

The Colts recovered Michaels's squib kick, and Unitas promptly led them to the Jets' 19-yard line. "We still were feeling the day could be salvaged," Shula says. "We would need another onside kick, of course. But first we needed that second touchdown."

On fourth down, Unitas looked for Orr. But linebacker Larry Grantham reached up and got a hand on the pass. It caromed beyond Orr, incomplete, with only 2:21 left.

At the final gun, Namath walked slowly off the field, head tilted downward. His only statement was the solitary index finger he waved along the way: number one.

Ewbank and Shula shook hands.

"We got all the breaks," Ewbank said.

"You have a fine team, Weeb," said Shula. "Enjoy this."

Showing total disregard for their coach's physical well-being, the Jets threw Ewbank into the shower. Their disregard for conformity had returned; the rebels were back. When Commissioner Pete Rozelle came into the room, tight end Pete Lammons yelled, "Hey, Pete, welcome to the AFL."

"That one game was perfect testament to the nature of the sport," Ewbank says. "We were playing, I suppose, for an entire league. But everyone else saw it that way. My team didn't. There was $15,000 a player at stake and there was this beautiful ring. But there were also the instincts of football in motion. And human nature—beat the man across from you. Especially if you keep getting told how much better he is than you.

"Sometimes you just respond."

IV

Kansas City 23, Minnesota 7

Fourth World Championship Game
Sunday, January 11, 1970 • 2:30 p.m.
Tulane Stadium, New Orleans, $15.00
NORTH END LOWER DECK

17 or
18   Z   4   11
GATE   SEC.   ROW   SEAT

Vital Statistics

Starting Lineups

Minnesota (NFL)	Offense	Kansas City (AFL)
Gene Washington	WR	Frank Pitts
Grady Alderman	LT	Jim Tyrer
Jim Vellone	LG	Ed Budde
Mick Tingelhoff	C	E.J. Holub
Milt Sunde	RG	Mo Moorman
Ron Yary	RT	Dave Hill
John Beasley	TE	Fred Arbanas
John Henderson	WR	Otis Taylor
Joe Kapp	QB	Len Dawson
Dave Osborn	RB	Mike Garrett
Bill Brown	RB	Robert Holmes
	Defense	
Carl Eller	LE	Jerry Mays
Gary Larsen	LT	Curley Culp
Alan Page	RT	Buck Buchanan
Jim Marshall	RE	Aaron Brown
Roy Winston	LLB	Bobby Bell
Lonnie Warwick	MLB	Willie Lanier
Wally Hilgenberg	RLB	Jim Lynch
Earsell Mackbee	LCB	Jim Marsalis
Ed Sharockman	RCB	Emmitt Thomas
Karl Kassulke	SS	Jim Kearney
Paul Krause	FS	Johnny Robinson

Substitutions

Minnesota-Offense: K-Fred Cox. P-Bob Lee. WR-Bob Grim. TE-Kent Kramer. LINE-Steve Smith, Ed White. QB-Gary Cuozzo. RB-Clint Jones, Bill Harris, Oscar Reed, Jim Lindsey. Defense: LINE-Paul Dickson. LB-Dale Hackbart, Mike McGill, Jim Hargrove. DB-Charlie West. DNP: T-Doug Davis. LB-Mike Reilly.
Kansas City-Offense: K-Jan Stenerud. P-Jerrel Wilson. WR-Gloster Richardson. TE-Curtis McClinton. LINE-George Daney, Remi Prudhomme. QB-Mike Livingston. RB-Warren McVea, Wendell Hayes, Ed Podolak. Defense: LINE-Gene Trosch, Ed Lothamer, Chuck Hurston. LB-Bob Stein. DB-Goldie Sellers, Willie Mitchell, Ceaser Belser. DNP: QB-Tom Flores.

Officials

Referee-John McDonough (AFL). Umpire-Lou Palazzi (NFL). Head Linesman-Harry Kessel (AFL). Field Judge-Charlie Musser (AFL). Back Judge-Tom Kelleher (NFL). Line Judge-Bill Schleibaum (NFL).

Scoring

Minnesota	0	0	7	0	—	7
Kansas City	3	13	7	0	—	23

KC-FG Stenerud 48
KC-FG Stenerud 32
KC-FG Stenerud 25
KC-Garrett 5 run (Stenerud kick)
Minn-Osborn 4 run (Cox kick)
KC-Taylor 46 pass from Dawson (Stenerud kick)
Attendance-80,562

FINAL TEAM STATISTICS

	Vikings	Chiefs
TOTAL FIRST DOWNS	13	18
Rushing	2	8
Passing	10	7
Penalty	1	3
TOTAL NET YARDAGE	239	273
Total Offensive Plays	50	62
Average Gain per Offensive Play	4.8	4.4
NET YARDS RUSHING	67	151
Total Rushing Plays	19	42
Average Gain per Rushing Play	3.5	3.6
NET YARDS PASSING	172	122
Pass Att.-Comp.-Int.	28-17-3	17-12-1
Sacks-Yards Lost	3-27	3-20
Gross Yards Passing	199	142
Avg. Gain per Pass (Incl. Sacks)	5.5	6.1
PUNTS-YARDS	3-111	4-194
Average Distance	37.0	48.5
Had Blocked	0	0
TOTAL RETURN YARDAGE	97	60
Kickoff Returns-Yards	4-79	2-36
Punt Returns-Yards	2-18	1-0
Interception Returns-Yards	1-0	3-24
TOTAL TURNOVERS	5	1
Fumbles-Lost	3-2	0-0
Had Intercepted	3	1
PENALTIES-YARDS	6-67	4-47
TOTAL POINTS SCORED	7	23
Touchdowns Rushing	1	1
Touchdowns Passing	0	1
Touchdowns Returns	0	0
Extra Points	1	2
Field Goals-Attempts	0-1	3-3
Safeties	0	0
THIRD DOWN EFFICIENCY	3/9	9/16
FOURTH DOWN EFFICIENCY	0/0	0/0
TIME OF POSSESSION	25:27	34:33

INDIVIDUAL STATISTICS

RUSHING

Minnesota	No.	Yds.	Avg.	Long	TD
Osborn	7	15	2.1	4t	1
Brown	6	26	4.3	10	0
Reed	4	17	4.3	15	0
Kapp	2	9	3.5	7	0

Kansas City	No.	Yds.	Avg.	Long	TD
McVea	12	26	2.2	9	0
Garrett	11	39	3.5	6	1
Hayes	8	31	3.9	13	0
Holmes	5	7	1.4	7	0
Pitts	3	37	12.3	19	0
Dawson	3	11	3.7	11	0

PASSING

Minnesota	Att.	Comp.	Yds.	Long	TD	Int.
Kapp	25	16	183	28	0	2
Cuozzo	3	1	16	16	0	1

Kansas City	Att.	Comp.	Yds.	Long	TD	Int.
Dawson	17	12	142	46t	1	1

RECEIVING

Minnesota	No.	Yds.	Long	TD
Henderson	7	111	28	0
Brown	3	11	10	0
Beasley	2	41	26	0
Reed	2	16	12	0
Osborn	2	11	10	0
Washington	1	9	9	0

Kansas City	No.	Yds.	Long	TD
Taylor	6	81	46t	1
Pitts	3	33	20	0
Garrett	2	25	17	0
Hayes	1	3	3	0

INTERCEPTIONS

Minnesota	No.	Yds.	Long	TD
Krause	1	0	0	0

Kansas City	No.	Yds.	Long	TD
Lanier	1	9	9	0
Robinson	1	9	9	0
Thomas	1	6	6	0

PUNTING

Minnesota	No.	Yds.	Avg.	TB	Long
Lee	3	111	37.0	1	50

Kansas City	No.	Yds.	Avg.	TB	Long
Wilson	4	194	48.5	1	59

PUNT RETURNS

Minnesota	No.	FC	Yds.	Long	TD
West	2	0	18	11	0

Kansas City	No.	FC	Yds.	Long	TD
Garrett	1	0	0	0	0

KICKOFF RETURNS

Minnesota	No.	Yds.	Long	TD
West	3	46	27	0
Jones	1	33	33	0

Kansas City	No.	Yds.	Long	TD
Hayes	2	36	18	0

FUMBLES

Minnesota	No.	Own Rec.	Opp. Rec.
Kapp	1	0	0
Henderson	1	0	0
West	1	0	0
Vellone	0	1	0

Kansas City	No.	Own Rec.	Opp. Rec.
Robinson	0	0	1
Prudhomme	0	0	1

KICKING

Minnesota	XP-A	FG-A	FG Made	FG Missed
Cox	1-1	0-1	--	56

Kansas City	XP-A	FG-A	FG Made	FG Missed
Stenerud	2-2	3-3	48,32,25	--

PLAY-BY-PLAY

Minnesota won the coin toss and elected to receive.

FIRST QUARTER

Stenerud kick into end zone, touchback.

Minnesota (15:00)

M 20	1-10	Osborn 2 run left tackle (Thomas).
M 22	2-8	Kapp 10 pass to Osborn left (Lanier).
M 32	1-10	Brown 3 run left end (Lynch).
M 35	2-7	Kapp 26 pass to Beasley middle.
KC 39	1-10	Osborn 1 run left tackle (Kearney).
KC 38	2-9	Kapp pass to Brown right flat, loss of 1 (Mays).
KC 39	3-10	Kapp pass to Beasley off his fingertips.
KC 39	4-10	Lee 22 punt out of bounds at KC 17.

Kansas City (10:58)

KC 17	1-10	Holmes 3 run left tackle (Hilbenberg).
KC 20	2-7	Dawson 17 pass to Garrett left (Sharockman).
KC 37	1-10	Holmes 3 run left (Page).
KC 40	2-7	Garrett 4 run right (Larsen).
KC 44	3-3	Dawson 20 pass to Pitts left (Hilgenberg).
M 36	1-10	Dawson sacked, loss of 8 (Winston).
M 44	2-18	Garrett 3 draw left tackle (Page).
M 41	3-15	Dawson pass to Garrett left broken up (Page).
M 41	4-15	Stenerud, 48-yard field goal (6:52).

Kansas City scoring drive: 42 yards, 8 plays, 4:06.
Kansas City 3, Minnesota 0

Stenerud kick into end zone, touchback.

Minnesota (6:52)

M 20	1-10	Brown 3 run up middle (Culp).
M 23	2-7	Kapp sacked, loss of 6 (Mays).
M 17	3-13	Brown 10 sweep left (Buchanan).
M 27	4-3	Lee 45 punt, Mitchell no return. Play nullified and KC penalized 15 for roughing the kicker.
M 42	1-10	Kapp 1 pass to Brown right (Kearney).
M 43	2-9	Kapp 1 pass to Osborn left (Lynch).
M 44	3-8	Kapp 6 pass to Henderson right (Marsalis).
50	4-2	Lee 50 punt into end zone, touchback.

Kansas City (3:18)

KC 20	1-10	Dawson 20 pass to Pitts middle (Krause).
KC 40	1-10	Dawson 9 pass to Taylor right flat (Krause).
KC 49	2-1	Garrett 3 run left (Larsen).
M 48	1-10	Garrett 5 run left tackle (Warwick).
M 43	2-5	Holmes draw, loss of 5 (Page).

END OF FIRST QUARTER:
Kansas City 3, Minnesota 0

SECOND QUARTER

M 48	3-10	Dawson pass to Pitts incomplete. Play nullified and Minn. penalized 17 for pass interference (Sharockman).
M 31	1-10	Dawson 7 pass to Taylor right (Mackbee).
M 24	2-3	Holmes run right, loss of 1 (Winston).
M 25	3-4	Dawson pass to Taylor deep broken up (Mackbee).
M 25	4-4	Stenerud, 32-yard field goal (13:20).

Kansas City scoring drive: 55 yards, 8 plays, 4:58.
Kansas City 6, Minnesota 0

Stenerud kick to M 13, West 19 return (Daney).

Minnesota (13:20)

M 32	1-10	Osborn run left, no gain (Culp).
M 32	2-10	Kapp 16 pass to Henderson, fumbled, recovered by KC at M 48, Robinson 2 return.

Kansas City (11:48)

M 46	1-10	Garrett run right tackle, loss of 1 (Page).
M 47	2-11	Dawson pass to Taylor deep intercepted at M 7, Krause no return (Taylor).

Minnesota (11:09)

M 7	1-10	Osborn 3 run right (Buchanan).
M 10	2-7	Kapp pass to Washington deep broken up (Thomas).
M 10	3-10	Minn. penalized 5 for delay of game.
M 5	3-12	Kapp pass to Grim deep incomplete.
M 5	4-12	Lee 39 punt, Garrett no return (Tingelhoff).

Kansas City (10:05)

M 44	1-10	Pitts 19 reverse right (Mackbee).
M 25	1-10	Minn. penalized 5 for offsides.

M 20	1-5	Dawson keeper middle, no gain (Larsen).
M 20	2-5	Hayes 1 run left (Marshall).
M 19	3-4	Hayes 2 draw left (Hilgenberg).
M 17	4-2	Stenerud, 25-yard field goal (7:52).

Kansas City scoring drive: 27 yards, 4 plays, 2:13.
Kansas City 9, Minnesota 0

Stenerud kick to M 11, West no return, fumbled, Prudhomme recovered for KC at M 19.

Kansas City (7:21)

M 19	1-10	Dawson sacked, loss of 8 (Marshall).
M 27	2-18	Hayes 13 draw up middle (Winston).
M 14	3-5	Dawson 10 pass to Taylor right (Mackbee).
M 4	1-goal	Garrett run left end, loss of 1 (Marshall).
M 5	2-goal	Dawson keeper middle, no gain (Dickson).
M 5	3-goal	Garrett 5 trap draw over left guard, touchdown (5:34). Stenerud kicked extra point.

Kansas City scoring drive: 19 yards, 6 plays, 1:47.
Kansas City 16, Minnesota 0

Stenerud kick to M 5, West 27 return (Prudhomme).

Minnesota (5:34)

M 32	1-10	Kapp 27 pass to Henderson middle.
KC 41	1-10	Kapp pass to Reed incomplete (Lanier).
KC 41	2-10	Kapp sacked, loss of 8 (Buchanan).
KC 49	3-18	Kapp pass to Henderson broken up (Marsalis).
KC 49	4-18	Cox's 56-yard field goal attempt was short, fielded at KC 7, McVea 17 return (Tingelhoff).

Kansas City (3:20)

KC 24	1-10	McVea run left, loss of 1 (Warwick, Page).
KC 23	2-11	McVea 2 sweep right (Page). Two-Minute Warning.
KC 25	3-9	McVea 9 sweep right (Eller).
KC 34	1-10	Pitts 11 reverse right (Eller).
KC 45	1-10	Dawson 3 pass to Taylor right (Mackbee).
KC 48	2-7	Hayes 3 run up middle (Warwick, Winston).
M 49	3-4	Dawson pass to McVea broken up (Hilgenberg).
M 49	4-4	Wilson 34 punt, Grim fair catch. Play nullified and KC penalized 5 for illegal procedure.
KC 46	4-9	Wilson 44 punt downed at M 10.

Minnesota (:23)

M 10	1-10	Kapp pass to Washington deep incomplete (Thomas).
M 10	2-10	Kapp 2 keeper up middle (Buchanan).

END OF SECOND QUARTER:
Kansas City 16, Minnesota 0

THIRD QUARTER

Cox kick 3 yards into end zone, Hayes 18 return (Harris).

Kansas City (15:00)

KC 15	1-10	McVea 5 sweep left (Marshall).
KC 20	2-5	Dawson 6 pass to Taylor right (Mackbee).
KC 26	1-10	Garrett 6 run right tackle (Winston).
KC 32	2-4	Hayes run right, loss of 2 (Hilgenberg).
KC 30	3-6	Dawson 8 pass to Garrett left (Sharockman).
KC 38	1-10	Dawson pass to Richardson broken up (Mackbee).
KC 38	2-10	Dawson 3 screen left to Hayes (Marshall).
KC 41	3-7	Dawson 8 pass to Arbanas. Play nullified and KC penalized 15 from spot of foul (KC 34) for holding.
KC 19	3-29	Dawson 6 sweep left (Warwick).
KC 25	4-23	Wilson 55 punt, West 11 return (Stein).

Minnesota (9:06)

M 31	1-10	Brown run left, no gain (Culp).
M 31	2-10	Kapp 15 pass to Beasley left (Kearney).
M 46	1-10	Brown 2 run right (Lanier).
M 48	2-8	Kapp 7 run evading pass rush (Bell, Lanier).
KC 45	3-1	Osborn 1 run left tackle (Lanier, Kearney).
KC 44	1-10	Brown 8 run left (Bell).
KC 36	2-2	Kapp 11 screen to Brown left (Buchanan).
KC 25	1-10	Kapp 9 pass to Henderson right (Marsalis).
KC 16	2-1	Kapp 12 pass to Reed left (Kearney).
KC 4	1-goal	Osborn 4 run off right tackle, touchdown (4:32). Cox kicked extra point.

Minnesota scoring drive: 69 yards, 10 plays, 4:34.
Kansas City 16, Minnesota 7

Cox kick to M 2, Hayes 16 return (Hackbart).

Kansas City (4:32)

KC 18	1-10	Garrett 5 run left (Hilgenberg).
KC 23	2-5	Hayes 6 draw up middle (Warwick).
KC 29	1-10	Garrett 4 run right (Hilgenberg).
KC 33	2-6	Dawson 3 pass to Pitts left. Play nullified and KC penalized 5 for illegal procedure.
KC 28	2-11	Hayes 4 draw up middle (Warwick).
KC 32	3-7	Pitts 7 reverse right (Mackbee).
KC 39	1-10	Dawson pass to Pitts deep overthrown. Play nullified and Minn. penalized 15 for personal foul.
M 46	1-10	Dawson 46 pass to Taylor right sideline, caught at M 41, broke two tackles and went down sideline, touchdown (1:22). Stenerud kicked extra point.

Kansas City scoring drive: 82 yards, 6 plays, 3:10.
Kansas City 23, Minnesota 7

Stenerud kick to M 4, Jones 33 return (Mitchell).

Minnesota (1:22)

M 37	1-10	Reed 1 run left tackle (Buchanan).
M 38	2-9	Kapp 9 pass to Henderson (Marsalis).

END OF THIRD QUARTER:
Kansas City 23, Minnesota 7

FOURTH QUARTER

M 47	1-10	Osborn 4 sweep left (Lanier).
KC 49	2-6	Reed 3 run left (Lanier).
KC 46	3-3	Kapp pass to Beasley intercepted at KC 34, Lanier 9 return (Vellone).

Kansas City (13:48)

KC 43	1-10	Dawson screen to Pitts, loss of 7 (Sharockman).
KC 36	2-17	McVea 4 run left (Warwick).
KC 40	3-13	McVea 1 sweep left (Hilgenberg).
KC 41	4-12	Wilson 59 punt into end zone, touchback.

Minnesota (11:29)

M 20	1-10	Kapp 2 pass to Reed. Play nullified and Minn. penalized 10 (half the distance) for illegal man downfield.
M 10	1-20	Kapp pass to Henderson deep incomplete.
M 10	2-20	Kapp 28 pass to Henderson right (Marsalis).
M 38	1-10	Kapp pass to Beasley intercepted at KC 40, Robinson 9 return (Grim).

Kansas City (10:22)

KC 49	1-10	McVea run left, loss of 1 (Warwick).
KC 48	2-11	McVea 4 sweep left (Sharockman).
M 48	3-7	McVea run left tackle, no gain (Hilgenberg).
M 48	4-7	Wilson 36 return, West 7 return (Belser).

Minnesota (7:52)

M 19	1-10	Kapp 9 pass to Washington left (Thomas).
M 28	2-1	Reed sweep left, loss of 2 (Brown).
M 26	3-3	Kapp 4 pass to Reed right (Bell).
M 30	1-10	Kapp sacked, loss of 13 (Brown), fumbled, Vellone recovered for Minn. at M 17. Kapp injured.
M 17	2-23	Cuozzo 16 pass to Henderson middle (Kearney).
M 32	3-8	Cuozzo pass to Washington overthrown.
M 48	1-10	Cuozzo pass to Henderson intercepted at KC 28, Thomas 6 return (Brown).

Kansas City (4:00)

KC 34	1-10	Dawson 11 run around left end (Hilgenberg).
KC 45	1-10	McVea run left tackle, loss of 1 (Warwick).
KC 44	2-11	McVea run right, no gain (Winston). Two-Minute Warning.
KC 44	3-11	Dawson sacked, loss of 4 (Eller). Minn. penalized 15 for personal foul.
M 45	1-10	McVea 4 run around left end (Marshall).
M 41	2-6	Hayes 4 run left tackle (Warwick).
M 37	3-2	Holmes 7 run right tackle (Warwick).

FINAL SCORE:
Kansas City 23, Minnesota 7
FINAL RECORDS:
Kansas City 14-3, Minnesota 14-3

Beyond an Unreasonable Doubt

He lay in his bed, toes squirming, the nausea coming in waves. His legs cramped, causing him to sit and moan softly. Len Dawson looked at the clock next to his bed. It was 4 in the morning.

He fell back against his pillow, disoriented, blanching at the pain. In less than 11 hours, Dawson was supposed to be the quarterback for the Kansas City Chiefs in Super Bowl IV. The toughest week of the toughest season of his career had come down to pro football's biggest game.

"I thought about trying to go back to sleep," Dawson says now. "Then the nausea came again."

A knee injury had sidelined him for six weeks during the season. His father had died two days before an important game. And his arrival in New Orleans, site for the final football game ever to be played between the American Football League and the National Football League was accompanied by the numbing discomfort of innuendo.

In the bed next to his, Dawson's roommate, Johnny Robinson, was sound asleep, snoring. Robinson had cracked two ribs in the AFL Championship Game against Oakland and he had complained about how hard it was to breathe easily. But a sleeping pill had put Robinson safely in a deep sleep. Dawson wondered if there was a pill that could make him relax.

But then the cramps hit his calf muscles again and his stomach churned and rolled. He limped quickly to the bathroom.

On Tuesday, January 6, 1970, the "Huntley-Brinkley Report" on NBC television led with a bulletin: "In Detroit, a special Justice Department Task Force, conducting what is described as the biggest gambling investigation of its kind ever, is about to call seven professional football players and one college coach to testify on their relationship with known gamblers…"

Len Dawson's world changed forever.

"…Among the players scheduled to appear is Len Dawson, quarterback for the Kansas City Chiefs, who will play the Minnesota Vikings in the Super Bowl this Sunday."

Suddenly, nobody wanted to talk about football. Snap conclusions were made. Guilt was assumed. It was simply a miserable way for a quarterback to prepare for a championship game. Dawson appeared at a hastily arranged press conference, listening to a barrage of tough questions and offering quick denials to all charges.

Commissioner Pete Rozelle came to Dawson's defense. Rozelle was a staunch opponent of sports gambling. Seven years earlier, he had made a strong stand, suspending two players, Paul Hornung and Alex Karras, for a year because they had bet on pro football games. And only a few months earlier, Rozelle had demanded that Joe Namath, hero of Super Bowl III, sell his part-ownership in a New York bar frequented by known gamblers.

NFL investigators had found no wrongdoing in Dawson's case; nothing had turned up after careful and thorough scrutiny. Rozelle said NBC's report was "totally irresponsible."

But the controversy was already out. Dawson should have been brimming with uncontrollable excitement. The game was his chance to erase the memory of Super Bowl I, when he and the Chiefs were defeated 35-10 by the Green Bay Packers. Now it would be a trial of ethics. Tulane Stadium would be filled with jurors who would watch an inverted justice system in which a man had to prove his innocence.

"It was, beyond a doubt, the toughest week of my life," Dawson says. "I don't know what the public would have thought if I'd had a really bad game. What if I had fumbled or thrown an interception with the game on the line? It was something I had to block out of my mind. I couldn't dwell on the bad that might happen."

He got out of bed that Sunday morning, walked to the window, and parted the curtains. It still was dark. It still was cold. Record freezing temperatures had hit New Orleans. Dawson began thinking about plays and formations; he concentrated on those that were safest and not likely to fail because of inclement weather. After what had happened that week, Dawson had to be ready for anything.

And he was. The Kansas City Chiefs beat the

Not much went right in the pregame festivities to Super Bowl IV. A planned hot-air balloon race fizzled when the one manned by a "Viking" failed to gain much altitude and floated into the stands in the end zone.

heavily favored Minnesota Vikings 23-7 in Super Bowl IV before 80,562 fans and a national television audience. Neither Chet Huntley nor David Brinkley had any comment. Neither did the Justice Department. Len Dawson was named the game's most valuable player.

The underdog Chiefs jumped ahead 9-0 in the second quarter on three Jan Stenerud field goals.

"It was one of the greatest, most courageous performances of all time," says Chiefs head coach Hank Stram.

Because of all the off-field drama and unfortunate allegations, Stram feels his team has been slighted by history, deprived of its fair share of recognition.

"It became a totally out-of-focus event," Stram says now. "The Chiefs played a great game that day...and not just Len Dawson. Len displayed an incredible amount of

character. He played an almost flawless game on a day when any and every mistake would have been held up for scrutiny. It was one of the greatest clutch performances I've ever seen under ridiculously unfair conditions. But that game has never been perceived for what it really was—namely, a great victory by a great team."

The Chiefs' defense was spectacular that day. The kicking game, perhaps the greatest in history, was conspicuously dominant. His innovative offense was productive. The Vikings, who had been 14-point favorites, were totally dominated.

"It still bothers me," Stram says. "The Vikings were a good team, called by some one of the best in NFL history.

"My personal feelings are of satisfaction and pride. We were the last AFL champions ever. We won the last game between the two leagues before the implementation of the merger. But it is almost tragic that one TV report caused the rest of the world to lose its perspective."

The 1969 football season was much like the rest of the world—chaotic, violent, emotional, pivotal. Man walked on the moon. People marched in protest against the Vietnam conflict. There was horrifying news about a madman named Charles Manson and his cult of

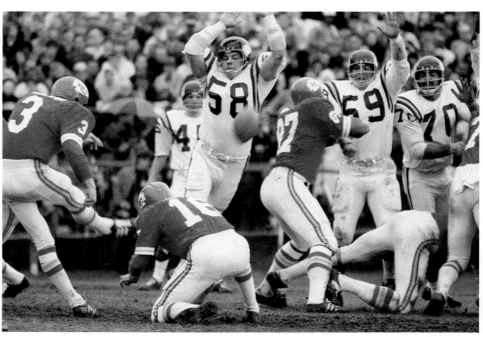

murderers. The nation cringed after a tragedy at Chapaquiddick, gasped at the details of My Lai and smiled at Big Bird on "Sesame Street." It was a decade of war, assassination, exploration, civil rights protests, and youthful turbulence. Perhaps it was only fitting that the biggest sporting event of the new decade would be shrouded in confusion and suspicion.

Bud Grant, the Vikings' head coach in Super Bowl IV, agrees the game became a sideshow to the main event, which was Len Dawson's personal melodrama.

Shrugging off the pressure of being unfairly linked to a gambling investigation, cool Len Dawson completed 12 of 17 passes for 142 yards and a touchdown, directed the Chiefs to victory, and was named the game's MVP.

"People do seem to look back on that game for the wrong reasons," Grant says today. "But it bothers me that when they talk about the game, it is called an upset. That was a fine football team that beat us. I think it becomes less and less of an upset as more and more of the Chiefs get inducted into the Hall of Fame. I think hindsight allows a better picture."

Len Dawson dressed in the dark that January 11 morning. He didn't want to wake his roommate.

Hank Stram woke up early, too.

"My eyes were really burning," he says. "You watch a lot of film as a coach. I was concerned with a lot of things that week, Lenny's thing, the Vikings. But I remember my first thoughts were about the weather."

On the second day after arriving in New Orleans, the fountain outside the Chiefs' team hotel had frozen. Like Dawson, Stram opened his curtains and peered out at the blackness.

Stram dressed quickly and called an old friend, Monsignor Vincent Mackey. He asked the priest to go for a walk with him, something they did often.

The skies were still swollen and foreboding. Minnesota weather, Stram joked. The Vikings already had every seeming advantage (if you believed the media). Now one more had materialized.

"I'm going to have to trade you," Stram joked to his friend about the weather.

As they walked, the temperature seemed to rise. Stram apologized to Monsignor Mackey, complimented him on his remarkable powers, and they shared a laugh. But when the two men got back to the hotel, they heard a report that a tornado warning had been posted for the area.

"What else could possibly happen?" Stram asked, not really wanting to hear any answer.

Outside of town, in the Vikings' hotel, Bud Grant slept peacefully. Grant always kept football in perspective. He believed in hard work and careful preparation...and then playing the game. Fretting wasn't in his game plan.

In the week before Super Bowl IV, Grant downplayed his team's reported superiority, neither out of modesty nor coaching caution. He also scoffed at Stram's *avant-garde* theories such as a triple-stack defense and a movable pocket offense.

"I don't think either team will be able to run away from the other on the scoreboard," Grant said. "Both defenses are very good, both very solid. I expect a low-scoring game."

Stram says he never worried about Dawson. Their relationship traced back 14 years, to Purdue, where Stram had been an assistant coach and Dawson an All-America quarterback.

"I knew this whole mess was eating away at

The powerful Chiefs' defense intercepted two of Joe Kapp's passes and sacked him three times, including this shirttail tackle by 6-foot-7 tackle Buck Buchanan. End Jerry Mays (75) came up to help out.

him," Stram says. "But he never complained. He always was at his best when things were toughest anyway."

Two days after Dawson's father died, he had passed for almost 300 yards in a victory over the New York Jets, then had rushed to catch a plane for the funeral.

Dawson's counterpart, the Vikings' Joe Kapp, also was "cool." But you'd never confuse either man for the other.

Kapp was a swaggering battler with a rebel image and a cackling laugh. He had spurned the NFL after his career at California and had gone to the Canadian Football League. He won a championship there and built a legend. In 1967 Kapp joined the Vikings, becoming their leader from day one. Before the 1969 season, Kapp came up with a battle cry.

The slogan "40 for 60" meant every player must devote every minute to the cause. Nobody took that to heart more than Kapp.

"Most quarterbacks look for somewhere to run out of bounds," Grant deadpanned in the week before the game. "Mine looks for someone to run into."

Kapp says now his reputation was warranted—"but also a little overblown. I was a little crazy but I wasn't insane. I might try to bowl over a linebacker once in a while. But as a rule, you don't survive if you try that stuff regularly."

Kapp has a face that is like a map of his life. Deep creases in his forehead, a nose that looks like a stepped-on biscuit, an intriguing scar that runs along his jaw. Kapp's playing style wasn't exactly pretty either. But he was a winner.

Teammates still talk about the scene he created in the locker room after the Vikings beat Cleveland in the NFL Championship Game. Kapp took one long, satisfying chug from a huge bottle of champagne, letting the wine run down his chin. Then he turned to the nearest locker and smashed the bottle to pieces. Kapp shouted he'd drink the whole bottle when the

The heavily favored Vikings didn't have much luck running on Kansas City, either, as they netted just 67 yards. Aggressive tackle Curley Culp (61) stuffed Dave Osborn with a little help from his friends.

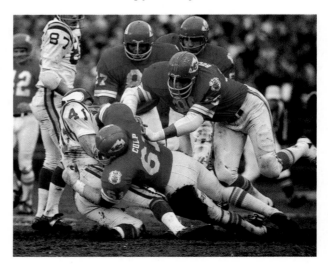

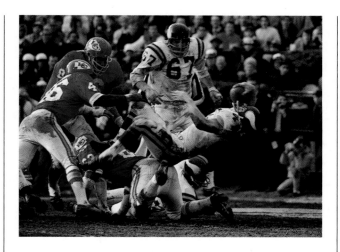

Minnesota made a third-quarter bid to get back in the game, driving 69 yards for a touchdown on Osborn's four-yard run and backward lunge to trim the score to 16-7. However, Kansas City scored on the next series.

Vikings won the whole championship.

Kapp was charismatic if not eloquent. He seethed with passion for victory, but he also resisted any temptation to make a Joe Namath-like guarantee of victory.

He was a long way from the lettuce fields of Salinas, California, where he'd learned the game. He also was a long way from British Columbia, where he'd led the Lions' team to a CFL championship.

When he first awoke on the day of the game, Kapp remembers, "I was hungry. I was *always* hungry. Hungry for it all. I wanted it all. First, breakfast. Then the world championship."

Dawson's breakfast was crackers and warm milk.

"I was lucky to keep that down," Dawson says. "In a city like New Orleans that's so famous for its food and restaurants, I ate like a man in prison. I guess I *was* something of a prisoner that week."

Room 858 of the Fountainbleu Hotel on Tulane Street became a dungeon. Dawson knew the game would have to be played anyway.

Stram and his staff studied and restudied the films.

"The Vikings' secondary played very far off the receivers, very soft, as much as nine yards deep," Stram says. "We couldn't understand at first why other teams didn't throw underneath

their zone. Why didn't opponents dink them to death?"

A film of the Vikings' game against the Browns provided the answer. Defensive ends Carl Eller and Jim Marshall constantly knocked down those short passes. Or else they pressured the quarterback.

"If we can keep those two occupied," Stram said, "they won't be able to put their arms up like they do. We'll double-team those two."

The Vikings' overall aggressiveness on defense also made them susceptible to traps.

"You don't get called the Purple People Eaters for nothing," Stram says. "They really came at you. We decided to use their strength to our advantage."

Defensively, the Chiefs had to prepare for the Vikings' inside running game. Bill Brown, Dave Osborn, and Oscar Reed were big running backs, perfect for a ball-control game. Center Mick Tingelhoff was a perennial all-pro selection, excellent at cutting down linebackers. Grant liked to run a lot of trap plays as a result.

"We must keep Tingelhoff occupied," Stram said. "Just like we have to keep Marshall and Eller busy."

The 3-4 defense was rare in the NFL but not in the AFL. It was a Chiefs' staple. Stram's plan was to borrow from the 3-4 by aligning tackles Buck Buchanan, (6 feet 7, 285) or Curley Culp (6-1, 295), in front of Tingelhoff, who was quick off the ball, but, at 237 pounds, small in comparison. If Tingelhoff was going to block the Kansas City linebackers, he'd have to get by Buchanan or Culp first.

The Vikings rushed for just two first downs in Super Bowl IV. Meanwhile, Dawson completed 12 of 17 passes, almost all of them underneath patterns—square-outs, hitches, and curls. Neither Marshall nor Eller got a hand on any of Dawson's passes.

It was a simple game plan, Stram says. The Vikings were typical of NFL teams then.

"The Vikings were like the Packers under Lombardi," Stram says. "In essence, they said, 'Here's what we do. Try to stop us.' If they executed they won. And if they didn't...well, that's how we beat them."

The skies were clearing quickly as the kickoff neared. . Stram squinted as a few brief rays of sunshine broke through. Across the field, Jerry Burns, the Vikings' offensive coordinator, stared at the sky, too. And at the punts of Chiefs kicker Jerrel Wilson.

"I don't believe I'd ever seen anyone kick the ball so well, so high," Burns says. "I was in awe of their kickers. Wilson was kicking them as high as the lights. And their placekicker [Jan Stenerud] was routinely kicking fifty-yarders.

"We were a team that depended upon field position. Our offense was not exceptional, but our defense was. It was the job, more or less, of the offense not to jeopardize things for the defense. But that punter...I remember thinking he was going to put us in trouble."

In Super Bowl IV, Wilson averaged 48.5 yards on four punts. Stenerud kicked field goals of 48, 32, and 25 yards and added two conversions.

"We kept them penned up," Stram says. "We had field position all day. When Jan kicked that first field goal from forty-eight yards out, the Vikings were staring in disbelief. They couldn't believe we weren't going to punt."

Football is a game of efficiency. Coaches hope for a minimum of mistakes. Not to mention field position and ball control.

Minnesota fumbled three times, losing two of them, threw three interceptions, and was penalized six times. "We made more mental mistakes in one game than we did in one season," said Vikings safety Karl Kassulke.

Before the game, the Chiefs received two emotional boosts. One was a patch sewn on their jerseys. It said "AFL-10," symbolizing the league's tenth and final year of existence.

"It lit us up," says Chiefs linebacker Willie Lanier. "We knew what it all meant."

The other inspiration came in a phone call.

On the play that virtually clinched the victory for the Chiefs, Otis Taylor took a short pass from Len Dawson, broke cornerback Earsell Mackbee's tackle at the sideline, and went 46 yards for a touchdown.

Stram listened as President Richard Nixon wished the Chiefs good luck. Then Nixon asked Stram to tell Dawson not to worry about the scandalous innuendo and allegations.

"I don't know that it constituted a Presidential pardon," Stram says. "But it sure made Leonard feel better."

In the pregame festivities, a planned hot-air balloon race turned into a fiasco when the balloon that was marked NFL and manned by someone in a Vikings suit took off prematurely. Never gaining altitude, the gondola crashed into a section of the end zone. Then actor Pat O'Brien was supposed to recite the Na-

One of the great head coaches in NFL history, Bud Grant took four teams to the Super Bowl, but never won.

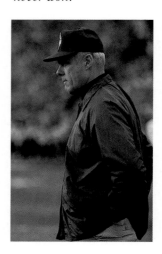

Minnesota drove to Kansas City's 46 early in the fourth quarter, but linebacker Willie Lanier broke up the short drive by intercepting a Joe Kapp pass. Linebacker Bobby Bell (78) threw a helpful block.

tional Anthem, accompanied by trumpeters Doc Severinsen and Al Hirt. But O'Brien's microphone was not turned on.

"We should have known something bad was about to happen," Carl Eller says now.

By the second quarter, the Chiefs were ahead 9-0, on the strength of the three field goals by Stenerud.

Stenerud's kickoff following his third field goal became one of the game's pivotal plays.

The weather had cleared. But the gusty wind remained. Minnesota's Charlie West tried to settle under the high kick, but West had to dive for the wind-blown ball.

Remi Prudhomme, a reserve lineman for the Chiefs, recovered at the Vikings' 19.

The Chiefs worked

Forced to pass on nearly every down, Kapp took a beating and left the game with a bruised shoulder.

the ball to the 5, where Stram sent in a play called 65 Toss Power Trap.

"We knew all about their great tackle, Alan Page," Stram says. "His quickness off the ball was very good. But we felt that if ever he lined up in the gap between guard and tackle, we could trap him. Our tackle, Jim Tyrer, would set the trap. Our guard, Mo Moorman, would close it. The problem was Page generally lined up in the gap between center and guard."

Stram called for the play anyway, because of the field position.

"When I saw Page move over between our guard and tackle, I almost squealed," Stram says.

Tyrer said after the game he tried not to smile. Moorman was afraid, he said, he'd lean or tip Page what was coming through some accidental means.

Running back Mike Garrett ran through the huge hole Page would have occupied to score the touchdown.

The crowd was stunned. The 16-0 lead was a bigger shock than the previous Super Bowl, when the New York Jets beat the Baltimore Colts. The Jets led only 7-0 at halftime.

Grant typically showed little emotion. He had no words of inspiration. There would be no major changes. "Just play better," he said.

After the Chiefs used up almost six minutes of the third quarter with a failed drive, the Vikings finally got something going. A 69-yard drive ended with Osborn running four yards for the touchdown that cut the score to 16-7. Vikings fans crackled with anticipation. Their team had rallied to beat the Rams in the first round of the playoffs. This was a team that had scored 50 or more points in three different games that season. Kapp had thrown seven touchdown passes in a single game. There was still enough time.

Stram huddled with Dawson. The coach had permitted NFL Films to wire him for sound. Stram's crisp confidence was recorded on the tape of the game.

"Let's put out that fire, Leonard," Stram said. "Let's make sure they don't get any closer."

The stoic Dawson nodded and trotted away.

A third-down situation developed quickly. Seven yards were needed for the first down. It was another critical play. The Vikings had come to life. And if the Chiefs did not get the first down, they would have to punt.

Spontaneity is part of coaching. Stram looked out on the field and shouted, "Reverse."

"We'd run it twice and it had worked each time," he says. "I don't know if the Vikings ever saw us run it on film. But they were just so darned aggressive, I just felt it'd work one more time for us."

Wide receiver Frank Pitts curled around at the snap of the ball, took the handoff…and raced for just over seven yards.

Another critical play came at the Vikings' 46.

"It was a quick hitch pass, right?" Dawson says, trying to remember. "Their safety [Paul Krause] was coming on the blitz. If I'd called for anything long or anything in the pocket, I would have been in trouble. It was a simple, quick pass, designed to gain six yards or so."

Dawson smiles. "But then Otis broke the tackle."

Otis Taylor braced when he saw cornerback Eärsell Mackbee close in for the tackle. Then he made a little swivel move.

Mackbee's arm was numb. He'd suffered a pinched nerve in the NFL title game. It suddenly had become numb again. "I couldn't feel anything," he said later.

Taylor spun away and raced down the sideline. Safety Karl Kassulke came flying up at the Vikings' 20, but Taylor faked Kassulke to the inside, broke his arm tackle inside the 15, and kept going. The touchdown snuffed out the Vikings' infant momentum.

Now things really *were* desperate. Now the Vikings' game plan would have to change radically. Now they had to resort almost exclusively to the passing game.

Kapp took a beating. Midway through the fourth quarter, he had to be helped off the field with a badly bruised shoulder.

There was less than two minutes left to play when backup quarterback Mike Livingston ran onto the field to replace Dawson.

"I wanted Lenny to hear the cheers, to know how everyone really felt," Stram says.

Even his teammates applauded as Dawson headed for the bench. The final moments of the game were uneventful. The message already had been delivered.

Grant also conceded the better team had won. Asked if he felt strange or embarrassed, Grant said, with his usual succinctness, "No. We played the best we could today. It wasn't good enough by a long margin. But God will forgive me—that's His job.

"It simply wasn't the end of the world to lose that game to Kansas City," Grant says. "What's older than yesterday's newspaper? The Super Bowl is one game, for the highest stakes, and that appeals to America. But losing that game isn't like dying."

Chiefs linebacker Bobby Bell felt a single tear slide into his smile as he screamed, "Go Chiefs, world champions!" Bell had been an All-America in college at the University of Minnesota. He had been drafted by both the Chiefs and Vikings.

"I knew I made the right choice," he said.

Stram and Dawson hugged. Stram told Dawson there was a phone call for him. It was the President again.

A finger stuck in his right ear so he could hear, his son at his side, Dawson listened and smiled as Nixon offered congratulations.

Moments later, Dawson told the press, "I'm kind of tired…I didn't get too much sleep last night…"

V

Baltimore 16, Dallas 13

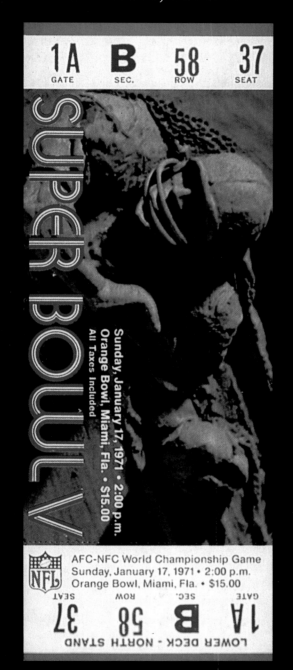

1A B 58 37
GATE SEC. ROW SEAT

SUPER BOWL V

Sunday, January 17, 1971 • 2:00 p.m.
Orange Bowl, Miami, Fla. • $15.00
All Taxes Included

NFL AFC-NFC World Championship Game
Sunday, January 17, 1971 • 2:00 p.m.
Orange Bowl, Miami, Fla. • $15.00

SEAT ROW SEC. GATE
37 58 B 1A
LOWER DECK - NORTH STAND

The mighty Dallas Dooms Day Defense faltered, allowing a 4th quarter T.D. on a two yard run by Tom Nowatzke.

SPORTS ILLUSTRATED: "Blunder Bowl... ...the Colts led in turnovers, 7-4; but the Cowboys won for penalties, 10-4 (133-31 yards)...and TV worried that situation comedy was dead."

JIM O'BRIEN (WHO KICKED THE WINNING FIELD GOAL): "I sat on the bench for the whole game hoping it wouldn't come down to me."

CLINT MURCHISON (REMEMBERING THE '67 CHAMPIONSHIP): "At least we're closing in. We got it down to five seconds from thirteen."

UNITAS: "Thank God I've got six months to rest."

DALLAS' ALL-PRO BOB LILLY (after throwing his helmet 40 feet): @★·!!＊⑨!

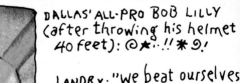

LANDRY: "We beat ourselves"

Vital Statistics

Starting Lineups

Baltimore (AFC)	Offense	Dallas (NFC)
Eddie Hinton	WR	Bob Hayes
Bob Vogel	LT	Ralph Neely
Glen Ressler	LG	John Niland
Bill Curry	C	Dave Manders
John Williams	RG	Blaine Nye
Dan Sullivan	RT	Rayfield Wright
John Mackey	TE	Pettis Norman
Roy Jefferson	WR	Reggie Rucker
John Unitas	QB	Craig Morton
Norm Bulaich	RB	Duane Thomas
Tom Nowatzke	RB	Walt Garrison
	Defense	
Bubba Smith	LE	Larry Cole
Billy Ray Smith	LT	Jethro Pugh
Fred Miller	RT	Bob Lilly
Roy Hilton	RE	George Andrie
Ray May	LLB	Dave Edwards
Mike Curtis	MLB	Lee Roy Jordan
Ted Hendricks	RLB	Chuck Howley
Charley Stukes	LCB	Herb Adderley
Jim Duncan	RCB	Mel Renfro
Jerry Logan	LS	Cornell Green
Rick Volk	RS	Charley Waters

Substitutions

Baltimore-Offense: K-Jim O'Brien. P-David Lee. QB-Earl Morrall. RB-Sam Havrilak, Jack Maitland, Jerry Hill. TE-Tom Mitchell, WR-Ray Perkins. LINE-Sam Ball, Cornelius Johnson, Tom Goode. Defense: LINE-Billy Newsome. LB-Bob Grant, Robbie Nichols. DB-Ron Gardin, Tom Maxwell. DNP: WR-Jimmy Orr. DT-George Wright.
Dallas-Offense: K-Mike Clark. P-Ron Widby. RB-Calvin Hill, Dan Reeves, Claxton Welch. WR-Dennis Homan. TE-Mike Ditka. LINE-Bob Asher. Defense: LINE-Pat Toomay, Ron East. LB-D.D. Lewis, Tom Stincic, Steve Kiner. DB-Richmond Flowers, Mark Washington, Cliff Harris. DNP: QB-Roger Staubach. T-Tony Liscio.

Officials

Referee-Norman Schachter. Umpire-Paul Trepinski. Head Linesman-Ed Marion. Field Judge-Fritz Graf. Back Judge-Hugh Gamber. Line Judge-Jack Fette.

Scoring

Baltimore	0	6	0	10	—	16
Dallas	3	10	0	0	—	13

Dal-FG Clark 14
Dal-FG Clark 30
Balt-Mackey 75 pass from Unitas (kick blocked)
Dal-Thomas 7 pass from Morton (Clark kick)
Balt-Nowatzke 2 run (O'Brien kick)
Balt-FG O'Brien 32
Attendance-79,204

FINAL TEAM STATISTICS

	Colts	Cowboys
TOTAL FIRST DOWNS	14	10
Rushing	4	4
Passing	6	5
Penalty	4	1
TOTAL NET YARDAGE	329	215
Total Offensive Plays	56	59
Average Gain per Offensive Play	5.9	3.6
NET YARDS RUSHING	69	102
Total Rushing Plays	31	31
Average Gain per Rushing Play	2.2	3.3
NET YARDS PASSING	260	113
Pass Att.-Comp.-Int.	25-11-3	26-12-3
Sacks-Yards Lost	0-0	2-14
Gross Yards Passing	260	127
Avg. Gain per Pass (Incl. Sacks)	10.4	4.0
PUNTS-YARDS	4-166	9-377
Average Distance	41.5	41.9
Had Blocked	0	0
TOTAL RETURN YARDAGE	159	65
Kickoff Returns-Yards	4-90	3-34
Punt Returns-Yards	5-12	3-9
Interception Returns-Yards	3-57	3-22
TOTAL TURNOVERS	7	4
Fumbles-Lost	5-4	1-1
Had Intercepted	3	3
PENALTIES-YARDS	4-31	10-133
TOTAL POINTS SCORED	16	13
Touchdowns Rushing	1	0
Touchdowns Passing	1	1
Touchdowns Returns	0	0
Extra Points	1	1
Field Goals-Attempts	1-2	2-2
Safeties	0	0
THIRD DOWN EFFICIENCY	5/14	2/13
FOURTH DOWN EFFICIENCY	0/1	0/0
TIME OF POSSESSION	28:36	31:24

INDIVIDUAL STATISTICS

RUSHING

Baltimore	No.	Yds.	Avg.	Long	TD
Bulaich	18	28	1.6	8	0
Nowatzke	10	33	3.3	9	1
Unitas	1	4	4.0	4	0
Havrilak	1	3	3.0	3	0
Morrall	1	1	1.0	1	0

Dallas	No.	Yds.	Avg.	Long	TD
Thomas	18	35	1.9	7	0
Garrison	12	65	5.4	19	0
Morton	1	2	2.0	2	0

PASSING

Baltimore	Att.	Comp.	Yds.	Long	TD	Int.
Unitas	9	3	88	75t	1	2
Morrall	15	7	147	45	0	1
Havrilak	1	1	25	25	0	0

Dallas	Att.	Comp.	Yds.	Long	TD	Int.
Morton	26	12	127	41	1	3

RECEIVING

Baltimore	No.	Yds.	Long	TD
Jefferson	3	52	23	0
Mackey	2	80	75t	1
Hinton	2	51	26	0

Havrilak	2	27	25	0
Nowatzke	1	45	45	0
Bulaich	1	5	5	0

Dallas	No.	Yds.	Long	TD
Reeves	5	46	17	0
Thomas	4	21	7t	1
Garrison	2	19	14	0
Hayes	1	41	41	0

INTERCEPTIONS

Baltimore	No.	Yds.	Long	TD
Volk	1	30	30	0
Logan	1	14	14	0
Curtis	1	13	13	0

Dallas	No.	Yds.	Long	TD
Howley	2	22	22	0
Renfro	1	0	0	0

PUNTING

Baltimore	No.	Yds.	Avg.	TB	Long
Lee	4	166	41.5	1	56

Dallas	No.	Yds.	Avg.	TB	Long
Widby	9	377	41.9	0	49

PUNT RETURNS

Baltimore	No.	FC	Yds.	Long	TD
Gardin	4	3	4	2	0
Logan	1	0	8	8	0

Dallas	No.	FC	Yds.	Long	TD
Hayes	3	0	9	7	0

KICKOFF RETURNS

Baltimore	No.	Yds.	Long	TD
Duncan	4	90	30	0

Dallas	No.	Yds.	Long	TD
Harris	1	18	18	0
Hill	1	14	14	0
Kiner	1	2	2	0

FUMBLES

Baltimore	No.	Own Rec.	Opp. Rec.
Gardin	1	0	0
Unitas	1	0	0
Duncan	1	0	1
Hinton	1	0	0
Morrall	1	1	0

Dallas	No.	Own Rec.	Opp. Rec.
Harris	0	0	1
Pugh	0	0	1
Flowers	0	0	1
Thomas	1	0	0

KICKING

Baltimore	XP-A	FG-A	FG Made	FG Missed
O'Brien	1-2	1-2	32	52

Dallas	XP-A	FG-A	FG Made	FG Missed
Clark	1-1	2-2	14,30	--

The first touchdown was on a pass from Unitas that caromed off Hinton & Renfro to Mackey.

UNITAS: "...I tried to force it between the linebackers."

LANDRY (TO MORTON): "You just have to get the ball over that guy. (Ted Hendricks)"

Duncan & Smith (of the Colts) & Manders (Cowboys) all claimed to have recovered a controversial fumble by Thomas on the goal line.

I.

After a Colt missed field goal...

the ball was allowed to roll, and died inside the one yard line.

VOGEL: I'd be concentrating so hard...

I missed the snap count.

REEVES: "we get paid to catch the hard ones. A thousand college players can catch an easy pass."

"Curtis gave us more problems than anyone he's able to check himse in the midd of a col mi tme

PLAY-BY-PLAY

Dallas won the coin toss and elected to receive.

FIRST QUARTER
O'Brien kick to D 10, Hill 14 return (Maitland).
Dallas (15:00)
D 24	1-10	Garrison 2 run off left tackle (Hilton).
D 26	2-8	Morton 6 pass to Thomas (May).
D 32	3-2	Morton pass to Hayes underthrown.
D 32	4-2	Widby 42 punt, Gardin fair catch.

Baltimore (12:50)
B 26	1-10	Bulaich 4 run off left tackle (Jordan).
B 30	2-6	Bulaich run right, loss of 5 (Adderley).
B 25	3-11	Unitas 5 pass to Mackey middle (Jordan).
B 30	4-6	Lee 35 punt, Hayes 2 return.

Dallas (10:46)
D 37	1-10	Thomas run off left tackle, no gain (Hilton).
D 37	2-10	Thomas 3 draw up middle (Curtis).
D 40	3-7	Morton sacked, loss of 3 (Hilton).
D 37	4-10	Widby 39 punt, Logan 8 return. Dal. penalized 15 for personal foul (Harris).

Baltimore (9:05)
B 47	1-10	Unitas pass to Bulaich intercepted at D 32, Howley 22 return (Unitas).

Dallas (8:53)
B 46	1-10	Thomas 2 run off left tackle (Miller).
B 44	2-8	Morton pass to Garrison underthrown.
B 44	3-8	Morton pass to Hayes incomplete. Play nullified and Dal. penalized 15 from spot of foul (D.46) for holding (Neely).
D 31	3-33	Garrison 11 run off left tackle (Curtis, Volk).
D 42	4-22	Widby 48 punt, Gardin no return, fumbled, Harris recovered for Dal. at B 9.
B 9	1-goal	Thomas 4 run right (Stukes).
B 5	2-goal	Thomas run off left tackle, loss of 2 (Curtis).
B 7	3-goal	Morton pass to Rucker overthrown.
B 7	4-goal	Clark, 14-yard field goal (5:32).

Dallas scoring drive: 2 yards, 3 plays, 1:40.
Dallas 3, Baltimore 0
Clark kick to B 15, Duncan 21 return (Washington).

Baltimore (5:32)
B 36	1-10	Bulaich run right, no gain (Lilly).
B 36	2-10	Nowatzke 7 draw up middle (Andrie).
B 43	3-3	Bulaich 1 run off right tackle (Pugh).
B 44	4-2	Lee 56 punt into end zone, touchback.

Dallas (3:04)
D 20	1-10	Garrison 6 run off right tackle (Logan).
D 26	2-4	Garrison 5 run right (Miller, May).
D 31	1-10	Thomas 3 run right (Stukes, Hendricks).
D 34	2-7	Morton 13 pass to Reeves (Stukes).
D 47	1-10	Morton 41 pass to Hayes deep right. Balt. penalized 6 (half the distance) for roughing the passer (Miller).
B 6	1-goal	Morton pass tipped away (Hendricks).
B 6	2-goal	Thomas run left, gain of 1 (Duncan).

END OF FIRST QUARTER:
Dallas 3, Baltimore 0

SECOND QUARTER
B 7	3-goal	Morton pass incomplete. Dal. penalized 15 and loss of down for intentional grounding (Morton).
B 22	4-goal	Clark, 30-yard field goal (14:52). Dal. declined offsides against Balt.

Dallas scoring drive: 58 yards, 8 plays, 3:12.
Dallas 6, Baltimore 0
Clark kick to B 3, Duncan 22 return (Welch).

Baltimore (14:52)
B 25	1-10	Unitas pass to Hinton broken up (Edwards).
B 25	2-10	Unitas pass to Jefferson underthrown.
B 25	3-10	Unitas 75 pass to Mackey off of Renfro's deflection, touchdown (14:10). O'Brien's extra point attempt was blocked.

Baltimore scoring drive: 75 yards, 3 plays, :42.
Dallas 6, Baltimore 6
O'Brien kick into end zone, touchback.

Dallas (14:10)
D 20	1-10	Thomas run off left tackle, loss of 2 (May).
D 18	2-12	Morton pass to Ditka underthrown, incomplete.
D 18	3-12	Morton pass to Garrison dropped, incomplete.
D 18	4-12	Widby 44 punt, Gardin no return (Washington).

Baltimore (13:06)
B 38	1-10	Balt. penalized 5 for illegal procedure (Vogel).
B 33	1-15	Bulaich 2 run off left tackle (Edwards, Pugh).
B 35	2-13	Bulaich 2 run left (Cole, Pugh).

B 37	3-11	Unitas pass to Hinton overthrown, incomplete.
B 37	4-11	Lee 37 punt, Hayes 7 return.

Dallas (11:38)
D 33	1-10	Thomas 2 run off left tackle (Miller).
D 35	2-8	Morton pass to Hayes underthrown.
D 35	3-8	Morton pass to Reeves, no gain (May).
D 35	4-8	Widby 43 punt, Gardin fair catch. Play nullified and Dal. penalized 5 for offsides.
D 30	4-13	Widby 49 punt, Gardin fair catch.

Baltimore (10:08)
B 21	1-10	Unitas pass to Bulaich overthrown.
B 21	2-10	Bulaich run left, no gain (Waters).
B 21	3-10	Unitas 4 run evading pass rush (Jordan), fumbled, Pugh recovered for Dal. at B 28.

Dallas (9:00)
B 28	1-10	Thomas 4 run right (Bu. Smith).
B 24	2-6	Morton 17 pass to Reeves (May).
B 7	1-goal	Morton 7 swing pass to Thomas right, touchdown (7:53). Clark kicked extra point.

Dallas scoring drive: 28 yards, 3 plays, 1:07.
Dallas 13, Baltimore 6
Clark kick to B 8, Duncan 30 return (Flowers).

Baltimore (7:53)
B 38	1-10	Unitas pass to Mackey incomplete. Play nullified and Dal. penalized 13 for pass interference (Adderley).
D 49	1-10	Unitas 8 pass to Jefferson (Adderley).
D 41	2-2	Bulaich 4 run right (Jordan).
D 37	1-10	Unitas pass to Hinton intercepted at D 15, Renfro no return.

Dallas (6:07)
D 15	1-10	Thomas 2 run off left tackle (May).
D 17	2-8	Thomas 6 run left (Volk, Curtis).
D 23	3-2	Balt. penalized 5 for offsides.
D 28	1-10	Morton 5 pass to Thomas (Logan).
D 33	2-5	Morton 10 pass to Rucker (Volk). Play nullified and Dal. penalized 15 for pass interference.
D 18	2-20	Morton 11 pass to Reeves (Logan).
D 29	3-9	Morton sacked, loss of 11 (Hilton, Miller).
D 18	4-20	Widby 36 punt, Gardin 2 return (Flowers).

Baltimore (2:48)
B 48	1-10	Morrall 26 pass to Hinton middle (Renfro).
D 26	1-10	Morrall pass to Hinton broken up (Renfro).
D 26	2-10	Morrall 21 pass to Jefferson right (Jordan). Dal. penalized 3 (half the distance) for personal foul (Jordan). Two-Minute Warning.
D 2	1-goal	Bulaich run left tackle, no gain (Jordan).
D 2	2-goal	Bulaich run right, no gain (Jordan).
D 2	3-goal	Bulaich run off right tackle, no gain (Edwards).
D 2	4-goal	Morrall pass to Mitchell end zone overthrown.

Dallas (:16)
D 2	1-10	Garrison 2 run off right tackle (Curtis).

END OF SECOND QUARTER:
Dallas 13, Baltimore 6

THIRD QUARTER
Clark kick to B 8, Duncan 17 return (Welch), fumbled, Flowers recovered for Dal. at B 31.

Dallas (14:43)
B 31	1-10	Thomas 7 run left (Curtis).
B 24	2-3	Garrison 9 run off right tackle (Volk).
B 15	1-10	Thomas 2 run right (B.R. Smith).
B 13	2-8	Garrison 6 run up middle (May).
B 7	3-2	Thomas 5 sweep right (Miller).
B 2	1-goal	Thomas 1 run off left tackle (Logan), fumbled, Duncan recovered for Balt. at B 1.

Baltimore (11:08)
B 1	1-10	Nowatzke 2 run left (Howley).
B 3	2-8	Bulaich 4 run off right tackle (Edwards).
B 7	3-4	Bulaich 8 run right (Waters, Edwards).
B 15	1-10	Morrall pass to Hinton broken up (Renfro).
B 15	2-10	Morrall 25 pass to Havrilak middle (Renfro).
B 40	1-10	Nowatzke 2 draw up middle (Pugh).
B 46	2-4	Havrilak 3 run right (Edwards).
B 49	3-1	Bulaich 2 run off right tackle (Green).
D 49	1-10	Morrall pass to Jefferson broken up (Adderley).
D 49	2-10	Morrall 5 pass to Bulaich (Waters).
D 44	3-5	Morrall pass to Perkins broken up (Jordan).
D 44	4-5	O'Brien's 52-yard field goal attempt was short, downed by Goode at D 1.

Dallas (5:14)
D 1	1-10	Morton 2 keeper up middle (Miller).

D 3	2-8	Garrison 1 run left (B.R. Smith).
D 4	3-7	Garrison run left, no gain (Hilton).
D 4	4-7	Widby 44 punt, Gardin 2 return (Welch). Balt. penalized 15 for clipping (Maitland).

Baltimore (3:01)
B 39	1-10	Nowatzke 1 run right (Adderley).
B 40	2-9	Morrall 45 pass to Nowatzke middle (Adderley).
D 15	1-10	Bulaich 3 run left (Lilly).
D 12	2-7	Morrall 1 keeper (Pugh).

END OF THIRD QUARTER:
Dallas 13, Baltimore 6

FOURTH QUARTER
D 11	3-6	Morrall pass to Bulaich intercepted in end zone by Howley, touchback.

Dallas (14:55)
D 20	1-10	Garrison 19 run left (Hilton).
D 39	1-10	Morton pass to Hayes dropped.
D 39	2-10	Morton 3 pass to Thomas (B.R. Smith).
D 42	3-7	Morton 5 pass to Reeves (Logan).
D 47	4-2	Widby 35 punt, Gardin fair catch.

Baltimore (12:30)
B 18	1-10	Morrall pass to Jefferson overthrown.
B 18	2-10	Morrall fumbled and recovered snap, pass to Jefferson overthrown.
B 18	3-10	Morrall pass to Hinton incomplete. Play nullified and Dal. penalized 13 for pass interference (Renfro).
B 31	1-10	Morrall 23 pass to Jefferson right (Adderley).
D 46	1-10	Nowatzke draw, no gain (Howley).
D 46	2-10	Morrall 2 pass to Havrilak (Adderley).
D 44	3-8	Morrall pass tipped away. Play nullified and Dal. penalized 5 for holding. Automatic first down.
D 39	1-10	Nowatzke 9 run right (Cole).
D 30	2-1	Havrilak 25 pass to Hinton (Green), fumbled, ball rolled out of end zone, touchback.

Dallas (9:11)
D 20	1-10	Garrison 3 run off right tackle (B.R. Smith).
D 23	2-7	Morton pass to Thomas overthrown.
D 23	3-7	Morton pass to Garrison tipped and intercepted at D 33, Volk 30 return (Rucker).

Baltimore (8:10)
D 3	1-goal	Nowatzke 1 run left (Stincic).
D 2	2-goal	Nowatzke 2 run off left tackle, touchdown (7:35). O'Brien kicked extra point.

Baltimore scoring drive: 3 yards, 2 plays, :35.
Dallas 13, Baltimore 13
O'Brien kick to D 17, Harris 18 return (Johnson).

Dallas (7:35)
D 35	1-10	Garrison 1 run right (Bu. Smith).
D 36	2-9	Morton 14 pass to Garrison (B.R. Smith).
50	1-10	Thomas run off left tackle, no gain (Bu. Smith).
50	2-10	Morton pass knocked down (Miller).
50	3-10	Morton 5 pass to Garrison (Miller).
B 45	4-5	Widby 40 punt downed at B 5.

Baltimore (4:03)
B 5	1-10	Nowatzke 4 run off left tackle (Jordan).
B 9	2-6	Nowatzke 1 run left (Jordan, Howley).
B 10	3-5	Bulaich run left, no gain (Howley, Pugh). Two-Minute Warning.
B 10	4-5	Lee 38 punt, Hayes no return (out of bounds).

Dallas (1:52)
B 48	1-10	Thomas run right, loss of 1 (Bu. Smith).
B 49	2-11	Morton sacked, loss of 9 (Miller). Play nullified and Dal. penalized 15 from spot of foul (D 42) for holding.
D 27	2-35	Morton pass to Reeves tipped and intercepted at D 41, Curtis 13 return (Homan).

Baltimore (0:59)
D 28	1-10	Bulaich 2 run right (Lilly).
D 26	2-8	Bulaich 1 run off right tackle (Lilly).
D 25	3-7	O'Brien, 32-yard field goal (:05).

Baltimore scoring drive: 3 yards, 2 plays, :54.
Baltimore 16, Dallas 13
O'Brien kick to D 38, Kiner 2 return (Gardin).

Dallas (:05)
D 40	1-10	Morton pass to Garrison intercepted at B 29, Logan 14 return (out of bounds).

FINAL SCORE:
Baltimore 16, Dallas 13
FINAL RECORDS:
Baltimore 14-2-1, Dallas 12-5

Dallas wanted to overcome a reputation for doing fine during the season then losing The Big Games.

The Colts all shared the nightmare of Super Bowl

LANDRY ON WHY HIS DECISION TO CALL EVERY PLAY WAS NOT PUNITIVE: "... Craig (morton) & I are very close."

The Colts had a 37 year old Quarterback backed up by a 36 year old.

GARRISON: "I'm not going to miss this one, ... 2, 3 days can make a big difference."

PUNT RETURNER RON GARDIN: "All I could think of was what my mother would think."

A Mad, Mad, Mad Super Bowl

Ed Pope of the *Miami Herald* wasn't sure if it was the best game he'd ever seen...or the worst.

Tex Maule, *Sports Illustrated*'s man on the scene, suggested it be renamed the Blunder Bowl.

Which left it to the President of the United States to establish some sort of workable perspective. Asked by reporters in Washington on the morning after for his assessment of Super Bowl V, Richard M. Nixon smiled, shook his head, and said, "I sure hope I don't make that many mistakes."

Not all who were there, however, held with that line of thinking.

Earl Morrall, a substitute who ended up as the winning quarterback, says, "It really was a physical game. I mean, people were flying into one another out there."

Tom Landry, who ended up as the losing coach, adds, "I haven't been around many games where the players hit harder. Sometimes people watch a game and see turnovers and they talk about how sloppy the play was. The mistakes in that game weren't invented, at least not by the people who made them. Most were forced."

Whatever...On a late Sunday afternoon, January 17, 1971, in the Orange Bowl at Miami, the Baltimore Colts defeated the Dallas Cowboys 16-13 when a gangly, long-haired rookie named Jim O'Brien kicked a 32-yard field goal with five seconds left to play.

But the story is a lot more complex than that.

Both teams approached Super Bowl V with less than immaculate laundry. Two years before, in the same stadium, the then old-line Colts of the National Football League had been bushwhacked 16-7 by Joe Namath and the upstart New York Jets of the American Football League. With the subsequent merger of the two leagues sandwiched between those appearances, the Colts now traveled on newly drawn AFC papers.

The new NFC Cowboys, for their part, packed four years worth of playoff miseries in their saddlebags, having lost twice to Green Bay and twice to Cleveland. People were saying Dallas Couldn't Win The Big One.

Taking things a step further, both teams had

problems along the way to Super Bowl V. Despite their 7-2-1 record at the time, the Colts fell behind to the Chicago Bears 17-0 in the second quarter. Baltimore's plight was pretty well summed up by offensive tackle Bob Vogel. "I was actually embarrassed to come back out of the locker room [after halftime]," he said.

But he did, and so did the rest of the Colts. They won 21-20, and they didn't look back until they were in Miami.

Dallas started the season poorly, going 5-4. It was gut-checking time. "We were at the bottom of the barrel, and we could stay there or go up," said Cowboys quarterback Craig Morton. "We went up." Former Dallas quarterback Don Meredith, working as an ABC television analyst in 1970, lamented the Cowboys' decline on *Monday Night Football*. But the Cowboys won five straight to win the NFC East, and added two more playoff victories on the road to Miami.

The game matched two strong defensive teams against two dissimilar offenses—Baltimore's pass-oriented attack built around the redoubtable Johnny Unitas, and the more conservative Cowboys scheme based on the running of crusty old Walt Garrison and the hugely talented, highly enigmatic rookie, Duane Thomas.

Well, both defenses showed up, and to a fare-thee-well. But somebody must have wrapped the trash in the offensive game plans.

Unitas limped off late in the second quarter with torn rib cartilage, a condition acquired from standing too close to George Andrie's helmet. Unitas's statistics, at that point, were three completions in nine attempts for 88 yards (75 on a tipped touchdown pass), two interceptions, and one fumble. And the Cowboys' ground game? Well, Garrison ended up with 65 yards, a game high for both sides. Thomas managed just 35 on 18 carries, although he scored one touchdown.

The second-quarter injury to Unitas was in keeping with the rest of the day.

The game just seemed to get curiouser and curiouser. When Unitas went down, the Colts' first-year head coach, Don McCafferty, had to turn to the 36-year-old Morrall, aging backup and scarred survivor of Baltimore's first Super Bowl fling in game III.

Morrall had started for the Colts against the Jets in 1969. Unitas, who had a bad arm, came in

Don McCafferty of the Colts became the first rookie head coach to take his team to the Super Bowl and win. The feat wasn't accomplished again until George Seifert led the 49ers to victory in Super Bowl XXIV, 19 years later.

Morrall was drafted by San Francisco out of Michigan State in 1956. After he spent a year behind Y.A. Tittle, the 49ers dealt him to Pittsburgh for a linebacker and two first-round draft choices. At Pittsburgh, Morrall started ahead of rookies Len Dawson and Jack Kemp. In 1958, the Steelers decided they wanted a more experienced quarterback than Morrall, so they traded him to Detroit for Bobby Layne, who had won two NFL championships and set up a third in his career with the Lions. Morrall was with the Lions through 1964, an off-again, on-again starter over the years, competing with Tobin Rote, Jim Ninowski, and Milt Plum. He missed the 1962 season because he cut off the top half of his left big toe with a power mower. In 1964, he went down after six games, his collarbone shattered by the Bears' huge defensive end, Doug Atkins.

The Lions sent Morrall to the New York Giants in 1965, and he started all year. A broken wrist sidelined him in 1966, and in 1967 the Giants traded for Minnesota's scrambling quarterback, Fran Tarkenton, making Morrall expendable once more during the 1968 preseason.

The Colts were looking for quarterback help

Baltimore tied the score 6-6 when tight end John Mackey raced 75 yards to score with a deflected pass from Johnny Unitas. The ball was tipped by both Eddie Hinton of Baltimore and Mel Renfro of Dallas.

late, but the two of them didn't add up to one Broadway Joe and a mistake-free Jets team that day. There were those along the Chesapeake who still thought poorly of Morrall, a much-traveled veteran.

Was he thinking about Super Bowl III in Super Bowl V?

"I think all the veterans were," Morrall says. "We talked about it a lot. By game time we were pretty well wired. We knew what that feeling was like and we did not want to experience it again."

Morrall had a remarkable football career. He played 21 years in the NFL. When he replaced Unitas in Super Bowl V, he was a mere 15-year veteran, a dandelion in the well-ordered lawn of the NFL. Nobody could finish him off. George Blanda—who is in the Pro Football Hall of Fame —was the only quarterback who outlasted him. "I couldn't kick," Morrall pointed out, "or I might have beaten George, too."

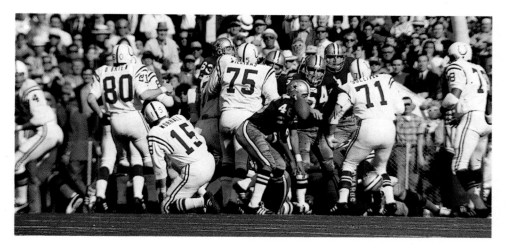

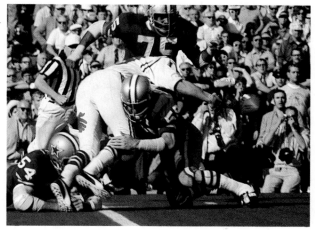

teams got comfortable in the national TV spotlight.

So much for decorum.

Midway through the first quarter, Unitas was intercepted by Cowboys linebacker Chuck Howley, who returned the ball to the Colts' 46. Howley later would collect a second interception in the end

The Colts failed to take a 7-6 lead after Mackey's touchdown when Jim O'Brien's extra-point try was blocked by Dallas cornerback Mark Washington (46). Earl Morrall (15), who later replaced Unitas, was the holder.

Midway through the second quarter, Unitas tried to scramble for a first down, but fumbled when hit by linebacker Lee Roy Jordan (55). Tackle Jethro Pugh's (75) recovery set up the Cowboys' only touchdown.

during the '68 preseason because Unitas had elbow problems. They were considering either Morrall or the aforementioned Ninowski, then at Washington, and, like Morrall, available. The Redskins were to play their final preseason game at home, and Don Shula, the Colts' head coach, wanted to attend the game, along with his offensive assistants, to scout Ninowski. Shula told the coaches to gather at a suburban Holiday Inn, where they would pile in one car and drive up to D.C. The assistants showed up at the Holiday Inn, and Shula went to a Holiday Inn, too…but not the same one. By the time the mixup was sorted out by phone, Shula was upset and said he was going home. His assistants decided to go to the game, where Ninowski turned in an outstanding performance.

When the staff met the next day, the offensive assistants raved about Ninowski. Shula, still piqued about the mixup, rolled his jaw out to battle stations and said Morrall was his man. Case closed.

Pretty bright guy, Shula. Morrall quarterbacked the Colts to a 15-1 record en route to Super Bowl III, where disaster struck. Unitas came back healthy in 1969, so Morrall returned to backing up until the following season…in the second quarter of Super Bowl V.

Things started off normally enough in V. There were three sets of three-and-out as both

zone and, still later, earn distinction as the only player from the losing team ever to be named most valuable player in the Super Bowl.

Dallas faltered, but Baltimore's Ron Gardin mishandled a punt by Ron Widby. The Cowboys recovered at the Colts' 9, and eventually got a 14-yard field goal by Mike Clark. Eight seconds into the second quarter, Dallas extended its lead to 6-0. Another field goal by Clark capped a 58-yard march. The big play was a 41-yard pass from Craig Morton to Bob Hayes, the former Olympic sprint champion and "world's fastest human."

Baltimore responded promptly, and right off the wall. On third down from his own 25-yard line, Unitas tried to hit Eddie Hinton, crossing shallow. Hinton leaped, and touched the ball, but couldn't handle it. Cowboys cornerback Mel Renfro was dogging Hinton ("I might have got a fingernail on it"), and he touched the deflected ball. It fell into the hands of Colts tight end John Mackey, rumbling without escort in the deep middle. Mackey took the ball in stride and went on to score uncontested.

"I was just supposed to clear the zone for Hinton," Mackey said of the 75-yard scoring play. "We called that play 'individual to the flanker.' Guess we'll have to start calling it 'individual to the flanker to the tight end.'"

"Renfro's contact with the ball was minute, but it was contact," Landry says. "It couldn't have been closer."

Dallas blocked O'Brien's conversion attempt to leave the issue square at 6-6.

The big play notwithstanding, Unitas was back in the soup soon enough.

Forced to run two possessions later, Unitas fumbled as he was flattened by middle linebacker Lee Roy Jordan. Defensive tackle Jethro Pugh recovered for Dallas at the Colts' 28. Morton needed just three plays, the last a seven-yard touchdown pass to Thomas. Dallas led 13-7 with 7:53 to play in the first half.

Unitas had the Colts moving on the next series, but, on third down from the Cowboys' 37, he took a hard shot from Andrie as he released the ball. To make matters worse, Renfro intercepted at the Dallas 15. Unitas was helped to the sideline, done for the day.

The Colts had one more shot before halftime. Morrall's passes to receivers Hinton and Roy Jefferson carried them to a first down at the Cowboys' 2-yard line. But after Dallas stuffed fullback Norm Bulaich three straight times, Morrall's fourth-down fade pass for tight end Tom

Mitchell failed. "Tom stepped on somebody's foot clearing the line, and lost his balance," Morrall says. "He was stumbling and he couldn't get to the ball."

At halftime, both the Colts' doctor and Unitas told McCafferty that Unitas could return despite the injury. McCafferty said he'd stick with Morrall.

Baltimore's luck seemed no better at the start of the second half. Jim Duncan fumbled the opening kickoff, and Dallas had the ball at the Colts' 31, which was 30 yards from where the game probably was decided.

Thomas and Garrison hacked their way to the Colts' 2, where Thomas tried to slant off left tackle for the score, but fumbled.

"There was just a pile of people," Landry says. "Our center, Dave Manders, said he had the ball under him on the ground. Craig [Morton] said the same thing. But somebody dug it out, once they were down. I know the officials couldn't see it. Nobody could.

"Then, all of a sudden, here's Billy Ray Smith, jumping up out of the pile and pointing the other

The Cowboys were bidding to take a 20-6 lead in the third quarter, when Duane Thomas (33) lost a fumble on the Baltimore 1-yard line, one of 11 turnovers in the game. Colts cornerback Jim Duncan recovered.

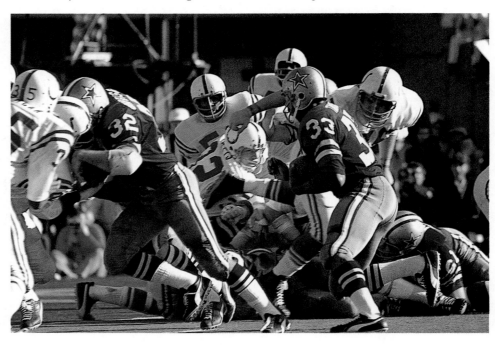

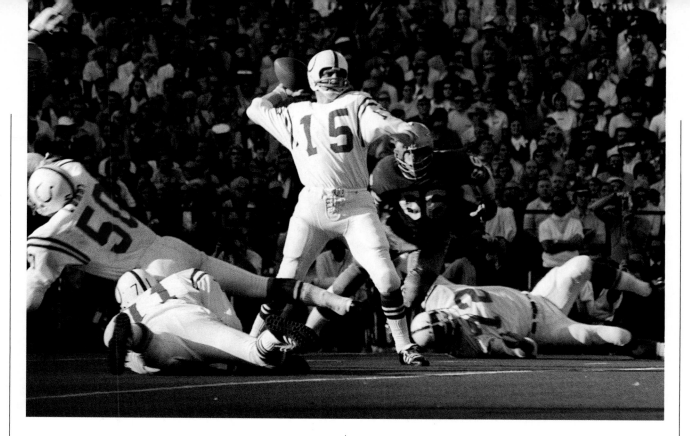

way. The officials went for it, I guess. That was the biggest play Billy Ray made all day."

Earlier in the week, Smith, a defensive tackle out of Arkansas who retired after the game, had the media chuckling with his stories. One suddenly seemed pertinent.

"Sunday will be my last game unless I turn into a referee," he said. "Those guys have been telling me what to do for so many years, I'd like to tell someone else what to do for a change."

The fumble was crushing for the Cowboys.

"We go up two touchdowns, they weren't going to get no two touchdowns off of us," was the way Bob Lilly, Dallas's all-pro defensive tackle, put it.

O'Brien missed a 52-yard field-goal try, and the third quarter ended with Dallas still clinging to a 13-6 lead. Baltimore was on the Cowboys' doorstep at the end of the period, but Howley squelched that chance on the first play of the final period, intercepting a pass by Morrall in the end zone.

Howley says, "I was backing up in coverage, and I must have gotten tangled with someone, and then, boom! there it was."

Baltimore was back within range in short order. Morrall drove the Colts 52 yards to the Dallas 30, where McCafferty called for his "gimmick" play.

Morrall tossed a lateral to halfback Sam Havrilak, who was to toss back to Morrall, setting up a flea-flicker pass to Hinton. But Morrall was cut

Earl Morrall replaced the injured Johnny Unitas and completed 7 of 15 passes for 147 yards.

off from a return toss, guarded by Andrie. Seeing this, Havrilak, a former quarterback at Bucknell, passed downfield to a wide-open Hinton.

"I was thinking six, six, six," Hinton said. "Then I felt something from behind, and it wasn't a tackle. All of a sudden the ball wasn't there any-

On the first play of the fourth quarter, Cowboys linebacker Chuck Howley stopped a Colts drive with an end-zone interception. Howley was named the game's most valuable player, despite his team's 16-13 loss.

105

Baltimore squandered several scoring opportunities, losing the ball on the Dallas 5 when Eddie Hinton (33) had it punched from his grasp by safety Cornell Green. The ball rolled through the end zone for a touchback.

more, and I'm thinking, What in the world?"

What happened was Cowboys safety Cornell Green. He punched the ball out of Hinton's grasp in a diving effort. The ball rolled lazily goalward. Hinton, among others, crawled after it.

"I was down by then, crawling," Hinton says. "Then I couldn't crawl anymore...Renfro had hold of me." The ball rolled through the end zone for a touchback.

If the Colts anguished at this latest turn of events, they didn't have much time to mope.

The Colts finally tied the score at 13-13 midway through the fourth quarter after safety Rick Volk (above) returned an interception 30 yards to the Dallas 3. Tom Nowatzke scored the touchdown on a two-yard run off left tackle.

Three plays later, they made the first of their three fourth-quarter interceptions.

Safety Rick Volk had help making the first one.

"Roy Hilton got a good rush and got his hands

Nowatzke's touchdown, after a handoff from Earl Morrall, came with 7:35 to go in the game and ended a three-yard drive. Rookie Jim O'Brien tied the score at 13-13 with the conversion, the first of his two big kicks.

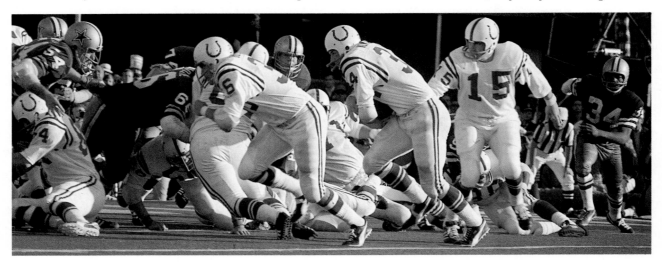

up high, in Morton's face," Volk says. "Ted Hendricks got up, too. Morton had to get the ball higher than he wanted, I'm sure. Garrison jumped and reached back, but he couldn't hold it. It fell right to me."

Volk intercepted at the Cowboys' 33 and returned it to the 3.

"I was on the ground, right in Rick's path," Hendricks said. "I just stayed there and he jumped over me. I was afraid if I tried to get up he'd trip on me."

Defensive tackle Fred Miller wanted to help, but his intentions were short lived. "I wheeled around, looking for someone to hit," he said, "and that big Rayfield Wright knocked me right on my can."

Fullback Tom Nowatzke, a Detroit castoff who had been claimed on waivers before the season, gained a yard on first down.

"I went too tight," he said. "I asked Earl to run it again in the huddle and told him I'd go a little wider and get in."

Tight end Mitchell, blocking on that side, lined up just outside Dallas linebacker Howley. "He let me get to his legs," Mitchell says, "and I got him on the ground." Nowatzke cut past Howley to score.

Morrall calls Volk's interception the play of the game.

"It let us punch in a touchdown," Morrall says. "We'd been trying so long, and it really lifted us."

"I ran for my life," Volk says. "Then once we got the touchdown to tie, we knew they'd have to throw. And that's what we were waiting for."

Cowboys quarterback Morton had been nursing arm injuries through the three games leading to Miami. With Roger Staubach on the bench, critics had rapped his playoff performances. Landry called Morton's plays from the sideline, and, given the halftime lead, the coach didn't call a pass in the third quarter. Unfortunately for Dallas, Morton's fourth-quarter passing log—when they needed it—showed 4 completions in 10 attempts, three interceptions, and just 27 yards.

With the score tied 13-13, the teams traded possessions before Baltimore punted to Dallas at the Colts' 48 with 1:52 remaining. The Cowboys appeared to be in great position to retake the lead, or, at worst, to assure overtime.

They did neither. Thomas lost a yard on their

With nine seconds left, O'Brien (1) took aim on the potential game-winning field goal. All eyes on both teams watched the flight of the ball (2), and O'Brien celebrated (3) when his 32-yard kick was good, prompting Cowboys defensive tackle Bob Lilly (4) to hurl his helmet in disgust.

first play. Calamity struck on second down when Morton was sacked as a Cowboys blocker was penalized for holding. They lost 24 yards back to the Dallas 27-yard line because the 15 yards was stepped off from the point of the foul.

It was one more bad break for the Cowboys. The next year, they would not have suffered a devastating 24-yard loss. The rules were amended so that the offending team would be penalized from the line of scrimmage, not from the spot of the foul. Thus, the Cowboys would have lost either nine yards on the sack (making it third down) or 15 yards on the penalty.

But on second-and-35, Morton's pass for player-coach Dan Reeves was high.

"A back fresh out of college could have caught it," said Reeves. "I went as high as I could...the ball just went through my hands."

It did not go through the hands of Colts middle linebacker Mike Curtis. "I almost squeezed the air out of it," Curtis said. "My only thought was: Don't fumble."

He didn't, and Baltimore set up shop at the Dallas 28-yard line with 59 seconds to play.

The Colts had Bulaich squirm in the middle for three yards on two carries before calling time with nine seconds remaining.

Morrall came to the sideline where McCafferty asked him to "calm the kid down a little."

O'Brien, a rookie receiver and kicker out of the University of Cincinnati, had beaten 13-year veteran Lou Michaels out of a job in training camp, thus alienating some of the Colts' veterans. Then there was O'Brien's long hair...they called him "Lassie."

"In the huddle, Billy Ray Smith pointed at O'Brien and reminded him his kick would be worth three-hundred grand [the 40-man squad's total for the difference between winning, $15,000 each, and losing, $7,500]," says Morrall, now a Florida golf club operator. "I don't think that calmed him down any.

"When we broke the huddle, Jim was trying to pull up grass blades and throw them to check the wind. I reminded him we were on artificial turf. I just told him to forget the wind and hit it square."

He did. O'Brien's 32-yard kick out of Morrall's hold of center Tom Goode's snap sailed six feet inside the right upright, marking the first time the Colts had led. Dallas had time for one play, a Morton rainbow that was intercepted by Baltimore's Jerry Logan.

And then it was over, and the crowd of 79,204 was left with ample material for post-mortems.

Winning Baltimore had fumbled five times (four were recovered by Dallas), had thrown three interceptions, and had one conversion attempt blocked.

The two teams had a total of 11 turnovers. Their combined six interceptions remains a single-game Super Bowl record.

The difference was that the three interceptions by the Colts came in the fourth quarter, when they counted. That, and the overall passing—Morrall was better than Morton. And the penalties: Dallas was flagged 10 times for 133 yards, to 4 for 31 levied against the Colts.

Was it really the Blunder Bowl?

We go back to Tom Landry's remark about the mistakes not being invented by the people who made them.

Looking back with the wisdom of two decades, Dallas MVP Howley says his team was positive going into V. "But there still was this little voice in the back of my head," he says. "It kept saying, 'I hope, I hope....' After playing in the next Super Bowl [Dallas won], I can see where we had some room for doubt."

Colts safety Volk speaks from the same vantage point: "Going to the game a second time took away some of the awe. I think we were able to focus better. There was no way we were going to let ourselves get beat again."

Meanwhile, Jim O'Brien was the postgame center of attention.

"I had this dream early in the week," he said. "I saw the winning field goal go sailing through the uprights. The problem was, I didn't know if it was me or [Dallas kicker] Mike Clark who kicked it."

A final thought: Waived by Baltimore after the 1971 season, Earl Morrall was claimed by Miami, where Shula had gone to coach. Morrall stayed with the Dolphins through five seasons and two Super Bowl victories. The 1972 Dolphins posted a perfect 17-0 record, winning Super Bowl VII. Regular quarterback Bob Griese missed 11 of those 17 wins with injuries. Who do you suppose replaced him?

VI

Dallas 24, Miami 3

Z 68 50
SEC. ROW SEAT

SUPER BOWL VI

SUPER BOWL VI

 SUNDAY, JANUARY 16, 1972
KICKOFF 1:30 P.M. $15.00
ALL TAXES INCLUDED

AFC-NFC WORLD CHAMPIONSHIP GAME
SUNDAY, JANUARY 16, 1972 KICKOFF 1:30 P.M.
TULANE STADIUM, NEW ORLEANS, LOUISIANA • $15.00

SEAT ROW SEC.
50 68 Z

Vital Statistics

Starting Lineups

Dallas (NFC)	Offense	Miami (AFC)
Bob Hayes	WR	Paul Warfield
Tony Liscio	LT	Doug Crusan
John Niland	LG	Bob Kuechenberg
Dave Manders	C	Bob DeMarco
Blaine Nye	RG	Larry Little
Rayfield Wright	RT	Norm Evans
Mike Ditka	TE	Marv Fleming
Lance Alworth	WR	Howard Twilley
Roger Staubach	QB	Bob Griese
Duane Thomas	RB	Jim Kiick
Walt Garrison	RB	Larry Csonka
	Defense	
Larry Cole	LE	Jim Riley
Jethro Pugh	LT	Manny Fernandez
Bob Lilly	RT	Bob Heinz
George Andrie	RE	Bill Stanfill
Dave Edwards	LLB	Doug Swift
Lee Roy Jordan	MLB	Nick Buoniconti
Chuck Howley	RLB	Mike Kolen
Herb Adderley	LCB	Tim Foley
Mel Renfro	RCB	Curtis Johnson
Cornell Green	SS	Dick Anderson
Cliff Harris	FS	Jake Scott

Substitutions

Dallas-Offense: K-Mike Clark. P-Ron Widby. TE-Bill Truax. RB-Dan Reeves, Calvin Hill, Joe Williams, Claxton Welch. LINE-John Fitzgerald. Defense: LINE-Pay Toomay, Tody Smith, Bill Gregory. LB-D.D. Lewis, Tom Stincic. DB-Issac Thomas, Charlie Waters. DNP: QB-Craig Morton. G-Forrest Gregg. WR-Gloster Richardson.
Miami-Offense: K-Garo Yepremian. P-Larry Seiple. WR-Karl Noonan, Otto Stowe. TE-Jim Mandich. RB-Eugene Morris, Terry Cole, Hubert Ginn. LINE-Wayne Moore, Jim Langer. Defense: LINE-Frank Cornish, Vern Den Herder, Jesse Powell. DB-Lloyd Mumphord, Bob Petrella. DNP: QB-George Mira. WR-John Richardson.

Officials

Referee-Jim Tunney. Umpire-Joe Connell. Head Linesman-Al Sabato. Field Judge-Bob Wortman. Back Judge-Ralph Vandenberg. Line Judge-Art Hoist.

Scoring

Dallas	3	7	7	7 — 24
Miami	0	3	0	0 — 3

Dal-FG Clark 9
Dal-Alworth 7 pass from Staubach (Clark kick)
Mia-FG Yepremian 31
Dal-D. Thomas 3 run (Clark kick)
Dal-Ditka 7 pass from Staubach (Clark kick)
Attendance-80,591

FINAL TEAM STATISTICS

	Cowboys	Dolphins
TOTAL FIRST DOWNS	23	10
Rushing	15	3
Passing	8	7
Penalty	0	0
TOTAL NET YARDAGE	352	185
Total Offensive Plays	69	44
Average Gain per Offensive Play	5.1	4.2
NET YARDS RUSHING	252	80
Total Rushing Plays	48	20
Average Gain per Rushing Play	5.3	4.0
NET YARDS PASSING	100	105
Pass Att.-Comp.-Int.	19-12-0	23-12-1
Sacks-Yards Lost	2-19	1-29
Gross Yards Passing	119	134
Avg. Gain per Pass (Incl. Sacks)	4.8	4.4
PUNTS-YARDS	5-186	5-200
Average Distance	37.2	40.0
Had Blocked	0	0
TOTAL RETURN YARDAGE	74	143
Kickoff Returns-Yards	2-34	5-122
Punt Returns-Yards	1-(-1)	1-21
Interception Returns-Yards	1-41	0-0
TOTAL TURNOVERS	1	3
Fumbles-Lost	1-1	2-2
Had Intercepted	0	1
PENALTIES-YARDS	3-15	0-0
TOTAL POINTS SCORED	24	3
Touchdowns Rushing	1	0
Touchdowns Passing	2	0
Touchdowns Returns	0	0
Extra Points	3	0
Field Goals-Attempts	1-1	1-2
Safeties	0	0
THIRD DOWN EFFICIENCY	6/13	2/9
FOURTH DOWN EFFICIENCY	1/1	0/0
TIME OF POSSESSION	39:12	20:48

INDIVIDUAL STATISTICS

RUSHING

Dallas	No.	Yds.	Avg.	Long	TD
D. Thomas	19	95	5.0	23	1
Garrison	14	74	5.3	17	0
Hill	7	25	3.6	13	0
Staubach	5	18	3.6	5	0
Ditka	1	17	17.0	17	0
Hayes	1	16	16.0	16	0
Reeves	1	7	7.0	7	0

Miami	No.	Yds.	Avg.	Long	TD
Kiick	10	40	4.0	12	0
Csonka	9	40	4.4	9	0
Griese	1	0	0.0	0	0

PASSING

Dallas	Att.	Comp.	Yds.	Long	TD	Int.
Staubach	19	12	119	21	2	0

Miami	Att.	Comp.	Yds.	Long	TD	Int.
Griese	23	12	134	27	0	1

RECEIVING

Dallas	No.	Yds.	Long	TD
D. Thomas	3	17	11	0
Alworth	2	28	21	1
Ditka	2	28	21	1
Hayes	2	23	18	0
Garrison	2	11	7	0
Hill	1	12	12	0

Miami	No.	Yds.	Long	TD
Warfield	4	39	23	0
Kiick	3	21	11	0
Csonka	2	18	16	0
Fleming	1	27	27	0
Twilley	1	20	20	0
Mandich	1	9	9	0

INTERCEPTIONS

Dallas	No.	Yds.	Long	TD
Howley	1	41	41	0

Miami	No.	Yds.	Long	TD
None				

PUNTING

Dallas	No.	Yds.	Avg.	TB	Long
Widby	5	186	37.2	1	47

Miami	No.	Yds.	Avg.	TB	Long
Seiple	5	200	40.0	0	45

PUNT RETURNS

Dallas	No.	FC	Yds.	Long	TD
Hayes	1	1	-1	-1	0
Harris	0	2	0	0	0

Miami	No.	FC	Yds.	Long	TD
Scott	1	0	21	21	0

KICKOFF RETURNS

Dallas	No.	Yds.	Long	TD
I. Thomas	1	23	23	0
Waters	1	11	11	0

Miami	No.	Yds.	Long	TD
Morris	4	90	37	0
Ginn	1	32	32	0

FUMBLES

Dallas	No.	Own Rec.	Opp. Rec.
Hill	1	0	0
Howley	0	0	1
Cole	0	0	1

Miami	No.	Own Rec.	Opp. Rec.
Csonka	1	0	0
Griese	1	0	0
Fernandez	0	0	1

KICKING

Dallas	XP-A	FG-A	FG Made	FG Missed
Clark	3-3	1-1	9	--

Miami	XP-A	FG-A	FG Made	FG Missed
Yepremian	0-0	1-2	31	49

PLAY-BY-PLAY

Miami won the coin toss and elected to receive.

FIRST QUARTER
Clark kick to M 6, Morris 20 return (Harris).
Miami (15:00)

M 26	1-10	Griese pass to Twilley right broken up (Jordan).
M 26	2-10	Kiick 7 run left (Andrie).
M 33	3-3	Kiick sweep right, no gain (Edwards).
M 33	4-3	Seiple 45 punt, Hayes return, loss of 1 (Humphord).

Dallas (12:59)

D 21	1-10	Staubach 5 pass to Hayes right flat (Anderson).
D 26	2-5	D. Thomas 8 run off right tackle (Kolen).
D 34	1-10	Staubach sacked, loss of 6 (Fernandez).
D 28	2-16	Staubach 1 run evading pass rush (Riley).
D 29	3-15	Staubach pass to Alworth deep overthrown.
D 29	4-15	Widby 29 punt downed at M 42.

Miami (10:16)

M 42	1-10	Csonka 12 sweep left (Cole).
D 46	1-10	Csonka fumbled handoff, loss of 2, Howley recovered for Dal. at D 48.

Dallas (9:11)

D 48	1-10	D. Thomas 2 sweep left (Fernandez).
50	2-8	Staubach 5 run evading pass rush (Fernandez).
M 45	3-3	Staubach 4 run evading pass rush (Heinz).
M 41	1-10	Garrison 8 run right (Kolen).
M 33	2-2	Garrison 10 run off right tackle (Johnson).
M 23	1-10	Staubach sacked, loss of 13 (Riley).
M 36	2-23	Staubach 18 pass to Hayes middle (Scott).
M 18	3-5	Staubach 11 pass to D. Thomas (Foley).
M 7	1-goal	D. Thomas 3 run up middle (Heinz).
M 4	2-goal	Garrison 2 run left (Kolen, Riley).
M 2	3-goal	Staubach pass to D. Thomas, no gain (Anderson).
M 2	4-goal	Clark, 9-yard field goal (1:23).

Dallas scoring drive: 50 yards, 11 plays, 7:48.
Dallas 3, Miami 0
Clark kick to M 5, Ginn 32 return (Renfro).
Miami (1:23)

M 37	1-10	Kiick 1 run right (Green).
M 38	2-9	Griese pass to Warfield broken up (Renfro).
M 38	3-9	Griese sacked, loss of 29 (Lilly).

END OF FIRST QUARTER:
Dallas 3, Miami 0

SECOND QUARTER

M 9	4-38	Seiple 45 punt, Hayes fair catch.

Dallas (14:44)

D 46	1-10	Garrison 5 run right (Kolen).
M 49	2-5	D. Thomas 5 run right (Buoniconti).
M 44	1-10	Staubach pass to Hayes deep broken up (Foley).
M 44	2-10	Staubach 4 screen pass to Garrison (Buoniconti). Dal.-first time out.
M 40	3-6	Staubach pass to Alworth overthrown.
M 40	4-6	Widby 40 punt into end zone, touchback.

Miami (12:03)

M 20	1-10	Kiick 9 sweep left (Harris).
M 29	2-1	Kiick 2 run left (Jordan).
M 31	1-10	Griese 20 pass to Twilley right (Harris).
D 49	1-10	Csonka 3 run right (Cole, Edwards).
D 46	2-7	Griese pass to Warfield deep incomplete.
D 46	3-7	Griese 4 pass to Kiick right (Howley).
D 42	4-3	Yepremian's 49-yard field goal attempt was short.

Dallas (10:03)

D 20	1-10	D. Thomas 10 run right (Foley).
D 30	1-10	Garrison 17 run off right tackle (Foley).
D 47	1-10	Garrison run left, no gain (Fernandez).
D 47	2-10	Garrison 2 run left (Kolen).

D 49	3-8	Staubach pass to Ditka dropped, incomplete.
D 49	4-8	Widby 24 punt downed by I. Thomas.

Miami (7:15)

M 27	1-10	Griese pass to Warfield middle incomplete.
M 27	2-10	Csonka 2 run left (Pugh).
M 29	3-8	Griese 6 pass left to Kiick (Harris).
M 35	4-2	Seiple 41 punt out of bounds.

Dallas (6:15)

D 24	1-10	D. Thomas 5 run right (Swift).
D 29	2-5	Staubach 6 pass to D. Thomas right (Johnson).
D 35	1-10	D. Thomas 5 run left (Heinz).
D 40	2-5	D. Thomas 6 sweep left (Anderson).
D 46	1-10	Garrison 1 run up middle (Buoniconti).
D 47	2-9	Staubach 21 pass to Alworth middle (Anderson).
M 32	1-10	Hill 13 run left (Scott, Swift).
M 19	1-10	Hill 7 run right (Riley). Two-Minute Warning.
M 12	2-3	Hill 5 reverse left (Kolen).
M 7	1-goal	Staubach 7 pass to Alworth left corner of end zone, touchdown (1:15). Clark kicked extra point.

Dallas scoring drive: 76 yards, 10 plays, 5:00.
Dallas 10, Miami 0
Clark kick out of bounds. Dal. penalized 5 for illegal procedure (Clark). Clark kick to M 20, Morris 12 return (Waters).
Miami (1:15)

M 32	1-10	Griese 5 pass to Warfield left sideline (Green).
M 37	2-5	Griese 11 pass to Kiick middle (Jordan).
M 48	1-10	Griese pass to Mandich incomplete. Play nullified and Dal. penalized 5 for offsides.
D 47	1-5	Griese 23 pass to Warfield (Harris).
D 24	1-10	Griese pass to Warfield at D 2 dropped.
D 24	2-10	Yepremian, 31-yard field goal (:04).

Miami scoring drive: 44 yards, 4 plays, 1:11.
Yepremian kick to D 33, Waters 11 return (Mumphord).
END OF SECOND QUARTER:
Dallas 10, Miami 3

THIRD QUARTER
Yepremian kick to D 6, I. Thomas 23 return (Mumphord).
Dallas (15:00)

D 29	1-10	Garrison 3 run left (Stanfill).
D 32	2-7	D. Thomas 4 run right (Buoniconti).
D 36	3-3	Staubach 12 pass to Hill right (Kolen).
D 48	1-10	D. Thomas 7 sweep right (Anderson).
M 45	2-3	D. Thomas 23 run right (Kolen).
M 22	1-10	Hayes 16 reverse right (Heinz).
M 6	1-goal	Garrison 3 run left (Fernandez).
M 3	2-goal	D. Thomas 3 sweep left, touchdown (9:43). Clark kicked extra point.

Dallas scoring drive: 71 yards, 8 plays, 5:17.
Dallas 17, Miami 3
Clark kick to goal line, Morris 37 return (Harris).
Miami (9:43)

M 37	1-10	Kiick 3 run right (Lilly).
M 40	2-7	Csonka 2 run off right tackle (Jordan).
M 42	3-5	Griese pass to Warfield middle incomplete.
M 42	4-5	Seiple 32 punt, Harris fair catch.

Dallas (7:24)

D 26	1-10	Garrison 3 run right (Fernandez).
D 29	2-7	D. Thomas 4 sweep right (Buoniconti).
D 33	3-3	Staubach 7 pass to Garrison middle (Buoniconti).
D 40	1-10	D. Thomas sweep right, loss of 5 (Foley).
D 35	2-15	Dal. penalized 5 for delay of game.
D 30	2-20	Staubach 3 run evading pass rush (Swift).
D 33	3-17	Staubach pass to Hayes right incomplete.

D 33	4-17	Widby 46 punt, Scott 21 return (Harris, Lewis).

Miami (3:45)

M 42	1-10	Griese pass to Kiick broken up (Howley).
M 42	2-10	Griese pass to Kiick deep broken up (Adderley).
M 42	3-10	Griese pass to Warfield middle incomplete.
M 42	4-10	Seiple 37 punt, Harris fair catch.

Dallas (3:10)

D 21	1-10	Garrison 2 run right (Den Herder).
D 23	2-8	D. Thomas 2 sweep left (Stanfill).
D 25	3-6	Staubach pass to Hayes deep overthrown.
D 25	4-6	Widby 47 punt downed at M 28.

Miami (1:36)

M 28	1-10	Csonka 2 run off left tackle (Lilly).
M 30	2-8	Kiick 6 sweep left (Renfro).

END OF THIRD QUARTER:
Dallas 17, Miami 3

FOURTH QUARTER

M 36	3-2	Griese 7 pass to Warfield right (Adderley).
M 43	1-10	Kiick 2 run up middle (Howley).
M 45	2-8	Griese pass to Warfield middle (Green).
M 49	3-4	Griese pass to Kiick right intercepted at 50, Howley 41 return.

Dallas (12:35)

M 9	1-goal	D. Thomas run left, no gain (Riley). Miami declined illegal motion against Dal.
M 9	2-goal	Hill 2 run left (Kolen).
M 7	3-goal	Staubach 7 pass to Ditka right end zone, touchdown (11:42). Clark kicked extra point.

Dallas scoring drive: 9 yards, 3 plays, :53.
Dallas 24, Miami 3
Clark kick to M 2, Morris run left (Harris).
Miami (11:42)

M 23	1-10	Griese 16 swing pass to Csonka (Jordan).
M 39	1-10	Kiick 3 run off right tackle (Jordan).
M 42	2-7	Griese 27 pass to Fleming middle (Harris).
D 31	1-10	Csonka 6 draw up middle (Edwards).
D 25	2-4	Griese pass to Fleming broken up (Green).
D 25	3-4	Griese 9 pass to Mandich (Green).
D 16	1-10	Griese fumbled snap, Cole recovered for Dal. at D 20.

Dallas (8:33)

D 20	1-10	D. Thomas 4 run left (Johnson).
D 24	2-6	D. Thomas 2 run right (Kolen).
D 26	3-4	Staubach 21 pass to Ditka right (Anderson).
D 47	1-10	D. Thomas 7 run off left tackle (Johnson).
M 46	2-3	Garrison 17 run up middle (Johnson).
M 29	1-10	Staubach 5 run evading pass rush (Matheson).
M 24	2-5	Garrison 1 run left (Riley).
M 23	3-4	Hill 3 run left (Kolen).
M 20	4-1	Reeves 7 run right on fake field goal attempt (Scott).
M 13	1-10	Hill sweep left, loss of 5. Two-Minute Warning.
M 18	2-15	Ditka 17 reverse left (Fernandez).
M 1	1-goal	Hill dive left, no gain, fumbled, Fernandez recovered for Miami at M 4.

Miami (1:48)

M 4	1-10	Kiick 7 run left (Toomay).
M 11	2-3	Csonka 11 sweep right (Thomas).
M 22	1-10	Griese 2 screen pass to Csonka (Gregory).
M 24	2-8	Csonka 4 sweep right (Lewis).

FINAL SCORE:
Dallas 24, Miami 3
FINAL RECORDS:
Dallas 14-3, Miami 12-4-1

111

The National Football League doesn't list a record for Longest Helmet Throw, One Game, but if it did, the name that would be listed would be Bob Lilly, who played defensive tackle for the Dallas Cowboys and played it with distinction for a long time.

Lilly threw his helmet from Miami to New Orleans or, if history is more your thing, from Super Bowl V to Super Bowl VI.

There's some poetic license in this…but not much.

In the final seconds of Super Bowl V in Miami, a number of veteran Cowboys, including Lilly, felt the darkness never would lift. The loss to Baltimore in Super Bowl V marked the fifth year in a row the Cowboys had charged into the playoffs, only to be blown out of their saddles. The loss to Baltimore was rock bottom.

So, as Jim O'Brien's winning field goal cleared the crossbar, Cowboys defender Lilly pulled off his own helmet in agony, turned, and hurled it more than 50 yards downfield.

Years later, photographer Bob Lilly was interrupted while he was constructing a new darkroom in Mesilla, New Mexico. He has developed into a fine photographer, and his work, which focuses mostly on nature, has a large following in Texas and the Southwest.

Lilly was asked about his epic helmet toss.

"You know," he said, "I don't remember it. I mean, I know I did it…Lord, enough people have told me about it to where I know I did it…but I sure don't remember doing it. But one thing I do know is we were heading off the field after the game and just feeling awful, and some young Colts player, he had to be a rookie, came up to me, holdin' out my helmet. He just said 'I think this is yours, Mr. Lilly.'

"So, in addition to feeling awful, I felt like an idiot."

Feeling awful, it developed, was not wasted on the 1971 Cowboys. Feeling the five years of playoff miseries against Green Bay and Cleveland and Baltimore was what led the Dallas Cowboys into Super Bowl VI, where the bad news finally turned good.

"We didn't get sorted out right away," Lilly says, "but that feeling of frustration was what kept us going the next year."

They didn't start fast, however. Midway through the 1971 season, the Cowboys fell to 4-3 after losing to the Chicago Bears, 23-19. Receiver Lance Alworth recalls Lilly stalking into the Soldier Field visitors' dressing room after that game. "He looked around," Alworth says, "and he said 'Now, maybe everybody will start playing!'"

Everybody did, including a young quarterback named Roger Staubach who had spent the early part of the season dividing time with veteran Craig Morton. After the loss to Chicago, Dallas head coach Tom Landry took Staubach aside and told him he was going to be the quarterback the rest of the way. The Cowboys ran off 10 victories in a row en route to their first world championship.

Looking back, Lilly talks about the way the defense came together.

"We weren't going to let people into the end zone," he says. "We developed this tremendous closeness and confidence. From that point on, we didn't play with fear. We played with anticipation."

Landry, the Cowboys' head coach from 1960-1988, looks back from the vantage point of today.

"You have to understand the way it was for that team," he says. "They were seasoned, tough football players. I mean, really tough. These fellows had been down, they'd been kicked around, they'd been criticized, they'd been made fun of. They had lived with a lot of adversity for a long time and that made them very tough-minded people.

"Once we were in New Orleans to play the Dolphins, they were very confident. When they talked among themselves they said there was no way they were going to lose that game."

Super Bowl VI was played on artificial turf in raw, 39-degree weather in Tulane Stadium on Sunday, January 16, 1972. It matched Dallas and its less-than-grand playoff past against the upstart Miami Dolphins, a 1966 American Football League expansion team, a team that had survived a near-slapstick infancy to reach pro football's biggest game in just two seasons

While balloons soared toward the sky, Phantom jets streaked over Tulane Stadium just after the National Anthem in the colorful pregame ceremonies. It was the second of seven Super Bowls played in New Orleans.

under new head coach Don Shula.

In the weeks before Super Bowl VI, Miami had outlasted Kansas City 27-24 on Christmas day in a record 22 minutes of overtime, pro football's longest game, and had shut out defending Super Bowl champion Baltimore 21-0. Dallas had beaten Minnesota and San Francisco, allowing just one touchdown.

It was Miami's fine young offense against Dallas's salty old defense, and Miami's small "no-name" defense against Dallas's underrated offense.

Miami ran the ball with Larry Csonka and Jim Kiick, powerful backs who had averaged a total of 129 yards a game in 1971 and had lost only one fumble between them (by Kiick). Smart quarterback Bob Griese could throw to the gifted Paul Warfield and sure-handed Howard Twilley. Kicker Garo Yepremian, an Armenian who was raised on Cyprus, also was an important contributor. It was Yepremian's field goal that ended the overtime classic against the Chiefs. And then there was the Dolphins' defense—anonymous, efficient, and unyielding.

Dallas's offense had a running game that featured Duane Thomas, Calvin Hill, and swingman Walt Garrison. The 1971 season would be the second and last for Thomas at Dallas. Displeased with his contract going into '71, Thom-

as held out during the preseason and blasted Dallas management after it refused to renegotiate the contract. Thomas finally ended his holdout after former NFL great Jim Brown told him he should honor his contract.

But, off the field, Thomas spurned almost all contact with others, both inside and outside the team. He was traded to San Diego the next season.

"If we had Duane Thomas and Calvin Hill [who left Dallas to sign with a WFL team while in his prime] for normal careers in the seventies, I think we would have been something," Landry says. "Don't get me wrong—we had good backs over the years, but those two were big backs with terrific talent. We could have been consistently up there for a long time, like Pittsburgh was."

But Landry had both runners in 1971, along

The game was scoreless when Miami's Larry Csonka fumbled a handoff from Bob Griese, and Dallas linebacker Chuck Howley recovered. The lost fumble, Csonka's first of the season, led to a Cowboys' field goal.

with Staubach throwing to former Olympic gold medal-winning sprinter Bob Hayes, veteran Lance Alworth, and tough old tight end Mike Ditka.

The Doomsday Defense, anchored by Lilly and middle linebacker Lee Roy Jordan, had allowed only 92 points in the Cowboys' run of nine successive victories.

But it was the offensive line that proved to be the winning ingredient in Super Bowl VI—even without Pro Bowl tackle Ralph Neely, who had broken his leg riding a dirt bike.

"You know how players are," Ditka says, "always gotta try something new or different. I mean, like little kids, you know?

"Well, that year we were into dirt bikes. We'd go out riding together, go in the woods, anywhere so it was off-road. Tom [Landry] knew about them and he didn't like us having them, but he couldn't say no to everything. Well, it's November, and we're riding after a meeting. Neely's in the middle, with me on one side and Danny Reeves on the other. That was when Ralph fell off his bike and broke his leg.

"You talk about a bad day! Me and Dan had to first take Ralph to the hospital, then we had to call coach Landry to tell him we were at the hospital and why we were there. I've seen Tom Landry mad over the years, but never as mad as that."

Landry patched the hole for two weeks with veterans Don Talbert and Forrest Gregg, but then they were injured. That left Dallas coming down the stretch with just one tackle, Rayfield Wright.

During the offseason, the Cowboys had traded veteran tackle Tony Liscio to San Diego. Told during the Chargers' training camp that he was to be traded on to Miami, Liscio opted to retire in Dallas.

Down to one tackle by mid-November, Landry called Liscio, by then a commercial real estate salesman.

On the last play of the first quarter, defensive tackle Bob Lilly of the Cowboys chased Griese all the way back to his own 9-yard line and sacked him for a 29-yard loss. Miami netted only 185 yards.

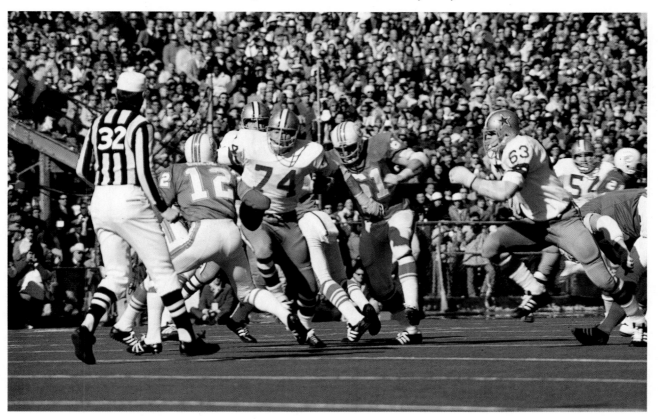

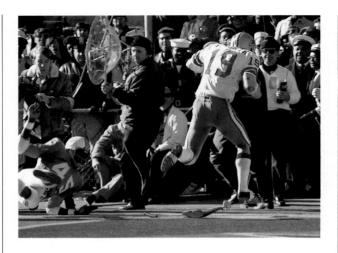

Lance Alworth gave the Cowboys a 10-0 lead when he caught a seven-yard touchdown pass from Roger Staubach in the left corner of the end zone. A 21-yard pass to Alworth helped set up the touchdown.

"He said he needed me, or he'd have to shuffle everybody on the line, play everybody out of position," Liscio says. "I told him I thought he was crazy to be calling me." That was Monday, November 15. Liscio thought about it for two days, then showed up for practice on Wednesday. He started on Sunday against Washington.

"Tony solved the problem," Ditka says. "He came out of retirement and just played great. It was a neat thing to see. And none of us rode dirt bikes anymore."

As the game began, Miami took the opening kickoff and was not pleased with what it saw.

"Dallas had changed its coverage," Dolphins

Miami's Paul Warfield couldn't hold a pass inside the Dallas 5 late in the second quarter, and the Dolphins got only a field goal on the drive. The ball was deflected by Cowboys safety Cornell Green (not in the picture).

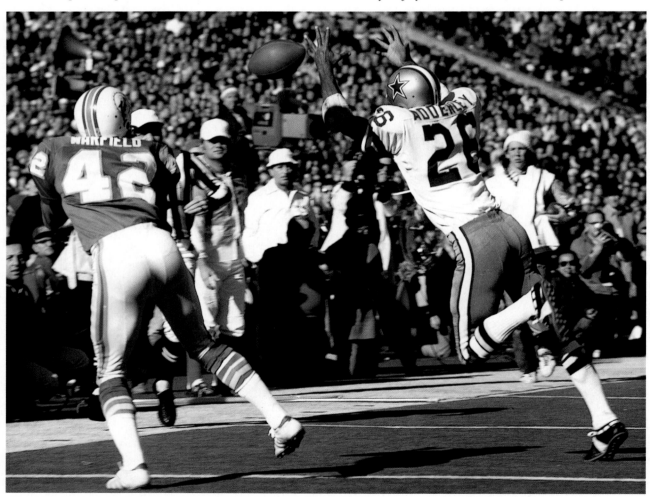

wide receiver Twilley says. "They came out in a double-single—doubled both wide receivers and used a linebacker to cover the tight end. Taking me away from our offense wasn't going to hurt, but taking Warfield away sure was. What we did depended on getting the ball to Warfield."

But Miami didn't corner the early market on confusion. Staubach had problems with the Dolphins' zone, in which linebacker Nick Buoniconti buzzed around the middle and safeties Dick Anderson and Jake Scott lurked in the secondary.

But then something happened that hadn't happened all year: Larry Csonka fumbled.

"I was reading the hole and I had my eyes too high," Csonka says. "Griese's handoff was fine, I just hit it with my knee." Dallas linebacker Chuck Howley, the most valuable player in a losing cause in Super Bowl V, recovered near midfield.

On Staubach's short passes and the running of Garrison, who had started in place of a gimpy Calvin Hill, the Cowboys marched from their

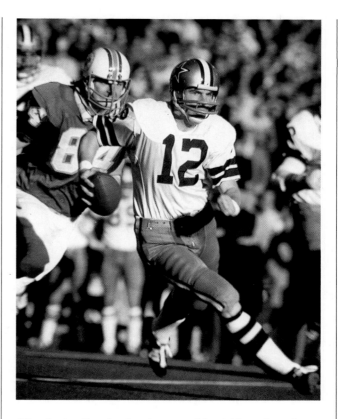

The elusive Staubach, who passed for 119 yards and two touchdowns and ran five times for 18 more yards, was named the game's most valuable player. He led the Cowboys to three more Super Bowls in the 1970s.

The Cowboys rushed for a Super Bowl-record 252 yards, led by "Silent" Duane Thomas, who gained 95 on 19 carries. Thomas also scored on a three-yard run in the third quarter to boost his team's lead to 17-3.

48-yard line to the Dolphins' 7. But Miami resisted there, forcing Mike Clark to kick a field goal. Dallas led 3-0 after 13:37.

The last play of the first quarter hurt Miami.

On third-and-9 at his own 38, Griese faded to pass and quickly saw that the Cowboys' rush was going to be a problem.

"I looped outside of George Andrie, our left end, and Larry Cole beat his man on the right side," Lilly says. "Griese kept giving ground, turning little loops. He was trying to buy time, clear a receiver, make something happen. Cole and me just kept herding him back. It was like how riders hem up a cow they want to take. I think Griese was okay until he realized how much ground he'd given. He might have gotten a little nervous then." Lilly sacked him at the Miami 9, a stunning 29-yard loss.

The first four possessions of the second quarter resulted in nothing more than a missed long

whichever way he wanted to go," Niland says.

With 6:15 to go in the half, Dallas went 76 yards in 10 plays. A Staubach-to-Alworth collaboration over the middle was good for 21 of them, and Hill came off the bench to add 25 yards on three carries.

"One thing we did to confuse them was to be less confusing," Ditka says. "I mean, our reputation was to shift a lot before the snap to confuse the defense. We cut out a lot of the shifting and went right now from straight sets. The Dol-

Linebacker Chuck Howley's 41-yard interception return to the Miami 9 set up Dallas's final score.

With 1:53 left in the game, the Cowboys led 24-3 and were bidding for one last touchdown, when Calvin Hill fumbled on the goal line and Miami's Manny Fernandez recovered. The lost fumble ended a 79-yard drive.

field-goal attempt by Yepremian. But the Cowboys' ground game was beginning to click. Dallas rushed for 43 yards in the first quarter, 81 in the second. Going in, the Cowboys' strategy had been to attack the heart of the Dolphins' defensive middle, with counter plays behind guards John Niland and Blaine Nye and center Dave Manders.

"Our backs made a false start away from the hole, then countered back," Niland says. "Buoniconti was very quick, and we wanted to make his quickness run him out of the play."

Two of the three linemen would work in tandem, one taking the nose tackle, the other slipping through to Buoniconti. "We took him

Tight end Mike Ditka scored on a seven-yard touchdown pass to give the Cowboys a 24-3 lead. Fourteen years later, Ditka was the head coach of the Chicago Bears when they won Super Bowl XX, also in New Orleans.

them," says Miami defensive end Bill Stanfill. "All we talked about was staying in our lanes on defense, not overplaying our pursuit because they were cutting back so much."

"Duane Thomas was really a good back," Ditka says. "And the thing he did best was cut back. He'd get in a hole quick, he would clear it, and then he'd look, right away, to cut back across the pursuit grain. [Gale] Sayers, and maybe Hugh McElhenny, were the best cutback runners I ever saw, but I'll tell you, Duane Thomas wasn't far behind them."

Dallas took the second-half kickoff and drove 71 yards to score again, 37 of the yards coming on runs by Thomas. He ran three yards for a touchdown on a pitchout from Staubach, the only audible the Cowboys' quarterback would call all day, and Dallas led 17-3.

By now, the pressure was taking its toll on the Miami defense. The Dolphins' bid to stay home and stop the inside counters was answered quickly by Landry, who sent Thomas and Hill wide. On one toss, Niland knocked down Buoniconti with a crushing block.

phins weren't expecting it."

With Hill's runs setting the table, Staubach fired a seven-yard bullet to Alworth in the corner, and Dallas led 10-0 after the extra point.

Then Miami's only real chance to get back in the game glanced off Warfield's fingers. Griese had hurried the Dolphins to the Cowboys' 24, where he went deep for Warfield on a first-down play. Cowboys safety Cornell Green deflected the ball, and it skidded off Warfield's hands at the 2. Miami had to settle for a field goal. The Dolphins trailed 10-3 at halftime.

"We thought we were still in it at half, but we had to stop

Bouncing back from their disappointing loss in Super Bowl V, the happy Cowboys carried head coach Tom Landry off the field after overpowering Miami. Landry led the Cowboys to five Super Bowls in the 1970s.

Buoniconti remained on the field until early in the fourth quarter, but he was out on his feet. The Dolphins' defense toughed it out, even with its leader dazed, but Griese and the offense were, to use Shula's word, "destroyed." The longest advance Miami had in the third quarter was to its own 42-yard line.

The Dolphins made it to the Cowboys' 16 in the fourth quarter, but that was after the score had mounted to 24-3, and the possession ended there when Griese fumbled to Dallas defender Cole.

The 17-3 third-quarter count went to 24-3 early in the final period. Operating from his own 49, Griese flipped a pass in the flat intended for Kiick, but got, instead, the ubiquitous Howley.

"We practiced getting up off the ground in a hurry," Howley says. "On the play, I had thrown myself at Twilley, to cut him at the line. I went down, but I bounced up again, quick."

Too quick for Miami. Griese threw the ball right to him.

Howley returned the interception 41 yards to the Dolphins' 9, where he stumbled and fell despite a blocking convoy. On third down, Staubach intended to throw to Hayes after first looking off to Ditka. "But when I looked to Mike, he was open, so I just went to him," Staubach says.

"I was an old guy, you know?" Ditka says. "I mean, I'd been around…Chicago, then Philadelphia, finally Dallas. I wasn't a kid anymore. I caught the first touchdown of the preseason and the last touchdown in the Super Bowl. I felt pretty good about that."

Griese's fumble later in the quarter set up a final Cowboys drive, but it failed when Hill fumbled going in from the 1. "That was the only mistake they made all day," Shula says.

Ditka almost had a second touchdown on that drive—he took an end-around 17 yards to the Dolphins' 1 before falling.

"I lost track of where I was," Ditka says. "I thought the five was the goal line. Here, I got Niland in front of me, I could walk in, and I'm stumbling and staggering and I fell right in front of the goal line."

It ended 24-3.

Afterwards, Landry said he was happiest for guys such as Lilly and Howley, the guys who had been there through all of the bad times. His list also might have included himself. Cowboys owner Clint Murchison was a bit droller: "It was just the successful conclusion of our twelve-year plan."

Dallas rushed for 252 yards, a Super Bowl record. Thomas, after a shaky showing against Baltimore in Super Bowl V, ran for 95 yards and caught three passes for 17 more. Miami's Csonka and Kiick managed a total of just 80 yards rushing, less then half Miami's season average. Staubach, with modest numbers (119 yards passing for two touchdowns, 18 yards rushing) was named the game's most valuable player.

"We learned one thing," the Dolphins' Twilley says, "when it's over, it's over. All week, we'd had media people up to our ears. But once that game was over the media just wanted to talk to one team and it wasn't us.

"It's so hard to figure. We went in confident. We really thought we'd win and win handily. Something happened, though, during the week. I guess it was that week. The week has its own momentum, like nothing we'd been in before.

"But afterwards, when Shula talked to us, I'll never forget that. He said we'd been embarrassed. He said we didn't even compete. I mean, it was hard to hear, but he had a point. That's the sickest feeling I've ever had.

"Why'd we lose? Because we were people. We made mistakes. We were influenced by emotion and events. We started to question ourselves and then we tried to do more, to take on more than we were prepared for—call it pressing. It's when everything goes south on you."

Then Twilley started talking about how the Dolphins had used despair to build upon, talked about how maybe the lessons most deeply learned are those taken from enduring pain.

He talked about going on, which the Dolphins surely did.

It sounded familiar.

There's no record of anybody on the Miami team throwing a helmet in frustration after Super Bowl VI, but, if it had happened, Bob Lilly would have understood.

VII

Miami 14, Washington 7

50 SEC. **90** ROW **51** SEAT

SUPER BOWL VII

Sunday, January 14, 1973
Kickoff 12:30 pm $15:00
all taxes included

AFC-NFC World Championship Game
SUNDAY, JANUARY 14, 1973 KICKOFF 12:30 P.M.
LOS ANGELES MEMORIAL COLISEUM • $15.00

51 SEAT **90** ROW **50** SEC.

Vital Statistics

Starting Lineups

Miami (AFC)	Offense	Washington (NFC)
Paul Warfield	WR	Charley Taylor
Wayne Moore	LT	Terry Hermeling
Bob Kuechenberg	LG	Paul Laaveg
Jim Langer	C	Len Hauss
Larry Little	RG	John Wilbur
Norm Evans	RT	Walter Rock
Marv Fleming	TE	Jerry Smith
Howard Twilley	WR	Roy Jefferson
Bob Griese	QB	Billy Kilmer
Jim Kiick	RB	Larry Brown
Larry Csonka	RB	Charley Harraway
	Defense	
Vern Den Herder	LE	Ron McDole
Manny Fernandez	LT	Bill Brundige
Bob Heinz	RT	Diron Talbert
Bill Stanfill	RE	Verlon Biggs
Doug Swift	LLB	Jack Pardee
Nick Buoniconti	MLB	Myron Pottios
Mike Kolen	RLB	Chris Hanburger
Lloyd Mumphord	LCB	Pat Fischer
Curtis Johnson	RCB	Mike Bass
Dick Anderson	SS	Brig Owens
Jake Scott	FS	Roosevelt Taylor

Substitutions

Miami-Offense: K-Garo Yepremian. P-Larry Seiple. TE-Jim Mandich. WR-Marlin Briscoe. LINE-Doug Crusan, Howard Kindig. RB-Eugene Morris, Ed Jenkins, Hubert Ginn, Charles Leigh. QB-Earl Morrall. Defense: LINE-Maulty Moore. LB-Bob Matheson, Larry Ball, Jesse Powell. DB-Henry Stuckey, Charles Babb. DNP: WR-Otto Stowe.

Washington-Offense: K-Curt Knight. P-Mike Bragg. WR-Clifton McNeil, Mack Alston. LINE-George Burman, QB-Sam Wyche. RB-Herb Mul-Key, Bob Brunet, Mike Hull. Defense: LINE-Mike Fanucci, Manuel Sistrunk. LB-Rusty Tillman, Harold McLinton. DB-Ted Vactor, Alvin Haymond, Jeff Severson, Jon Jaqua. DNP: G-Ray Schoenke.

Officials

Referee-Tom Bell. Umpire-Lou Palazzi. Line Judge-Bruce Alford. Head Linesman-Tony Veteri. Back Judge-Tom Kelleher. Field Judge-Tony Skover.

Scoring

Miami	7	7	0	0 —	14
Washington	0	0	0	7 —	7

Mia-Twilley 28 pass from Griese (Yepremian kick)
Mia-Kiick 1 run (Yepremian kick)
Wash-Bass 49 fumble recovery return (Knight kick)
Attendance-90,192

FINAL TEAM STATISTICS

	Dolphins	Redskins
TOTAL FIRST DOWNS	12	16
Rushing	7	9
Passing	5	7
Penalty	0	0
TOTAL NET YARDAGE	253	228
Total Offensive Plays	50	66
Average Gain per Offensive Play	5.1	3.5
NET YARDS RUSHING	184	141
Total Rushing Plays	37	36
Average Gain per Rushing Play	5.0	3.9
NET YARDS PASSING	69	87
Pass Att.-Comp.-Int.	11-8-1	28-14-3
Sacks-Yards Lost	2-19	2-17
Gross Yards Passing	88	104
Avg. Gain per Pass (Incl. Sacks)	5.3	2.9
PUNTS-YARDS	7-301	5-156
Average Distance	43.0	31.2
Had Blocked	0	0
TOTAL RETURN YARDAGE	132	54
Kickoff Returns-Yards	2-33	3-45
Punt Returns-Yards	2-4	4-9
Interception Returns-Yards	3-95	1-0
TOTAL TURNOVERS	2	3
Fumbles-Lost	2-1	1-0
Had Intercepted	1	3
PENALTIES-YARDS	3-35	3-25
TOTAL POINTS SCORED	14	7
Touchdowns Rushing	1	0
Touchdowns Passing	1	0
Touchdowns Returns	0	1
Extra Points	2	1
Field Goals-Attempts	0-1	0-1
Safeties	0	0
THIRD DOWN EFFICIENCY	3/11	3/13
FOURTH DOWN EFFICIENCY	0/0	0/1
TIME OF POSSESSION	32:17	27:43

INDIVIDUAL STATISTICS

RUSHING

Miami	No.	Yds.	Avg.	Long	TD
Csonka	15	112	7.5	49	0
Kiick	12	38	3.2	8	1
Morris	10	34	3.4	6	0

Washington	No.	Yds.	Avg.	Long	TD
Brown	22	72	3.3	11	0
Harraway	10	37	3.7	8	0
Kilmer	2	18	9.0	9	0
C. Taylor	1	8	8.0	8	0
Smith	1	6	6.0	6	0

PASSING

Miami	Att.	Comp.	Yds.	Long	TD	Int.
Griese	11	8	88	28t	1	1

Washington	Att.	Comp.	Yds.	Long	TD	Int.
Kilmer	28	14	104	15	0	3

RECEIVING

Miami	No.	Yds.	Long	TD
Warfield	3	36	18	0
Kiick	2	6	4	0
Twilley	1	28	28t	1
Mandich	1	19	19	0
Csonka	1	-1	-1	0

Washington	No.	Yds.	Long	TD
Jefferson	5	50	15	0
Brown	5	26	12	0
C. Taylor	2	20	15	0
Smith	1	11	11	0
Harraway	1	-3	-3	0

INTERCEPTIONS

Miami	No.	Yds.	Long	TD
Scott	2	63	55	0
Buoniconti	1	32	32	0

Washington	No.	Yds.	Long	TD
Owens	1	0	0	0

PUNTING

Miami	No.	Yds.	Avg.	TB	Long
Seiple	7	301	43.0	1	50

Washington	No.	Yds.	Avg.	TB	Long
Bragg	5	156	31.2	0	38

PUNT RETURNS

Miami	No.	FC	Yds.	Long	TD
Scott	2		4	4	0
Anderson	0	1	0	0	0

Washington	No.	FC	Yds.	Long	TD
Haymond	4	0	9	7	0
Vactor	0	2	0	0	0

KICKOFF RETURNS

Miami	No.	Yds.	Long	TD
Morris	2	33	17	0

Washington	No.	Yds.	Long	TD
Haymond	2	30	18	0
Mul-Key	1	15	15	0

FUMBLES

Miami	No.	Own Rec.	Opp. Rec.
Scott	1	0	0
Anderson	0	1	0
Yepremian	1	0	0

Washington	No.	Own Rec.	Opp. Rec.
Brown	1	0	0
Bass	0	0	1

KICKING

Miami	XP-A	FG-A	FG Made	FG Missed
Yepremian	2-2	0-1	--	42

Washington	XP-A	FG-A	FG Made	FG Missed
Knight	1-1	0-1	--	32

124

PLAY-BY-PLAY

Miami won the coin toss and elected to receive.
FIRST QUARTER
Knight kick to M 7, Morris 17 return (Brunet).
Miami (15:00)
M 24	1-10	Kiick 2 run up middle (McDole).
M 26	2-8	Csonka 2 run off left tackle (Biggs).
M 28	3-6	Griese swing pass to Csonka, loss of 1 (Pardee).
M 27	4-7	Wash. penalized 5 for illegal procedure.
M 32	4-2	Seiple 50 punt, Haymond 7 return.

Washington (12:05)
W 25	1-10	Brown 3 run around right end (Den Herder).
W 28	2-7	Brown 2 run off right tackle (Heinz).
W 30	3-5	Kilmer 7 swing pass to Brown right (Scott).
W 37	1-10	Brown 5 run up middle (Heinz).
W 42	2-5	Harraway run left, loss of 2 (Fernandez).
W 40	3-7	Kilmer rushed, pass to Brown incomplete.
W 40	4-7	Bragg 28 punt, Scott fair catch.

Miami (8:27)
M 32	1-10	Csonka 7 run off left tackle (Hanburger).
M 39	2-3	Griese 7 pass to Warfield left flat (Bass).
M 46	1-10	Morris run right, loss of 1. Play nullified and Miami penalized 15 for illegal use of hands.
M 31	1-25	Griese sacked, loss of 13 (Biggs).
M 18	2-38	Morris 3 run around left end (Bass).
M 21	3-35	Morris 4 run up middle (Talbert).
M 25	4-31	Seiple 35 punt, Vactor fair catch.

Washington (5:05)
W 40	1-10	Harraway 3 run left (Swift).
W 43	2-7	Brown 1 sweep left. Wash. penalized 15 from spot of foul (W 44) for holding.
W 29	2-21	Brown 2 run off left tackle (Fernandez).
W 31	3-19	Kilmer swing pass to Brown, no gain (Matheson).
W 31	4-19	Bragg 34 punt, Scott no return (Vactor), fumbled, Anderson recovered for Miami at M 37.

Miami (2:55)
M 37	1-10	Kiick 3 run left (Pottios).
M 40	2-7	Kiick 8 run around right end (Pardee).
M 48	1-10	Griese 18 pass to Warfield left sideline (Owens).
W 34	1-10	Csonka 2 run right (McDole).
W 32	2-8	Kiick 4 run left (Mcdole).
W 28	3-4	Griese 28 pass to Twilley deep right (caught at W 5), touchdown (:01). Yepremian kicked extra point.

Miami scoring drive: 63 yards, 6 plays, 2:54.
Yepremian kick to W 13, Haymond 18 return (Mandich).
END OF FIRST QUARTER:
Miami 7, Washington 0
SECOND QUARTER
Washington (15:00)
W 31	1-10	Brown 1 run right (Den Herder).
W 32	2-9	Harraway 1 run up middle (Heinz).
W 33	3-8	Kilmer pass to C. Taylor intercepted at M 45, Scott 8 return (Hermeling).

Miami (13:10)
W 47	1-10	Griese 20 pass to Fleming. Play nullified and Miami penalized 15 for illegal man downfield (Kuechenberg).
M 38	1-25	Morris 3 run up middle (Pottios).
M 41	2-22	Csonka 6 run up middle (Riggs).
M 47	3-16	Griese 4 pass to Kiick (Pardee).
W 49	4-12	Seiple 49 punt into end zone, touchback.

Washington (10:40)
W 20	1-10	Brown 2 run off right tackle (Anderson).
W 22	2-8	Kilmer 11 pass to Brown (Scott).
W 33	1-10	Brown 3 run up middle (Den Herder).
W 36	2-7	Kilmer pass to C. Taylor incomplete.
W 36	3-7	Brown draw middle, loss of 2 (Fernandez).
W 34	4-9	Bragg 38 punt, Scott 4 return (Alston).

Miami (7:35)
M 32	1-10	Csonka 13 run up middle (R. Taylor).
M 45	1-10	Kiick 8 sweep right (Pottios).
W 47	2-2	Griese 47 pass to Warfield deep, touchdown. Play nullified and Miami penalized 5 for illegal procedure (Briscoe).
M 48	2-7	Morris 1 sweep right (Fischer).
M 49	3-6	Griese sacked, loss of 6 (Talbert).
M 43	4-12	Seiple 42 punt, Haymond 2 return (Ginn).

Washington (5:41)
W 17	1-10	Kilmer 8 swing pass to Jefferson (Mumphord).
W 25	2-2	Harraway 8 run up middle (Anderson).
W 33	1-10	C. Taylor 8 reverse right (Mumphord).
W 41	2-2	Harraway 4 run up middle (Kolen).
W 45	1-10	Harraway 1 run up middle (Fernandez).
W 46	2-9	Brown 6 run left (Anderson). Two-Minute Warning.

| M 48 | 3-3 | Kilmer rushed, pass to Brown intercepted at M 41, Buoniconti 32 return. |

Miami (1:51)
W 27	1-10	Kiick 3 run up middle (Talbert).
W 24	2-7	Csonka 3 run around right end (Sistrunk).
W 21	3-4	Griese 19 pass to Mandich, diving catch right sideline.
W 2	1-goal	Kiick 1 run right tackle (Hanburger).
W 1	2-goal	Kiick 1 run over right guard, touchdown (:18). Yepremian kicked extra point.

Miami scoring drive: 27 yards, 5 plays, 1:33.
Miami 14, Washington 0
Yepremian kick to W 21, Haymond 12 return.
Washington (:18)
| W 33 | 1-10 | Kilmer pass to Harraway off of Stanfill's deflection, loss of 3. |
| W 30 | 2-13 | Brown 3 run around left end (Stanfill). |

END OF SECOND QUARTER:
Miami 14, Washington 0
THIRD QUARTER
Yepremian kick to W 15, Mul-Key 15 return (Stuckey).
Washington (15:00)
W 30	1-10	Kilmer 11 pass to Smith (Kolen).
W 41	1-10	Brown 2 run right tackle (Den Herder).
W 43	2-8	Kilmer pass to C. Taylor incomplete.
W 43	3-8	Kilmer 15 pass to C. Taylor (Mumphord).
M 42	1-10	Kilmer 15 pass to Jefferson (Johnson).
M 27	1-10	Kilmer 7 pass to Jefferson right (Mumphord).
M 20	2-3	Harraway 3 run right (Den Herder).
M 17	1-10	Kilmer pass to C. Taylor right (at M 2) broken up (Scott).
M 17	2-goal	Kilmer screen pass to Harraway right incomplete.
M 17	3-10	Kilmer sacked, loss of 8 (Fernandez).
M 25	4-18	Knight's 32-yard field goal attempt was wide right, no good.

Miami (10:21)
M 20	1-10	Csonka run left tackle, no gain (Pottios).
M 20	2-10	Csonka 5 run right end (Fischer).
M 25	3-5	Csonka 2 run up middle (McDole).
M 27	4-3	Seiple 49 punt, Haymond return, loss of 6 (Ginn).

Washington (8:17)
W 18	1-10	Brown 7 sweep right (Fernandez).
W 25	2-3	Harraway 6 run up middle (Den Herder).
W 31	1-10	Brown 9 run right end (Buoniconti).
W 40	2-1	Brown 3 run right tackle (Heinz).
W 43	1-10	Kilmer 13 pass to Jefferson left (Anderson).
M 44	1-10	Kilmer pass to Jefferson deep incomplete.
M 44	2-10	Kilmer pass to C. Taylor incomplete.
M 44	3-10	Wash. penalized 5 for false start.
M 49	3-15	Kilmer pass to McNeil underthrown, incomplete.
M 49	4-15	Bragg 32 punt, Scott fair catch.

Miami (5:09)
M 17	1-10	Morris 6 run around left end (Hanburger).
M 23	2-4	Csonka 12 run left tackle (Taylor).
M 35	1-10	Csonka 49 run up middle after breaking several tackles (Pardee, Owens).
W 16	1-10	Morris 4 run around right end (Sistrunk).
W 12	2-6	Morris 5 run up middle (Pottios).
W 7	3-1	Kiick 2 run up middle (Riggs).
W 5	1-goal	Csonka run right tackle, no gain (Talberg).
W 5	2-goal	Griese pass to Fleming underthrown, intercepted by a leaping Owens in end zone, touchback.

Washington (:25)
| W 20 | 1-10 | Brown reverse left, loss of 6 (Swift). |

END OF THIRD QUARTER:
Miami 14, Washington 0
FOURTH QUARTER
W 14	2-16	Brown 1 run left end (Kolen).
W 15	3-15	Kilmer 12 swing pass to Brown right (Anderson), fumbled, ball rolled out of bounds.
W 27	4-3	Bragg 24 punt, Anderson fair catch.

Miami (14:05)
M 49	1-10	Morris 2 run right end (Biggs).
W 49	2-8	Griese pass to Warfield incomplete.
W 49	3-8	Griese 2 swing pass to Kiick (Hanburger).
W 47	4-6	Seiple 36 punt, Vactor fair catch.

Washington (12:26)
W 11	1-10	Kilmer 7 pass to Jefferson left (Johnson).
W 18	2-3	Brown 6 run up middle (Kolen).
W 24	1-10	Smith 6 reverse right (Matheson).
W 30	2-4	Brown 11 sweep left (Buoniconti).
W 41	1-10	Kilmer 9 run evading pass rush (Matheson).
50	2-1	Harraway 8 run right tackle (Fernandez).

M 42	1-10	Harraway 5 run left (Matheson).
M 37	2-5	Brown 4 run up middle (Stanfill).
M 33	3-1	Brown 5 run right (Kolen).
M 28	1-10	Kilmer 9 run evading pass rush (Matheson).
M 19	2-1	Kilmer 5 pass to C. Taylor (Mumphord).
M 14	1-10	Brown 4 sweep right (Anderson).
M 10	2-6	Kilmer pass to Smith end zone hit crossbar, incomplete.
M 10	3-6	Kilmer pass to C. Taylor middle intercepted 3 yards into end zone, Scott 55 return (Harraway).

Miami (5:08)
W 48	1-10	Csonka 7 run up middle (McDole).
W 41	2-3	Kiick 4 run right (Talbert).
W 37	1-10	Kiick 3 run up middle (Pardee).
W 34	2-7	Csonka run left tackle, no gain (Riggs).
W 34	3-7	Griese pass to Twilley deep incomplete.
W 34	4-7	Yepremian's 42-yard field goal attempt was blocked by Brundige, recovered by Yepremian, rollout right, fumbled, recovered by Wash., Bass 49 return down sideline, touchdown (2:07). Knight kicked extra point.

Miami 14, Washington 7
Knight kick to goal line, Morris 16 return (Owens). Two-Minute Warning.
Miami (2:07)
M 16	1-10	Morris 3 run around right end (out of bounds).
M 19	2-7	Griese 11 pass to Warfield left sideline (Owens).
M 30	1-10	Kiick run right tackle, loss of 1 (Owens). Wash.-first time out (1:39).
M 29	2-11	Csonka run around left end (Matheson). Wash.-second time out (1:31).
M 33	3-7	Morris 3 sweep right (Pardee). Wash.-third time out (1:23).
M 36	4-4	Seiple 40 punt, Haymond 6 return (Ginn).

Washington (1:14)
W 30	1-10	Kilmer pass to Brown incomplete (Kolen).
W 30	2-10	Kilmer pass to C. Taylor overthrown (1:04).
W 30	3-10	Kilmer swing pass to Brown, loss of 3 (Stanfill).
W 26	4-14	Kilmer sacked, loss of 9 (Stanfill).

FINAL SCORE:
Miami 14, Washington 7
FINAL RECORDS:
Miami 17-0, Washington 13-4

In Super Bowl VI, the year before, the opposing head coach, Tom Landry of the Dallas Cowboys, said he couldn't name any of the Miami Dolphins' defensive players and a nickname was born. So was a feeling.

"We lost the game, got steamrolled pretty good," fullback Larry Csonka says. "And the feeling was just miserable. I really believe the whole perfect-season idea began that day. It became a launching pad for us, a call to arms, a real impetus. The next season, we just made the ball bounce our way every week.

"I mean, nobody's perfect, right? But we were. For one season, we sure were."

Going into Super Bowl VII, the Dolphins were undefeated, untied, and apparently unappreciated. Incredibly, the Washington Redskins were favored by three points.

"That was the final indignity," remembers Csonka, one of the most recognizable Dolphins. "A great surge of arousal overcame us. Our pride factor was hyperactive. The two superlatives that team had were pride and intelligence.

"And, oh yeah, Don Shula."

How those odds were determined—some said Miami had played an easy schedule, others claimed the Dolphins had been lucky in the playoffs—did not matter to the Dolphins' players. Only that they were the underdogs.

"Sure, we resented the heck out of that," says linebacker-defensive end Bob Matheson, a key factor in the Dolphins' 53 defense. "I mean, how can you be undefeated after sixteen games and not be favored to win in the seventeenth?"

It was an easy flag to rally around. But it was not the reason they won the game. Former all-pro guard Larry Little says that the slight may have offered "a speck of motivation," but the essence of what the Miami Dolphins were all about was "a supreme inner confidence. We believed in ourselves first and foremost. We took a lot of satisfaction in being able to self-motivate. That thing about us not being favored to win when we were undefeated, that was nothing but a little extra push. To me the real motivation was losing Super Bowl VI. We started

the season determined to get back to the scene of the crime, so to speak. But the real reason we went undefeated was we were simply a damn good team."

Little laughs at the memory. He speaks of subtle domination, of intense focus, and of immense motivation. And he talks of the final punctuation, the exclamation point of victory in Super Bowl VII, "the most one-sided 14-7 victory ever recorded."

On the cross-country flight to Los Angeles, Marv Fleming, the tight end who'd played for Green Bay in the first two Super Bowls, made a fist for the benefit of the several players who were gathered around him. It made the huge ring on his finger protrude even more.

"Super Bowl rings have special powers," Fleming said. "This is one of the ones I got when I was with the Packers. Win one of these and you're the best. To win it all…man, you've just got to know what it's like."

They stared, like children at a pet store window. Fleming sensed their awe and tried to turn it into inspiration.

"Take a good look, fellas," he said. "You know we have a chance to be the best ever. *Undefeated Miami Dolphins.* We can get rings like nobody else ever had."

Meanwhile, on another chartered flight bound for Los Angeles, George Allen, who never met a motivational ploy he didn't like, was busy thinking about running backs. The Redskins' head coach had decided Csonka was the key to the game. Stop him and the Redskins could win. Miami was not a one-dimensional team—"They were so efficient in every facet that you could understand why they were a dynasty," Allen says today—but he felt that the one thing Miami could not live without was ball control. And Csonka was the key element to that.

Of course, the Redskins could run the ball well, too. Larry Brown had rushed for a team-record 1,216 yards, barely missing the NFL rushing title. Wide receivers Charley Taylor and Roy Jefferson and tight end Jerry Smith were skilled, dangerous pass catchers. Quarterback Sonny Jurgensen had been lost for the season with an Achilles tendon injury in late October, but Billy Kilmer had led Washington to an 8-2 record down the stretch, including two playoff wins.

But Allen also worried. His team had played so well, so emotionally, in winning the NFC Championship Game against the Cowboys. Were the Redskins' emotional wells dry? What could he do to get his team back to the same emotional peak? The talk that his team was favored to win disturbed him. George Allen hat-

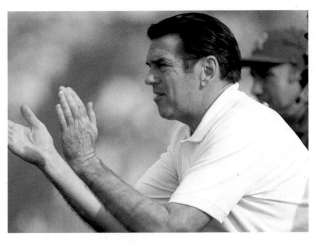

Miami quarterback Bob Griese, making his first start since suffering a broken leg in October, completed 8 of 11 passes. He threw a 28-yard touchdown pass to wide receiver Howard Twilley in the first quarter.

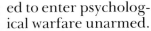
Inspirational George Allen coached the Redskins to the Super Bowl in his second season.

ed to enter psychological warfare unarmed.

When he checked into the team hotel and saw the blue and white bedspreads, he almost smiled. At the Redskins' practice field, where blue and white shoes and blue and white duffel bags were waiting for each player, Allen turned the smile into a forced frown of anger.

"I think someone was expecting the Dallas Cowboys to be here," Allen announced in calculated disgust. "Nobody respects my bunch of old-timers, my Over the Hill Gang."

Informed again that his team was favored to win, Allen said, "It's nice to know some people have faith in my bunch of old men. I know I sure do."

The Redskins had lost three games during the season but they appeared to have momentum on their side during the playoffs. In consecutive games against Green Bay and Dallas, Allen's senior citizens had not allowed a touchdown. In contrast, Miami had seemed sluggish in its victories, relying on a blocked punt and then a fake punt to pull out victories over Cleveland and Pittsburgh.

So the unbeaten looked beatable. Allen said this only to his team, of course. He told a different story to the rest of the world in the week leading up to the seventh Super Sunday.

"Miami is the best team I've seen in my career," he told the media. "We'll be lucky to stay on the same field with them."

Shula would not to be forced into any corners by such a flood of syrup. "George Allen said the other day that his team had never lost a game when it was raining," Shula said. "So if it does rain on Sunday, we plan to forfeit."

Mind games do not win football games, however. While Allen and Shula jousted daily for public consumption, real football was going on behind closed doors.

Shula had a problem. Whom would he start at quarterback? In the fifth game of the season, San Diego's Ron East and David (Deacon) Jones had sandwiched Bob Griese as he tried to pass. Griese's right leg was broken, his ankle dislocat-

Larry Brown led the Redskins with 72 rushing yards, but it took him 22 carries to do it as the Dolphins played outstanding defense. Brown was the NFL's second-leading rusher in 1972 with 1,216 yards.

ed. Shula turned to a familiar face for help.

Earl Morrall, who had been Shula's starting quarterback in Super Bowl III when the two were at Baltimore, had been a waiver addition for this very reason. In between his stints with Shula, he had been the winning quarterback in Super Bowl V after replacing the injured Johnny Unitas.

Morrall lumbered off the bench and the Dolphins won. And kept winning.

Guard Bob Kuechenberg says today that anyone who still underestimates and doesn't appreciate what the 1972 Dolphins were, should ask how many teams could survive the loss of a quarterback of Bob Griese's stature, an eventual Pro Football Hall of Fame quarterback, and still make it to the Super Bowl.

Kuechenberg, who, like Little, became an all-pro guard, says, "We went nine-and-oh in the regular season without our Hall of Fame quarterback. Earl did a great job. But the beauty of that team was the totality of team concept."

Shula struggled with his dilemma on the eve of the game. Morrall had been flat in the game against Pittsburgh and Griese had come on to pull out the victory. Shula realized he would be opening himself up for second-guessing, but he decided to go with Griese. Morrall, gracious, gallant, and loyal as always, accepted the decision gracefully.

The Redskins said it did not matter who Miami played at quarterback. If Miami had to rely on either Griese or Morrall to pass a lot, it meant the Dolphins were in trouble.

Miami's Paul Warfield was all alone when he caught a 47-yard touchdown pass from Bob Griese in the second quarter, but it was nullified by an illegal procedure penalty. Warfield caught three passes that counted.

Washington quarterback Billy Kilmer spent a frustrating afternoon in the Coliseum. He passed for only 104 yards, threw three interceptions, was sacked twice, and was unable to produce a touchdown.

"It's their running game that scares me most," Allen said.

Miami had set an NFL record by running for 2,960 yards. Csonka and Eugene (Mercury) Morris had become the first two players from the same team to gain 1,000 yards each in the same season. In addition, Shula had the extra dimension of Jim Kiick, a tough inside runner who also had great hands. Kiick had lost his starting position to Morris at the outset of the season, but Allen predicted that Miami would go to its bench and use the veteran in key situations.

Kiick remembers that season as one of both extreme frustra-

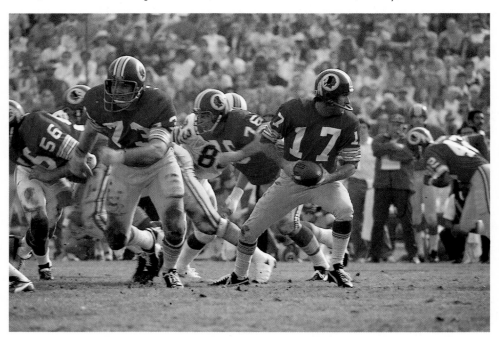

tion and great satisfaction.

Jim Mandich flipped the ball to an official after his 19-yard catch set up Miami's second score.

aged to put everyone together. Everyone had their own personalities until we hit the field. Then everyone became best friends. And we gave the man one-hundred percent."

Kiick scored the winning touchdown against Cleveland in the first playoff game, then scored the go-ahead touchdown against Pittsburgh in the AFC Championship Game.

In the week before Super Bowl VII, Kiick said, "I consider myself a money player. And this game is for all the money. Yeah, I'd like to have a hand in the outcome. I'd like to contribute."

Kiick scored what turned out to be the winning touchdown of the Super Bowl. It was, remembers Kiick, "my specialty—the one-yard gallop."

As far as football games go, the Dolphins' seventeenth victory of the season was not exceptionally gorgeous. In other words, it was vintage Dolphins football.

Griese threw just 11 passes, completing 8. One of the completions was a 28-yard touchdown pass to Howard Twilley in the first quarter.

"It's a tough position for a coach, playing people, not playing people," Kiick says today. "I hated it, not playing, and Shula knew that. But Merc [Morris] and I got along remarkably well. We understood the most important thing, which was to win the Super Bowl.

"We had a lot of rebel people on that team. There was a lot of turmoil. Lots of players were trying to get in the lineup. There was complaining everywhere except on the field. Somehow Shula man-

On the second play after Mandich's catch, Jim Kiick followed a block by Bob Kuechenberg (67) and went a yard for the touchdown that boosted Miami's lead to 14-0. Kiick gained 38 yards on 12 carries.

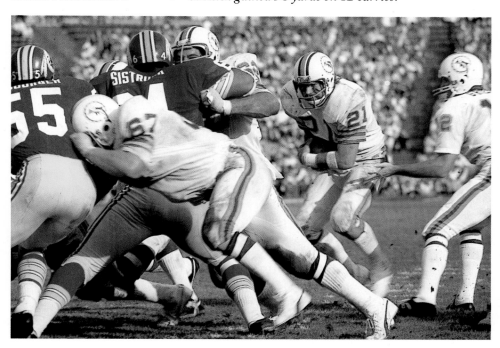

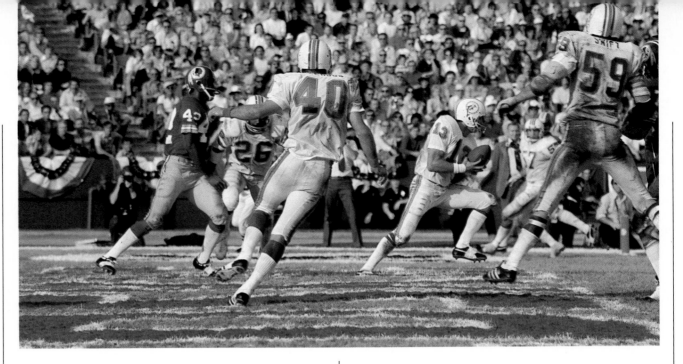

Dolphins safety Jake Scott was named most valuable player, thanks to two big interceptions. In the fourth quarter, he jumped in front of Charley Taylor (42, rear) in the end zone and returned the errant pass 55 yards.

It was, both thrower and catcher recall, a play designed during the week.

"It was third-and-short," explained Griese after the game. "I thought they'd be in man-to-man coverage. The Redskins doubled Paul Warfield. That left Twilley in single coverage."

Twilley, a possession-type receiver who had no speed but who managed to hold onto his job for 11 seasons, says the Dolphins had gone to slant patterns to the inside to ensure the first down all season long.

"But talking during the week," Twilley says now, "Bob and I figured Pat Fischer [Redskins cornerback] had spotted the tendency on film and would be ready for it. So I did a little three-step move inside and then broke to the outside. Fischer bit."

Fischer concedes it was "a great move by a smart receiver. He'd been running down and inside almost every play till then. Then he just changed directions on me. I recovered and was closing on him while the ball was still in the air, and I had a choice to make—tackle him or go for the ball. I got greedy and tried to knock the ball away and I didn't get it. If I'd gone for the tackle, I think I could have kept him out of the end zone. But I don't know—with their runners, they might have scored anyway."

The 7-0 lead looked as if it might stand up. Washington could not do anything against the No Name Defense. The Redskins' running attack was ineffective. Miami's defensive line held ground and waited for the Redskins' running backs to commit themselves. That nulli-

Powerful fullback Larry Csonka was the game's leading rusher as he rumbled for 112 yards on just 15 carries. In the third quarter, he broke several tackles on a 49-yard run to the Washington 16.

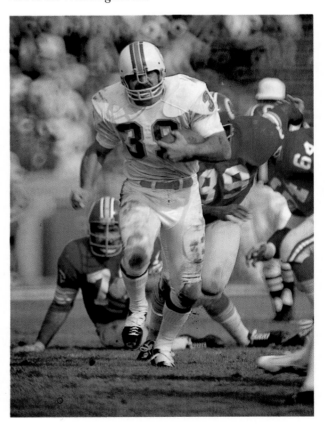

VII

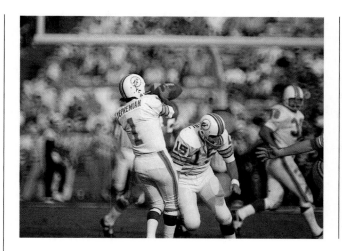

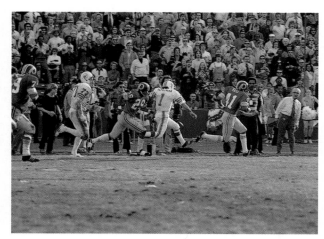

fied Washington's trap plays, neutralizing the cut back skills of Larry Brown.

The Redskins made it into Miami territory only once in the first half, and that mini-drive was aborted by one of quarterback Billy Kilmer's three interceptions, this one picked off by middle linebacker Nick Buoniconti.

Miami took that second-quarter miscue and marched to its second touchdown. Earlier, an apparent touchdown pass from Griese to Warfield had been called back because of a procedure penalty. This time, typical Miami precision and balance led to seven more points. Griese, who completed all six of his pass attempts in the first half, connected with tight end Jim Mandich, who rolled out of bounds at the Washington 2-yard line.

On his second try, Kiick scored.

"It was 14-0 and it

Late in the game, after he had a field-goal attempt blocked, Miami kicker Garo Yepremian (1, left) tried to pass the ball. But it squirted to the Redskins' Mike Bass (41, right), who ran 49 yards for a touchdown.

Don Shula had good reason to smile. He had just coached Miami to the NFL's first perfect season.

should have been 21-0," Kuechenberg remembers. "What'd they have for yardage at the half? Seventy-something yards? We were in the process of dominating them. But it was our nature to control games. We knew we didn't need any more points. Our defense was in control there. And then we come up for the field goal in the last couple of minutes. That would have made it 17-0, right? Gee, that would have been a nice final score, wouldn't it? Perfect score, in fact.

"Then Garo did his little thing."

VII

Garo's "little thing" occurred in the fourth quarter, after safety Jake Scott's second interception had foiled Washington's second serious threat of the half. (Curt Knight had missed a 32-yard field goal in the third quarter.) After Scott returned his end-zone interception 55 yards, the Dolphins moved to the Washington 34-yard line before stalling. Yepremian came in to attempt a 42-yard field goal.

"I thought I was doing something good, something that might help. It turned into tragedy," Yepremian says today.

The kick was low. Washington's Bill Brundige blocked it. Suddenly the ball bounced up and Yepremian had it.

Morrall, the holder for the kick, remembers that he was trying to get to the ball before Yepremian.

"I felt I was a little more experienced in such situations," Morrall says. "The smart thing to do, of course, is to fall on the ball."

But Yepremian got there first and enterprise overruled common sense.

Washington defensive back Mike Bass saw Yepremian grab the ball and immediately he knew the kicker wasn't going to try to run with it.

"We were on the same taxi squad in Detroit," Bass says. "I'd seen Garo run. I knew he couldn't run."

Bass rushed toward Yepremian, who held up the ball and tried to pass it. Only it slipped from his hands and wobbled into the air...directly to Bass at the Dolphins' 49-yard line.

"It was pretty much a straight line from there," Bass says.

If it'd been anywhere else but the Super Bowl, it would have drawn roars of laughter. A comedy routine, a Max Sennett short subject, the Keystone Kops. But the sudden 14-7 margin was no joke. And there were more than two minutes left to play.

Allen and his Redskins still had a chance. The Dolphins anticipated an onside kick.

But Allen ordered Knight, his kicker, to send it deep.

"We had all our time outs remaining," he says. "We couldn't risk giving them good field position."

In the huddle after the kickoff, Csonka said,

"This is it, guys—what we've been waiting for. Kill the clock."

Tackle Norm Evans added, "We don't have to say anything. Let's just do it."

There still was more than a minute left, however, when the Dolphins were forced to punt.

"I was praying the whole time on the sideline," Yepremian says.

Two passes by Kilmer were incomplete. Then a pass to Larry Brown lost four yards. Finally, in a fitting finale, Kilmer was sacked by a couple of No-Names—Bill Stanfill and Vern Den Herder.

"This is the ultimate," Shula said. "This team has gone into an area no other team has gone. It is...the ultimate."

The ensuing years have identified the '72 Dolphins not only as a great unit or team but also as individual stars. There are now four of them in the Pro Football Hall of Fame—Griese, Warfield, Csonka, and center Jim Langer.

Kuechenberg finds great irony in this.

"Just take our offensive line as an example," he says. "Four out of five members were at one time or another Pro Bowlers. And we were castoffs and retreads. Me—I was cut three different times from teams. Jim Langer was cut by the Browns. Wayne Moore, we got him when the 49ers tried to sneak him through waivers. Larry Little was a defensive end who weighed about a thousand pounds for San Diego. Norm Evans was left unprotected by Houston in the '66 expansion draft. And Monte Clark did the best job of offensive line coaching I've ever seen."

Kuechenberg remembers one day late in the season, when he and Langer allowed themselves to talk out loud about the unbeaten streak.

"We were in the weight room lifting," Kuechenberg says, "and I said, 'Okay, Jim, which one are we gonna lose?' We were nine-oh or ten-oh at the time and I said, 'We gotta lose one game or else we'll jinx ourselves for the playoffs. Nobody goes undefeated in the NFL.' That's just what I said that day. We were not dedicated to the proposition of being perfect, only to getting back to the Super Bowl and getting rid of the empty feeling. Perfection just came with it."

T

he hot new angle for the first—and so far only—Super Bowl to be played in Texas was this: For the first time, a team with American Football League roots was favored.

The Miami Dolphins, the defending world champions, beaten only twice that season and not at all the year before, were a six-point pick over the Minnesota Vikings in Super Bowl VIII in Houston's Rice Stadium. It was a match made in handicapper's heaven, giving birth to what became known as John Madden's Law. Said Madden, the coach whose Raiders would face the Vikings three years later (and also beat them), "Look for the team that complains first. That team will lose. It never fails."

Fair enough. The Vikings broke in front by griping about the condition of the locker room at their training facility, a high school stadium in Houston. Players and coaches had to change clothes in one cramped room, uncarpeted, with no lockers. Most of the shower heads did not function, and the Vikings hesitated to use the few that did for fear of disturbing a family of sparrows nesting in the area.

But the Madden Method of Super Bowl forecasting also said you should take note of the team that seemed to be the more distracted. There were reports of dissension among the Dolphins, the result of owner Joe Robbie's decision to allow the players to bring their wives at the club's expense.

Safety Jake Scott argued that the bachelors, for whom he was the spokesman, should have been able to invite their mothers. Robbie held firm: wives only.

Dolphins head coach Don Shula thought the story was "blown out of proportion," indicating how little coaches understand Super Bowl coverage. Imagine the tabloid headlines:

"LOCKER ROOM SCANDAL: Vikings Must Dress on Bare Floor! Hang Underwear on Nail. One Table for Eight Coaches!"

"SEX DISCRIMINATION! Wives of Miami Players Flown in by Team. Single Players Want Their Mommies."

In less than a decade, it had been established that the two most nagging distractions at a Super Bowl were tickets and personal arrangements. John Madden warned his players to dispose of their tickets no later than one week before the game, no matter how many they held or who begged for them. Madden's other hard rule limited each player to one guest: "Wife, mother, girl friend, favorite grade school teacher, whatever. That's it."

The pregame fussiness appeared to be a tie, but months after the game head coach Bud Grant would admit that his complaints about Minnesota's treatment were calculated. He had even taken a verbal swat at the commissioner's office. "This is the Super Bowl, not a pickup game," he said. "The league is responsible and Pete Rozelle runs the league."

As the designated home team, the Dolphins had access to the Oilers' practice complex, a few blocks from their hotel. The angry Grant pointed out that the Vikings had a 20-minute bus ride to a field that lacked blocking sleds. "I don't think our players have seen anything like this since junior high school," he muttered.

For his uncharacteristic display of temper, the usually impassive Grant, known around the NFL as the only coach who smiled less than Dallas's Tom Landry, drew a $1,500 fine. Actually, Grant was play-acting, tossing a few scraps to the media in the hope of sheltering his players.

If either side harbored any real concern, it was the Dolphins, who were troubled by the spongy conditions of the playing surface at Houston's Rice Stadium. Running teams prefer fast tracks, and Miami's offense, which featured the footwork of Larry Csonka, Eugene (Mercury) Morris, and Jim Kiick, was so run oriented it was almost collegiate. The Dolphins had all but buried the forward pass like an old bone.

The game promised an old-fashioned dust-up, the Dolphins' relentless ground attack against the Vikings' defense, which was in its prime. Three of the front four—Carl Eller, Alan Page, and Jim Marshall—would stay intact through most of the 1970s as the heart of the Purple People Eaters. The fourth, Gary Larsen, retired at the end of the 1974 season.

That vivid label was in almost comic relief to

Miami's No-Name Defense, inspired by a quote from Tom Landry two years earlier: "I can't recall the names of the Miami defensive unit."

Minnesota quarterback Fran Tarkenton, then with the Giants, was in the stands the day Kansas City upset the Vikings in Super Bowl IV. After his stint in New York, he was back where he belonged, where his pro career had begun 12 years earlier.

The teams, coaches, and quarterbacks who would be on display in Houston on January 13, 1974, disputed two of the popular myths about the NFL: The players were cloned, and coaches copied last year's successful coach.

Bob Griese was a cool Hoosier, scholastic, ideal for Shula's stiff discipline and directness. The Miami offense thrived not on the big play, but on avoiding the fatal mistake. Griese didn't dazzle you with his raw gifts, but he won with consistency, adroitly orchestrating the talent around him.

"In a game," Dolphins linebacker Nick Buoniconti says, "he was like a real general in a real war. Distant. Didn't talk to anybody on the sidelines, except maybe Shula." Griese made himself into a take-charge guy, overcoming his mild-mannered appearance, the first quarterback in memory to wear eyeglasses in a game.

Like Griese, Tarkenton looked smaller than 6 feet. He was quick, the prototype of the scrambling quarterback. Fran breaking out of the pocket was a lineman's nightmare. The threat made him a record-setting passer.

Yet, all his career, Tarkenton had to overcome the rap against him expressed by his first pro coach, Norm Van Brocklin: "He will win games he should lose, and lose games he should win, but he will never win the games he *has* to win."

It was cool, cloudy, and foggy when Miami and Minnesota met in Rice Stadium in the only Super Bowl played in Houston. The first seven Super Bowls alternated among Los Angeles, Miami, and New Orleans.

Of course, that knock was lurking out there in the shadows of Super Bowl VIII. Yet Tarkenton never lacked respect from opposing players. One of the key matchups would be between Tarkenton and Scott, Miami's safety, both of whom lived in, Athens, Georgia, in their youth.

The Dolphins—here stacking up Oscar Reed—shut out the Vikings for the first three quarters, leading 24-0.

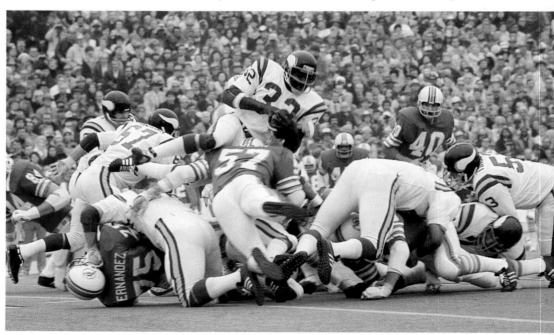

Five years older, Tarkenton was the star of the high school football team when Scott was in the eighth grade. "He was just the same then—a real leader," Scott said. "I knew his two brothers. Years later, Fran recruited me for the University of Georgia."

In college, Tarkenton took a course in psychology from Scott's mother. He watched Jake play YMCA football, and, years later, rated him with Green Bay's Willie Wood as the best free safeties he ever faced.

Students of the game wrung their hands in anticipation at the idea of Tarkenton taking on the defensive scheme that had helped the Dolphins to a 17-0 record a year earlier—the inventive "53 defense." The prospect excited the Dolphins, as well. Scott snapped his fingers and said, "Fran could turn a bad play into a good one, just like that."

"He had a sixth sense," Buoniconti says. "He seemed to know where the pressure was and he moved away from it so fast that he never took a shot from the blindside. He did everything by instinct, so we never knew where he'd be. So the whole thing had to start with our defensive ends, Bill Stanfill and Vern Den Herder. They had to control Tarkenton. If they let him roll outside, it would be a long afternoon."

Linebacker Bob Matheson, who once had played defensive end for Cleveland, was what made the "53 defense" click. Matheson could drop off and help with pass coverage, or enable the Dolphins to send as many as six people on a blitz (Matheson's jersey number was 53; coach-

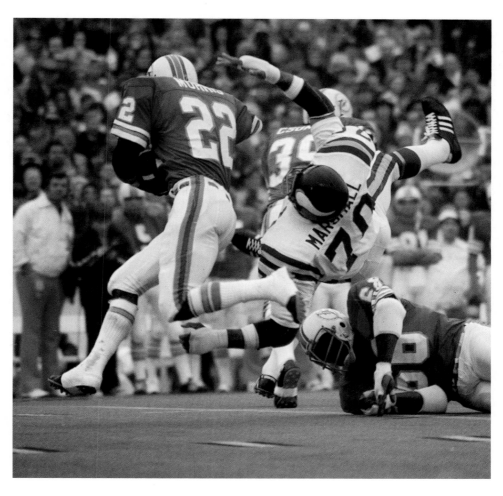

As guard Larry Little sent Vikings end Jim Marshall flying with a big block, Miami's Mercury Morris gained some of his 34 yards. The efficient Dolphins controlled the ball on the ground, rushing for 196 yards.

es usually aren't very creative with monikers).

Shula, with a 1-2 record in the Super Bowl, was the only coach to lose with different teams, the Colts (in III) and the Dolphins (in VI). The Vikings were making their second unsuccessful trip to what had become the crowning game. After this one, no one would need to ask who was buried in Grant's Tomb.

Shula was a born organizer and a perfectionist. As a high school baseball player in a small town in Ohio, he corrected mistakes before his coach did. But he was not a great athlete. He had to earn a full scholarship his second year at John Carroll University in Cleveland.

John Carroll used the Browns' playbook,

On his way to winning most-valuable-player honors, Miami running back Larry Csonka shredded the Vikings' defense for a Super Bowl record 145 yards on 33 carries. He ran for 112 yards in Super Bowl VII.

which was provided by Paul Brown, who lived in the neighborhood. When Brown later drafted Shula as a defensive back, Shula's command of the system enabled him to make the squad.

He was too slow to cover the speed burners and too small to back up the line.

In practice, he had to cover Cleveland's great receiver, Mac Speedie. "He'd lose me every time," Shula says now. "He'd fake out and go in, or fake in and go out. It didn't make any difference; he'd lose me. Once, when he cut in, I stayed with him and he said, 'What did you do, kid, guess right?'"

The fact that Shula lasted seven seasons in the NFL is testimony to his intelligence and tenacity. Sold by Baltimore to Washington in 1957, he returned six years later to replace Weeb Ewbank, the coach who had sold him. He was 33, the youngest coach in the modern era of the NFL.

Then, in early 1970, despite protests by Colts owner Carroll Rosenbloom, Shula left to coach Miami. He was now in his third successive Super Bowl with the Dolphins.

Bud Grant was that rare athlete, a pro in two sports. In the early 1950s, he was a forward with the Minneapolis Lakers in the NBA, and later a receiver with the Philadelphia Eagles of the NFL. He played his last pro football seasons with Winnipeg in the Canadian Football League, and he began coaching there.

In a league in which the 90-hour work week was not uncommon, Grant's methods were almost alien. He did not let the game consume him, or his players. He reported to his office at 9:30 A.M. and usually departed by 6 P.M. The hours allowed him to pursue a backyard hobby of studying wildlife that he cared for in captivity. The habits of ducks, quail, pheasants, and ravens fascinated him. It also allowed him to fish, to hunt, to relax.

There was no traditional rivalry between the teams, no Sicilian vendettas. There was nothing more heated than a crack by Vikings cornerback Bobby Bryant, who would have to cover Paul Warfield. When the swift wide receiver pulled a hamstring in practice, Bryant was quoted as wishing him a full recovery, "because I don't want to hear any of his excuses. I want him to be at full speed."

For Notre Dame fans, there was a clash of former Fighting Irish teammates, Miami guard Bob Kuechenberg and Minnesota defensive tackle Alan Page. Otherwise, all the props, all the names and no-names, were in place.

The game began in a gray mist that hung like

gauze over Rice Stadium, reducing the office towers of downtown Houston to ghostly silhouettes. The mist was nothing compared to the fog that soon enveloped the Vikings.

Garo Yepremian watched his 28-yard field goal sail through the uprights as he extended Miami's lead to 17-0 in the second quarter. The Dolphins are the only team to play in three successive Super Bowls.

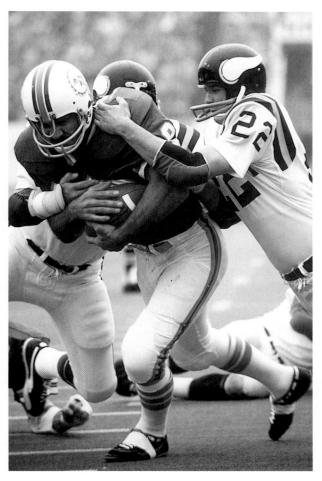

Tackling Csonka was like trying to tackle a moving Coke machine. When he opened the game's scoring with a five-yard touchdown run in the first quarter, he dragged Vikings safety Paul Krause (22) with him.

Setting the tone for the day, Miami took the opening kickoff and methodically charged into the heralded Minnesota defense. The Dolphins needed 10 plays to travel 62 yards for the game's first touchdown. Except for passes to Jim Mandich and Marlin Briscoe, the diligent Griese stuck to the good AstroTurf, sending Morris wide and letting Csonka pound the middle for 16 yards, then five, eight, and five more, the last for the touchdown. Csonka crossed the goal line with Minnesota's Paul Krause and Jeff Siemon wrapped around him.

The Vikings ran three plays and punted.

Here came the Dolphins again, like an 11-man street sweeper working its way up the block. This drive covered 56 yards, again in 10 plays. Griese passed for two first downs before Kiick, the third man in Miami's running attack, plunged the last yard for his first touchdown of the season.

At the end of the quarter Miami led 14-0. The Vikings had run a total of six plays and advanced as far as their own 23-yard line.

The second quarter featured a 28-yard field goal by Garo Yepremian, the balding little kicker from Cyprus. For Miami, a Super Bowl without Yepremian and his size 7½ shoe would have been unthinkable.

The Dolphins' drive to the Minnesota 21 to set up Yepremian was helped by a 15-yard unsportsmanlike conduct call on linebacker Wally Hilgenberg. Csonka also had five more carries on the march.

That was all the point production in the first half, although Tarkenton moved the Vikings from their own 20 to the Miami 6 with one minute left. The Dolphins had taken control so early and so completely that there was little feeling of tension when the Vikings lined up on fourth-

Minnesota's Chuck Foreman didn't find much room to run. Although he gained 801 yards during the regular season, he was held to 18 on seven carries by the Dolphins. As a team, Minnesota ran for only 72 yards.

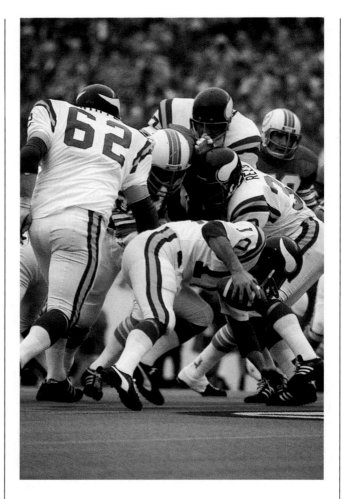

Fran Tarkenton completed 18 of 28 passes and ran four yards for Minnesota's only touchdown, but was frustrated most of the day. Despite help from two Vikings, he was brought down by Miami's Vern Den Herder (center).

and-inches, down by 17 and desperately needing points.

Close to the first down, running back Oscar Reed encountered linebacker Buoniconti, whose jarring tackle forced a fumble that safety Scott recovered. End of threat. For all practical purposes, end of game.

That call was one of the few worth second guessing. Some observers thought the Vikings, in view of their disadvantage, should have taken a field goal. "No," Tarkenton said. "We had the first down. We just fumbled."

To replicate the start of the game, the Dolphins also scored on their first series of the second half. The big play was a 27-yard pass from

from Griese to wide receiver Warfield, who had to be touched down by Bryant, the cornerback whose pregame hope had been that Warfield would be "at full speed." He wasn't, of course. If he had been more than 50 percent, Warfield claimed, he would not have been caught by Bryant.

Csonka scored the touchdown on a play that may have been the day's most symbolic.

At the 2, crouched over center, the usually astute Griese forgot the snap count. So he turned his head over one shoulder and whispered to Csonka: "Hey, what's the count?"

"Two," said a confident Csonka.

From the other side of the backfield, Jim Kiick said, "No, no…it's one."

It was among the most amazing conversations that ever took place in a Super Bowl. Griese decided to believe Csonka, but he learned that he had guessed incorrectly when he started his count and center Jim Langer snapped the ball on "one."

Griese bobbled the ball, but still was able to get it to Csonka, who punched it across for his second touchdown.

Yepremian's third extra point made the Miami lead 24-0. Griese would not attempt another pass the rest of the day. He finished with 6 of 7 for 73 yards.

"We wanted a shutout," said Manny Fernandez, Miami's fine defensive tackle, "but Tarkenton is no quitter."

Tarkenton set what then was a Super Bowl

Csonka plunged two yards for Miami's final touchdown, which boosted the Dolphins' lead to 24-0 in the third quarter. He was consistent, rushing for 78 yards in the first half and 67 in the second for his total of 145.

record for completions—18 of 28 for 182 yards—but he could get his team on the board only once. Early in the fourth quarter, he topped off a 10-play, 57-yard drive by rolling around right end from the 4. He tumbled into the end zone.

The Vikings threatened one more time, but Curtis Johnson intercepted a pass by Tarkenton under the Miami goal post. The Dolphins chewed up the game's final 6½ minutes with Csonka and Kiick alternating running plays.

Having demolished the men from the icelands 24-7 and having won the Super Bowl for the second year in a row, the Dolphins moved into the company of Vince Lombardi's Packers, who won games I and II. "You're living in a classy neighborhood," Csonka says, "when you've done something only one team has done before. We can compare ourselves with any team that's ever played this game."

So wounded and frustrated were the Vikings that they shed their tempers and composure completely in the final turns of the clock. With less than four minutes to play, defensive tackle Alan Page simply leveled Griese after a handoff. It was more than a cheap shot. It was a petty tantrum, and it cost the Vikings 15 yards.

Moments later, in what may have been another Super Bowl record, there were offsetting personal fouls as Page and Kuechenberg acted out a few bars of the Notre Dame Fight Song.

If any one player had overpowered a Super Bowl to this point, it was Csonka. The harder he ran, the lower his right shoulder got to the ground, until he began to look like a guy pushing a Fiat. His 145 yards rushing on 33 carries broke the records set by Matt Snell of the Jets in Super Bowl III.

When Csonka accepted the game's most valuable player trophy he said, dryly, "I want to thank Bud Grant for staying in that same four-three defense all day."

If anyone could afford to gloat, the big Miami fullback could. *Zonk-a*! Let the name roll off your tongue and it sounds like something a karate expert grunts as he breaks bricks.

Csonka's blockers handled the Vikings' front four with stunning ease, blowing them off the line of scrimmage. Then Csonka came at them like a wrecking ball.

"It's not the collision that gets you," said dejected Vikings linebacker Siemon. "It's what happens after you tackle him. His legs are just so strong he keeps moving. He carries you. He's a movable weight."

Csonka reviewed his work with a wryness that was refreshing. Reporters wondered how he received the black eye and swollen nose he sported in the locker room. Without identifying his assailant, he replied, "It was a cheap shot, but an honest cheap shot. He came right at me and threw an elbow right through my mask. I could see the game meant something to him."

If he did not enjoy getting slugged, you could tell that as a professional he admired the aesthetics of it.

This was the year, 1974, when one of the nation's catch phrases was good news/bad news. The Vikings provided several sporting examples of how it worked:

The good news was that John Gilliam returned the second-half kickoff 65 yards.

The bad news was that a clipping penalty rubbed it out.

The good news was that the Vikings, after finally scoring in the first two minutes of the fourth quarter, and trying to make the game respectable, recovered an onside kick.

The bad news was that they were offside.

The good news was that the Vikings forced the Dolphins to punt on one of those rare occasions when they contained their running game.

The bad news was that Miami's Larry Seiple got off a beauty, and the Dolphins' Tim Foley downed it at the Minnesota 3.

If Minnesota had suffered a blocked kickoff, it hardly could have been more painful than the misfortunes that actually befell them. Every break that came loose went the Dolphins' way.

Miami played a game so pure you almost would have to call it virtuous. As clean and obedient as the Boy Scouts who helped seat the 68,142 customers, they did not lose the ball once on a fumble or interception, nor did they draw a single penalty in the first 52 minutes.

The best team ever?

With good conduct, a quick defense, Csonka's raw power, and 32 victories in 34 games over the 1972 and 1973 seasons, the Dolphins made a strong claim.

PLAY-BY-PLAY

Pittsburgh won the coin toss and elected to receive.

FIRST QUARTER

Cox kick to P 22, Pearson 15 return (Martin).

Pittsburgh (15:00)

P 37	1-10	Bleier 3 run off left tackle (Sutherland).
P 40	2-7	Harris run right, slipped, loss of 1 (Winston).
P 39	3-8	Bradshaw sacked, loss of 4 (Lurtsema).
P 35	4-12	Walden 52 punt, McCullum 5 return (Bradley).

Minnesota (13:03)

M 18	1-10	Tarkenton 16 pass to Gilliam right (Wagner).
M 34	1-10	Tarkenton pass to Voigt middle overthrown.
M 34	2-10	Osborn 1 run left (White).
M 35	3-9	Tarkenton pass to Gilliam right incomplete.
M 35	4-9	Eischeid 40 punt, Swann 17 return (Kingsriter).

Pittsburgh (11:52)

P 42	1-10	Pitt. penalized 5 for false start (Mullins).
P 37	1-15	Bleier 18 run right (Krause).
M 45	1-10	Harris 4 run left (Page).
M 41	2-6	Harris run right, loss of 3. Play nullified and Pitt. penalized 15 for clipping.
P 44	2-21	Bradshaw 12 pass to Lewis left (Sutherland).
M 44	3-9	Bradshaw sacked, loss of 8 (Page).
P 48	4-17	Walden 39 punt, N. Wright 1 return (Bradley).

Minnesota (9:17)

M 14	1-10	Foreman run right, loss of 2 (Ham).
M 12	2-12	Tarkenton 4 pass to Osborn (Ham).
M 16	3-8	Tarkenton pass batted down at line (Greenwood).
M 16	4-8	Eischeid 37 punt downed at P 47. Play nullified and Minn. penalized 8 (half the distance) for clipping (McClanahan).
M 8	4-16	Eischeid 36 punt, Edwards no return (Blair).

Pittsburgh (7:21)

M 44	1-10	Bradshaw pass to Lewis middle incomplete.
M 44	2-10	Harris 3 run up middle (Sutherland).
M 41	3-7	Bradshaw 15 pass to Brown right (Poltl).
M 26	1-10	Bleier 4 run left (Hilgenberg).
M 22	2-6	Harris 2 run left (Siemon).
M 20	3-4	Bradshaw pass to Lewis left overthrown.
M 20	4-4	Gerela's 37-yard field goal attempt was wide left.

Minnesota (4:32)

M 20	1-10	Foreman 1 run left (Russell).
M 21	2-9	Tarkenton rushed, pass to Voigt incomplete.
M 21	3-9	Tarkenton pass to Gilliam left incomplete.
M 21	4-9	Eischeid 31 punt downed at P 48.

Pittsburgh (3:37)

P 48	1-10	Bleier 4 run right (Siemon).
M 48	2-6	Shanklin reverse, no gain. Play nullified and Minn. penalized 5 for offsides.
M 43	2-1	Harris 14 run off right tackle (Marshall).
M 29	1-10	Bradshaw 11 bootleg right (N. Wright).
M 18	1-10	Harris run, no gain (Sutherland).
M 18	2-10	Harris 2 run left (Page).
M 16	3-8	Bradshaw pass to Lewis end zone broken up (Wallace).
M 16	4-8	Attempted field goal, bad snap from center, holder Walden recovered own fumble, loss of 7.

Minnesota (:32)

M 23	1-10	Osborn run left, no gain (White).

END OF FIRST QUARTER:
Minnesota 0, Pittsburgh 0

SECOND QUARTER

M 23	2-10	Tarkenton 12 pass to Foreman right (Wagner).
M 35	1-10	Tarkenton pass to Lash deflected (Holmes).
M 35	2-10	Osborn run left, loss of 1 (Holmes).
M 34	3-10	Tarkenton pass to Gilliam left incomplete.
M 34	4-11	Eischeid 38 punt, Edwards 2 return. Pitt. penalized 15 for clipping.

Pittsburgh (13:36)

P 15	1-10	Harris 5 run around right end (Siemon).
P 20	2-5	Bradshaw pass to Stallworth broken up (Wallace).
P 20	3-5	Bradshaw 16 pass to Swann. Play nullified and Pitt. penalized 10 for pass interference (Swann).
P 10	3-15	Bleier 8 run right, fumbled, Poltl recovered for Minn. at P 24.

Minnesota (13:10)

P 24	1-10	Osborn 2 run left (Ham).
P 22	2-8	Tarkenton pass to Foreman right incomplete.
P 22	3-8	Tarkenton pass to Foreman at P 5 overthrown.

P 22	4-8	Cox's 39-yard field goal attempt was wide right.

Pittsburgh (12:09)

P 22	1-10	Bleier run left, loss of 1 (Siemon).
P 21	2-11	Harris 3 run off right tackle (Winston).
P 24	3-8	Bradshaw 22 pass to Stallworth left (Wallace).
P 46	1-10	Bleier 6 run off right tackle (Siemon).
M 48	2-4	Harris 2 run right (Sutherland).
M 46	3-2	Bleier sweep right, no gain (Siemon, Winston).
M 46	4-2	Walden 39 punt, McCullum no return (Shell).

Minnesota (7:56)

M 7	1-10	Foreman 3 run off left tackle (Russell).
M 10	2-7	Tarkenton recovered fumbled handoff in end zone and was downed by White, safety (7:11).

Pittsburgh 2, Minnesota 0

Eischeid free kick to P 35, Harrison no return (out of bounds).

Pittsburgh (7:11)

P 35	1-10	Bradshaw 5 pass to Bleier right (Winston).
P 40	2-5	Harris 2 run around left end (Hilgenberg).
P 42	3-3	Bradshaw screen pass left to Stallworth, loss of 6 (Wallace).
P 36	4-9	Walden 50 punt, McCullum 6 return (Garrett).

Minnesota (5:16)

M 20	1-10	Tarkenton pass incomplete. Play nullified and Pitt. penalized 15 for pass interference (Blount).
M 35	1-10	Osborn run left, loss of 1 (White).
M 34	2-11	Tarkenton 10 pass to Foreman right (Thomas).
M 44	3-1	Foreman 2 run up middle (Lambert).
M 46	1-10	Tarkenton rushed, pass out of bounds.
M 46	2-10	Foreman 2 run up middle (Lambert).
M 48	3-8	Tarkenton 17 pass to Foreman middle (Thomas).
M 35	1-10	Foreman 4 run (Greenwood). Two-Minute Warning.
P 31	2-6	Tarkenton 3 pass to Voigt (out of bounds).
P 28	3-3	Tarkenton 3 pass to Osborn right (Lambert).
P 25	1-10	Tarkenton pass middle deflected by Gilliam and intercepted at goal line, Blount 10 return.

Pittsburgh (1:05)

P 10	1-10	Bradshaw run right, loss of 1 (Marshall).
P 9	2-11	Harris 25 run left (Krause).
P 34	1-10	Bleier run right, loss of 1 (Siemon).
P 33	2-11	Bradshaw 17 run right (Page).

END OF SECOND QUARTER:
Pittsburgh 2, Minnesota 0

THIRD QUARTER

Gerela kick to M 28, B. Brown 2 return, fumbled, Kellum recovered for Pitt. at M 30.

Pittsburgh (14:49)

M 30	1-10	Bleier run right, no gain (Eller).
M 30	2-10	Harris 24 run off left tackle (Sutherland).
M 6	1-goal	Harris run right, loss of 3 (Hilgenberg).
M 9	2-goal	Harris 9 sweep left, touchdown (13:25). Gerela kicked extra point.

Pittsburgh scoring drive: 30 yards, 4 plays, 1:24.

Pittsburgh 9, Minnesota 0

Gerela kick to M 2, McCullum 26 return (Kellum).

Minnesota (13:25)

M 28	1-10	Osborn 2 run right (Holmes).
M 30	2-8	Foreman 1 run right (Greene).
M 31	3-7	Tarkenton 6 pass to Foreman left (Russell).
M 37	4-1	Tarkenton tried to draw Pitt. offsides, both teams ruled offsides, penalties offset.
M 37	4-1	Eischeid 42 punt, Swann 6 return (J. Wright).

Pittsburgh (11:16)

P 27	1-10	Harris recovered own fumble, 9 run right (Page).
P 36	2-1	Harris 4 run right (Winston).
P 40	1-10	Bradshaw 8 pass to Stallworth left (Wallace).
P 48	2-2	Harris 4 run left (Winston).
M 48	1-10	Bradshaw 5 run evading pass rush (Page).
M 43	2-5	Bradshaw 1 run up middle (Page).
M 42	3-4	Bleier run left, no gain (Eller).
M 42	4-4	Walden 42 punt into end zone, touchback.

Minnesota (6:49)

M 20	1-10	Foreman run left, loss of 1 (Russell).
M 19	2-11	Tarkenton pass batted back, caught by Tarkenton, then 41 pass to Gilliam. Completion to Gilliam nullified and Minn. penalized loss of down for illegal forward pass.
M 19	3-11	Foreman 12 run right (Toews).
M 31	1-10	Osborn 1 run right (Holmes).

M 32	2-9	Osborn run left, loss of 5 (Greenwood).
M 27	3-14	Tarkenton 28 pass to Voigt right (Edwards).
P 45	1-10	Foreman run right, loss of 2 (Bradley).
P 47	2-12	Tarkenton pass deflected and intercepted at P 45, Greene 10 return. Pitt. penalized 15 for clipping.

Pittsburgh (2:31)

P 40	1-10	Harris 6 run left (Krause).
P 46	2-4	Harris run left, no gain (Page).
P 46	3-4	Bradshaw pass intercepted at M 49, Siemon 6 return. Play nullified and Minn. penalized 5 for offsides.
M 49	1-10	Harris 1 run left (Hilgenberg).
M 48	2-9	Harris 3 sweep left (Eller).

END OF THIRD QUARTER:
Pittsburgh 9, Minnesota 0

FOURTH QUARTER

M 45	3-6	Bradshaw pass to Brown right incomplete.
M 45	4-6	Walden 21 punt, Wallace fair catch.

Minnesota (14:40)

M 24	1-10	Tarkenton 5 pass to Foreman left (Holmes).
M 29	2-5	Foreman sweep left, no gain (Blount).
M 29	3-5	Tarkenton pass to Foreman broken up (Edwards).
M 29	4-5	Eischeid 36 punt, Swann 11 return (Tingelhoff).

Pittsburgh (13:05)

P 46	1-10	Harris run left, no gain, fumbled, Krause recovered for Minn. at P 47.

Minnesota (12:59)

P 47	1-10	Tarkenton pass to Gilliam deep incomplete. Play nullified and Pitt. penalized 42 for pass interference (Wagner).
P 5	1-goal	Foreman run right, loss of 2, fumbled, Greene recovered for Pitt. at P 7.

Pittsburgh (12:44)

P 7	1-10	Harris 8 run right (Eller).
P 15	2-2	Harris run right, no gain (Siemon).
P 15	3-2	Bleier run right, no gain (Page).
P 15	4-2	Walden's punt blocked by Blair, T. Brown recovered for Minn. in end zone, touchdown (10:33). Cox's extra point attempt hit the left upright.

Pittsburgh 9, Minnesota 6

Cox kick to P 17, Harrison 17 return (McClanahan).

Pittsburgh (10:18)

P 34	1-10	Harris run right, no gain (Siemon).
P 34	2-10	Harris 8 run off left tackle (Eller).
P 42	3-2	Bradshaw 30 pass to Brown right (Wallace).
M 28	1-10	Bleier 5 run right. Play nullified and Pitt. penalized 5 for illegal motion.
M 33	1-15	Bleier run left, no gain (Page).
M 33	2-15	Bleier 17 run off right tackle (Krause).
M 16	1-10	Harris 4 run right (Eller).
M 12	2-6	Harris 1 run right (Winston).
M 11	3-5	Bradshaw 6 pass to Bleier middle (Krause).
M 5	1-goal	Harris 2 run up middle (Siemon, Winston).
M 3	2-goal	Harris sweep left, loss of 1 (Siemon).
M 4	3-goal	Bradshaw rollout right, 4 pass to Brown end zone, touchdown (3:31). Gerela kicked extra point.

Pittsburgh scoring drive: 66 yards, 11 plays, 6:47.

Pittsburgh 16, Minnesota 6

Gerela kick to M 17, McClanahan 22 return (Allen).

Minnesota (3:31)

M 39	1-10	Tarkenton pass to Gilliam middle intercepted at P 33, Wagner 26 return (Yary).

Pittsburgh (3:07)

M 41	1-10	Harris 2 run left (Krause).
M 39	2-8	Harris 1 run left (Marshall). Two-Minute Warning.
M 38	3-7	Harris 15 run off right tackle (Hilgenberg).
M 23	1-10	Bleier 6 run off right tackle (Hilgenberg).
M 17	2-4	Swann reverse right, loss of 7 (Eller).
M 24	3-11	Bleier 7 run right (Larsen). Minn.-first time out (:41).
M 17	4-4	Bleier run left, loss of 6 (Marshall).

Minnesota (:37)

M 23	1-10	Tarkenton pass deflected at line (Greenwood).
M 23	2-10	Tarkenton swing pass to Reed left, loss of 2 (Toews).

FINAL SCORE:
Pittsburgh 16, Minnesota 6
FINAL RECORDS:
Pittsburgh 13-3-1, Minnesota 12-5

For the romantic, or even the marginally prescient, the horse's silks would have given it away. Right then, Elijah must have taken one quick look, smiled at the occasionally ironic ways of his Boss, and told the nearest Cherubim, "Get me twenty bucks down on the Steelers."

In retrospect, the moment didn't demand a prophet's eye. Even a tout with a bit of intuition and sense of the dramatic should have been able to guess all that would follow: the Pittsburgh star finally beginning its ascent to a height that eventually would result in four Lombardi trophies; Minnesota being caught once again with its karma down; Fran Tarkenton's shoulder going lame; a Pittsburgh assistant coach creating a bizarre-looking but strangling defensive alignment; and, mostly, two NFL teams, headed in different directions, meeting on the same path.

Okay, so maybe you don't believe in prophecy. Will you buy destiny? A draft, still talked about in awe, taking immediate hold? God repaying a few Vikings for dumping a bucket of water from a balcony onto Howard Cosell's toupee? And that horse should have told you something.

There was Art Rooney, the NFL's beloved loser, standing patiently in a New Orleans racetrack winner's circle. A legendary horseplayer, he'd been invited to present the trophy for the featured race a day before his football team was to play Minnesota in Super Bowl IX. Rooney could think of no finer place to be. And when he saw that horse, he was sure of it. A devout Catholic who had attended Mass every morning since childhood, he knew God would not taunt him with the color of racing silks. Besides, he knew his football team.

Next to him, Mrs. Kathleen Rooney decidedly was not so sure. She was shot-through Irish, and she put the sort of stock in Celtic folklore that she did in Mother Church. This horse was wearing—the saints preserve them all—purple and white.

"That's a bad omen," she whispered of the Vikings' colors.

No, her husband replied, it was anything but. The colors were Super Bowl colors. Besides, nothing but good had ever befallen him at a racetrack. Indeed, on successive days at two New York tracks, he had won somewhere between a quarter- and a half-million dollars.

But for 41 winters after they were purchased with $2,500 won on another good day at the racetrack, the Steelers won absolutely nothing. And while they were doing so, quarterbacks named Sid Luckman, John Unitas, Len Dawson, and Jack Kemp slipped from their inept clutches. One year they dealt a number-one pick to Chicago that the Bears used to acquire Dick Butkus. In short, they were a laughingstock. Even in their forty-first winter it took a last-second freak of a play, historically known as the Immaculate Reception, to give them their most important win.

Not that the 1974 Vikings seemed likely to provide a second, you understand.

"We knew that if we played up to our ability, or maybe just a little bit beyond it, we would win," says Ron Yary, the Vikings' great offensive tackle.

Minnesota had a defensive line that earned the grandest tribute the game can bestow, a nickname (the Purple People Eaters). It had the state-of-the-art scrambling quarterback, the elusive Tarkenton. The Vikings, who had six Pro Bowl players, had finished 10-4 in 1974, defeating the Cardinals and the Rams in the playoffs to reach the Super Bowl for the second consecutive season.

January 12, 1975, dawned unusually biting and windy for that time of year in New Orleans. An NFC champion that had won 26 of its 33 previous encounters was matched against an AFC representative armed with a strange-looking defensive front, a quarterback (Terry Bradshaw) who still had rough edges, and a ball-control offense that seemed to be nothing special.

Still, the Steelers were, if anything, cocky approaching IX. Just prior to the AFC Championship Game, defensive end L.C. Greenwood slouched in front of a TV set. Asked what he was doing, he replied, "Just watching to see who we're going to play in the Super Bowl."

Pittsburgh had survived a winter of discontent that included the "No Freedom, No Foot-

As the Steelers were introduced, the confident Franco Harris (far left) gave the thumbs-up sign.

ever did get to the Super Bowl, Terry'd be so shook we wouldn't get a first down."

Still, sweet youth had ridden to the Pittsburgh rescue following a 1973 season in which the Steelers were unceremoniously bumped from the playoffs by the Oakland Raiders.

After four decades of comedy, laughter at the Steelers had gone silent in 1972 when they reached the playoffs for the first time. But the real key to their success in the fall and winter of 1974 began in the spring with a draft that only can be described as wondrous. That spring, the Steelers chose Lynn Swann, Jack Lambert, John Stallworth, and Mike Webster, and signed Donnie Shell as a free agent—28 Pro Bowl appearances, 20 Su-

ball" training camp strike, a quarterback controversy pivoting on *three* contenders, an offense comprising a respectable infantry but a suspect air force, and the infusion that year of no fewer than 14 rookies.

"We knew what sort of talent we had. We had to go for it," Steelers head coach Chuck Noll says. "But we had some things to overcome."

Noll hated the 1974 strike so much that he wouldn't use the word with the media. He refused to speak the names of veterans not in camp. Further disunity occurred after the players held a meeting in which third-year quarterback Joe Gilliam gave an impassioned speech in behalf of the holdouts, and then immediately reported to the Steelers' training camp.

The quarterback controversy revolved around Gilliam, who was extroverted and talented; Terry Hanratty, a former Notre Dame star and hometown favorite; and Bradshaw, a brilliant talent whose football acumen was suspect even to his teammates. All three would play before Bradshaw won the job from Gilliam at midseason en route to a 10-3-1 season.

While the Vikings boasted balance enhanced by Tarkenton's elusiveness, the Steelers' offense was built largely on field position and the run. Bradshaw's passing and poise were so inconsistent that one Steelers veteran is kidded to this day for saying off-the-record then, "If we

Pittsburgh scored on a safety when Fran Tarkenton's fumbled handoff bounced behind the Vikings' goal line. Tarkenton beat the Steelers' Jack Lambert (58) and L.C. Greenwood (68) to the ball and recovered it.

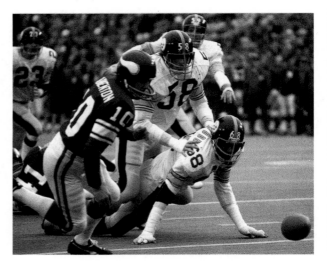

The Steelers stretched their lead to 9-0 when Harris shook off linebacker Jeff Siemon and scored on a nine-yard run. Harris rushed for a Super Bowl-record 158 yards and was named the game's most valuable player.

per Bowl rings, and maybe five Pro Football Hall of Fame selections among them—and chose seven other worthies who became, as they say, contributors. Pluck played a role.

"You guys blew it," Noll raged at his scouts, after they convinced him to take Swann in the opening round and wait to tap Stallworth. "He'll be gone," Noll said. Stallworth lasted until the fourth round.

Fate had a role in the selection of Swann, who had run a slow 40-yard time for scouts. Only the Steelers knew Swann had a pulled leg muscle and returned to time him again.

The second round brought Lambert, an undersized linebacker whom a Steelers scout had seen dive at a teammate during a parking-lot practice and then stand there quietly picking cinders out of his bleeding face. Noll gambled on toughness overcoming a lack of heft.

Given the draft transfusion, it's small wonder that Noll was confident enough before Super Bowl IX to let the players sleep with their wives the night before the game. "An act of faith," defensive tackle Joe Greene says today.

The strongest recollection Noll carried away from Super Bowl IX was his fear of Minnesota's relentless defensive pressure.

"That's what I remember the most—that they could pass rush like *hell*," he says. "They made things happen...good things...We *had* to be able to run the ball."

Minnesota head coach Bud Grant had similar concerns—concerns that were the product of the innovative mind of young Steelers defensive line coach George Perles, who had drawn up a bizarre-looking defensive front and convinced Noll to employ it.

With Greene so sprinter-quick off the ball, Perles found the perfect vehicle for the Steelers' defense: a front that set a defensive tackle, usually Greene, snug up on the center but at a 45-degree angle.

In practice, late in the season, the Steelers worked to refine it; Noll sprung it in the playoffs. Running

Defensive tackle Joe Greene helped lead the Steelers to four Super Bowl victories in four tries.

159

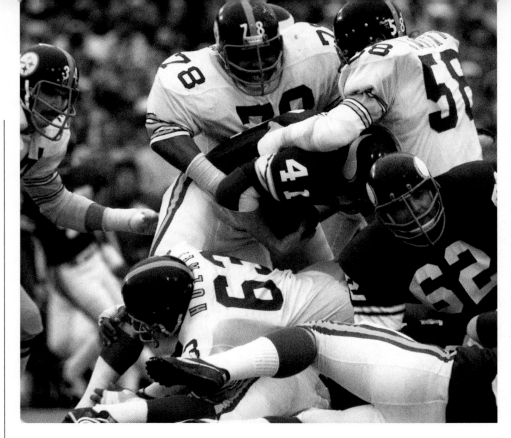

The Steelers' defense overwhelmed the Vikings' offense, holding Minnesota to 119 total yards and nine first downs. Jack Lambert (58) and Dwight White (78) smothered running back Dave Osborn on this play.

for 49 yards, the Raiders 29.

"I can't tell you why I did it," Perles says now. "If you threw it into a computer, it wouldn't look too good. The fifteenth game in a season isn't usually where you experiment."

But Perles's ingenious "Stunt 4-3" worked—and Grant had a puzzle to solve. To that end, Vikings assistant Jerry Burns, a friend of Perles's, telephoned Paul Roach, a Raiders assistant, and asked, "What the hell happened to the Raiders?" Roach wasn't precisely sure. Greene charging from the odd angle had managed two accomplishments: It popped what coaches call a "bubble"— a linebacker's route to the ball carrier usually is impeded by a defensive lineman—and it

stunts designed not to harry the passer but to trap the runner, the Steelers smothered Buffalo 32-14 and then beat Oakland 24-13. Against Perles's creation, O.J. Simpson of the Bills ran

Fran Tarkenton (fleeing L.C. Greenwood) completed 11 of 26 passes and had three interceptions.

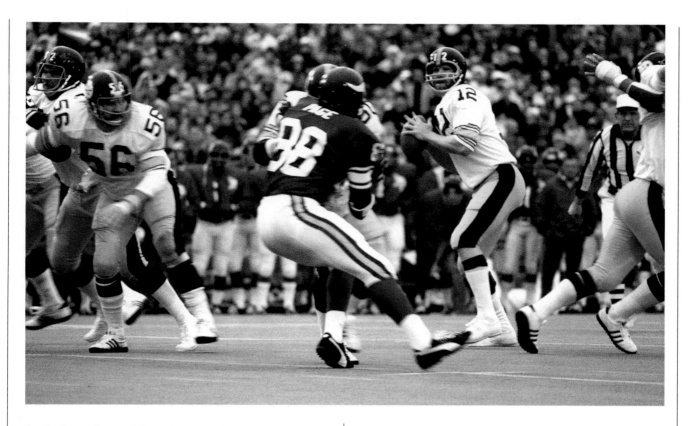

Pittsburgh was a run-oriented team in Super Bowl IX, with Terry Bradshaw attempting only 14 passes and completing 9. Minnesota's Alan Page tried to fight off a blocker to get to Bradshaw on this play.

fouled up the Raiders' blocking assignments.

"All through the playoffs," Perles says, "I'm not nervous, I'm *scared*. It's not like I had stayed up all night thinking it up. I just fell into it. The defensive line had fun with it."

Minnesota did not.

Meanwhile, Noll was repeating the charge he'd given the troops the day he began pulling Pittsburgh from the muck five years before: "Whatever it takes."

"We heard that so often we always said he had it embroidered on his shorts," Steelers center Ray Mansfield says.

Against Minnesota, what it mostly took was unrelenting defense. The defense was personified by end Dwight White.

White had contracted pleurisy on the flight to New Orleans, and he compounded it by eating "a mess of oysters and gumbo" on arrival. He spent all but a few hours of the week before the game in a hospital bed. He lost 18 pounds, and the Pittsburgh coaching staff had a bet that he wouldn't survive the pregame warmups. Instead, he missed only a handful of plays.

Only slightly less critical against the Vikings were two young reserve linebackers, Marv Kellum and Ed Bradley. Andy Russell, by then a five-year Pro Bowl player, fell prey to a pulled hamstring early in the third quarter and was more than adequately replaced by Kellum, a rookie who said, "When the Vikings saw me come out onto the field, they probably were saying, 'Who's this turkey?'"

Bradley was no more recognizable. The son of a Chicago Bears defensive end who had put a football in Ed's crib the day he was brought home from the hospital, Bradley ably filled in for Lambert, middle linebacker and linchpin, when Lambert was lost with a sprained ankle in the waning moments of the first half. Playing without Lambert and Russell for much of the game, the Steelers' defense didn't miss a beat.

No one suggested this was the birth of a dynasty, but the signs all were there.

Ironically, the real beginning to the dynasty

had taken place five years before in a New Orleans hotel ballroom not far from Tulane Stadium. There the Steelers won a coin flip with the Chicago Bears to determine who would get the first pick in the 1970 draft. "Tails" was worth Terry Bradshaw. Steelers president Dan Rooney gave the coin, a 1921 silver dollar, to Noll for luck...and four years later, the luck took hold.

The Steelers' 1974 draft became a veritable mother lode—what former 49ers head coach Bill Walsh still refers to as "maybe the best draft ever"—and the undoing of the Minnesota Vikings, a team destined to lose four Super Bowls.

Still, that destiny hadn't begun to haunt the Vikings yet. In fact, the Vikings were a very loose team in New Orleans. A few days before the game, Tarkenton spent $3,000 on a dinner for his offensive linemen at Antoine's, the famous French Quarter restaurant. Fred Dryer, who would become more celebrated as a TV actor than he had been as a Los Angeles Rams defensive end, and one-time Vikings receiver Lance Rentzel spent the week as court jesters for the Vikings, dressing in absurd 1930s re-

porter costumes. They broke up a Minnesota practice with laughter after asking Tarkenton why he couldn't win the big games. "Well, I guess I'm just not a dedicated athlete," Tarkenton replied with a straight face.

Later, at a Grant press conference, they asked the bemused coach, "Is the zone defense on its way out, and if so, where is it going?"

Late in the week, Tarkenton led a foray that resulted in the dumping of a bucket of water on broadcaster Howard Cosell's head as he tried to conduct a radio interview at the team hotel. "Washed his wig right off," Yary says.

In retrospect, Dryer and Rentzel should've hung around for the game. Super Bowl IX was, alas, the stuff of ennui, memorable not for what took place that day, but for what it heralded: the birth of a true dynasty and one more example of the Vikings' Super Bowl blues. The Min-

More than 10 minutes remained when Vikings linebacker Matt Blair blocked a Pittsburgh punt, and reserve safety Terry Brown (24) scooped it up and carried it in for a touchdown that reduced Pittsburgh's lead to 9-6.

Chuck Noll celebrated after finally accomplishing what no other Steelers coach ever had—winning an NFL championship. Noll was in only his sixth season as a head coach when he won Pittsburgh its first Super Bowl.

Even that early, the Stunt 4-3 front had rendered Minnesota's running game ineffective. The Vikings would average just under one yard per rushing attempt in the first half and total only 17 on 21 carries for the game. In three postseason games, Pittsburgh yielded a total of just 146 yards rushing.

To all assembled in Tulane Stadium, a grimy, old Erector Set of a place, the game's outcome seemed ordained: Unless the elusive Tarkenton could become an apparition, the Vikings were doomed. Understandably, he refuses to discuss Super Bowl IX to this day.

nesota offense proved resistible; the Steelers' defense was largely immovable.

From any vantage, the statistics bear it out. The Vikings could retard the Steelers for much of the day, but the Minnesota offense couldn't move on the Pittsburgh defense with anything resembling consistency. Tarkenton's shoulder was hurting, and he couldn't throw. He couldn't hide, either.

"They didn't give us much," Greene says. "We gave them less."

Almost nothing, in fact. Early in the first quarter, Greenwood slithered around Yary's block, flushed Tarkenton into awkward retreat, and slapped his pass aside like it was a bothersome fly.

Steelers defensive linemen would deflect five passes—three by Greenwood.

The Vikings were unable to advance beyond their 35-yard line in their first four possessions. Early in the second quarter, Tarkenton began the fifth on the Pittsburgh 24 after a fumble recovery. It failed, too, when Dave Osborn ran for just two yards, Tarkenton threw incomplete twice, and Fred Cox missed a 39-yard field goal.

"I have no interest in talking about it," Tarkenton says. "Once you're out of the game, people think you *want* to talk about it. I don't have time for it."

Nor, in Super Bowl IX, did Tarkenton have the arm for it.

Minnesota wide receiver John Gilliam was left to ponder the Vikings' third Super Bowl loss.

"The fact is that I couldn't throw a football five yards with any velocity," he says.

"I got hurt in the fourth game of the season and it got worse. There was horrible pain, but we got there anyway."

And perished there.

"Francis could make things happen," Noll says. "He could scratch where it itched. We *had* to contain him."

Outside pressure from Greenwood and White, with an occasional blitz inside from a linebacker, did just that. Minnesota finished with a mere 119 yards in total offense for the day. Tarkenton threw three interceptions.

Midway through the second quarter, Tarkenton botched a handoff at the Vikings' 10. The ball hit running back Osborn in the left hip and was kicked toward the end zone by Greenwood. Tarkenton recovered the careening ball just beyond the goal line as White touched him down for a Steelers safety.

Still, the only difference on the scoreboard was the safety. Inspired by the slender deficit, Minnesota's offense shook itself to life in the second quarter for the only time. Fueled by a pair of passes by Tarkenton to running back Chuck Foreman and a 15-yard pass-interference penalty, the Vikings reached the Pittsburgh 25. There, they were halted by The Blade, the nickname for free safety Glen Edwards.

Running free over the middle at the Pittsburgh 5, Tarkenton's favorite target, John Gilliam, had a pass in his hands when Edwards, the Steelers' nastiest hitter, rammed a shoulder pad into the receiver's chinstrap.

"Ball must've gone ten yards in the air," Mel Blount recalls. When it came down, Blount, probably the game's top cornerback, was camped under it. The Vikings' bid was ended.

Before it, Minnesota had life and hope; after it, the Vikings were impotent. Except for a fourth-quarter pass-interference call on strong safety Mike Wagner that was worth 42 yards, they would not advance more than a few feet beyond midfield again.

Thus gashed, the Vikings began to bleed profusely. Minnesota's Bill Brown fumbled away the opening kickoff of the second half, and Kellum fell on it at the Vikings' 30. In four plays, one a 24-yard run by Franco Harris, Harris was in the end zone, and the Steelers owned a 9-0 lead.

Beyond running nine yards for the game's first touchdown, Harris set two Super Bowl records by rushing 34 times for 158 yards. He was named the game's most valuable player.

Early in the fourth quarter, the Vikings' Matt Blair blocked a punt by the Steelers' Bobby Walden, and Terry Brown recovered it in the end zone for Minnesota's only points. Trailing 9-6 with more than 10 minutes left, the Vikings never threatened again.

"Everyone searches for a reason," Yary says with a sigh. "For some games, there isn't one. They dominated us. We just didn't perform. It's funny. It's like a disease. Something goes wrong and it's like a virus...it spreads."

On the series following the blocked punt, the fat lady began clearing her throat. The Steelers drove 66 yards and scored again on Bradshaw's four-yard pass to tight end Larry Brown, a play that was suggested by forgotten quarterback Joe Gilliam.

"You could see it in their eyes; we were going to be number one," Noll says.

After Brown's catch, even the Vikings knew it. Minnesota defensive tackle Alan Page, who later would bitterly lay the loss at the feet of the Vikings' offense, threw his elbow pads at Steelers guard Jim Clack and said, "Hell, Clack, I'm all through."

With the score 16-6, the Steelers began smiling at one another.

"Late in that season," Greene remembers, "We would look at each other and we knew. We simply weren't going to lose."

If the cornerstone of a Pittsburgh dynasty had been laid, so had Minnesota's still-indelible reputation as a team incapable of the ultimate triumph.

"If we had played them in another game, it all might've been another story," Yary says, a lament still humming softly in his voice after all the years. "Everyone still asks the same question: *Why did you lose all four of them?*"

Bradshaw has decided why Minnesota had lost the third one: "We wanted it, Jack!" he says with a laugh.

Oh, about that horse in purple and white. After Super Bowl IX, Art Rooney told a friend: "Despite what my wife said at the track that day, I *knew* they'd have to get lucky to beat us."

A Classic Shootout—for Men Only

Reminded of the conversation for the first time in 15 years, he drops his eyes to the fish sandwich he's slathering with ketchup, and his happy-face-button grin is at once embarrassed and delighted.

"It wasn't really Landry," he says. "It was Tex Schramm. I like Tex…but you know, they never just lost one. It was always the officials…or the weather…or something else."

Mother Teresa does more standup routines than Chuck Noll. A reflective man, his approach to life is perhaps best summed up by a former player who says, "If you died, you'd want Chuck to raise your kids in your place… but you wouldn't want to go out for a beer with him."

Noll reserves jokes for making a point. In the spring of 1976, he made one at the expense of the Dallas Cowboys and club president Tex Schramm, whose incessant complaining in the wake of Super Bowl X had irritated him. If it was out of character, and if the gag was restricted to only a few people, it still spoke volumes about how his Pittsburgh Steelers teams played the game and what they thought of those who played it differently.

Noll's only documented standup routine went like this: The day the Steelers got their Super Bowl X rings, he told a couple of admirers of the jewelry, "It has a little button on the side. Push it and the top flips up. Inside is a miniature tape recorder. Listen…

"You can hear Tom Landry crying."

And that tells you what the Pittsburgh Steelers thought of the Dallas Cowboys—and still think of them—and why, more than anything else, Super Bowl X was a genuine collision of attitudes and football philosophies, of value systems, and people who genuinely didn't like one another.

"To me, football is executing, just blocking and tackling better, not fooling people," says Joe Greene, the rock-hard tackle around whom the Pittsburgh defense was built.

So it was no surprise that after the Super Bowl X encounter, Cowboys tight end Jean Fu-gett spoke for all Dallas partisans, uniformed and civilian, when he observed:

"The really unfortunate thing is that that team of asses is the world champions."

Behind the hype and hoopla, the Cowboys and the Steelers represented a clash of styles. Pittsburgh spoke for the old values. Pro set offense, pound inside the tackles. Standard 4-3 defense—with a twist: Don't outthink them, kill them.

By necessity, Dallas had been forced to abandon its version of power football that year. The Cowboys stood for the New Order: Shotgun offense; more men in motion than a shipboard fire; the Flex defense, with linemen a yard off the football. In other words: Don't bludgeon them, fool them.

If the Steelers were a stiff finger in your eye, the Cowboys were an unfelt hand lifting your wallet. To Pittsburgh, football was muscle and meanness; to Dallas, it was guile and trickery. The Cowboys wouldn't have wanted to live in Pittsburgh's neighborhood, and the Steelers knew it.

"Hot dogs," Cowboys linebacker D.D. Lewis called them, while Dallas receiver Golden Richards complained afterwards that Pittsburgh cornerback Mel Blount had fractured his ribs "with a punch."

The hostility between the teams had unusual and diverse roots: a cornerback named John Rowser, traded by Pittsburgh to Denver in 1974; the excessive practice time needed by the Steelers in the two weeks before the Super Bowl to learn the complexities of Dallas's Flex defense and motion-oriented offense; a widespread belief shared by NFL insiders that the Steelers would not be able to cope with the Cowboys' pass rush.

Ironically enough, Rowser, nicknamed "Dirty John," triggered the animosity that grew in the week before the game.

"It all started with D.J.," Noll says with a sigh.

When Denver lost to Pittsburgh in the fourth game of the 1975 season, Rowser brutally worked over Lynn Swann, the young Steelers receiver who was on the verge of blossoming into a superstar. Other Pittsburgh opponents quickly followed Rowser's lead, and in the AFC Championship Game against the Oakland

Dallas began the game with a trick play as kickoff returner Preston Pearson handed the ball to Thomas (Hollywood) Henderson on a reverse, and Henderson raced 48 yards to the Steelers' 44-yard line.

Raiders, Swann suffered a severe concussion.

"John went for Swann's head and started all of that stuff," Noll says. "The idea was that Swann could be intimidated. He couldn't be, but it went around the league. 'What can you do to stop him? Intimidate him!'"

Dallas players made no attempt to disguise their intent to adopt a similar strategy in the Super Bowl.

"Getting hit while he's running a route across the middle," Dallas safety Cliff Harris repeatedly said to reporters, "must be in the back of his mind."

In the back of Noll's mind was the talk around the NFL that the Steelers' undersized offensive line wouldn't be able to protect quarterback Terry Bradshaw.

"We talked a lot about that, how they had a great pass rush," Noll says, "and then getting ready for them was not easy. They tried to fool you as much as beat you physically. We needed the two weeks to get ready and we used all of it. That sort of worked on our people, too."

Even the accommodations in Miami seemed to fuel the growing hostility between the teams. The Cowboys were housed amid the glitz of Fort Lauderdale's beachfront at the Galt Ocean Mile Hotel, while the Steelers were assigned to the quaint but cramped Miami Lakes Inn in a distant suburb. An interviewer for a crew shooting a *cinéma vérité* TV documenta-

172

ry was told by Pittsburgh defensive lineman Ernie (Fats) Holmes: "I hate this place. I feel like eating palm trees. People come here to play golf and die."

As early as midweek, the Steelers' game faces were frozen in place.

"I remember telling a reporter I hoped a shark would bite off one of Roger Staubach's arms," says Steelers middle linebacker Jack Lambert, the chief stoker of the Steelers' fires.

Even the taciturn Landry was drawn into the acrimony, telling a Dallas reporter, "The Steelers are an arrogant team. They haven't learned humility, but they will."

Some years later, the Steelers did, but it would not come in the 1970s and it wasn't the Cowboys who taught it to them.

Despite the unusual dislike between the teams, there was more similarity between them

Terry Bradshaw retaliated on the next series, driving the Steelers 67 yards to the tying touchdown, which he got on a seven-yard pass to tight end Randy Grossman. Bradshaw passed for 209 yards and two touchdowns.

The Cowboys jumped to a 7-0 lead, scoring on Roger Staubach's 29-yard pass to Drew Pearson. On the previous play, Pittsburgh punter Bobby Walden bobbled the snap and was tackled at the 29.

than either cared to admit. Prior to 1975, Dallas had played the Steelers' brand of right-cross football. But when power backs Calvin Hill and Walt Garrison left the Cowboys—the former to go to the World Football League and the latter to retirement with a body battered by both the field and the rodeo arena—Landry was obliged to retool with 12 rookies and an increasing dependence upon the trickery of Shotgun and motion plays. The Steelers got an infusion of new blood the year before as 14 first-year players assisted in the throttling of Minnesota in Super Bowl IX.

During the 1975 regular season, the Steelers, behind the power running of Franco Harris and arguably the finest defense the sport has known, won 11 consecutive games en route to a 12-2 season, and then defeated Baltimore and Oakland in the playoffs.

"Our best team ever was '75," says Greene, who missed more than half that year with nerve damage in his right shoulder. "They didn't even need me. The easiest of them all was that second time. We knew from day one where we were going."

For Dallas, the road to Miami was significantly bumpier, or enough so that many of the players came to refer to 1975 as "our miracle season." The offense had to be rebuilt almost from scratch in training camp, and the Cowboys

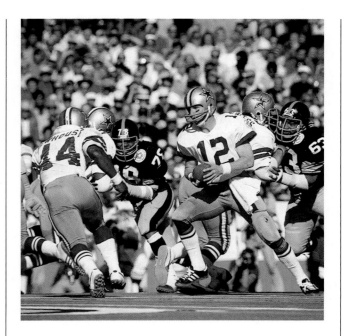

Dallas and Roger Staubach took a 10-7 lead in the second quarter, marching 46 yards to a field goal by Toni Fritsch. Robert Newhouse (44) ran for 30 yards on the drive, which stalled at the Steelers' 19.

didn't know if they were going anywhere. But, after failing to make the playoffs for the first time in nine years in 1974, they went 10-4 to finish a game behind St. Louis in the NFC East.

Then the gods smiled on America's Team. A 50-yard desperation pass from Roger Staubach to Drew Pearson—forever known as the Hail Mary—with 24 seconds to play provided a 17-14 upset of Minnesota in the divisional playoffs. In the NFC Championship Game, Staubach threw four touchdown passes—three to ex-Steeler Preston Pearson—as Dallas thumped the Los Angeles Rams 37-7 to become the first wild-card team to reach the Super Bowl.

While Landry was restructuring the Cowboys with X's and O's, Noll was fine-tuning the Steelers. The previous season, assistant coach George Perles had devised the Stunt 4-3 defensive front, which placed the intimidating Greene tight on the center but at a disconcerting 45-degree angle. In 1975, another unheralded assistant, offensive line coach Dan Radakovich, had brought some more new wrinkles.

In his first six years, Noll had put together a staff whose strength was teaching. Radako-

vich's was innovation…and the sort of single-minded work ethic that saw him rush home one night that winter, grab a can of beer from the refrigerator, and sit down at the kitchen table over the team playbook just in time to be greeted by a woman, not his wife, who coolly informed him that his house was a block away. So intense was Radakovich that his charges nicknamed him "Bad Rad." (His wife came to be known, somewhat proudly, as "Mrs. Bad Rad.")

The Steelers had smallish linemen, so Radakovich had an equipment man's mother-in-law tailor their jerseys skin-tight to prevent them from being thrown around. At the time, officials called holding if offensive linemen fully extended their arms while pass blocking, but Radakovich believed no call would be made if they simply struck out with their fists. When he discovered he was right, he issued his linemen the boxing workout gloves that came to be *de rigueur* in the NFL. Radakovich also instituted the concept of area blocking—sloughing off a stunting defender to the next blocker. All of Radakovich's innovations caused Dallas grief. With nothing to grab and punched off balance, Dallas defensive linemen sacked Bradshaw only twice and rarely hurried him. The blocking scheme also bought Pittsburgh valuable yardage on draws against the Flex defense.

While Jethro Pugh (75) and Ed (Too Tall) Jones (72) soared high in the air to try to block the ball, Pittsburgh's Roy Gerela sailed this 36-yard field-goal attempt wide to the left at the end of the first half.

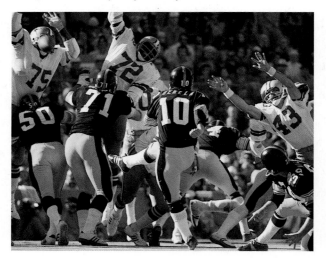

Pittsburgh's defense in 1975 was so good it was called the Steel Curtain. Dallas running back Preston Pearson found out why as linebackers Andy Russell (34) and Jack Ham made a sandwich out of him.

score, Pittsburgh punter Bobby Walden fumbled away a snap and the "ooohs" still were reverberating when Staubach, who would spend much of the day staring up at the azure blue sky, gunned a 29-yard touchdown strike to wide receiver Drew Pearson. It provided Dallas with an early 7-0 lead, but later proved the wisdom of that adage dealing with the inadvisability of returning to the well too often.

Linebacker Jack Lambert inspired the Steelers by both word and deed, such as this tackle of Newhouse.

From that moment on, the glory of Super Bowl X belonged largely to Swann, the ignominy to Cliff Harris.

Almost always, Super Bowl hype merely pro-

The day was sunny and crisp on January 18, 1976, when Dallas and Pittsburgh met on the slippery new Polyturf of the Orange Bowl to match their discordant approaches to the game.

"Gadget team," sneered the Steelers. "Thugs," snickered the Cowboys. And then they conspired to produce the very best of the first 10 Super Bowls.

Finesse took the first bite. Dallas used a reverse on the opening kickoff and almost broke rookie linebacker Thomas Henderson loose for a touchdown. He ran 48 yards to the Pittsburgh 44. On the Steelers' first series, after Dallas failed to

Pittsburgh's Lynn Swann won most valuable player honors after a game of catches such as this remarkable 53-yarder to the Dallas 37. The Steelers failed to score after this one, however, as Gerela missed a field goal.

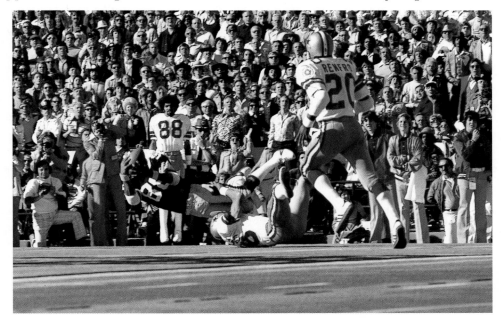

vides distraction for the players and thin fodder for the media. Occasionally, a pregame comment will boomerang, as Harris discovered.

When the Steelers arrived in Miami, Swann still was suffering the effects of the concussion he received at the hands, forearms, and elbows of Oakland safeties George Atkinson and Jack Tatum—who the following year would be branded by Noll a part of the NFL's "criminal element" (Tatum subsequently sued him over the remark). Doctors in Miami told Swann, hospitalized for two days after the game against the Raiders, that another heavy blow to the head might result in permanent damage.

A thoughtful man who would retire after only nine years in the league, presumably concerned about his health, Swann practiced only on the day before the game. He consistently dropped passes and seemed to run with a stiff gait. But Harris's ill-advised attempt to rattle Swann did Dallas a severe disservice.

"He was trying to intimidate me," Swann says. "I read all that stuff he was saying all week. He said that I'd be afraid. I said, 'The hell with it, I'm going to play.' "

Swann celebrated in the end zone after scoring on the 64-yard pass with 3:02 left that ultimately clinched the victory. The Steelers' wide receiver caught four passes from Terry Bradshaw for 161 yards.

Swann played with a vengeance. And it was he who would stomp on the Cowboys' fingers each time Dallas seemed to get a handhold on the proceedings (the Cowboys owned leads of 7-0 in the first quarter, 10-7 at halftime, and 10-9 in the fourth quarter).

After Dallas moved ahead early, Swann provided the equalizer just minutes later. Making an adagio move along the right sideline to free himself from the coverage, he reached inside Cowboys cornerback Mark Washington's arms and snatched a pass by Bradshaw. The 32-yard completion put Pittsburgh at the Cowboys' 16-yard line, setting up the tying touchdown, Bradshaw's seven-yard pass to reserve tight end Randy Grossman.

"That catch seemed to boost me," Swann says. "I never had a day in my life when I felt so loose."

The Steelers received another dose of inspiration early in the third quarter, after Roy Gerela missed a 33-yard field goal with his team trailing 10-7. Harris taunted him, lightly slapping the Pittsburgh kicker's helmet. Lambert, the fire in the Steelers' belly, threw Harris to the ground.

"That guy's gotta learn the Steelers don't get intimidated," Lambert said after the game.

"There was a time when things weren't going good for the defense," Greene says. "Lambert made the hard licks that got us moving. He pulled us together."

If Swann was the epic Steeler, the heroic one who would collect the MVP trophy after catching four passes for 161 yards, and Lambert was the leader of the defense, it was left for a man called Boobie to play another significant role.

Staubach tried to rally the Cowboys, throwing one touchdown pass, but was intercepted on the last play.

Still owning a 10-7 lead and the game's momentum thanks to a second-quarter field goal by Toni Fritsch, the Cowboys lost both to Reggie Harrison, probably the most anonymous Steeler on the field and a caddy for Franco Harris who rarely played except on special teams. If Reggie Harrison— Boobie to his intimates—had remained with the Steelers largely due to his special-teams enthusiasm and a hugely agreeable personality, he would know one long moment of celebrity before returning to oblivion. He got it by sticking his tongue in front of a football.

Early in the fourth quarter of one of those games that seem forever to hang there for the taking, Dallas had to punt from its 16. For the first time in several years, Noll ordered a 10-man rush. Harrison blocked Mitch Hoopes's kick with his face and it rolled out of the end zone for a safety that cut Dallas's lead to 10-9 and seemed to strip the Cowboys of control.

"I still don't know what happened, but it split my tongue down the middle," says Harrison of the only punt he blocked in 14 years of playing organized football. "I was always afraid to block a kick for fear of someone kicking *me*."

The play had several effects, not the least of which was galvanizing the Steelers for the decisive last 11 minutes.

"I could see the balloon collapsing right then," veteran Cowboys defensive tackle Jethro Pugh says.

There was other evidence that Pugh's intuition was correct. A minute or two before Harrison's heroics, a woman had left the stands and run into the Dallas huddle, trying to give Cowboys tackle Rayfield Wright a silver horseshoe good-luck charm. Wright refused to accept it.

"It [the blocked punt] got us back to business," Greene recalls.

Certainly it excited the Steelers, and none more than Harrison. "I was yelling and screaming so much, I didn't realize we'd gotten some [more] points," he says. "I looked at the scoreboard and we were leading 12-10 and I asked someone, 'What happened?'"

What happened was that the Steelers quickly drove to the Dallas 19 after the free kick, and Gerela—who had broken a rib tackling Henderson on the opening kickoff—kicked a 36-yard field goal.

Two minutes later, Gerela added another field goal after Staubach went back to the play that produced the first-quarter touchdown pass to Drew Pearson, only to have Steelers strong safety Mike Wagner step in front of his throw at the Dallas 26 and return it to the 7.

Still, with 6:26 left and Pittsburgh clutching an uneasy 15-10 edge, Super Bowl X remained there for the taking.

Three minutes later, Swann took it.

The afternoon's pivotal play occurred in the middle of the Dallas defense, the turf patrolled by Cliff Harris. And, to add a touch of irony, it came on a blitz by Harris and linebacker Lewis.

"Once, Harris came over to me after an earlier play and told me I was lucky because he'd just missed me with a hard shot," Swann says. "He said he was going to get me if I came across the middle."

But Harris wasn't there to keep his promise. Instead, he was wrapping his arms around Bradshaw's legs while defensive tackle Larry Cole hit him in the head. It was a classic case of the-operation-was-a-success-but-the-patient-died, as Cole knocked Bradshaw into unconsciousness just as the pass was released. Downfield, Swann abandoned his pass route and simply outran the coverage to the deep middle. Again, the victim was Washington, who says, "It will take a lifetime to forget that day." With Bradshaw on his back, out cold, Swann caught the long pass in stride at the Cowboys' 5 and loped into the end zone for the touchdown that put Pittsburgh ahead 21-10.

The clock, though, was a familiar enemy to Staubach, who was sacked for the seventh time in the next series, but still managed to breathe life into the fading Cowboys with a 34-yard touchdown pass to little-used receiver Percy Howard. Ironically, it was Howard's only catch of his entire career.

In some ways, the pregame forecasts of an encounter essentially pitting the Dallas offense against the Pittsburgh defense were accurate. If Staubach was consistently harassed, his passing and scrambling kept the Cowboys always within reach of victory. And if the Steelers' defense had bent more than usual, Noll was only too willing to leave the outcome in its hands. Which he did with arguably the most second-guessed decision in the history of the Super Bowl.

With 1:28 left in the game, the Steelers had a 21-17 lead and were looking at fourth-and-9 from the Dallas 41. Noll—incredibly, some thought, and still think—decided against a punt. Rocky Bleier ran right for only two yards, and Staubach, from his own 39-yard line, once more faced his old adversary, the clock.

"I'd do it again," Noll says of his decision. "They had no time outs left, they had to have a touchdown to win, and they had to throw.

"We like our defense to have a team in a position like that." He didn't mention that his punter was having a bad day.

With almost everyone in the Orange Bowl reminding one another of the Cowboys' dramatic last-second win over Minnesota in the playoffs, Staubach scrambled for a first down, and then threw four straight passes. Steelers free safety Glen Edwards caught the last one in the end zone and returned it 35 yards as time ran out, and Pittsburgh joined Green Bay and Miami as winners of consecutive Super Bowls.

Noll still is asked about his unorthodox strategy.

"I have a great deal of faith in fate," he says. "I used to know a guy who worried about getting hit by a car every time he crossed the street.

"He never did...but he did have a nervous breakdown."

The trouble with Super Bowls, Gene Upshaw says, is "nobody remembers who lost the darn game." That's true to a point. The Minnesota Vikings crossed that point in Super Bowl XI. By losing their fourth Super Bowl, 32-14 to Upshaw's Oakland Raiders, the Vikings indelibly etched themselves in sports fans' memories.

The Vikings had a regular-season record of 87-24-1 from 1969-1976, an average record of 11-3 for eight years, and still they're remembered mainly for four games they lost. They're more vividly remembered as losers than the Bears and the Eagles, who averaged 4-9-1 seasons for those eight years and never had a winning record.

"It's so unfair in some cases," Upshaw says years later, by now a member of the Pro Football Hall of Fame and the NFL Players Association's executive director. "You only get one chance. It's a single-elimination tournament."

Upshaw wasn't talking about the Vikings, though. He was talking about the Raiders. People tend to forget the Raiders also went into Super Bowl XI as a team that Couldn't Win the Big One. Heck, they couldn't even *get* to the big one after Super Bowl II. In the eight years after that, the Raiders played in six AFL or AFC Championship Games and lost all of them.

So the 1976 Raiders identified with the Vikings, having to wear that big red L on their chests wherever they went. They even sort of envied the Vikings. At least the Vikings had played in Super Bowls. Of the first 11 Super Bowls, Minnesota was the only team to play in four of them. The Raiders had to keep watching. But they paid attention.

"One thing always stuck in our minds about Super Bowls," Upshaw says. "They were always so one-sided. It seemed like the big reason was momentum. A team gets an early lead, and there's so much riding on it, the momentum doesn't swing. You get it and you keep it."

That was the story of the Vikings' lives in Super Bowls. It happened again against the Raiders. Late in the first quarter, with the game still scoreless, Minnesota took over on the Raiders' 3-yard line after a blocked punt. Two plays later, Oakland had the ball on a Vikings fumble. The Raiders drove 90 yards and kicked a field goal, then scored touchdowns on their next two possessions. It was 16-0 at halftime and 19-0 before Minnesota scored.

"We score early and it's a different ball game," says Vikings safety Paul Krause, one of 10 Vikings to play in four Super Bowls. "It was early in the game, I know. You still have to play the remaining game. But when we didn't score, it changed the whole complexion."

It kept the Vikings' defense on the defensive. An early lead is especially valuable to a team with a great pass rush, a team that can attack an offense once it's down. The Vikings were that kind of team. "We played with a kind of wild abandon," Krause says. But in Super Bowls, Minnesota's defense always was chained to an empty scoreboard.

"We never had a lead in a Super Bowl game," Krause says. "That's not to say we would have beaten the Raiders, but it would have changed the complexion. We were a dominating defense, and in all four of our Super Bowls, we were never able to play that type of game."

The Vikings never cleared seven points in a Super Bowl until their meaningless second touchdown against Oakland, with 25 seconds left in the game. They lost to Kansas City 23-7, to Miami 24-7, and to Pittsburgh 16-6. They failed to score in the first halves of all four Super Bowls, and only Pittsburgh led them by fewer than 16 points at halftime.

"We never scored enough points to win a Super Bowl," linebacker Wally Hilgenberg says. "Everybody says you win with great defense. I don't believe that. Great defense can keep you in the game, but you win with great offense. Most of the winning Super Bowl teams had great offensive games."

The Raiders sure did, probably the greatest of the early Super Bowl era, before the 1978 rules changes helped blockers and receivers make big passing games easier. Oakland set Super Bowl records with 266 rushing yards and 429 total yards. Increased passing has obliterated the total yardage record, but the rushing total still is within 14 yards of the record, and the total yardage broke the record at the time by 71 yards.

Oakland's Clarence Davis ran 16 times for 137 yards, a career high. "If we'd have kept him in the game, he probably would have set a rushing record that would still be standing," tackle Art Shell says. Davis had gains of 20, 35, 13, 18, and 16 yards, usually to his left, behind Shell, Upshaw at guard, and tight end Dave Casper.

"There is no defense you can run against a great-blocking offensive line," Vikings linebacker Jeff Siemon said after the game.

"Our problem was that we couldn't force them to throw the ball," Vikings head coach Bud Grant said.

Taking a lead would have done it. Shutting down the run would have done it. The Vikings couldn't do either. It didn't matter that the pass rush was the strength of their team. No pass rush is great when it cannot anticipate a pass.

"We felt going into the game we could move the ball on the left side," Shell says. The Raiders had good reason to believe that, even though the Vikings had allowed the second-fewest points in the NFL that season and their pass defense ranked first in fewest yards and touchdowns allowed. Against the run, however, Minnesota gave up 4.3 yards per attempt, twenty-first in the NFL that year.

Ken Stabler (12) and the Raiders controlled the game by rushing for a Super Bowl-record 266 yards—mostly to the left side of the line where tackle Art Shell (78) and guard Gene Upshaw (63) lined up.

In the first quarter, Minnesota's Fred McNeill blocked a punt and recovered it at the Raiders' 3. But the Vikings wasted the opportunity when Willie Hall recovered Brent McClanahan's (33) fumble.

"I always felt, and I still feel to this day, that the toughest part is getting to the Super Bowl," Shell says. "Once you get there, it's easy, because we know how to win. I felt at the time, once we got to the Super Bowl, we were not going to be denied."

The Raiders even could have told themselves those AFC Championship Games they lost were more competitive than the Super Bowl. All six teams that beat them went on to win the Super Bowl. They were a 13-1 team in 1976, and their 36-6 record from 1974-76 was one of the best three-year records in the history of the NFL.

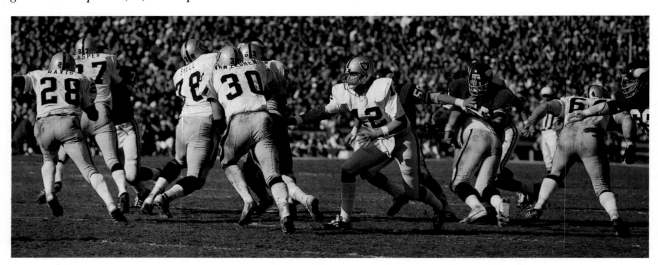

Both teams long had dominated their divisions. This was Oakland's ninth AFC (or AFL) West championship in 10 years, and Minnesota's eighth NFC (or NFL) Central championship in nine years. But the Raiders had dominated better competition. The 1976 season was the fourth consecutive year in which Minnesota was the only NFC Central team over .500. In going 11-2-1 in the regular season, the Vikings were only 1-1-1 against teams with winning records, compared to Oakland's 4-1. Minnesota's offense ranked third in NFC scoring, but it was only ninth in the NFL, 45 points behind Oakland's.

Still, the Vikings did have a strong offense, built around a short passing game that Grant liked to call the "off-tackle pass." Quarterback Fran Tarkenton directed it masterfully. His 61.9 completion percentage ranked second in the NFL to Kenny Stabler's 66.7 for Oakland, and the Vikings' 10 interceptions thrown tied the league low.

The Vikings could run, too. Chuck Foreman's 1,155 rushing yards ranked sixth in the league that year, and he tied for the lead with 14 touchdowns. But the quick fullback also ranked fifth with 55 catches, trailed closely by two new Minnesota wide receivers—ex-Bills and Cardinals veteran Ahmad Rashad with 53, and rookie deep threat Sammy White with 51. And this was a year when the whole league had only 14 players with at least 50 catches.

The knock on the Vikings was their age. Nine starters were in their 30s. But this was a different, more emotional team, Grant said. White and Rashad had brought

Six Raiders carried the ball, including Pete Banaszak, who lunged for two touchdowns.

exuberance, and the Vikings had drawn fiery resolve from Dallas's Hail Mary pass that eliminated them in the 1975 playoffs. It was as though, after getting cuffed upside the head by three Super Bowl trophies, Roger Staubach's desperate touchdown pass to Drew Pearson was the final straw that made the stoic Vikings say, "All right. Now you made us *mad*."

Oakland also was more of a passing team, but, unlike Minnesota, its offense far outshone its defense. In fact, Stabler outshone the whole NFL galaxy that year. He led the league in both completion percentage and touchdown passes, with 27, and he added a league-high 9.4 yards per attempt to that rare double. His 103.7 passer rating was the sixth best of all time. Casper and future Hall of Fame member Fred Biletnikoff were Stabler's possession targets. His long-ball target, Cliff Branch, led the league with 12 touchdown catches and fell one yard short of the receiving yardage lead.

The Raiders' only loss was a blowout in the fourth game, 48-17 to New England. The Patriots nearly knocked them out of the playoffs, too. Stabler directed two late touchdown drives to save the game 24-21, and the last one needed a roughing-the-passer penalty to nullify a third-down failure with 52 seconds left. Oakland beat Pittsburgh easily, 24-7 in the cham-

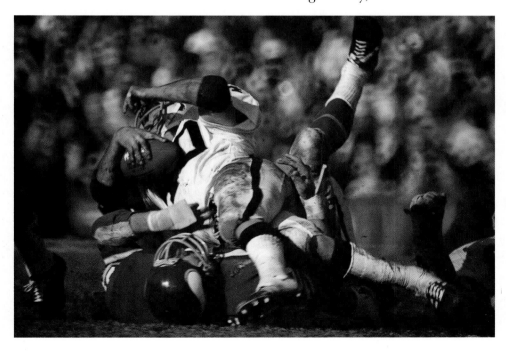

Oakland's sticky-fingered Fred Biletnikoff earned MVP honors by catching four passes for 79 yards. But that doesn't tell the whole story. Three of his catches led directly to touchdowns from the 1- and 2-yard lines.

pionship game, although injuries to both starting Pittsburgh running backs stripped some of the luster from the victory.

If New England seemed to have the Raiders' number, it was because the Patriots had their defense, and had been using it longer than Oakland. The Raiders had just begun using a 3-4 alignment a few weeks earlier. They had to. "We were down to three defensive linemen," says Bob Zeman, the Raiders' defensive backfield coach. Linemen Tony Cline, Horace Jones, and Art Thoms all were injured. "We always had the three-four as a pass defense," Zeman says. "We just incorporated our regular defense into it."

The emergency gave birth to two prime examples of Raiders lore. Scrambling for defensive linemen, they signed controversial castoff John Matuszak, who wound up starting most of the season and came to be considered the poster boy of the Raiders' reclamation projects. And in their hunt for a fourth pass rusher off the 3-4, they created a new position for Ted Hendricks, the 6-7 linebacker who had played defensive end in college.

"Hendricks started moving around, like a roving linebacker," Shell says. "He'd find a spot where he felt he could get a good run at the quarterback. When people started seeing it, people started copying it."

In NFL genealogy, Hendricks begat defensive end Fred Dean and linebacker Lawrence Taylor, two more lineman-linebacker hybrids who rushed the passer from every which way. Eventually, nearly every team had a pass rusher who moved around.

"People have expanded on what we did then, but the principles are still the same," Zeman says. Unleashing a rover keeps an offense wondering who will rush the passer and who will drop into coverage, and it gives the best pass rusher a chance to line up across from the worst blocker.

Against the Vikings, the Raiders' edge might have stemmed largely from the latitude head coach John Madden gave them to relax during the week. "Before we went, he talked to a lot of other coaches who had been there," Upshaw says. "He really picked their brains."

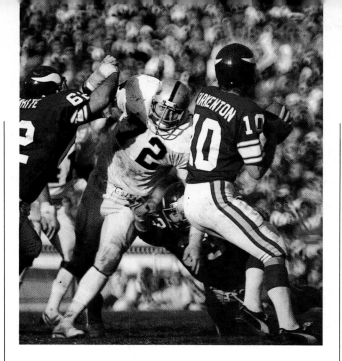

Minnesota's Fran Tarkenton passed for 205 yards, but produced just one touchdown in three and a half quarters of action. Pressure from Oakland defenders like end John Matuszak (72) helped keep him in check.

"I remember big John saying, 'We're going to go down there [to Los Angeles] and we're going to have some fun. But we're not going to forget what we're down there for,' " says Shell. "We read and heard some things about how the Vikings were uptight, how they didn't like dealing with the press. We were more prepared for that. The coaches told us the press is part of it. You've got to deal with it, so enjoy it."

The Vikings did not appear to be happy campers during the week in southern California. Foreman demanded a new contract. Tarkenton, with a sore knee, talked about the possibility of retirement. The edginess Shell heard about went beyond the press sessions, defensive tackle Alan Page recalls, and was another recurring Super Bowl problem.

"You never had more than two hours alone," Page says. "There were either meetings or meals or practices every day for however long a time. That creates a tension that doesn't have to be."

The only controversy that seeped into the Raiders' camp has gained irony through the years. Page and Upshaw were union leaders at the time, and the NFL was without a collective bargaining agreement, so Page slyly told reporters the Raiders were thinking of striking the game. "After years of trying to get to the Super Bowl," Upshaw said in reply, "can you imagine me going to our guys and telling them we are going to strike? They'd kill me."

On Saturday, the Raiders even spent much of practice playing baseball, using helmets for bats and wadded-up tape for a ball. "That was the way we had done things throughout the year," Upshaw says. "Loose and carefree."

"I knew by the end of practice on Thursday that we were going to have a great game," Shell says. Wednesday had been the defense's practice day, and it went quite well, "I didn't even want to practice against our defense," Shell says. "Then the next day was offensive day, and

The Vikings had trouble stopping Clarence Davis all day long as the Oakland running back—here rolling along behind Mark van Eeghen—gained 137 yards on just 16 carries. He had runs of 35, 20, and 18 yards.

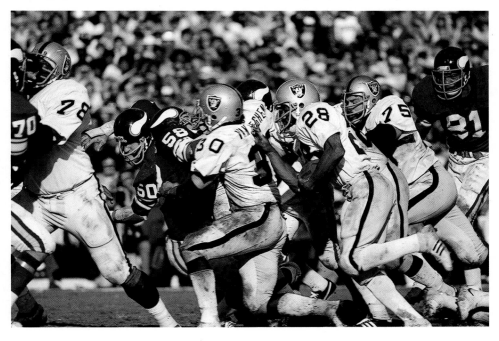

Running back Pete Banaszak was one of four Raiders who played on the Oakland team that lost to Green Bay in Super Bowl II. He was willing to do anything to score from the 1-yard line—even stand on his head.

it was uncanny. Ken Stabler had one ball hit the ground, and the receiver just happened to drop it. That guy was so accurate, it was eerie. I said, 'Hey, these guys are in big trouble.' "

Shell and Upshaw have vivid memories of watching the Vikings warm up before the game, which was the first Super Bowl to be played in the Rose Bowl. Shell recalls seeing them "playing around like they think it's going to be a cakewalk," and telling Upshaw, "They just don't realize what they're in for today."

Upshaw remembers the pregame introductions of Minnesota's defense. "The front four, the Purple Gang, were all leading cheers," Upshaw says, "and I said, 'That's got to be false chatter.'"

Upshaw felt even better after Minnesota's first possession, which ended on Tarkenton's badly thrown short pass toward Foreman on third-and-four. "I was thinking, 'If that's the best he can throw, they're going to be in for a long day,' " Upshaw says.

Before long, though, it was the Raiders' day that looked longer than 5 o'clock shadows. Minnesota had blocked 13 kicks during the regular season, including five by Page on placekicks. In one four-game stretch, the Vikings blocked three field goals, three extra points, and one punt. Then they beat the Rams for the NFC championship primarily with blocked kicks. On

an 18-yard field-goal attempt, cornerback Nate Allen deflected the kicked ball to Bobby Bryant, whose 90-yard return gave the Vikings a 7-0 lead, and they made it 10-0 when linebacker Matt Blair's blocked punt set up a field goal.

The Raiders thought they were different. Ray Guy had punted for four NFL seasons without having one blocked. But the first time came on Oakland's third possession. With the ball on the Raiders' 34, Vikings linebacker Fred McNeill broke through the middle to block the kick, then recovered the high-bouncing ball inside the 5. McNeill stumbled to the ground and Guy touched him down.

Even so, Minnesota had the ball on the Raiders' 3. "If we move the wrong way, it's a touchdown," Matuszak said.

"That was a tight time for us," Oakland cornerback Willie Brown says. "But you've got to do your job wherever the ball is. It didn't even cross my mind that they might score."

Minnesota's first play gained one yard. On second down, halfback Brent McClanahan took the ball and headed between guard Ed

The game was already decided, but Oakland's Willie Brown didn't relax. He intercepted a Fran Tarkenton pass and raced 75 yards for the fourth-quarter touchdown that boosted his team's lead to 32-7.

White and tackle Ron Yary on the right side. Raiders nose tackle Dave Rowe got there first. Left linebacker Phil Villapiano, who had been caught outside Yary on first down, drove his body lower this time and joined Rowe in the hole. He hit the ball with his helmet and heard McClanahan yell an obscenity, "so I knew he had lost it," Villapiano said. Willie Hall, the extra inside linebacker who became a starter when the Raiders went to four linebackers, saw the ball roll through someone's legs. He dived and recovered it.

"They lined up in a formation where they had a big tendency to run to our left, and we slanted to it," Zeman says. "They'd been successful running it all year, but fortunately we were ready and we executed. Sometimes, you're ready and you don't execute."

However, the Raiders still were back on their

Oakland wide receivers Cliff Branch (left) and MVP Fred Biletnikoff embraced as time ran out. Biletnikoff retired after two more seasons, but Branch went on to play for two more Raiders Super Bowl winners.

Raiders head coach John Madden wore a smile as big as the Lombardi Trophy as his team won its first Super Bowl. Oakland never trailed, jumping to a 16-0 halftime lead and keeping on the pressure to win 32-14.

own 3. "We just wanted to move the ball out and get some good punting position," Shell says. But on third-and-seven, Davis broke free around left end for 35 yards to the Oakland 41.

"They were in a formation where they ran the same play every time," Page says, "and we knew it. Or at least we should have known it. I can remember coming out of the huddle, thinking, 'We're going to stop this one dead.' After that, the air went out." The Raiders drove to Minnesota's 7, taking a 3-0 lead on Errol Mann's 24-yard field goal.

"Isn't it ironic?" said Mark van Eeghen, the Raiders' 1,000-yard fullback. "Somebody blocks our punt and it turns the game around for us."

It sure did. Hilgenberg remembers looking at the Raiders' bench after the block. "You could almost see the fear in their eyes," he says. "But they made it a ten-point turnaround. Just as they had gone from a real low to a real high, we knew we had lost a tremendous opportunity. The momentum swing was so great, I don't think we ever came back from that."

Madden was yelling on the sideline when Stabler joined him before the field goal. He wanted seven points from the drive. "Don't worry," Stabler told Madden. "There's a lot more where that came from."

He was right. Oakland's next two drives went

for touchdowns—64 yards in 10 plays, then 35 in five plays after Neal Colzie's 25-yard punt return. Stabler's one-yard pass to tight end Dave Casper made it 10-0 with 7:10 left in the half, and his 17-yard pass to Biletnikoff set up Pete Banaszak's one-yard scoring run less than four minutes later. Mann missed his first of two wide-right extra-point tries to keep the score 16-0.

The Raiders had 166 rushing yards at halftime. "Those two are the best in football," defensive end Jim Marshall said of Shell and Upshaw. Upshaw overpowered Page, and Shell kept the 240-pound Marshall from making so much as an assist on a tackle. "The guy didn't have a stat," Upshaw says. "We were too big and strong. And we knew when we went into the game, if we got through the front four and the linebackers, not too many people in their secondary were too anxious to tackle."

Defensively, Oakland found its 3-4 ideally suited to cut off short passes to Vikings backs. "When they hooked, we hooked with them," Villapiano said. "The way Tarkenton scrambles, we weren't going to sack him anyway, so we didn't lose anything by having only three linemen." When the Vikings split Foreman wide to match him one-on-one against a linebacker, the Raiders were ready for that, too. Safety Jack Tatum covered him.

So the Vikings tried to take advantage of the Raiders' man-to-man cornerback coverage and threw deep more than usual. It wasn't their game, though, and their longest pass all day to a wide receiver gained 25 yards. "They got impatient and kept trying to get a big play," Zeman says. "Our guys were able to cover them, which was fortunate."

In the first 30 minutes, the Raiders controlled the ball for 21:30. They had 16 first downs to the Vikings' 4, 48 plays to 22, and 288 yards to 86. "I felt at halftime we had total control of the football game," Shell says. "But we warned each other during halftime that we're playing a great team. They're not going to give up. I don't take anything away from the Vikings. We played a great football team that day."

Late in the third quarter, after Mann's 40-yard field goal made it 19-0, the Vikings drove 68 yards to a touchdown. They scored on Tarkenton's eight-yard pass to White. Then they threatened to cut Oakland's lead to 19-14. They drove 41 yards to the Raiders' 37 before Hall surfaced again to intercept a pass by Tarkenton.

Three plays later, Biletnikoff ran to the Vikings' 2 on a 48-yard pass play, and Banaszak scored on the next play. Biletnikoff set up three scores with his four catches for 79 yards, earning him the game's most valuable player award. Brown made it 32-7 against Minnesota's hurry-up offense when he anticipated White's short sideline route, broke out of his deep zone, and picked off the ball with a clear field ahead for a 75-yard touchdown return.

That was it for Tarkenton. Bob Lee directed the last touchdown drive, getting a score from the 13 on a pass to tight end Stu Voigt. Tarkenton would play two more seasons, but he never made it to another Super Bowl. More than any other Vikings player, he has lamented that he's still haunted by the Super Bowl losses, three in Tarkenton's case. He won't talk about them anymore.

"I blocked them out of my mind," he says.

But even now, the losses seem to be an obstacle at the Hall of Fame's door that only Tarkenton and Page have been able to clear. Other former Vikings deserve consideration, certainly. Yary and center Mick Tingelhoff were all-pro seven times, Krause and defensive end Carl Eller six times. Krause's 81 interceptions are an NFL career record. Marshall and Tingelhoff set NFL records for consecutive games on defense and offense, respectively. Those seven men started in all four Vikings Super Bowls, and kicker Fred Cox, guard Ed White, and linebacker Roy Winston played in them. And, of course, Bud Grant was at the helm for all of them. He won 168 games and a remarkable 11 division championships in 18 years at Minnesota.

"You could speculate for a lifetime and never really come up with the reasons we lost them," Krause says. "We had good football teams. It just so happened it wasn't our time to win a Super Bowl. That's past history, and the sun will come up tomorrow. At least we were there, doggone it. A lot of other teams would love to have been in a Super Bowl."

When Super Sunday Was Doomsday

Hindsight should have told us what was coming. It doesn't always work that way, though, which is a testimony to just how far emotion can carry a pro football team.

In Super Bowl XII, there were the Dallas Cowboys, who were at the top of their considerable game, and the Denver Broncos, who were…well, to tell the truth, the Broncos probably weren't all that sure just what they were…and couldn't quite believe where they were. The Broncos rode to New Orleans on a tide of emotion. Fact is, they had been frequently outmanned along the route. Fact is, they hadn't been outfought.

"I think we probably had a better team in game twelve than we had in six," says Roger Staubach, who quarterbacked Dallas in both of those victories.

"We were a younger team, and, meaning no disrespect to the guys who won in Super Bowl six, we probably had more dangerous people at the skill positions in Super Bowl twelve, more ways to hurt an opponent. For one thing, we had more speed."

The Cowboys' offense had younger receivers with younger legs. In Super Bowl VI, Bob Hayes and Lance Alworth had been near the end of illustrious careers. The Super Bowl XII receivers—Drew Pearson, Butch Johnson, and Golden Richards—were on the way up. And the running game featured the brilliant rookie, Tony Dorsett, along with Robert Newhouse, a vastly underrated back. The Cowboys' defense in Super Bowl XII, nicknamed "Doomsday II" after that hard-handed bunch from Super Bowl VI, was just as nasty, but a whole lot quicker.

The point is, Dallas was expected to be in Super Bowl XII. Denver wasn't. Dallas was coached by the disciplined and painstakingly thorough Tom Landry. Mike Ditka, who played and coached for Landry, says, "Nobody prepared more thoroughly than Tom… nobody."

Dallas also had Staubach, a remarkably resourceful field leader. Staubach was the Heis-man Trophy winner his junior year at the Naval Academy, but after his senior season he went off to honor his military commitment. Four years later, he returned to football. Did the lay-off hurt? Not really.

"You have to understand," Landry says, "when you're talking about Roger Staubach, you're talking about one of the best ever at that position."

Looking back at Super Bowl XII, Landry adds, "Oh, and we also had a great defense."

"We didn't have all that much talent," former Denver head coach Robert (Red) Miller says now.

In 1977, Red Miller coached the Broncos as Elmer Gantry might have…with a passion.

Miller had a quarterback, too, and the Cowboys knew him well because he once was one of them.

"First thing I did when I got the job that year [1977] was make a trade with the Giants for Craig Morton," Miller says. Morton had quarterbacked Dallas before Staubach, then had been dealt to the New York Giants. Before he came to Denver, his reviews had been mixed at best. Dallas lost to Baltimore in Super Bowl V with Morton on the field and Staubach on the bench. Craig Morton labored under the reputation of not being able to win the big one.

"Craig didn't have much left in the way of knees, but he still had an arm," Miller says. "He could throw the hell out of the ball."

Denver also had a solid defense in 1977. To put a finer point on it, Denver had what football-wacky Colorado had come to know as the "Orange Crush."

"They fought like a bunch of alley cats," Miller says.

Miller was a first-year head coach in 1977, having replaced John Ralston.

"I took over a team of individuals," he says. "They had revolted against Ralston. If I did one thing for that team, I made them a team. I taught them to fight for one another. Well, they did that…they played hard."

"Red drew the team together in a hard time," says Broncos defensive end Lyle Alzado. "He gave us discipline. I remember the first meeting we had with him after he was named coach. All of us came slopping into the meeting room,

Super Bowl XII was the first one played without a sky. Dallas and Denver met indoors—under the lights of the Louisiana Superdome—as this wide-angle shot, taken with a "fish-eye" lens during the game, reveals.

drinking soda pop or eating candy bars like we always had. Red just looked at us and said, 'This is a working room, not a dining room. Don't ever let me see you come in here again eating or drinking. And I mean it!' Nobody ever did, either."

Miller grew up in downstate Illinois. His grandfather had been a muleskinner and his father had worked in the coal mines. Because he was good in athletics, Red escaped the coal fields. But he remained a blue-collar football coach. His

Noting the Denver fans, a Dallas player said, "It looked like the whole stadium was orange."

dossier showed long service at the high school, college, and pro levels—before he ever got his shot as a head coach.

"What we did in Denver that year was relaxed and enjoyable," Morton says. "And Red was the reason we felt good about what we were doing. He got us believing in ourselves, believing in each other."

"I felt good about our chances," Miller says. "We'd won games we weren't supposed to win just to get to New Orleans. We'd played Dallas in the last regular-season game that year, played 'em tough. We lost 14-6."

Going into Super Bowl XII, Dorsett remem-

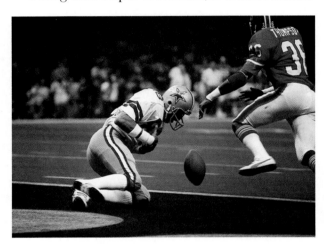

Dallas led 13-0 at halftime, but squandered several scoring chances. One was this touchdown pass dropped by Drew Pearson (with safety Billy Thompson covering). Efren Herrera missed a subsequent field goal.

bered his team's regular-season meeting with Denver.

"Great pursuit," he said. "I tried some little shake-and-bake moves on them. I got the shake, but they'd come across and nail me before I ever got to any bake. The only way to run on that defense is north and south, nothing fancy."

Miller's "alley cats" burst upon the Super Bowl scene with a fervor not easily forgotten by those who were there. The Denver defense was introduced prior to Super Bowl XII and it's doubtful that any starting unit for this game ever took the field with a greater show of emotion. The Broncos' fans practically crushed one another in their enthusiasm.

"Looked like the whole stadium was orange," recalls Dallas defensive tackle Jethro Pugh. "Folks were just going crazy, and those players...I never saw a bunch of players so excited as that."

"People wondered why we weren't a more emotional team," says Randy White, the Cowboys' other defensive tackle. "We were. It didn't show on the surface, but it showed in the way we played."

Pugh is asked for his assessment of Morton. "Smart... smart's the first thing I think of when I think of Craig," Pugh says. Pugh wasn't the only Cowboy who felt that way. "I believe he was the most intelligent quarterback I ever had," Landry says.

"He was smart but he wasn't able to run much," Pugh adds.

"Films we studied, you could see where Craig was hurting—he had a hip bothering him, I think. He just looked like he couldn't get around much. The strength of our defense was our pass rush, so our thinking, going in, was to shut down their run and make them pass. We figured we could get to Craig."

"I don't think he'll finish," said Cowboys safety Cliff Harris before the game. "Craig looks like he's hurting and if he takes a good hard lick, he's not going to be there at the end."

For Staubach, the week before Super Bowl XII had been emotional. "It was the aspect of playing against Craig Morton," he says. "We'd been rivals for the job when I got to Dallas. Now, here we were, rivals again."

Morton had helped Staubach when Roger joined the Cowboys. "Craig was a good guy,"

Dallas rookie Tony Dorsett scored the game's first touchdown by bouncing three yards off left tackle. An interception by safety Randy Hughes at the Denver 25—one of four Cowboys interceptions—set up the touchdown.

Staubach says, "a very giving person."

The game began, not with a bang, not even with a whimper. It was more like banana cream pies at ten paces.

Dallas tried a double-reverse on the first play from scrimmage. Tony Dorsett handed to Butch Johnson, who fumbled, recovered, and went down for a nine-yard loss. Dallas ended up punting.

Denver went from its own 47 to the Cowboys' 33 before Randy White ended the drive by sacking Morton for an 11-yard loss.

White played right defensive tackle for Dallas. His nickname was "Manster"—half man, half monster. White and the defensive end on his side, Harvey Martin, would end up sharing most valuable player honors for XII. The ballot box they stuffed was Craig Morton.

"Obviously, I wanted us to win the game," Staubach says, "and I was glad when we did.

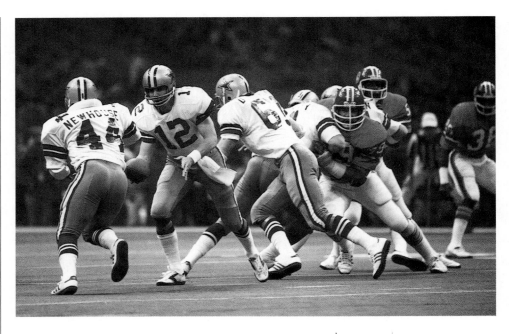

The Cowboys more than doubled Denver's yardage, out-gaining the Broncos 325-156. Stumpy Robert New-house (44), taking the ball from Roger Staubach, carried 14 times for 55 yards. Tony Dorsett ran for 66.

But I wish Craig had done well and the score had been close—I really do. When we went to our first Super Bowl [V], Craig went all the way, but he'd been playing hurt since midseason. When we played against him and Denver, he had a bad hip and a leg muscle pull. But he played.

"I feel badly because people only remember winners, and when they think of Craig Morton, they think of him as the quarterback who lost in those Super Bowl games. They don't think about the phenomenal seasons he had just getting his teams to those games. Watching what happened to him in twelve was one of the saddest things I can remember in football."

What happened to Morton was Doomsday II, the Dallas defense.

"Going in," Miller says, "I felt like we matched up with them in every area except one. I didn't like our offensive line against their defensive line. I felt like we were overmatched there. Hell, I'd picked up our left offensive tackle off of the waiver wire."

Andy Maurer, who was across from Randy White or Harvey Martin, depending upon which way the Cowboys' defensive scythe opted to swing, was the left offensive tackle.

"I was real surprised when I saw they weren't going to double on me," Martin says. "They left that tackle out there to take me alone. I felt real good when I saw it was just going to be me and him."

Pugh, White, Martin, Ed (Too Tall) Jones, Bill Gregory, Bob Breunig, D.D. Lewis, and the garrulous Thomas (Hollywood) Henderson overwhelmed the Denver offense.

Morton was sacked two times and intercepted four times, but even that doesn't begin to tell the story. On virtually every one of his 15 pass attempts (4 completions), he was savaged by the Dallas rush.

"Rushing the passer was the key to it, as far as we were concerned," Landry says. "We knew if

Red Miller of Denver became only the second head coach to take a team to the Super Bowl in his first year. His inspired Broncos won 14 of 16 games in the regular season and playoffs to get to the Super Bowl.

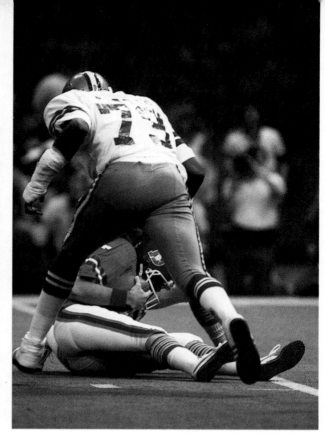

Dallas defenders Randy White (left) and Harvey Martin made life miserable for Craig Morton, helping to harass him into four interceptions and sacking him once each. Morton completed only 4 of 15 passes.

we gave Craig time, he could hurt us. So we wanted a big rush. Craig didn't have a chance. Our rush was on him before he could respond."

Super Bowl XII proved that a quarterback's life isn't all champagne and roses. It showed us, chillingly, the fearsome price a man may be called to pay for dropping back into the pocket.

"I see the rush, I don't watch it," said Morton afterwards. "But I knew it was there, because I didn't get the ball to people who were open, and we had them open. I just didn't hit them. It's disappointing and I wish we could have made a better showing, but we didn't. It's hard to accept, but I have to accept it.

"There was a lot to this year that was good. We overcame a lot just to get here. Do I worry that people will say I was the guy who didn't win the Super Bowl? No, there's more to my life than that."

In his way, Morton was a gallant figure, swept away by circumstance in his two opportunities to go the final mile.

"Craig was a fine quarterback," Landry says. "He had a great arm, intelligence, and toughness. He did a lot for the Dallas Cowboys and for Denver."

Denver punted after the first sack by Randy White, and that's where Miller figures the Broncos lost the game.

Cowboys rookie Tony Hill unwisely chose to field Bucky Dilts's punt at the Dallas 3. Hill fumbled, but was ruled to have regained possession in a wild scramble at the Cowboys' 1.

"Our man had it, but I guess it squirted out," Miller says. "I believe if we get that one, we win the game."

To be sure, Dallas seemed to be trying to fulfill Miller's hopes. Although they led 13-0 at halftime, the Cowboys had fumbled four times, had been penalized five times, and had seen quarterback Staubach sacked four times. Throw in three missed field-goal attempts by Efren Herrera, too.

"At one point in the first half," Staubach says, "Robert Newhouse got hold of my arm and said, 'Roger, you've got to get hold of this team.' I told him, 'Robert, I'm trying to get hold of myself.' Eventually, we did. Both offenses were very spotty to start with. We finally got settled down, but Denver never did."

Dallas scored first with less than five minutes remaining in the first quarter. Morton's first interception launched that short drive (25 yards). A 13-yard pass from Staubach to Billy Joe Du-

It was a long day for Denver's defense, which spent much of the game lining up in the shadow of its own goal line. The Broncos' offense put the defense in trouble by turning over the ball a Super Bowl-record eight times.

Pree and Dorsett's runs were the weapons. Dorsett slanted over from the Denver 3 on fourth-and-1 behind a shattering block by Newhouse to give Dallas a 7-0 advantage. Two plays later, linebacker Breunig tipped Morton's pass over the middle, and cornerback Aaron Kyle intercepted. The Cowboys were in business again at the Broncos' 35.

Newhouse and Dorsett ran their way to the Broncos' 8, but Alzado sacked Staubach back to the 18, and Dallas had to settle for a 35-yard field goal by Herrera for a 10-0 lead at the end of the first period. Morton's first quarter included two completions in six attempts for 14 yards, one sack, and two passes intercepted.

Desperate for the breaks to run their way, the Broncos seemed to get one early in the second quarter. Scrambling from the Broncos' 19, Staubach's pass was intercepted...but officials ruled Staubach had stepped out of bounds before the errant throw. Dallas retained possession, and Herrera kicked a 43-yard field goal.

The rockslide of Broncos mistakes continued. Two plays after the field goal, Haven Moses was open deep, but Morton threw short,

and Benny Barnes intercepted. The Cowboys couldn't score then, nor could they score moments later when they got the ball back after Denver fumbled a punt. Denver turned the ball over five times within an 11-minute stretch of the second quarter. Two of Morton's four completions for the day came in that period—and both were fumbled after the catch and recovered by Dallas safety Randy Hughes. But the three botched field-goal attempts by Dallas kept the halftime score at 13-0.

In the Cowboys' locker room, Landry reminded his players that Denver had done most of its winning that season in the second halves of games. In the Broncos' locker room, Miller wrote on the blackboard: No More Turnovers, Offense Break the Ice, Defense Keep Working. Attack, Attack, Attack!

Norris Weese replaced Craig Morton at quarterback for Denver in the third quarter, but didn't fare much better. Aggressive linebacker Thomas (Hollywood) Henderson blasted him just after he released this pass.

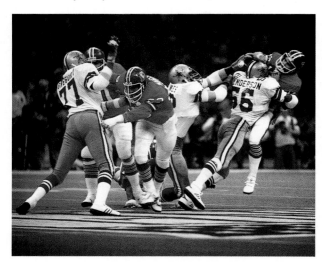

Dallas was leading only 13-3 in the third quarter, when Butch Johnson made a spectacular, 45-yard, fingertip catch for a touchdown. He beat safety Bernard Jackson (29) and cornerback Steve Foley on the play.

Denver broke the ice early in the third quarter, moving 35 yards to enable Jim Turner to kick a 47-yard field goal, second longest in Super Bowl history. But it really shouldn't have happened. Denver lost four yards on a fourth-down fake at midfield, but got a first down on a Dallas penalty.

The Cowboys replied two series later, going 58 yards in five plays to stretch their lead to 20-3, and 45 of the yards came on one play. Facing third-and-10 at the Broncos' 45, Dallas broke its huddle with a pass play called to wide receiver Pearson. But, as the Cowboys left the huddle, Staubach had a word for Butch Johnson, the opposite wide receiver. Johnson was to run a clear-out route on the play.

"Run a post," Staubach told Johnson.

"I'm supposed to run an in."

"Just run a post, will you…and if Jackson wavers in the middle, run by him. And keep going!"

Denver free safety Bernard Jackson hesitated on Pearson's deep route while Johnson flew past him in the middle. Johnson made a spectacular reception, grabbing Staubach's 45-yard pass on his fingertips as he dived over the goal line. He lost the ball upon impact, but it was ruled that he had broken the plane of the goal.

"I was getting upset," Staubach says. "We had the lead at halftime, so we went conservative. I thought we should keep attacking."

Denver's Rick Upchurch followed Johnson's scoring catch with a 67-yard kickoff return to the Cowboys' 26.

On the first play from scrimmage, Morton's pass in the flat for Rob Lytle went square into the considerable torso of Ed (Too Tall) Jones.

"I had a touchdown, probably, if I had held on," Jones says. "But just as I got the ball I looked to see where Craig was. I figured it'd be a footrace, him and me. I don't know if I could have beat him, but it would have been interesting. Instead, I dropped the ball."

At that point, Miller had seen all he needed to see of Morton, although he said later that the halftime dis-

Randy White (left) and Harvey Martin are the only co-MVPs in Super Bowl history.

cussion had included using reserve quarterback Norris Weese in long-yardage situations because Weese could scramble.

"We're taking you out," Miller told Morton. Today, Miller says, "Craig and I had a good relationship. All he said was 'All right.'"

Lytle and Jim Jensen got the Broncos a touchdown in four plays, with Lytle scoring from the 1. With 5:39 to play in the third quarter, Denver had pulled to within 20-10.

The 1977 Broncos had done their best work in the fourth quarter of almost every game. Miller held up four fingers on the sideline as the fourth quarter began, and orange-clad Broncomaniacs in attendance went nuts.

It was like one of those golf tournaments in which the contenders don't do much, but the leader keeps backing up, getting closer to them. Dallas took what looked like a very large step backwards two plays into the final period when Staubach, back to pass, fumbled at the Broncos' 45, and Denver nose tackle Rubin Carter recovered.

Staubach broke the index finger on his passing hand on the play. He came back to play, even though he couldn't pass very well. But it didn't matter because Dallas had another man who could throw the ball.

On Denver's second possession after Staubach's fumble, Norris Weese went from the Shotgun on third down from the Broncos' 30.

"The guy I played on [Maurer] backed up, waiting to take me on," Harvey Martin says. "I used his momentum against him, got up under him going back, made him knock the quarterback down."

Weese went down under the Martin-Maurer tangle and fumbled, and Kyle recovered for Dallas at the Broncos' 29.

Before the game, Landry had suggested to running back Newhouse that he throw a few practice passes, just in case.

Halfbacks throwing passes in warmups tend to attract attention, so Newhouse, being wise as well as short, threw his warmup tosses into the artificial turf.

After Weese's fumble, Landry, feeling the Denver defense would be down because of the turnover, called for a halfback pass.

"I wasn't expecting it," Newhouse says. "I had stickum all over my hands, so I licked that stuff off my fingers in the huddle."

Newhouse's throw to receiver Golden Richards was good for a 29-yard touchdown. It was 27-10, and over.

Randy Gradishar was a linebacker for the 1977 Broncos, and a good one.

"Looking back," he says, "nobody believed we'd get that far. I can remember sitting in the locker room with other linebackers, and we'd say, 'This team is going to the Super Bowl?'

"We did, and we played hard to get there. I think the real excitement was what it meant to the people of Colorado. Maybe we didn't play as well as we could have, but Dallas had a lot to do with that."

Denver had compiled only three winning seasons in its history, the best of which was 9-5 in 1976. Then came 1977 and the 12-2 year and AFC Western Division Championship, then the AFC title, and finally the Super Bowl after 17 years of mostly bottom-of-the-barrel finishes. It was heady stuff.

The "first-time" syndrome one sees so often in the Super Bowl was a factor.

"We thought we were ready, but it was different," Broncos wide receiver Jack Dolbin says. "Something...concentration, or just being nervous. We didn't make the plays we had made to get there."

Gradishar alludes to the pressure of a team's first Super Bowl appearance, but he adds that another circumstance—his severely sprained ankle—kept him from worrying about it much.

The Denver defense was as fierce as advertised, but too often it had to solve problems created by its own offense.

"People look back and figure the game was lopsided," Landry says. "I don't. Their history was one of coming back and I was very much aware of it. In the fourth quarter, the difference was only ten points."

Was Landry worried?

"You bet."

The worry abated when Weese fumbled, and Newhouse fired that sticky strike to Richards.

"Super Bowl six was special because people had said we couldn't win the big one," Landry says. "But I felt pretty darned good after twelve, too."

Feelings That Even Time Can't Heal

A full decade later, midlife crises surfacing on the horizon, many of them gone to fat, hair graying or gone, competitive fires supposedly long since banked, fortysomething men with *responsibilities*—and damned if they still weren't at it. It was as if time had stood shock-still.

Cliff Harris still was running his shuck on Lynn Swann; Swann still was catching it so deep the Dallas secondary was only a rumor. Franco Harris still was laying down tracks. Roger Staubach still was getting it away clean as the rush eddied against him. Dallas still was opting for slick, Pittsburgh still was putting its chips on savage. They were talking about one another's mothers, about poking each other in the eyes. There were elbows in the face and knuckles in the groin and cries of "cheap shot *me*, sucka!"

And not a one of them had worn a jockstrap in anger in years.

Forget their Super Bowl engagements. Forget Super Bowl XIII—the exciting sequel to Super Bowl X in which the guys in black got the girl again and the only things that changed were the heroes and the postgame complaints about being robbed. We're talking *recent*.

The rematch was flag football in 1988, a charity deal. The old antagonists got together in Pittsburgh the night before to have a few drinks, share a few laughs, and dabble in nostalgia…and the next day they tried to destroy each other the same way they had twice when it counted, back when they despised one another like rival herd bulls.

"Everyone laughed about the old days the night before," recalls Preston Pearson, the halfback who played five seasons in Pittsburgh before blooming in Dallas as a third-down receiver out of the backfield. "Even just before the game, there was nothing but kidding. Then the flag game started and it was, 'I'm going to get you for everything you ever did to me.'"

For the indignities and abuse heaped on them in what may have been the two best Super Bowls ever played, the Cowboys finally got even. Sort of.

The Pittsburgh post-flag football injury list suggested a midair collision: Franco Harris suffered what Dallas free safety Cliff Harris calls "the worst broken nose I've ever seen." Linebacker Andy Russell tore an Achilles' tendon. Running back Frenchy Fuqua broke an ankle.

"I looked around at what was happening," Pearson says, "and I said 'the hell with this' and went over and sat down."

All those years…and they discovered they didn't like each other any more in 1988 than they had in 1976 or 1979.

Hadn't in Super Bowl X, when the Steelers won largely on the strength of Swann's brilliance; didn't when they met again three years later in the first Super Bowl rematch. Ironically, both games were decided by four points, both produced furious and futile Dallas rallies, both pitted Cowboys guile against Pittsburgh grit, and both ended in real acrimony. Only the victims of funky fate—Cowboys tight end Jackie Smith and field judge Fred Swearingen—were different in XIII.

"Yeah, we disliked them," says Cliff Harris. "The rough, rugged, basic Steelers…the clean, cosmopolitan, finesse Cowboys. The guys in the ties and dark suits against the guys in the hardhats and rolled-up sleeves. That contrast …that was the thing between us."

The second time they met in the Super Bowl, the Cowboys were in Miami to defend the Vince Lombardi Trophy, having thrashed Denver 27-10 in Super Bowl XII. Dallas also was riding an eight-game winning streak.

"We should have won our first game against them," Cliff Harris says. "But in the second Super Bowl we over-prepared, over-planned. We thought too much. Pittsburgh ran a simple, basic offense and we never matched their aggressiveness. I was mad about it then. I still am."

Back in the Super Bowl for the third time, the Steelers were convinced that only injuries in the 1976 playoffs, and then a season of distractions in 1977, had prevented them from collecting even more Super Bowl hardware.

"I'm telling you," Joe Greene said at breakfast the day before Super Bowl XIII, "we're going to kick their ass. Put it in the bank!"

Elsewhere, there was considerably less confidence over Pittsburgh's chances. The Steelers

213

The game was barely five minutes old when Pittsburgh's Terry Bradshaw and John Stallworth hooked up on a 28-yard touchdown pass. Arriving too late were cornerback Aaron Kyle and safety Cliff Harris.

had climbed the pro football mountain in 1978 with a defense that eventually should put five players into the Pro Football Hall of Fame, plus a running game spearheaded by a relatively small offensive line that included rookie tackle Ray Pinney, a late-season replacement for the injured Larry Brown. Pinney would have to block Ed (Too Tall) Jones, a defensive end who was quick enough to retire temporarily after the game to pursue a career in boxing.

Super Bowl XIII began with a coin toss by Hall of Fame member George Halas (standing in car).

"Oh, yeah," Chuck Noll says today. "That's

Dallas tied the score 7-7 on the last play of the first quarter as Roger Staubach fired a 39-yard touchdown pass to Tony Hill, who sprinted down the left sideline with safety Donnie Shell in pursuit.

what the so-called *experts* around the league were saying. We weren't going to be able to handle the Cowboys' defensive ends."

As it turned out, Steelers tackles Pinney and Jon Kolb got nothing worse than a standoff with Jones and Harvey Martin. What did in the Cowboys wasn't their defensive ends. The Dallas fall from Super Bowl grace can be directly traced to several things: a pass interference call that two years later got field judge Swearingen fired; a pass dropped in the end zone by Dallas tight end Jackie Smith that still lives in his worst nightmares; a rules change ironically triggered by a Steelers defender.

Mostly, the Cowboys' loss can be hung on the coming of age of quarterback Terry Bradshaw. Those were Bradshaw's fingerprints they found on the neck of the Dallas team on that cloudy January 21, 1979, afternoon in Miami.

Thought even as late as the previous season

214

to lack sufficient intellect—"He thinks a Rhodes Scholar is a hitchhiker going to school," a teammate once had snickered—the Bradshaw of 1978 discovered the one ingredient that had kept him from greatness: poise.

Bob Adams knew it was coming a few years before, even though an anxiety attack had caused Bradshaw to throw up on the former Steelers tight end's hands in a huddle. "Watching him play quarterback," Adams says years later, "was like seeing a rose bloom in slow motion."

By 1978, Bradshaw was in full flower. Meanwhile, the NFL's Competition Committee, on which Cowboys president Tex Schramm was chairman, was inspired—to a large degree by the dominance of Pittsburgh cornerback Mel Blount—to make a rules change that worked wonderfully to the Steelers' benefit.

For years, Blount and other Pittsburgh cornerbacks had littered the secondary with half-conscious receivers. But in the offseason prior to 1978, the rules were changed and it was illegal to have defensive contact with receivers five yards beyond the line of scrimmage.

On the way to being sacked in the second quarter, Bradshaw had the ball stripped from him by the Cowboys' Thomas (Hollywood) Henderson. Mike Hegman (left) picked it up and ran 37 yards for a touchdown.

"I don't know if I caused it," says Blount, "but they always called it the 'Mel Blount Rule.'"

A rose by any other name, the rule alteration that raised the premium on the passing game caused Noll to move the Steelers' offensive emphasis away from the running of Franco Harris. Bradshaw *After Hegman's score, Bradshaw was treated on the sideline for a shoulder injury, but he returned.*

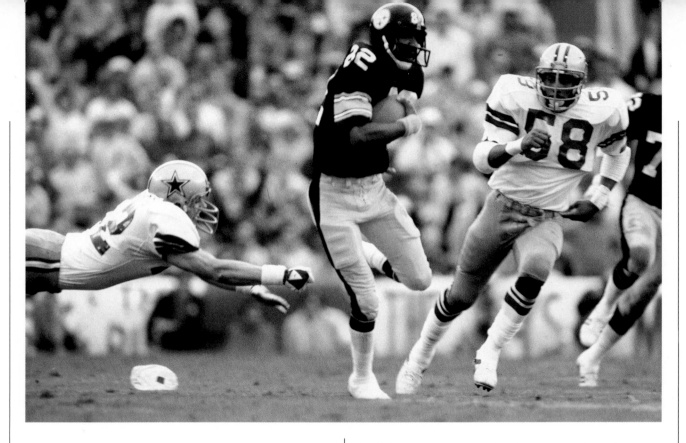

The Steelers tied the score at 14-14 when John Stallworth caught a 10-yard pass from Bradshaw at the right sideline, turned toward the middle, and raced 75 yards for his second touchdown. Pittsburgh led 21-14 at halftime.

threw roughly 15 percent more often in 1978 than he had in the seasons when Pittsburgh won its first two Super Bowls.

"That year, Terry came into his own," says Steelers linebacker Andy Russell. "He wasn't ever dumb. He was just a kid. Right after he signed, I had him over to my place with some of the other guys before camp started, just to get him acquainted. He tried to be one of the guys, even telling dirty jokes. There was a lot of pressure on him. And he was *so* young."

A long-time Steelers official reads Bradshaw's maturity differently: "He learned to play quarterback in the NFL the way I learned to be a Catholic...by rote."

Whatever the impetus for improvement, the Bradshaw that Dallas had seen in Super Bowl X was far less formidable than the one it faced in Super Bowl XIII.

"Bradshaw told me later that in Super Bowl thirteen, he had keyed on me," says Cliff Harris, the centerfielder at safety in the Cowboys' Doomsday II defense. "He told me he'd throw where I wasn't because I was a strength. And that makes sense, because I would always be helping out a cornerback on a receiver."

As he had in Super Bowl X, Harris again tried to play mind games with Swann. "Subtle stuff," Harris says. "Like walking back after a play and saying, 'Hey, Lynn, you had that bad concussion, c'mon.' Or, 'Lynn, game's on the line now, don't come in my area or I'm going to have to knock you out. *Got* to, man!'"

The mental strategy had no more success

Still trailing 21-14 in the third quarter, Dallas failed to tie the score when tight end Jackie Smith dropped Staubach's perfect 10-yard pass in the end zone. The frustrated Cowboys settled for a field goal.

On the game's pivotal play in the fourth quarter, field judge Fred Swearingen (reaching for flag) penalized Dallas cornerback Benny Barnes 33 yards for tripping wide receiver Lynn Swann on a pass play.

than it had in X, when Swann won the Super Bowl MVP award.

"All you want them to do is think a little, make them realize they're vulnerable," Harris says. "Didn't work much on Swann."

Not noticeably. The decision in the Cliff Harris-Lynn Swann rematch again went to the Steelers' receiver, who torched Dallas for seven receptions worth 124 yards. Swann scored the touchdown that determined the outcome.

The day, overcast and humid even by Miami standards, began badly for Dallas. On Dallas's fifth play, Tom Landry called for a reverse, Drew Pearson botched a handoff from Tony Dorsett, and the Steelers recovered, setting up their first touchdown.

"If Tom hadn't gotten cute with that reverse..." Preston Pearson sighs over the memory. "That turno-

ver put a lot of doubt in our minds. We never really recovered from it."

If their first Super Bowl meeting had ultimately turned on defense—Pittsburgh's Steel Curtain falling on a last-minute Dallas rally—the second time around featured the offenses. Bradshaw and Staubach took turns punching the other guys silly.

Bradshaw threw 28 yards to John Stallworth, who turned around Cowboys cornerback Aaron Kyle 360 degrees with a shoulder fake, to open the scoring. Staubach countered by going 39 yards to Tony Hill to tie it. Then, Bradshaw was stripped of the ball by blitzing linebacker Thomas (Hollywood) Henderson, and linebacker Mike Hegman returned the fumble 37 yards for a 14-7 Cowboys lead. Bradshaw again found Stallworth, this time on a 75-yard play, and it was tied again. Bradshaw later tossed to Rocky Bleier in the end zone on a roll-out to give Pittsburgh a 21-14 halftime lead, turning up the lights for the second-half theatrics that decided the game.

The first came with just under three minutes

Three plays after the pass-interference penalty, Pittsburgh's Franco Harris charged 22 yards up the middle for the touchdown that made it 28-17. An official accidentally screened off Dallas safety Charlie Waters (41).

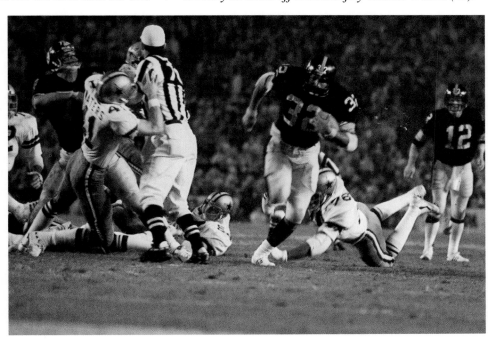

The Steelers took an almost insurmountable 35-17 lead when Bradshaw took advantage of a lost Dallas fumble and threw an 18-yard touchdown pass to Lynn Swann (left), who was mobbed by his Steelers teammates.

left in the third quarter. Dallas was driving for the equalizer. The Pittsburgh offense suddenly had gone dead in the water, failing to get a first down since intermission.

Looking at a third-and-3 situation from the Steelers' 10 and sensing that control of the game was there for the taking, Staubach called a time out to confer with Landry. He wanted no confusion on the call. Late in the first half, with

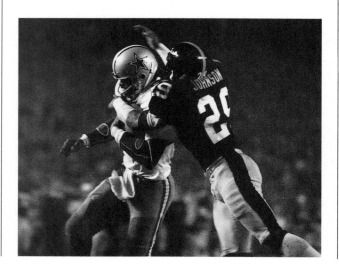

Staubach running a two-minute drill, Landry had interrupted the flow by sending in a play that resulted in an interception by Blount. The quarterback and the coach had argued on the sideline afterwards, Landry asking, "Why didn't you throw late to the tight end?" and Staubach firing back, "Why did you call that ridiculous play?"

The brief conference produced a decision to throw to backup tight end Jackie Smith on a delayed route to the inside. After all, hadn't just such an occasion prompted the Cowboys to bring the 38-year-old Smith out of retirement that summer after a neck condition had ended his fine career with the St. Louis Cardinals?

On the pivotal play, Smith came wide open over the middle near the end line, and the pass that Staubach still calls "the one that will haunt me the longest" was a strike. But the hands that once held everything they touched failed Jackie

Dallas didn't go quietly as Staubach rallied the Cowboys to within four points of Pittsburgh with two touchdown passes in two minutes, the first one to tight end Billy Joe DuPree with 2:27 left in the game.

After recovering the Cowboys' final onside kickoff, the Steelers ran out the clock to win 35-31. Head coach Chuck Noll, who had won his third Super Bowl in five years, was given a victory ride by his team.

XIII not on Jackie Smith, but on Swearingen. Years later, accustomed to controversy that refuses to die, he greets a writer telephoning from Pittsburgh with a chuckle: "I thought you were calling from *Dallas*."

With nine minutes remaining in the last big game he would work in his 21-year career—six years as a referee—Swearingen saw his fate intermingled with that of the Steelers for a second time. Six years before, he had presided over one of the most disputed plays in professional football history—the Immaculate Reception.

On fourth down, with 22 seconds left in a 1972 AFC playoff game between Pittsburgh and Oakland, Bradshaw threw a desperation pass that deflected off either Steelers running back Frenchy Fuqua or Raiders safety Jack Tatum, or both of them. In any case, it rebounded a full 20 yards to where Franco Harris scooped it up, just before it hit the turf, and raced into the end

Smith. If the official play-by-play describes what occurred bluntly, no writer has ever been more trenchant: "Staubach passes for Smith alone in end zone. He drops ball."

Rafael Septien followed Smith's gaffe with a field goal, chopping the Steelers' edge to 21-17, but it left the Cowboys feeling empty.

"I just missed it," Smith says now. "I dropped passes before, but never one that important."

Blaming himself for taking something off the throw to the wide-open Smith, Staubach sighs years later, "I could've punted it to him."

Still, in Dallas, they always put the goat horns for Super Bowl

As the crowd filed out, Pittsburgh's Franco Harris celebrated the Steelers' Super Bowl victory. The powerful running back led his team in rushing with 68 yards on 20 carries, and scored a touchdown.

zone. Swearingen, who didn't see the play, had to rule on its legality. If Fuqua had deflected the pass, it would have been an incompletion and the Raiders would have won. Swearingen conferred with his crew and league supervisor of officials Art McNally, and ruled it a touchdown, giving the Steelers the most important victory in the franchise's then-39-year history.

"I never saw Bradshaw's pass," Swearingen says. "But I had to make the call, and I did."

A half-dozen seasons later, another crucial call fell to Swearingen, who had been reassigned to a field judge position in 1976.

Even Smith's misfortune hadn't shaken the Steelers' offense awake into the fourth quarter, until Swann broke outside on a deep route with Dallas in a blitz, alongside Cowboys cornerback Benny Barnes. Bradshaw threw a high lob. The feet of Swann and Barnes became entangled as Swann tried to cut inside to catch the under-thrown ball, and both fell hard at the Cowboys' 23. Swearingen threw a yellow flag.

After 51 peaceful quarters, the Super Bowl had its very first raging controversy. It howls on to this very day. Swann still says, "It definitely was pass interference." Barnes still says, "I couldn't believe the call; when I saw the flag I thought it was on him." Landry still says Swearingen's call was "the kiss of death" and "the ball game for Pittsburgh." Swearingen still says it was a correct call, but claims that it cost him his job at the hands of a vengeful Schramm.

"It was a lob pass to Swann, a timing pattern," Swearingen says. "They were running side-by-side and there was some contact, but Swann didn't push Barnes. Barnes actually tripped himself, and his legs came up when he hit the ground and he tripped Swann. There was no intent on Barnes's part, but intent wasn't part of the rule.

"The way the rule was written then, the defenders couldn't touch the receiver in any way. So I just flipped the flag, really not thinking it would be a momentous call."

In retrospect, "momentous" is not an understatement. The 33-yard penalty gave the Steelers a first down at the Dallas 23. On third down, Franco Harris bolted through another Dallas blitz from the 22 and scored the touchdown that made it 28-17.

Swearingen barely had gotten his yellow hanky back in his pocket when the Steelers put Super Bowl XIII in theirs. The kickoff following Franco Harris's touchdown run was shanked, and then fumbled at the Dallas 24 by Randy White, the Cowboys' great defensive tackle who was part of the blocking wedge.

The Steelers recovered at the Cowboys' 18. On the next play, Bradshaw, who would be named the game's MVP after passing for a Super Bowl-record and personal-best 318 yards, threw a strike to Swann at the back edge of the end zone. The Steelers led 35-17. Staubach threw two touchdown passes in the next 6:30, but the title of his autobiography, *Time Enough to Win*, proved to be a cruel bit of irony. After the Cowboys' last score, Pittsburgh cleanly handled Dallas's onside kick with 22 seconds remaining and Super Bowl XIII was over. Almost.

"So, after all that time, we play that flag game back in Pittsburgh...and it all starts up again," Preston Pearson says. "Nothing had changed."

No, nothing had. As those groups of aging antagonists dressed in the same locker room, Cliff Harris and Swann talked face-to-face for the first time.

"There is still some...we get along, let's say," Harris says. "He was the perfect receiver—looked great, dressed just right, shoes shined. I was a headhunter. Got all dirty. Hey, DBs are tougher!"

On that sunny 1988 afternoon, they sure were. Cliff Harris ran into Franco Harris and broke his nose. "The Steelers got behind and were trying to catch up," Harris says, "and it got physical."

It also was close and exciting again. Dallas won this time, 24-22, as Staubach threw three touchdown passes—the same number he had tossed in Super Bowl XIII.

And, for the last time, Swann burned Harris on a touchdown pass.

"Afterwards, Lynn came over and handed me his game jersey," Harris says. "He wanted to swap. He said, 'I want you to have this.'

"I said, 'Swann, you got me, again.'"

For a moment, some part of the enmity that defined the Steelers-Cowboys relationship dissolved.

For a moment.

XIV

Pittsburgh 31, Los Angeles 19

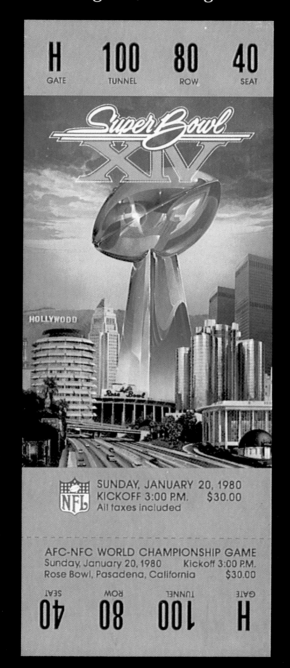

Vital Statistics

Starting Lineups

Los Angeles (NFC)	Offense	Pittsburgh (AFC)
Billy Waddy	WR	John Stallworth
Doug France	LT	Jon Kolb
Kent Hill	LG	Sam Davis
Rich Saul	C	Mike Webster
Dennis Harrah	RG	Gerry Mullins
Jackie Slater	RT	Larry Brown
Terry Nelson	TE	Bennie Cunningham
Preston Dennard	WR	Lynn Swann
Vince Ferragamo	QB	Terry Bradshaw
Wendell Tyler	RB	Franco Harris
Cullen Bryant	RB	Rocky Bleier
	Defense	
Jack Youngblood	LE	L.C. Greenwood
Mike Fanning	LT	Joe Greene
Larry Brooks	RT	Gary Dunn
Fred Dryer	RE	John Banaszak
Jim Youngblood	LLB	Dennis Winston
Jack Reynolds	MLB	Jack Lambert
Bob Brudzinski	RLB	Robin Cole
Pat Thomas	LCB	Ron Johnson
Rod Perry	RCB	Mel Blount
Dave Elmendorf	SS	Donnie Shell
Nolan Cromwell	FS	J.T. Thomas

Substitutions

Los Angeles-Offense: K-Frank Corral. P-Ken Clark. RB-Eddie Hill, Lawrence McCutcheon, Jim Jodat. TE-Charle Young. WR-Ron Smith, Drew Hill. LINE-Dan Ryczek, Bill Bain, Gordon Gravelle. Defense: LINE-Jerry Wilkinson, Reggie Doss. LB-Joe Harris, George Andrews, Greg Westbrooks. DB-Jackie Wallace, Eddie Brown, Dwayne O'Steen, Ivory Sully. DNP: QB-Jeff Rutledge, Bob Lee. CB-Ken Ellis.

Pittsburgh-Offense: K-Matt Bahr. P-Craig Colquitt. RB-Greg Hawthorne, Anthony Anderson, Sidney Thornton, Rick Moser. TE-Randy Grossman. WR-Theo Bell, Jim Smith. LINE-Thom Dornbrook, Ted Peterson, Steve Courson. LINE-Steve Furness, Tom Beasley, Dwight White. LB-Tom Graves, Loren Toews, Zack Valentine. DB-Larry Anderson, Dwayne Woodruff. DNP: QB-Mike Kruczek, Cliff Stoudt. LB-Jack Ham.

Officials

Referee-Fred Silva. Umpire-Al Conway. Line Judge-Bob Beeks. Head Linesman-Burl Toler. Back Judge-Stan Javie. Side Judge-Ben Tompkins. Field Judge-Charley Musser.

Scoring

Los Angeles	7	6	6	0 —	19
Pittsburgh	3	7	7	14 —	31

Pitt-FG Bahr 41
LA-Bryant 1 run (Corral kick)
Pitt-Harris 1 run (Bahr kick)
LA-FG Corral 31
LA-FG Corral 45
Pitt-Swann 47 pass from Bradshaw (Bahr kick)
LA-Smith 24 pass from McCutcheon (kick failed)
Pitt-Stallworth 73 pass from Bradshaw (Bahr kick)
Pitt-Harris 1 run (Bahr kick)
Attendance-103,985

FINAL TEAM STATISTICS

	Rams	Steelers
TOTAL FIRST DOWNS	16	19
Rushing	6	8
Passing	9	10
Penalty	1	1
TOTAL NET YARDAGE	301	393
Total Offensive Plays	59	58
Average Gain per Offensive Play	5.1	6.8
NET YARDS RUSHING	107	84
Total Rushing Plays	29	37
Average Gain per Rushing Play	3.7	2.3
NET YARDS PASSING	194	309
Pass Att.-Comp.-Int.	26-16-1	21-14-3
Sacks-Yards Lost	4-42	0-0
Gross Yards Passing	236	309
Avg. Gain per Pass (Incl. Sacks)	6.5	14.7
PUNTS-YARDS	5-220	2-85
Average Distance	44.0	42.5
Had Blocked	0	0
TOTAL RETURN YARDAGE	104	209
Kickoff Returns-Yards	6-79	5-162
Punt Returns-Yards	1-4	4-31
Interception Returns-Yards	3-21	1-16
TOTAL TURNOVERS	1	3
Fumbles-Lost	0-0	0-0
Had Intercepted	1	3
PENALTIES-YARDS	2-26	6-65
TOTAL POINTS SCORED	19	31
Touchdowns Rushing	1	2
Touchdowns Passing	1	2
Touchdowns Returns	0	0
Extra Points	1	4
Field Goals-Attempts	2-2	1-1
Safeties	0	0
THIRD DOWN EFFICIENCY	5/14	9/14
FOURTH DOWN EFFICIENCY	1/2	0/0
TIME OF POSSESSION	29:30	30:30

INDIVIDUAL STATISTICS

RUSHING

Los Angeles	No.	Yds.	Avg.	Long	TD
Tyler	17	60	3.5	39	0
Bryant	6	30	5.0	14	1
McCutcheon	5	10	2.0	6	0
Ferragamo	1	7	7.0	7	0

Pittsburgh	No.	Yds.	Avg.	Long	TD
Harris	20	46	2.3	12	2
Bleier	10	25	2.5	9	0
Thornton	4	4	1.0	5	0
Bradshaw	3	9	3.0	6	0

PASSING

Los Angeles	Att.	Comp.	Yds.	Long	TD	Int.
Ferragamo	25	15	212	50	0	1
McCutcheon	1	1	24	24t	1	0

Pittsburgh	Att.	Comp.	Yds.	Long	TD	Int.
Bradshaw	21	14	309	73t	2	3

RECEIVING

Los Angeles	No.	Yds.	Long	TD
Waddy	3	75	50	0
Bryant	3	21	12	0
Tyler	3	20	11	0
Dennard	2	32	24	0
Nelson	2	20	14	0
D. Hill	1	28	28	0
Smith	1	24	24t	1
McCutcheon	1	16	16	0

Pittsburgh	No.	Yds.	Long	TD
Swann	5	79	47t	1
Stallworth	3	121	73t	1
Harris	3	66	32	0
Cunningham	2	21	13	0
Thornton	1	22	22	0

INTERCEPTIONS

Los Angeles	No.	Yds.	Long	TD
Elmendorf	1	10	10	0
Brown	1	6	6	0
Perry	1	-1	-1	0
Thomas	0	6	6	0

Pittsburgh	No.	Yds.	Long	TD
Lambert	1	16	16	0

PUNTING

Los Angeles	No.	Yds.	Avg.	TB	Long
Clark	5	220	44.0	0	59

Pittsburgh	No.	Yds.	Avg.	TB	Long
Colquitt	2	85	42.5	1	50

PUNT RETURNS

Los Angeles	No.	FC	Yds.	Long	TD
Brown	1	0	4	4	0

Pittsburgh	No.	FC	Yds.	Long	TD
Bell	2	0	17	11	0
Smith	2	0	14	7	0

KICKOFF RETURNS

Los Angeles	No.	Yds.	Long	TD
E. Hill	3	47	27	0
Jodat	2	32	16	0
Andrews	1	0	0	0

Pittsburgh	No.	Yds.	Long	TD
L. Anderson	5	162	45	0

FUMBLES

Los Angeles	No.	Own Rec.	Opp: Rec.
None			

Pittsburgh	No.	Own Rec.	Opp: Rec.
None			

KICKING

Los Angeles	XP-A	FG-A	FG Made	FG Missed
Corral	1-2	2-2	31,45	--

Pittsburgh	XP-A	FG-A	FG Made	FG Missed
Bahr	4-4	1-1	41	--

That Chaucer, he's never around when you need him.

Still, how to tell this tale? Not a fable, you understand.

Not a fantasy, spun from whole cloth, not even a fairy tale. Fact, to be sure. But, a *tale* really, and one best told through the eyes and restored ego and nerve ends of John Stallworth. Not that he is the entire story, mind you, for this tale also includes a lot of disparate characters (Chaucer would *demand* that) plus a few thousand Terrible Towels.

Stallworth once was a wallflower, but in the last act he was asked to dance by the prettiest girl at the senior prom. Or, as Stallworth puts it, "I always felt I was as good as any receiver in the game, but that I didn't get the ball enough. And then I did."

But we're giving the ending away here and, anyway, all good tales must have a beginning. Even if it has to be filtered through that's-how-I-remember-it sort of reflections.

The beginnings of this tale are clear, anyway. Time and place and circumstance. Summer of 1979. A steamy night in early August. A dorm room at the Steelers' training camp in a valley 60 miles east of Pittsburgh. Idle conversation.

"You think we can do it again? Get it back like we did last year?" That's Stallworth, putting down a magazine and asking the question they'd all been thinking about since the Steelers had tightened the cinch on the Dallas Cowboys again the previous January, winning Super Bowl XIII.

"Yeah...then we'll get one for the thumb!" That's Joe Greene, undaunted optimist, speaking over Gladys Knight and the Pips.

Then somebody started talking about ordering pizza, Greene wound up the volume on the Pips, and grumbling about the weather pushed the future from the conversation. But it hung in the mind that hot summer, like the humidity clung to the Ligonier Valley. To every thing there is a season, the Bible says. And time seemed ready to call a halt to the Steelers.

"We haven't peaked yet," head coach Chuck Noll had insisted after his charges defeated Dallas. No, the near-future would prove that. But they were about to, and some of them sensed they had only one more dance on their cards.

"I recall thinking 'Gosh, we've done it three times,'" Stallworth says. "You would think that eventually the odds have to come up *against* you."

Indeed, there was evidence that, if not in 1979, then soon after, the Steelers would throw snake-eyes.

The defense, which by then privately considered itself the very best the game had known, was beginning to show signs of wear, exposed the year before by the Cowboys in the 35-31 Super Bowl triumph that largely was a victory for Pittsburgh's offense. Greene, ends L.C. Greenwood and Dwight White, and cornerback Mel Blount all were over 30. Terry Bradshaw was in his tenth camp, Franco Harris his eighth.

"We realized that was the last go-round," says linebacker Jack Ham, who suffered a broken foot late in the 1979 season that pushed him into retirement. "We could see the handwriting on the wall."

"We were tired," Bradshaw says of the 1979 Steelers.

And, finally, they were distracted. Through the seven previous seasons, the Steelers never had lost more than five games in a season, and their popularity in Pittsburgh was immense.

Unknown players were getting $2,000 to just stand around a corporate cocktail party for an hour. More than 20 had made national television commercials. Bradshaw and Greene had made movies, and it even was possible to purchase Terry Bradshaw Peanut Butter in your supermarket.

Early in training camp, Noll proffered his usual warning: What you did last year doesn't mean anything. "But we knew we wouldn't dominate teams the way we had for more than that one year," says a 1979 Steeler. "And I bet Chuck knew it, too."

Not that Noll would admit it, but indications existed that the Steelers' sun was starting to set. From the four drafts that followed the rich lode of 1974 came only a handful of players who would ever make important contributions, and

Owner Art Rooney, who founded the Steelers' franchise in 1933, tossed the coin before the game.

two of them would not do so until the 1980s. Injuries to key players, which the Steelers had managed to avoid almost completely in the first two Super Bowl seasons, had begun to take a toll. And the AFC Central had become one of the league's strongest divisions.

"Teams were starting to catch up to us," Greene recalls.

Still, there was time for a last hurrah, maybe even time to pursue Green Bay's record of five NFL championships in seven years. Time for all that talent to coalesce around a still-potent offense and leave an indelible mark for some future would-be dynasty to contemplate.

"I'll tell you this," Bradshaw says. "We sure did hate to lose."

And in that curtain-call of a season, the Steelers still did it only rarely. Houston made a stretch run at Pittsburgh in the division, but the Steelers went 12-4 to win it, then upended Miami and Houston in the playoffs.

Irony stuck its head in the door when the Los Angeles Rams—with three former Steelers assistant coaches on their staff—became the NFC representative in Super Bowl XIV.

Los Angeles had been forced to play four different quarterbacks during the regular season and had struggled to a 9-7 record, the poorest any team ever had taken to the big game. In the playoffs, the Rams squeezed by Dallas by two points, then defeated Tampa Bay 9-0 with three field goals, but oddsmakers were not convinced. Noting that young Los Angeles quarterback Vince Ferragamo would be making only his eighth pro start in the Super Bowl, they made the Steelers 12-point favorites.

"We had some problems early that year," says Nolan Cromwell, the Rams' soap-opera handsome free safety. "But we had a veteran

team. No question in our minds that we weren't going to win."

Except for some heroics from Stallworth, an interception made by Jack Lambert, and a potential interception that was dropped by Cromwell, the Rams could have won.

"We had them by the jugular and we let them go," says former Rams defensive coordinator Bud Carson. "They got to where they only had

Three months before Super Bowl XIV, Pittsburgh Pirates first baseman Willie Stargell batted .400 to lead his team to victory over the Baltimore Orioles in the 1979 World Series. Before the kickoff, Stargell stopped by to talk to Steelers quarterback Terry Bradshaw.

Bradshaw, who would be named most valuable player for the second successive Super Bowl, got the Steelers off to a 3-0 lead when he directed a drive to a field goal by Matt Bahr.

one receiver they wanted to throw to and it should've been all over."

That it wasn't can be traced largely to Stallworth, and only marginally less so to Lambert, the Steelers' resident ogre at middle linebacker.

For Stallworth, Super Bowl XIV was a coming-out party of sorts. Throughout his career, he had been hidden so deeply in the shadow of Lynn Swann that some Steelers called Stallworth "Other" (as in other receiver). Both came from the rich 1974 draft, but the similarities ended there. Swann was glitz, Stallworth grit. The gregarious Swann was a number-one pick from USC who seemed born for the spotlight; Stallworth was a number-four from tiny Alabama A&M and as shy as a fawn. Swann always seemed to be standing at the end of the runway with the flashes popping; Stallworth perennially won the Congeniality Award. And even early on, there was tension between them.

"We were friends, got along," says Stallworth, "but down deep there was some jealousy there. Bradshaw was tuned into Swann, but how could I complain? It just made me want to

After Bahr's field goal, the Rams retaliated with a 59-yard touchdown drive on the next series. Cullen Bryant hammered one yard up the middle for the score, which was signaled by his teammates, as well as the officials.

be better. But it also put a wall between us."

The year before, in Super Bowl XIII, Stallworth was having a marvelous afternoon—three catches for 115 yards and two touchdowns—only to be struck with leg cramps. While Stallworth played sporadically in the second half, Swann turned brilliant.

"Stall was the guy, the better receiver," says Preston Pearson, a former Steeler and Cowboy, "but the national TV people loved Swann."

Lambert was somewhat less lovable. His smile, rare as a harvest moon, exposed a large gap between two incisors that Dracula would have admired. Early in 1979 he was having a

Elusive Wendell Tyler led the Rams in rushing with 60 yards. He carried three times and caught an 11-yard pass as the Rams drove to Frank Corral's 31-yard field goal and tied the score at 10-10 in the second quarter.

Behind 7-3, the Steelers drove 53 yards and regained the lead on a one-yard touchdown sweep of right end by Franco Harris. Although the Rams limited him to 46 yards on 20 carries, Harris scored twice in the game. In four Super Bowls, he ran for four touchdowns.

quiet beer in a Pittsburgh bar when he was accosted from behind by a notorious Pittsburgh drug dealer who later would be convicted of a contract murder. The killer almost tore off Lambert's ear with a heavy beer mug. The Steelers' linebacker countered by knocking him over a table. Ironically enough, the place was called The Happy Landing. A Pittsburgh cop, who was a friend of Lambert's, halted the brawl through the simple device of sticking the barrel of his service revolver in the mouth of the attacker.

Almost from the day he was drafted in 1974, Jack Lambert epitomized how the Steelers played the game. If Terry Bradshaw was their sword and Joe Greene their heart and Franco Harris their power, Lambert was their spirit. And when that fourth Super Bowl ring began to slip from their fingers against the Rams, Lambert was their conscience, shouting up their resolve in the defensive huddle.

"Jack had a role," Greene says. "I was never sure what it was, but he had a role."

In essence, it probably was a combination of builder of the fire in the belly and stern headmaster. When Cliff Harris taunted Pittsburgh kicker Roy Gerela after he missed a field-goal attempt in Super Bowl X, it was Lambert who flung the Cowboys' safety to the ground. And when the Steelers failed to throttle the Rams when they had them by the neck, it was Lambert who went into a tirade.

"It was like when you got in a fight when you were a kid and you were getting beat up and your big brother came along," Steelers center Ray Mansfield says.

In the gloaming of a late January 20, 1980, afternoon in Pasadena that was so lovely it should have been preserved, and with the

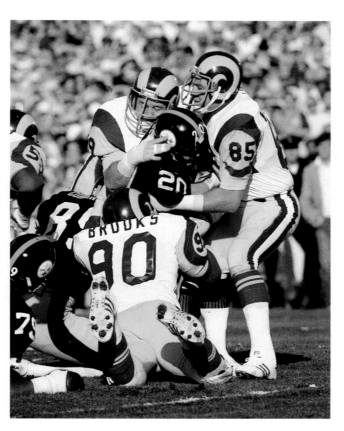

The Rams were inspired by defensive end Jack Young-blood (85), who played the entire game with a fractured fibula suffered in a playoff game. He made three tackles, including this stop of Rocky Bleier.

It was sunny and 67 degrees when 103,985 fans jammed the Rose Bowl for Super Bowl XIV. The surrounding mountains still were visible as the Steelers and Rams lined up for the second half kickoff.

mighty Steelers double-clutching it for all they were worth and trailing 19-17, Stallworth and Lambert came along just in the nick of time.

In the space of seven minutes early in the fourth quarter, all the Rams had bought with their grit turned to dust. It was sworn by Pittsburgh partisans that the Terrible Towel—a simple black-and-gold hand towel invented by sportscaster Myron Cope as the ultimate good-luck charm—had undone the plucky Rams. Given what happened to Los Angeles, it might have.

For roughly 45 minutes, all had gone swimmingly for the Rams of head coach Raymondo Guiseppi Giovanni Baptiste Malavasi.

Every time the Steelers scored, they

got counter-punched between the eyes. Rookie Matt Bahr gave Pittsburgh a 3-0 edge with a 41-yard field goal 7:29 into the game; Wendell Tyler scooted 39 yards to set up the touchdown that put the Rams ahead 7-3. Bradshaw's passes moved Pittsburgh 53 yards to recapture the lead 10-7. Ferragamo did likewise to provide a 10-10 stalemate, and a second field goal by Frank Corral gave the Rams a three-point lead at halftime.

Of course, what would a Steelers Super Bowl be without Swann stuffing Stallworth back into the shadows? Which is what Swann seemed to be doing as he made a marvelous leaping catch of a touchdown pass by Bradshaw—tipped by the unlucky Cromwell—on the opening series of the second half.

On the next series, Ferragamo continued to prove his mettle by throwing 50 yards to wide receiver Billy Waddy, but then came a bit of Rams guile. It came in the form of an option pass off the sweep by running back Lawrence McCutcheon, whose ugly floater dropped 24 yards into the arms of reserve receiver Ron Smith at the goal line to accomplish two things —give the Rams a 19-17 lead, and, after Bradshaw had thrown interceptions on Pittsburgh's next two series, absolutely convince Carson that Los Angeles was in control of the proceedings.

"That was the point when I thought, 'If we lose it now, it's a total giveaway,'" Carson says.

The thought has occurred to Cromwell. Often. Shortly after Los Angeles took its final lead, Bradshaw foolishly forced a pass to

On the fourth play of the second half, Pittsburgh jumped ahead 17-13 on Bradshaw's 47-yard touchdown pass to acrobatic Lynn Swann, who caught the ball despite safety Nolan Cromwell's desperate leap.

Swann back across the field and against the grain. Cromwell had it in his usually reliable hands...momentarily. Ahead of him there was nothing but grass.

The Rams regained the lead in the third quarter as running back Lawrence McCutcheon (30, left) took a handoff and lobbed a 24-yard touchdown pass to Ron Smith (84, right). The Los Angeles touchdown was set up by Vince Ferragamo's 50-yard pass to Billy Waddy.

"I had it...and then I didn't," he says. "When I looked up and saw where I was, I was sick. We could've had a nine-point lead and that might've changed the outcome."

The Rams' defense, orchestrated by Carson and assistant Dan Radakovich from their knowledge of Noll's basic offense (both had coached for the Steelers in Super Bowls IX and X along with Rams offensive coordinator Lionel Taylor), had choked off Pittsburgh's running game in the second half and, after Swann had been driven from the game by a third-quarter concussion, had the Steelers' air force right where it thought it wanted it.

"We'd shut their ass *down*," Carson says. "We'd knocked Swann and that kid receiver from Michigan, Jimmy Smith, out of the game. Then we decided to double-cover Stallworth on every passing down."

Catchy idea. And it almost worked. But it didn't take into account a play the Steelers still fondly call 60-Prevent-Slot-Hook-And-Go.

"I never liked that play," Stallworth says. "Neither did Bradshaw. First time it was called, he wouldn't use it. When we tried it in practice, it never worked."

Bradshaw liked it much better when it was called a second time and he saw Rams cornerback Rod Perry creep toward the line of scrimmage, where Stallworth was lined up in the slot.

"Stall faked the

Still trailing 19-17 in the fourth quarter, the Steelers shocked the Rams on a third-and-8 play as Bradshaw threw a 73-yard touchdown pass to John Stallworth, who barely beat cornerback Rod Perry.

hook, the safety [Eddie Brown] missed the coverage and Stall took off. The DB couldn't recover," Bradshaw says. Stallworth caught Bradshaw's pass over the leaping Perry, who had

The Rams' final bid to regain the lead was rebuffed by Pittsburgh linebacker Jack Lambert (58), who intercepted Ferragamo's pass intended for Ron Smith at the Steelers' 14. The Steelers then scored again.

stuck with Stallworth all the way. Stallworth raced the last 32 yards to the end zone all alone, and Los Angeles was suddenly looking at a 24-19 deficit. Bud Carson was cursing at Nickel back Brown, and people were frantically waving their Terrible Towels in the Rose Bowl and asking, "Lynn Who?"

For the reticent Stallworth, "it was the culmination of my career." For Carson, it was a nightmare that still lingers.

"Until that pass to Stallworth, I would've bet my right arm that we had them under control," he says. "That was the most sickening play of my entire career. We had him doubled all the way. But in the hole underneath him…Eddie Brown was supposed to cover over the top. He just blew it."

Yes, but it put John Stallworth where he long had been entitled to be. And just when the Rams seemed ready to climb back into it, driving from their 16 to the Pittsburgh 32 with less than 6 minutes to play, Lambert tore a storybook ending out of the book and crumpled it.

His earlier contributions had included a tirade. "He came into the huddle when we weren't playing well in the first half and bellowed so loud he scared me," safety Donnie Shell says. His second contribution was an interception.

From the Steelers' 32, Ferragamo went looking for Ron Smith again on a play-action pass designed to freeze the linebackers.

"Didn't hold anyone," Ferragamo said later.

Certainly not Lambert, who went up high in front of Smith and killed the Rams' last hope.

Fittingly, a few minutes later, Stallworth and good, old 60-Prevent-Slot-Hook-And-Go provided the nails for Los Angeles's coffin.

"We couldn't believe we went back to it and they stayed in the same formation," Stallworth says.

But the Rams did, and Bradshaw, who would claim his second consecutive Super Bowl MVP award on the strength of a 309-yard passing performance, arched one 45 yards and high over the middle of the field. Looking up for it through a fine, misty rain, Stallworth made a smashing, over-the-head, falling-to-the-ground, he-didn't-really-catch-it-did-he? grab before being brought down at the Los Angeles

22. With 1:49 left, Franco Harris bolted from a yard out for the final 31-19 score. There was nothing left of the business at hand except for determining how high "up" really was.

"How good were we?" Ham asks. "Well, we were at Kansas City in the middle of the '79 season and I could've played the first half in a tank top and shorts. It's almost the end of the second quarter…and I haven't been hit yet. Our defense had a kind of incredible chemistry."

Were they the very best of the NFL best? Maybe. What essentially was the same football team won four Super Bowls in six years, coming from behind in three.

"There's never been a better defense since I've been around," Carson says. "And it's an offensive game today."

Something of an NFL nomad, Carson still is given to identifying with the Steelers although he left the team in 1977.

"They legislated us out of business," says the principal architect of the Steelers' great defenses. "The chuck rule, not hitting a receiver five yards past the line…liberalizing the rule allowing the offensive linemen to extend their arms and protect the passer…only calling holding on running plays at the point of attack. We brought most of that to be."

Greene retired in 1981. Ham was nothing more than a bad imitation of himself after the 1979 injury that kept him out of Super Bowl XIV. He retired in 1982. Bradshaw hurt his right elbow and packed it in after the 1983 season, along with Blount. Lambert followed a year later. All of them now are in the Pro Football Hall of Fame.

Stallworth and Shell stayed on through 1987. "After Brad left, I realized how hard it had become to win," Stallworth says. "It had been so much easier before. I thought we'd always have a Joe Greene, a Franco, a Hammer, a Mel Blount…that those types of guys always would be there."

When they weren't, mediocrity set in. But time brought perspective, and Shell now says, "It's amazing how good we were."

Stallworth smiles in wonderment. "I look at the 49ers now and I think they're unbelievable," he says, "and then people will say, 'Hey, you guys were just like that.' And we were."

The Eagles Go Ker-Plunkett

The history books say the Oakland Raiders and Philadelphia Eagles played Super Bowl XV on Sunday, January 25, 1981.

There are those, however, who claim the game was decided long before that. They point to the day the two conference champions arrived in New Orleans: Monday, January 19.

The Eagles—the ultimate work-ethic team—went straight from the airport to practice.

The Raiders—being, well, the Raiders—went directly to the French Quarter and stayed there much of the week.

It was pretty obvious which team had the better idea. The Raiders stomped all over the Eagles 27-10 in the Louisiana Superdome, then hustled back to Bourbon Street to pick up where they left off.

So much for the work ethic.

"Just because you make bed check doesn't mean you show up ready to play," says linebacker Matt Millen, who started as a rookie on that Oakland team. "The Eagles weren't ready to play that day and we were. That was the difference.

"I could see it in [quarterback Ron] Jaworski's eyes on the very first series. He looked like a guy who realized he was in over his head and didn't know what to do about it. The other players had the same look. Very tight, very nervous.

"I knew if we got a quick lead on them, it would be all over. That's how it turned out."

It was a bitter disappointment for the Eagles, who went into the game favored by three points. They weren't the most talented team in the NFL—indeed, they had 14 free agents on their Super Bowl roster—but they rolled through a 12-4 regular season with a solid defense and an unshakable resolve.

In week 12, the Eagles had defeated the Raiders 10-7 in Philadelphia, sacking quarterback Jim Plunkett eight times. They were confident they could do it again in the Super Bowl, but they fell behind early (14-0) and never recovered. Plunkett burned the Philadelphia defense with three touchdown passes and was voted the game's most valuable player.

The intensity that characterized the Eagles' play all season was strangely lacking in Super Bowl XV. Were they worn out by their workaholic head coach Dick Vermeil? Were they unnerved by their first trip to the Biggest Game?

Years later, the answer still is unclear.

"I don't think we were physically tired, but we may have been emotionally drained," linebacker Frank LeMaster says now, looking back. "The week leading up to the game, all the hype and the pressure kind of sapped us.

"I think the Raiders' experience [they had 11 Super Bowl veterans] really helped them. They knew how to handle it. We didn't."

Vermeil has heard this for years, ever since he retired from coaching in 1983, citing emotional burnout as the reason. People say he wound his team up so tight for Super Bowl XV that he snapped the mainspring.

Maybe if Vermeil had lightened up in practice, lifted his curfew, let his guys have a little fun—who knows?—they might have played better in the Super Bowl.

"Or worse," Vermeil says, refusing to second-guess himself almost a decade later. "I didn't tell the players they couldn't go downtown that week. And I didn't work them any harder than I did the rest of the year. A lot of those theories are just that...theories.

"I've had people tell me our players looked tense during the [TV] introductions. I didn't see that. I thought we were ready to play. I think if we would have made a couple of big plays early, we would have been okay. But we fell behind and we seemed to sag emotionally. That happens in football.

"I think you have to give all the credit to the Raiders. They were a much better team that day. We didn't play at the level we played most of the season, but that's because the Raiders didn't let us. They beat our butts. Plunkett, especially."

Plunkett certainly was the hero of the piece, and there was a large measure of irony in that. The 32-year-old quarterback, written off by two other NFL teams, basically was forgotten until the fifth week of the 1980 season, when Oakland starter Dan Pastorini broke his leg and Plunkett took over. He became the starter in week 6.

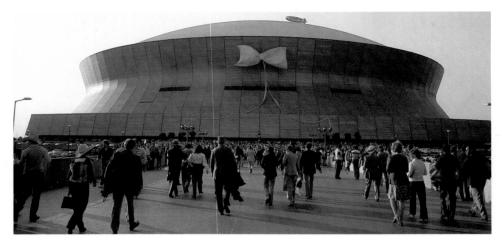

Plunkett led Oakland to 13 victories in 15 starts, including the postseason, as the Raiders became the first wild-card team to win the Super Bowl. Against the Eagles and their number-two-ranked defense, Plunkett completed 13 of 21 passes for 261 yards.

The Louisiana Superdome wore a yellow ribbon for the recently freed American hostages in Iran.

Vermeil was one of the first to congratulate Plunkett after the game.

Vermeil had been the quarterbacks coach at Stanford when Plunkett was a sophomore. They spent hours together on the practice field.

Little did Vermeil realize that years later that same quarterback would lay waste to his dream of an NFL championship. "If I had to lose to anyone," Vermeil says now, "I'm glad it was Jim. He is a great quarterback and a helluva man."

Plunkett was the last of the Oakland players to arrive in the interview room following the victory. He had showered and dressed, although he had not bothered to tuck his shirttail inside his corduroy trousers. He looked like someone who had just pulled on a pair of slacks to answer the doorbell.

Plunkett was led to a small platform that was surrounded by more than 100 newsmen. As Plunkett stepped onto the platform, he caught his foot on a TV cable and stumbled. A reporter reached out and grabbed the Super Bowl MVP to keep him from falling on his face.

"Seems appropriate," Plunkett said, smiling.

After all the misadventures that had befallen the veteran quarterback, it was almost fitting he arrived that way. A theatrical bow might have been fine for, say, Broadway Joe Namath, but not Hard Luck Jim.

Born of blind parents, stricken with a malignant neck tumor as a teen-ager, discarded by the New England Patriots in 1975 and the San Francisco 49ers in 1977, Plunkett made it to Super Bowl XV the hard way. He became a champion because he refused to quit when quitting would have been the easy, logical thing to do.

Plunkett was released by the 49ers and claimed by the Raiders, but he spent two years riding the bench behind Ken Stabler. In 1980, the Raiders traded Stabler to Houston for another veteran quarterback, Dan Pastorini. When head coach Tom Flores awarded Pastorini the starting job during the preseason, Plunkett asked to be traded.

"I didn't think I was being treated fairly," Plunkett says today. "Nothing against Dan, but I had been with the team for two years, I knew the offense, I felt I could do the job. When [Flores] passed me over, I thought I would be better off elsewhere. At thirty-two, I needed to play."

The Raiders denied Plunkett's request for a trade, citing the need for an experienced back-up. It was one of the best moves Al Davis never made.

The team got off to a wobbly 2-2 start with Pastorini at quarterback, but in the first quarter of the fifth game, Pastorini went down with a broken leg. Plunkett took over, and, although the Raiders lost 31-17, they were about to catch fire.

Plunkett won his first start the next week against San Diego 38-24, then blew away Pittsburgh 45-34 the following week. Those were the most points scored against the Steelers' defense in a decade. Suddenly, behind Plunkett,

the Raiders looked like a playoff team again.

One of Plunkett's two defeats was the 10-7 loss in Philadelphia on November 23. He was 10 for 36 passing that day with two interceptions. "We made some mistakes," Plunkett said after that game, "but it's not the end of the world. We'll bounce back."

He was right. First the Raiders won the AFC wild-card berth with an 11-5 record, and then they won three successive playoff games en route to New Orleans. After breezing past Houston 27-7, they went on the road to surprise Cleveland (14-12) and San Diego (34-27), and Oakland was in the Super Bowl.

The Raiders felt they could handle the Eagles in a rematch. They were the underdogs, but they were accustomed to that.

The inspired Raiders took a 14-0 lead in the first quarter and never trailed, running and passing for 377 yards. Future Pro Football Hall of Fame guard Gene Upshaw (63) blocked for Arthur Whittington on this sweep.

Oakland running back Kenny King (33) raced down the sideline on a record 80-yard first-quarter touchdown pass play.

The frustrated Eagles scored their only touchdown on Ron Jaworski's eight-yard, fourth-quarter pass to tight end Keith Krepfle. The Raiders still led by a healthy margin, 24-10, and went on to win 27-10.

No one thought the Raiders could beat the Browns in frigid Cleveland either. And they were supposed to have run out of gas in San Diego.

It didn't happen. Oakland kept finding new ways to win. With 41 seconds left, safety Mike Davis intercepted a pass by Brian Sipe in the end zone to preserve a narrow victory over Cleveland. Plunkett threw for two touchdowns and ran for another to upset the Chargers in the AFC Championship Game.

"We were a team of destiny," linebacker Rod Martin says. "We felt like nobody could stop us."

The Raiders displayed that breezy confidence all week in New Orleans. The Eagles were typically solemn and focused. When asked what he would do if he caught one of his players breaking curfew, Vermeil replied, "I'd ship his butt home."

"I don't think that approach would work with our team," said John Matuszak, the late Oakland defensive end who saw the sun rise over Bourbon Street several times that week. "We have a bunch of rugged individualists, and the

Raiders understand that. We don't have a lot of rules. We just play football."

"We were getting phone calls from other [NFL] players, saying we had to win this game," Millen says. "Guys were saying, 'If the Eagles win, then every owner will want a coach like that. We'll all be practicing four hours a day next year.' Nobody wanted that.

"To a man, we felt we would beat Philadelphia. We felt we should've beaten them the first time we played. Their offense did nothing in that game. We blew one coverage [Jaworski passed 43 yards to Leroy Harris] and that set up their only touchdown. We shut them down otherwise."

The Raiders' Cliff Branch scored two touchdowns, including this leaping 29-yard, third-quarter catch on which he took the ball away from rookie cornerback Roynell Young. Branch also caught a two-yard scoring pass.

Even as a rookie, Millen was a force against the run. The Raiders listed him at 255 pounds, but he was closer to 275. It took a little while for Millen to make the adjustment from college lineman to NFL linebacker, but, when he did, the Oakland defense came together. The Raiders allowed an average of 14.3 points per game the second half of the season, best in the league over that stretch.

The Raiders led the National Football League with 35 interceptions in 1980. Cornerback Lester Hayes had a career year with 18 interceptions, including five in the postseason games. Hayes coated his hands and forearms with "Stickum," a glue-like substance that turned him into a six-foot strip of flypaper. If Hayes got a hand—or elbow or jersey—on a football, it usually was his.

Linebacker Ted Hendricks, appearing in his third Super Bowl, was another big-play maker for Oakland. The 6-7 Hendricks lined up in various positions, sometimes slanting inside, sometimes blitzing, sometimes dropping off in zone coverage. Wherever he went, Hendricks usually found the ball and made something happen.

"We didn't match up very well against Oakland," Vermeil says now, an admission he would not—and could not—make in 1980. "They were a stronger team physically. Our best receiver was Harold Carmichael, but he had problems with bump-and-run coverage, which was what the Raiders played. [Still, he caught five passes]. Our other outside receiver [Charlie Smith] was playing with a broken jaw. [Smith made only two catches].

"We felt our only chance to break a big play was with tailback Wilbert Montgomery. We wanted to get him the ball in the flat and hope he could break one. We tried, but we just couldn't get it done.

"Falling behind the way we did really hurt because the Raiders were able to play pass [de-

Oakland linebacker Rod Martin (53) drove Jaworski crazy by intercepting three of his passes, a Super Bowl record. Linebacker Ted Hendricks (83) and safety Burgess Owens (44) escorted him on this steal.

fense] the whole second half. We were forced to take more chances and we wound up turning the ball over. We never could get momentum going our way."

Plunkett and Martin saw to that. Like Plunkett, Martin knew Vermeil from his college days. Vermeil tried to recruit the 6-2, 210-pound linebacker when he was head coach at UCLA, but Martin went to crosstown rival USC instead. That was the first time Martin complicated Vermeil's life.

Then came Super Bowl XV.

Martin intercepted three passes by Jaworski, exceeding his total for the entire season (two). He set the tone for the game when he intercepted the first pass Jaworski threw and returned it to the Eagles' 30-yard line. Plunkett took it from there, passing two yards to Cliff Branch for a touchdown and a quick 7-0 lead.

"I think they had a game plan designed to go

As the final seconds of the game ticked off the clock, Raiders players on the sideline signaled "3-2-1...". It was Oakland's second Super Bowl victory in five years and the first under head coach Tom Flores.

away from Ted Hendricks and I was usually the guy on the other side," says Martin. "I thought they might change after a while but they never did. They just kept running things my way and the balls kept dropping in my lap.

"I owe part of my record to Lester [Hayes] because he gave me an extra smear of Stickum right before we went out. I always wore a little bit, but Lester said I should wear more that day because it was the biggest game of the year. I'm glad I listened."

"I made some poor decisions," Jaworski says. "I tried to force a few balls into spots where I shouldn't. I read the coverage, I knew I should lay the ball off but I wanted to make the big play. When you play in that game [the Super Bowl] the first time, it makes you anxious.

"Anybody who says it's just another game is lying. It is not just another game. It is more like another world."

Like Jaworski, Plunkett was appearing in his first Super Bowl, but he had a much better grip on his passes and himself. Perhaps the many trials Plunkett endured earlier in his career steeled him for this moment. He couldn't explain it. He just knew when he walked on the field that day, and, in his words, "everything felt right."

Plunkett hit Branch with the first touchdown pass early, then lobbed a wobbly pass to running back Kenny King down the left sideline. The ball just cleared the fingertips of the Eagles' defender, cornerback Herman Edwards' and settled into King's hands. He raced away, untouched, to complete a Super Bowl-record 80-yard touchdown play. A 19-yard pass had turned into a 14-0 first-quarter lead.

The Eagles got a 30-yard field goal from

After passing for 261 yards and three touchdowns, Plunkett, who was named the game's most valuable player, relaxed on the sideline as time ran out. The strip of yellow tape on his helmet honored the freed hostages.

The Eagles sacked Jim Plunkett only once, after having brought him down eight times in a regular-season game. When end Claude Humphrey got his hands on Plunkett in the fourth quarter, he was cited for roughing the passer, and he hurled the official's flag at the referee.

Tony Franklin early in the second period, and they had a chance to climb back in the game just before halftime. They had a first down at the Oakland 11, but Jaworski misfired on three consecutive passes, and Franklin's 28-yard field-goal attempt was blocked by Hendricks.

"That hurt," Jaworski says. "If we could have picked up seven [points] there, we would have gone into the locker room with some confidence. But we just kept missing. It was one of those days."

Plunkett snuffed out any spark the Eagles

had left early in the second half, driving the Raiders 76 yards in five plays and finishing it off with a 29-yard touchdown pass to Branch, who outjumped rookie cornerback Roynell Young for the ball.

It wasn't a perfect throw—in fact, it was short and probably should have been intercepted—but it turned out just fine for Plunkett. His third touchdown pass of the game was a metaphor for his whole season.

"It was a matter of being in the right place at the right time," Plunkett says now. "I certainly didn't lead that team to the championship single-handedly. I was surrounded by a lot of great players who made my job easy. But I knew I could still play if I was given the chance. I hadn't lost my confidence.

"I thought the media overdramatized my story. Everything I read that week had the same theme: 'Plunkett resurrected...Plunkett back from the scrap heap.' I never thought I was that far gone. I mean, I didn't play for two years [in Oakland] because I was behind a Pro Bowl quarterback [Stabler]. I wasn't dead or anything."

Plunkett had seen the football world from every possible angle. He won a Heisman Trophy and a Rose Bowl at Stanford. He was lionized as a rookie with the Patriots. But then things went sour. He was battered and booed out of town, then additionally abused during two lean years in San Francisco.

Plunkett can recall lying in bed, staring at the ceiling, wondering if he wanted to keep playing after the 49ers waived him. One thought stuck in his mind: Al Davis wanted him. If the Raiders' owner thought he had something left, Plunkett figured it was worth going back.

"That was probably my last try," Plunkett admits. "If things hadn't worked out with the Raiders, I would have retired in 1978.

"But the Raiders looked like a great opportunity. They were a solid organization, a playoff team. I never had played in that kind of situation before. I wanted to give myself that chance before I walked away for good. I'm glad I did."

Plunkett was named the NFL's comeback player of the year in 1980. He threw 25 touchdown passes, including postseason. Said guard Gene Upshaw: "The motto of our team is 'Pride and Poise,' and Jim Plunkett represents the best of both. We never would have made it [to the Super Bowl] if it wasn't for him."

Another key to the Raiders' surprisingly easy win over the Eagles was the offensive line. Plunkett was sacked only once in the Super Bowl for a modest one-yard loss. What happened to the fierce Philadelphia rush that had Plunkett on his back eight times in November?

"We made some blocking adjustments," Upshaw said.

The opposition is more direct.

"They held more in the Super Bowl," Vermeil says. "They probably figured out that the officials aren't as likely to call holding in a Super Bowl, so they did it on almost every play.

"Look at the films. On the touchdown pass to King, [Eagles' defensive end] Carl Hairston is pulled down by the facemask. He was one step away from a sack and one of the Oakland linemen just dragged him down. The official was right there, but there was no call. They got a touchdown. A play like that just kills you."

The Eagles grew increasingly frustrated as the game wore on. When defensive end Claude Humphrey finally got his hands on Plunkett in the fourth quarter, he was called for roughing the passer. Humphrey, a 13-year veteran playing in his first and last Super Bowl, picked up the yellow flag and threw it at referee Ben Dreith.

That gesture pretty much summed up the Eagles' mood that day.

"I remember sitting in the locker room after the game, talking with our offensive linemen," Jaworski says now. "I remember saying we should be proud of what we accomplished that season. I mean, look at Merlin Olsen and O.J. Simpson. They were great players and they never even got to a Super Bowl.

"I was saying that but, deep down, I felt awful that we had the opportunity and we didn't do more with it. I really wish we had another chance. I think if we had gone back the next year or the year after, we would have been better prepared to deal with the whole atmosphere.

"As it turned out, we only had the one shot and we blew it. It's something I know I'll always regret."

XVI

San Francisco 26, Cincinnati 21

UPPER LEVEL			
NORTH	600	A	20
GATE	SECTION	ROW	SEAT

SUPER BOWL
XVI

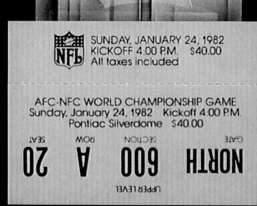

SUNDAY, JANUARY 24, 1982
KICKOFF 4:00 P.M. $40.00
All taxes included

AFC-NFC WORLD CHAMPIONSHIP GAME
Sunday, January 24, 1982   Kickoff 4:00 P.M.
Pontiac Silverdome $40.00

SEAT	ROW	SECTION	GATE
20	A	600	NORTH
		UPPER LEVEL	

Vital Statistics

Starting Lineups

San Francisco (NFC)	Offense	Cincinnati (AFC)
Dwight Clark	WR	Cris Collinsworth
Dan Audick	LT	Anthony Muñoz
John Ayers	LG	Dave Lapham
Fred Quillan	C	Blair Bush
Randy Cross	RG	Max Montoya
Keith Fahnhorst	RT	Mike Wilson
Charle Young	TE	Dan Ross
Freddie Solomon	WR	Issac Curtis
Joe Montana	QB	Ken Anderson
Ricky Patton	RB	Charles Alexander
Earl Cooper	RB	Pete Johnson
	Defense	
Jim Stuckey	LE	Eddie Edwards
Archie Reese	NT	Wilson Whitley
Fred Dean	DT-RE	Ross Browner
Dwaine Board	DE-LOLB	Bo Harris
Bobby Leopold	LLB-LILB	Jim LeClair
Jack Reynolds	MLB-RILB	Glenn Cameron
Keena Turner	RLB-ROLB	Reggie Williams
Ronnie Lott	LCB	Louis Breeden
Eric Wright	RCB	Ken Riley
Carlton Williamson	SS	Bobby Kemp
Dwight Hicks	FS	Bryan Hicks

Substitutions

San Francisco-Offense: K-Ray Wersching. P-Jim Miller. RB-Johnny Davis, Amos Lawrence, Bill Ring. WR-Mike Shumann, Mike Wilson. TE-Eason Ramson. C-Walt Downing. T-Allan Kennedy. G-John Choma. Defense: E-Lawrence Pillers. T-John Harty. LB-Dan Bunz, Willie Harper, Milt McColl, Craig Puki. DB-Rick Gervais, Lynn Thomas. DNP: QB-Guy Benjamin. RB-Walt Easley, Lenvil Elliott. DB-Saladin Martin.

Cincinnati-Offense: K-Jim Breech. P-Pat McInally. RB-Archie Griffin, Jim Hargrove. WR-Don Bass, Steve Kreider, David Verser. TE-M.L. Harris. C-Blake Moore. T-Mike Obrovac. Defense: E-Gary Burley, Mike St. Clair. NT-Rod Horn. LB-Tom Dinkel, Guy Frazier, Rick Razzano. DB-Oliver Davis, Mike Fuller, Ray Griffin, John Simmons. DNP: QB-Turk Schonert, Jack Thompson. G-Glenn Bujnoch.

Officials

Referee-Pat Haggerty. Umpire-Al Conway. Head Linesman-Jerry Bergman. Line Judge-Bob Beeks. Back Judge-Bill Swanson. Field Judge-Don Hakes. Side Judge-Bob Rice.

Scoring

San Francisco	7	13	0	6	— 26
Cincinnati	0	0	7	14	— 21

SF-Montana 1 run (Wersching kick)
SF-Cooper 11 pass from Montana (Wersching kick)
SF-FG Wersching 22
SF-FG Wersching 26
Cin-Anderson 5 run (Breech kick)
Cin-Ross 4 pass from Anderson (Breech kick)
SF-FG Wersching 40
SF-FG Wersching 23
Cin-Ross 3 pass from Anderson (Breech kick)
Attendance-81,270

FINAL TEAM STATISTICS

	49ers	Bengals
TOTAL FIRST DOWNS	20	24
Rushing	9	7
Passing	9	13
Penalty	2	4
TOTAL NET YARDAGE	275	356
Total Offensive Plays	63	63
Average Gain per Offenseive Play	4.4	5.7
NET YARDS RUSHING	127	72
Total Rushing Plays	40	24
Average Gain per Rushing Play	3.2	3.0
NET YARDS PASSING	148	284
Pass Att.-Comp.-Int.	22-14-0	34-25-2
Sacks-Yards Lost	1-9	5-16
Gross Yards Passing	157	300
Avg. Gain per Pass (Incl. Sacks)	6.4	7.3
PUNTS-YARDS	4-185	3-131
Average Distance	46.3	43.7
Had Blocked	0	0
TOTAL RETURN YARDAGE	98	87
Kickoff Returns-Yards	2-40	7-52
Punt Returns-Yards	1-6	4-35
Interception Returns-Yards	2-52	0-0
TOTAL TURNOVERS	1	4
Fumbles-Lost	2-1	2-2
Had Intercepted	0	2
PENALTIES-YARDS	8-65	8-57
TOTAL POINTS SCORED	26	21
Touchdowns Rushing	1	1
Touchdowns Passing	1	2
Touchdowns Returns	0	0
Extra Points	2	3
Field Goals-Attempts	4-4	0-0
Safeties	0	0
THIRD DOWN EFFICIENCY	8/15	6/12
FOURTH DOWN EFFICIENCY	0/0	1/2
TIME OF POSSESSION	32:13	27:47

INDIVIDUAL STATISTICS

RUSHING

San Francisco	No.	Yds.	Avg.	Long	TD
Patton	17	55	3.2	10	0
Cooper	9	34	3.8	14	0
Montana	6	18	3.0	7	1
Ring	5	17	3.4	7	0
Davis	2	5	2.5	4	0
Clark	1	-2	-2.0	-2	0

Cincinnati	No.	Yds.	Avg.	Long	TD
Johnson	14	36	2.6	5	0
Alexander	5	17	3.4	13	0
Anderson	4	15	3.8	6	1
A. Griffin	1	4	4.0	4	0

PASSING

San Francisco	Att.	Comp.	Yds.	Long	TD	Int.
Montana	22	14	157	22	1	0

Cincinnati	Att.	Comp.	Yds.	Long	TD	Int.
Anderson	34	25	300	49	2	2

RECEIVING

San Francisco	No.	Yds.	Long	TD
Solomon	4	52	20	0
Clark	4	45	17	0
Cooper	2	15	11t	1

		22	22	0
Wilson	1	22	22	0
Young	1	14	14	0
Patton	1	6	6	0
Ring	1	3	3	0

Cincinnati	No.	Yds.	Long	TD
Ross	11	104	16	2
Collinsworth	5	107	49	0
Curtis	3	42	21	0
Kreider	2	36	19	0
Johnson	2	8	5	0
Alexander	2	3	3	0

INTERCEPTIONS

San Francisco	No.	Yds.	Long	TD
Hicks	1	27	27	0
Wright	1	25	25	0

Cincinnati	No.	Yds.	Long	TD
None				

PUNTING

San Francisco	No.	Yds.	Avg.	TB	Long
Miller	4	185	46.3	0	50

Cincinnati	No.	Yds.	Avg.	TB	Long
McInally	3	131	43.7	0	53

PUNT RETURNS

San Francisco	No.	FC	Yds.	Long	TD
Hicks	1	0	6	6	0
Solomon	0	1	0	0	0

Cincinnati	No.	FC	Yds.	Long	TD
Fuller	4	0	35	17	0

KICKOFF RETURNS

San Francisco	No.	Yds.	Long	TD
Hicks	1	23	23	0
Lawrence	1	17	17	0

Cincinnati	No.	Yds.	Long	TD
Verser	5	52	16	0
Frazier	1	0	0	0
A. Griffin	1	0	0	0

FUMBLES

San Francisco	No.	Own Rec.	Opp. Rec.
Lawrence	1	0	0
Wright	1	0	0
Harper	0	1	0
Thomas	0	1	1
McColl	0	0	1

Cincinnati	No.	Own Rec.	Opp. Rec.
Collinsworth	1	0	0
A. Griffin	1	0	0
Simmons	0	0	1

KICKING

San Francisco	XP-A	FG-A	FG Made	FG Missed
Wersching	2-2	4-4	22,26,40,23	--

Cincinnati	XP-A	FG-A	FG Made	FG Missed
Breech	3-3	0-0	--	--

One Down...Three to Go

Super Bowl XVI was a game of firsts, a game of new faces and new ideas.

It marked the beginning of the San Francisco 49ers' decade of dominance in pro football. It introduced quarterback Joe Montana as a prime-time player. It popularized the notion of finesse football as taught by 49ers head coach Bill Walsh.

It also brought a change in Super Bowl ambience. The game was played at the Silverdome in Pontiac, Michigan, making it the first cold-weather Super Bowl. A grumpy press corps spent the week sloshing through rock salt, not beach sand. The suntan index was replaced by the wind-chill factor.

It was a different kind of game, all right. It brought together two teams, the 49ers and Cincinnati Bengals, that had finished with identical 6-10 records in 1980. Not since 1946 (Bears versus Giants) had the NFL's ultimate game matched two teams that had come back from losing seasons the year before.

The 49ers won 26-21, but it wasn't easy. First, they had to fight through a massive traffic jam to reach the Silverdome. They also had to survive a shaky second half in which the Bengals whittled away San Francisco's 20-point lead.

Cincinnati outgained the 49ers, 356 yards to 275, but lost the game on mistakes. The Bengals turned over the ball four times—twice on fumbles and twice on interceptions—and San Francisco turned them into 20 points.

The key was a goal-line stand in the third quarter in which the Bengals had three chances to score from the 1-yard line—and were thrown back each time by the San Francisco defense.

"That wasn't the most talented team we ever had [in San Francisco] but it was a team with some great individual players and tremendous chemistry," former 49ers Pro Bowl guard Randy Cross says today.

"We were so young, we didn't know we weren't supposed to win. The press would say, 'Well, you can't beat Dallas in a playoff game.' We'd say, 'Why not?' We were just naive enough to think that anything was possible, even a Super Bowl."

San Francisco's first NFL championship team was a melting pot of gifted youngsters, faceless role players, and recycled veterans. Twenty-one of the 45 players were gone within three years; 19 were out of pro football altogether. Yet they combined to make history in 1981.

The 49ers had three rookies in their defensive backfield—Ronnie Lott, Eric Wright, and Carlton Williamson. They had a 34-year-old warhorse named Jack Reynolds at linebacker. Their leading rusher, Ricky Patton, was a free agent. Although he passed for 3,565 yards, Montana was in his first full season as a starter.

The 49ers opened the season with one victory in the first three weeks, then caught fire. They won 15 of their last 16 games including the Super Bowl. They shocked Dallas 28-27 in the NFC Championship Game on one of the most memorable plays of all time. Wide receiver Dwight Clark made a miraculous, leaping fingertip catch of a six-yard pass from Montana for the winning touchdown.

"We weren't a great team that year," Walsh says, "but we made great plays."

On paper, the Bengals appeared more talented. Half of the Cincinnati starters (11 of 22) were either first- or second-round draft picks. Quarterback Ken Anderson led the NFL in passing in 1981. Cris Collinsworth, a lanky rookie, surpassed 1,000 yards receiving and scored eight touchdowns.

Head coach Forrest Gregg had taken the team from last place to first in just two seasons. Gregg had turned around the franchise with hard work and discipline, the same qualities he had embraced as a player under head coach Vince Lombardi at Green Bay in the 1960s.

The Bengals compiled the AFC's best record (12-4) during the 1981 season, and they defeated San Diego 27-7 in the AFC Championship Game on a day when the wind-chill factor was minus-59 degrees in Riverfront Stadium.

It was minus-12 degrees when the Bengals arrived in Michigan, January 18, to begin their Super Bowl preparations. Most players checked into their Dearborn hotel and didn't budge all week except to ride the bus to practices at the Silverdome, 30 minutes away.

The 49ers drew the early media session, which meant coaches and players had to be available for interviews at 8:30 A.M. That was 5:30 A.M., West

mixed reviews. Some scouts questioned his size (6-2, 190), others doubted his arm and his durability.

Walsh chose to focus on Montana's record at Notre Dame, his knack for winning big games and inspiring fourth-quarter comebacks.

Walsh drafted Montana in 1979 and brought him along slowly, finally installing him as the number-one quarterback late in the 1980 season. Walsh didn't want to sacrifice Montana—and risk shattering his confidence—before that. It was a wise move.

Montana had a superb season in 1981, leading the 49ers to their first playoff appearance in nine years. "Joe's comprehension

The 49ers seemed to have the game under control at halftime, leading 20-0. Quarterbacks coach Sam Wyche (left), who later became head coach of the Bengals, critiqued the offense as head coach Bill Walsh looked on.

Cincinnati's Ken Anderson rallied the Bengals in the second half, throwing two touchdown passes to tight end Dan Ross and running for another score. He completed a Super Bowl-record 25 passes for 300 yards.

and mastery of the system was the key," Walsh says. "He understood exactly what had to be done in a given situation and he adjusted if things broke down."

Typically, Walsh spent a lot of time adding new wrinkles in the days leading up to Super Bowl XVI.

He put in an unbalanced line, with Dan Audick, normally the left tackle, lining up between Cross, the right guard, and Keith Fahnhorst, the right tackle. The idea was to show it once or twice and give the Bengals something else to worry about.

Walsh also put in a new short-yardage play, a reverse with a lateral to the quarterback, who

passes to the tight end. Walsh called it on the first series against Cincinnati, and Montana hit Charle Young for 14 yards and a first down.

Walsh didn't stop there. He had place-kicker Ray Wersching practice a new kickoff, a hard squibber that bounced crazily along the Silverdome's artificial turf. Wersching did it in the game, and Cincinnati's Archie Griffin fumbled at his own 15-yard line, setting up the second of a record-tying four field goals by Wersching.

Walsh also revamped the 49ers' defense. He asked defensive coordinator Chuck Studley to put in more blitzes, something to disrupt Anderson's timing.

Studley came up with two packages. One was a safety blitz with Williamson rushing from the strongside; the other was a five-man line with Fred Dean, a defensive end, who moved like a big cat, roaming like a linebacker and looking for a lane to the quarterback.

"We called that our Cobra defense," Dean says. "They usually picked me up with two or three blockers, but it disrupted the rest of their line and allowed other guys to get through on Anderson. We had five sacks that day."

The 6-3, 230-pound Dean had played a leading role in the 49ers' surge to the title. He joined the team from San Diego following a contract dispute, then picked up 12 sacks in just 11 regular-season games. He was named NFC defensive player of the year by *United Press International* and was adored by the Candlestick Park faithful, who kept a "Dean's List" of fallen quarterbacks.

"The last piece in the puzzle," Walsh called him.

With Dean providing the pass rush, and Reynolds, who was claimed on waivers from the Rams in June, adding leadership at linebacker, San Francisco's defense had allowed just 250 points in

Joe Montana won the first of his three Super Bowl most-valuable-player awards with a calm, cool, efficient performance. He completed 14 of 22 passes for one touchdown and scored another touchdown from the 1.

1981, compared to 415 the previous year.

So Walsh had the plan and the personnel to win a Super Bowl—all he had to do was make sure everyone made it to the Silverdome on time. Ordinarily that would not be a concern, but it was for this game, with the uncertain weather (temperatures 11-below zero) and poor road conditions around the stadium.

Walsh urged the players to ride the team bus. He didn't want individuals taking cabs to Pontiac. Too risky, he said. A cab can break down, get stuck in traffic, maybe make a wrong turn. The bus, Walsh said, was the better way.

The trouble was that a handful of players, including Cross, Fahnhorst, and Lott, had a ritual about going to the stadium early. They had done it each Sunday during the regular season. Naturally, they were afraid to break the routine on the day of the Super Bowl.

"We showed up at the pregame meal, dressed and carrying our briefcases," Cross says. "We smiled at Bill and headed out the door [to the cabs]. There were about ten of us."

The players breezed to the Silverdome well ahead of the traffic. They arrived around 1 P.M.,

259

three and a half hours before kickoff. They had the locker room to themselves, as always.

Lott turned on his tape player. His musical selection for the day: "This Is It," by Kenny Loggins. The rookie thought it fit the occasion.

The San Francisco team bus left the hotel at 1:30. By the time it got within sight of the stadium, traffic was backed up in all directions, a state of pure gridlock. The 49ers were stuck on an off-ramp, a half-mile from the stadium. Police had blocked the road to allow Vice President George Bush's motorcade to pass.

It was almost 2:30 P.M. and the 49ers were supposed to be on the field for warmups at 3. On the bus, Walsh cracked a few jokes to ease the tension. "I've got the game on the radio," he said. "We're winning 7-0." Most of the players stayed cool.

"There wasn't any point in getting upset," Dean says. "There wasn't anything we could do except wait. I just kept looking at my finger, thinking how nice that [Super Bowl] ring was gonna look."

Inside the Silverdome, the early arrivals were trading jokes. "We were talking about who was gonna play both ways," Cross says, "and who was gonna call the plays. Chico Norton, our equip-

ment manager, volunteered to play quarterback. It was so ridiculous, you had to laugh."

The bus finally arrived at 2:50, giving the players just enough time to pull on their uniforms and hustle onto the field. No matter. They went through warmups without missing a beat and returned to the locker room full of confidence.

Young, the tight end, took a yellow legal tablet from his locker and began writing: "We are the

Cris Collinsworth caught a 49-yard pass from Ken Anderson in the third quarter, but the Bengals, failed to score.

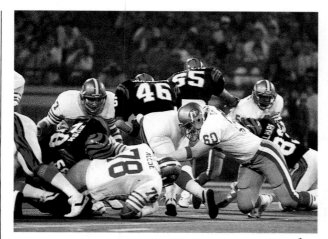

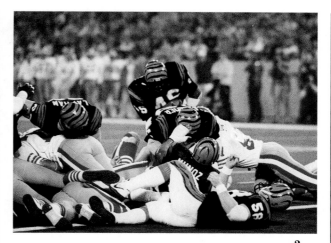

In the game's critical goal-line stand, the 49ers threw the Bengals back on four downs, three times from the 1. On first down (1), Pete Johnson was tackled by John Choma (60), Dan Bunz, and John Harty after a two-yard gain to the 1. Johnson was held for no gain on second down (2) by Harty and Jack Reynolds. Bunz tackled Charles Alexander on a third-down pass (3), and a mob stuffed Johnson on fourth down (4).

world champions. There is nothing in the world to describe the feeling. Thank you, Jesus."

"I had so much adrenaline pumping," linebacker Dan Bunz says, "that I could have run right through the side of the Silverdome, through all the snow outside, and just kept going. When we headed down the tunnel [to the field], the hair literally stood up on my neck. I never had that feeling before. I was tingling from head to foot."

Even a lost fumble by return man Amos Lawrence on the opening kickoff didn't shake the 49ers' confidence.

They got the ball back six plays later when free safety Dwight Hicks intercepted a pass by Anderson on the San Francisco 5-yard line and returned it to the 32. Montana immediately led his team to a touchdown, diving over from the 1 for the score.

The Bengals tried to retaliate in the second quarter as Anderson completed a 19-yard pass to Collinsworth at the 49ers' 8-yard line, but Wright stripped the ball and Lynn Thomas recovered the fumble. Montana capitalized again, driving his team 92 yards and hitting fullback Earl Cooper with an 11-yard touchdown pass.

Two field goals from Wersching pushed San Francisco's lead to 20-0 at halftime. The rout seemed to be on.

But the Bengals didn't quit. Cincinnati fought back in the second half, driving 83 yards to score on its first possession. Anderson went in on a five-yard run, breathing new life into his team.

Mixing in more blitzes, Cincinnati's defense shut down Montana and the 49ers. Eight plays and four yards was all the San Francisco offense could generate in the third quarter. The momentum had swung the Bengals' way.

Late in the period, Anderson hit Collinsworth with a 49-yard pass to the 49ers' 14. That set up the critical sequence: first-and-goal for the Bengals at the 3-yard line. The 49ers had a 20-7 lead, but it was in danger of erosion.

Studley went to his goal-line defense, with a backup offensive guard named John Choma, a first-year free agent, as the extra defensive tackle, and Bunz, normally a reserve, at inside linebacker next to Reynolds.

On first down, Anderson handed off to Pete Johnson, the 6-foot, 250-pound fullback. Choma shed two blockers and wrapped himself around Johnson's thighs, slowing him down enough for Bunz and tackle John Harty to make the stop at the 1.

On second down, Anderson sent Johnson off left tackle behind 6-6, 280-pound Anthony Muñoz. This time Harty filled the hole while Reynolds made the big hit on Johnson. No gain.

On third down, Anderson threw a swing pass to halfback Charles Alexander in the flat. The 6-1, 220-pound Alexander caught the ball at the 1, but was immediately slammed down by the 6-4, 220-pound Bunz.

"That was an unbelievable play for a linebacker," Studley said later. "Twenty times out of twenty that play is a touchdown. Bunz read it perfectly and made a great hit. He put his hat right down through [Alexander's] spinal column."

"I thought about going for the ball," Bunz says now. "Then I thought, 'What if I miss?' So I played it safe and went for the man. He tried to turn [into the end zone], but I had him wrapped up. He wasn't going anywhere but down."

Now it really became desperate—fourth-and-goal from the 1.

"I noticed they had a wider split between the guard and tackle on my side," Bunz says. "I caught Alexander looking at me [from his stance], like he was lining me up. I could tell they were coming my way again. Alexander was gonna lead.

"I shouted to Hacksaw [Reynolds], 'It's coming here. Watch for the lead blocker.' He saw it, too. He drew a bead on Johnson because he was gonna get the ball. All this happened in a couple of seconds.

"They snapped the ball, and I stuffed Alexander in the hole. Hacksaw, Archie [Reese, tackle], Choma, and a few other guys hit Johnson and stuffed him, too. I remember looking down and seeing the goal line at my chest. That's when I knew they hadn't gotten in."

The impact of the collision broke the chin strap on Bunz's helmet and snapped two of the screws that held his facemask in place. Bunz wobbled to his feet, a little shaken but otherwise all right. His place in 49ers history was secure.

The drive and goal-line stand took nearly six minutes off the clock and drained the fire from the Bengals. They cut the lead to 20-14 in the fourth quarter on a four-yard touchdown pass from Anderson to tight end Dan Ross, but the 49ers came back to add two field goals by Wersching and lock up the win.

Ross set a Super Bowl record with 11 receptions, two of them for touchdowns, but he wasn't in any mood to celebrate afterwards.

"The record doesn't mean a thing," Ross said. "We wanted to win the game and we didn't do it. I can't figure it out. We played tense and I don't know why."

"We had opportunities to score early and when we didn't, I think our players started thinking about what could have been instead of what was," Forrest Gregg said. "We came back and played pretty well in the second half, but we gave the 49ers too much of a cushion."

Montana completed 14 of 22 passes for 157 yards and accounted for both San Francisco touchdowns. He was voted the game's most valuable player, but he seemed embarrassed by the honor.

"I don't think I did that much," the quarterback said.

"Who would you give the award to?" someone asked.

"The team," Montana said. "The team was the MVP today."

No one knew it then, of course, but the happy locker room scene would be repeated three more times in the next eight Super Bowls.

XVII

Washington 27, Miami 17

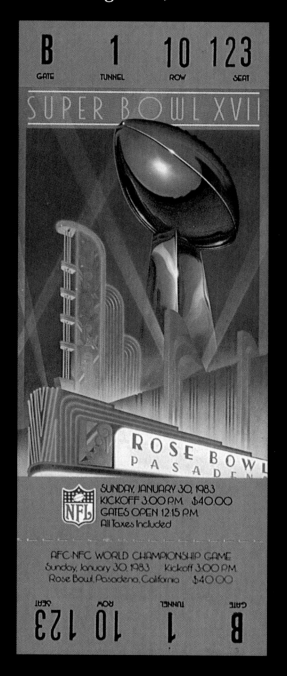

Vital Statistics

Starting Lineups

Miami (AFC)	Offense	Washington (NFC)
Duriel Harris	WR	Alvin Garrett
Jon Giesler	LT	Joe Jacoby
Bob Kuechenberg	LG	Russ Grimm
Dwight Stephenson	C	Jeff Bostic
Jeff Toews	RG	Fred Dean
Eric Laakso	RT	George Starke
Bruce Hardy	TE	Don Warren
Jimmy Cefalo	WR	Charlie Brown
David Woodley	QB	Joe Theismann
Tony Nathan	RB	John Riggins
Andra Franklin	RB-TE	Rick Walker
	Defense	
Doug Betters	LE	Mat Mendenhall
Bob Baumhower	NT-LT	Dave Butz
Kim Bokamper	RE-RT	Darryl Grant
Bob Brudzinski	LOLB-RE	Dexter Manley
A.J. Duhe	LILB-LLB	Mel Kaufman
Earnest Rhone	RILB-MLB	Neal Olkewicz
Larry Gordon	ROLB-RLB	Rich Milot
Gerald Small	LCB	Jeris White
Don McNeal	RCB	Vernon Dean
Glenn Blackwood	SS	Tony Peters
Lyle Blackwood	FS	Mark Murphy

Substitutions

Miami-Offense: K-Uwe von Schamann. P-Tom Orosz. QB-Don Strock, Jim Jensen. RB-Eddie Hill, Tom Vigorito, Woody Bennett, Rich Diana. WR-Vince Heflin, Nat Moore. TE-Ronnie Lee, Joe Rose. G-Roy Foster. T-Cleveland Green. C-Mark Dennard. Defense: E-Vern Den Herder. LB-Steve Shull, Ron Hester, Steve Potter, Charles Bowser. CB-Paul Lankford, William Judson, Fulton Walker. S-Mike Kozlowski. DNP: WR-Mark Duper. NT-Richard Bishop, Steve Clark.
Washington-Offense: K-Mark Moseley. P-Jeff Hayes. RB-Nick Giaquinto, Clarence Harmon, Otis Wonsley, Wilbur Jackson. WR-Virgil Seay. TE-Clint Didier. G-Mark May. T-Donald Laster. Defense: E-Tony McGee, Todd Liebenstein. LB-Larry Kubin, Monte Coleman, Pete Cronan, Quentin Lowry. CB-Joe Lavender, LeCharles McDaniel. S-Curtis Jordan, Greg Williams, Mike Nelms. DNP: QB-Bob Holly, Tom Owen. RB-Joe Washington. T-Garry Puetz. TE-Rich Caster.

Officials

Referee-Jerry Markbreit. Umpire-Art Demmas. Head Linesman-Bill Reynolds. Line Jude-Dale Hamer. Back Judge-Dick Hamtak. Field Judge-Don Orr. Side Judge-Dave Parry.

Scoring

Miami	7	10	0	0	— 17
Washington	0	10	3	14	— 27

Mia-Cefalo 76 pass from Woodley (von Schamann kick)
Wash-FG Moseley 31
Mia-FG von Schaman 20
Wash-Garrett 4 pass from Theismann (Moseley kick)
Mia-Walker 98 kickoff return (von Schamann kick)
Wash-FG Moseley 20
Wash-Riggins 43 run (Moseley kick)
Wash-Brown 6 pass from Theismann (Moseley kick)
Attendance-103,667

FINAL TEAM STATISTICS

	Dolphins	Redskins
TOTAL FIRST DOWNS	9	24
Rushing	7	14
Passing	2	9
Penalty	0	1
TOTAL NET YARDAGE	176	400
Total Offensive Plays	47	78
Average Gain per Offensive Play	3.7	5.1
NET YARDS RUSHING	96	276
Total Rushing Plays	29	52
Average Gain per Rushing Play	3.3	5.3
NET YARDS PASSING	80	124
Pass Att.-Comp.-Int.	17-4-1	23-15-2
Sacks-Yards Lost	1-17	3-19
Gross Yards Passing	97	143
Avg. Gain per Pass (Incl. Sacks)	4.4	4.8
PUNTS-YARDS	6-227	4-168
Average Distance	37.8	42.0
Had Blocked	0	0
TOTAL RETURN YARDAGE	244	109
Kickoff Returns-Yards	6-222	3-57
Punt Returns-Yards	2-22	6-52
Interception Returns-Yards	2-0	1-0
TOTAL TURNOVERS	2	2
Fumbles-Lost	2-1	0-0
Had Intercepted	1	2
PENALTIES-YARDS	4-55	5-36
TOTAL POINTS SCORED	17	27
Touchdowns Rushing	0	1
Touchdowns Passing	1	2
Touchdowns Returns	1	0
Extra Points	2	3
Field Goals	1-1	2-2
Safeties	0	0
THIRD DOWN EFFICIENCY	3/11	11/18
FOURTH DOWN EFFICIENCY	0/1	1/1
TIME OF POSSESSION	23:45	36:15

INDIVIDUAL STATISTICS

RUSHING

Miami	No.	Yds.	Avg.	Long	TD
Franklin	16	49	3.1	9	0
Nathan	7	26	3.7	12	0
Woodley	4	16	4.0	7	0
Vigorito	1	4	4.0	4	0
Harris	1	1	1.0	1	0

Washington	No.	Yds.	Avg.	Long	TD
Riggins	38	166	4.4	43t	1
Harmon	9	40	4.4	12	0
Theismann	3	20	6.7	12	0
Garrett	1	44	44.0	44	0
Walker	1	6	6.0	6	0

PASSING

Miami	Att.	Comp.	Yds.	Long	TD	Int.
Woodley	14	4	97	76t	1	1
Strock	3	0	0	0	0	0

Washington	Att.	Comp.	Yds.	Long	TD	Int.
Theismann	23	15	143	27	2	2

RECEIVING

Miami	No.	Yds.	Long	TD
Cefalo	2	82	76t	1
Harris	2	15	8	0

Washington	No.	Yds.	Long	TD
Brown	6	60	26	1
Warren	5	28	10	0
Garrett	2	13	9	1
Walker	1	27	27	0
Riggins	1	15	15	0

INTERCEPTIONS

Miami	No.	Yds.	Long	TD
Duhe	1	0	0	0
L. Blackwood	1	0	0	0

Washington	No.	Yds.	Long	TD
Murphy	1	0	0	0

PUNTING

Miami	No.	Yds.	Avg.	TB	Long
Orosz	6	227	37.8	0	46

Washington	No.	Yds.	Avg.	TB	Long
Hayes	4	168	42.0	1	54

PUNT RETURNS

Miami	No.	FC	Yds.	Long	TD
Vigorito	2	1	22	12	0

Washington	No.	FC	Yds.	Long	TD
Nelms	6	0	52	12	0

KICKOFF RETURNS

Miami	No.	Yds.	Long	TD
Walker	4	190	98t	1
L. Blackwood	2	32	17	0

Washington	No.	Yds.	Long	TD
Nelms	2	44	24	0
Wonsley	1	13	13	0

FUMBLES

Miami	No.	Own Rec.	Opp. Rec.
Woodley	1	0	0
L. Blackwood	1	1	0

Washington	No.	Own Rec.	Opp. Rec.
Butz	0	0	1

KICKING

Miami	XP-A	FG-A	FG Made	FG Missed
von Schamann	2-2	1-1	20	--

Washington	XP-A	FG-A	FG Made	FG Missed
Moseley	3-3	2-2	31,20	--

For a few seconds, it was a standoff.

The half-dozen reporters ringing the round table stared at their notepads.

John Riggins stared at his heavy, square hands, rested quietly on the table.

And nobody said a word. The silence was less than half a minute, but it was thick and uncomfortable.

It was midweek at the Washington Redskins' player interview sessions leading up to Super Bowl XVII.

Then Riggins looked up, and smiled. He was a good-looking man—curly, dark hair, clean features, a little bit of an impish tilt to his nose. When he leaned forward, his huge arms seemed ready to burst the sleeves of a black T-shirt.

"Anybody want to ask anything?" he said.

Still, the group was quiet.

It was because of Riggins's presence, which was considerable.

"Looks like it might be a decent day," Riggins offered. "Course, I ain't been out yet...."

A female reporter broke the media silence.

"The Dolphins...the Dolphins have outstanding linebackers," she said. "They've probably been the key to Miami's success."

Riggins looked attentive, but his smile receded. You got the notion he probably would have preferred talking about the weather. He moved a soda glass around, making wet rings on the table cloth.

"So how will you deal with the Miami linebackers?"

Riggins put the glass down and folded his oak tree arms across his chest.

"Won't," he answered, then smiled again. "I shouldn't have to deal with those linebackers ...not if the Hogs do their job.

"Hogs do what they're supposed to do, I ought to get on through to those defensive backs...that's who I should have to deal with. And they're quite a bit smaller."

Sunday, with darkness ringing the Rose Bowl as the fourth quarter wore on, the Redskins, trailing 17-13, ran "70 Chip" from the Miami 43 on fourth-and-one. It was a goal-line play, really, and it was designed by Joe Bugel, the Redskins' offensive coordinator.

"We tell John there's gonna be one guy we can't block," said Bugel. "You can't get everybody blocked because of the quarterback, so you start out eleven-to-ten in favor of the defense. We tell John he's going to be looking at one man."

The Dolphin Washington couldn't block on 70 Chip was a good one—right cornerback Don McNeal. But they *could* influence him.

Washington tight end Clint Didier went in motion inside, from left to right. Across the line of scrimmage, in the Dolphins' drawn-in secondary, McNeal mirrored Didier's progress, following inside. Then Didier reversed himself, moving back outside.

And McNeal slipped.

When McNeal reversed his motion, he hit a soft patch on a field that had been battling rain much of the week. He didn't fall all the way. He just dropped a hand to catch himself and it took a fraction of an instant to get his feet sorted out.

McNeal was moving back to where he should have been when the ball was snapped...when Riggins took a tight, crisp handoff from Joe Theismann...when the Hogs began to root ...when lead back Otis Wonsley, running in front of Riggins, sealed off the inside pursuit toward the hole...when Didier dropped his motion sham and went back to being what he really was—a blocker whose job was to block safety Glenn Blackwood.

In a testimony to his athletic ability, McNeal was able to make it back to the hole. But he made it sideways, made it diving, made it with one hand grabbing at Riggins's jersey and the other clawing futilely at his leg.

Don McNeal weighed about 190 pounds. John Riggins weighed about 250 pounds.

Maybe if McNeal had been able to stay back and had squared up in the hole ready to make a real hit with shoulders, back, and legs, and not a diving swipe... maybe if he could have slowed Riggins and held on until help arrived.

Maybe.

But Riggins blew through McNeal's frantic grasp much like an 18-wheeler rolling in from Barstow, and went 43 yards to score, which was when Washington won Super Bowl XVII.

The game was one of the most exciting offerings in the history of the spectacle, a turnabout from the regular season. A 57-day strike had stained the regular season, reducing it to nine games, followed by a postseason tournament that was reminiscent of professional hockey, in that more teams were included (16) than excluded (12).

In the NFC tournament, Washington upended Detroit, Minnesota, and Dallas. In the AFC, Miami defeated New England, San Diego, and the New York Jets.

The two teams had met in the Super Bowl before, also in California. The Dolphins beat the Redskins 14-7 in Super Bowl VII in the Los Angeles Memorial Coliseum to finish football's only perfect (17-0) season. The Dolphins still had the same head coach, Don Shula, which

The Redskins' offensive line not only was good, it was famous. Its members were called the Hogs, a nickname that stuck throughout the 1980s. The Hogs blocked for a Super Bowl-record 276 rushing yards.

was a major reason they were three-point favorites. The Redskins' head coach was Joe Gibbs, who had taken over in 1981. The Redskins had lost their first five games that season, but they had compiled a 19-4 record since then.

Ironically, both teams bore the stamp of the same man, Redskins general manager Bobby Beathard, who had been Miami's talent-hunter from 1972-77.

Both teams relied on strong defenses. Miami's had finished number one in the NFL, Washington's defense number four. Both had conservative offenses.

The week leading up to XVII was dominated

On their second series, the Dolphins struck for a quick 7-0 lead as Jimmy Cefalo took a short pass from David Woodley and broke it for a 76-yard touchdown. Miami led for most of the first three quarters.

by nicknames. Miami had the Killer Bees, Washington had the Hogs.

Behind a wall of Hogs, Joe Theismann completed 15 of 23 passes for 143 yards and two scores.

The Bees were the Dolphins' defensive starters, so named because six starters had last names beginning with the letter "B." The creation of assistant head coach Bill Arnsparger, the Dolphins' defense was built upon quickness, communication, movement, and discipline. It was intricate and beautifully crafted.

The Hogs were... well, a happening.

"Training camp," tackle George Starke says today, "is boring. You've got to remember that. I mean, you look for things to make it interesting. It started that year in camp when coach Bugel looked at Russ Grimm one day in drills and told him he looked like a hog, just big and kind of wallowing around in the dirt. A couple days later, Coach came out with T-shirts for us that had 'Hogs' on them. Then it was caps. I guess camp's as boring for the press as it is for players because they started writing about the Hogs.

Miami still led 7-0 late in the first quarter when Washington's Dexter Manley sacked Woodley and forced a fumble. Manley's teammate, Dave Butz, recovered the ball at the Dolphins' 46 to set up a field goal.

Both teams watched the flight of the ball as Washington's Mark Moseley kicked one of his two field goals (in the second and third quarters). Moseley hit an NFL-record 20 of 21 field goals during the regular season.

"And it just grew. During the season, we linemen [Starke, at right tackle, was the oldest Hog] would dress up in tuxes and go out to dinner at nice places. People really started to notice. It just grew... winning was a big part of it, of course. Everybody just went kind of crazy for the Hogs."

The Redskins tied the score at 10-10 on Alvin Garrett's short touchdown catch over Gerald Small.

The Hogs were tackles Joe Jacoby and Starke, guards Grimm, Mark May, and Fred Dean, and center Jeff Bostic. Because the Redskins' tight ends were blockers first, Don Warren and Rick Walker also became Hogs. And, because his running style had a lot of rooting to it, Riggins was granted honorary membership in the group.

They were big men, all of them. Starke says he played at about 260 and was, by far, the smallest Hog. "Most of 'em were up around three-hundred," Starke says. They were a line built to power-block, to make way for the shattering rushes of Riggins.

"We spent years in Washington trying to figure out how to block a three-man front," Starke says. "We'd chase those quick ends and linebackers, always trying to man-block 'em... never did get it. Until Joe Bugel."

Bugel's huge, powerful Hogs did not chase quick ends and linebackers. They simply would clear their area, usually at the snap of the ball. In XVII, they were remindful of road-graders, pushing aside Miami's precise, intricate defensive schemes.

And though Washington's offensive hopes rested largely with Riggins, Gibbs and his staff wanted to sow a little doubt for the Dolphins.

"It was our Wednesday night coaches' meeting, but it was Thursday morning by then," Bugel says. "Had to be three or after because Joe [Gibbs] was on about his fifteenth candy bar."

The Washington coaches were looking for something different, something to break the concentration of the Dolphins' defense. They already had reverses and a flea-flicker in their plan, but they wanted something extra.

Gibbs came up with their "explode" package. The plan was to put potential receivers in

Group celebrations were in with the Redskins as several receivers and running backs—known as the Fun Bunch —did high fives to celebrate touchdowns. This mob scene occurred after Garrett's scoring catch.

"wrong" positions in the original set, then move all of them to "right" positions before the snap.

"It was a mad scramble," says quarterback Joe Theismann. "When I hollered 'set!,' we'd have up to five guys switching spots.

"Think about it. You line up with a tight end in a wide receiver's spot. Linebacker's got him, so now the linebacker is set out wide. We switch…everybody runs around. Unless the linebacker moves, he's covering a wideout now,

and that's a bad matchup. If he moves back, he may be messed up at the snap of the ball."

It worked, too. "We got both touchdown passes on it," Theismann says.

If Riggins was the hero of XVII, and he was, and if the Hogs paved the way to Riggins's run to glory, and they did, it was left to Theismann to make all of that possible.

Theismann started as a sophomore at Notre Dame after Terry Hanratty was injured, and he was matched against arch-rival USC. Theismann's first pass went for a touchdown—USC intercepted and scored.

Returning to the Irish bench, Theismann had a few words for head coach Ara Parseg-

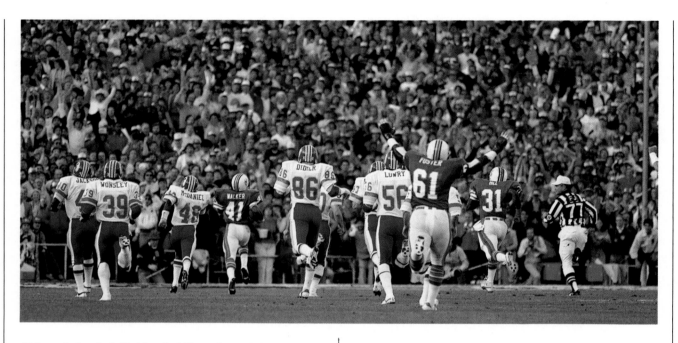

Although they led 17-10 at halftime, the Dolphins were shut out in the second half as quarterback David Woodley missed all eight of his passing attempts. Miami earned only two first downs in the second half.

The Dolphins took that 17-10 halftime lead on a 98-yard kickoff return for a touchdown by Fulton Walker (41, center). It was the first scoring kickoff return in Super Bowl history—and still is the longest play.

hian. "Don't worry, coach," he said, "we're going to win." He was close. They tied 21-21. But his confidence was infectious.

Coming out of college, Theismann was a fourth-round draft choice by the Dolphins.

Disappointed, he signed with Montreal of the Canadian Football League. Theismann was in the NFL three years later, the Dolphins having traded him to the Redskins.

Eight years after that, he came into Super Bowl XVII as the NFC's top-rated passer.

Ironically, his biggest play in XVII came as a defender. It permitted Washington to win.

Trailing 17-13 in the third quarter, and deep in his own end of the field, Theismann's pass toward the flat was deflected by Miami defensive end Kim Bokamper. The ball went straight up, then straight down...into Bokamper's waiting hands. He had only to walk about four yards for a touchdown.

"I thought, 'Ohmigod!'," Theismann says. "I don't remember thinking or deciding anything. I just dove at him. I whacked the ball out just as it fell into his hands."

"It was," Don Shula says, "an incredible play

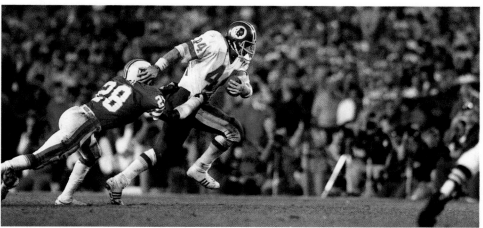

In the third quarter, Miami's Kim Bokamper (58) almost scored on a deflected Washington pass.

game belonged to Washington, unless you're one of those purists who go by the score. The Redskins gained more yards, ran more plays, and showed more muscle. Yet they went to their locker room trailing 17-10. Truth is, they were lucky it wasn't worse.

Miami struck first—and dramatically. Quarterback David Woodley hit Jimmy Cefalo on a modest little sideline route that turned into a 76-yard touchdown when the Redskins' Jeris White and Tony Peters goofed their coverages.

After the Redskins stalled, Miami took over with six minutes to play in the first quarter and punched the ball to the Washington 37 before

for a quarterback to make…a great reaction and play. It really hurt."

Instead of going up by 11, Miami clung to a 4-point lead. Instead of forcing Washington to go to the pass, it let them continue to hurl the hurtful Riggins at the Dolphins' tiring defense.

The first half of the

Alvin Garrett and Joe Theismann congratulated Charlie Brown after his six-yard touchdown catch.

John Riggins put the Redskins ahead to stay in the fourth quarter when he broke an attempted tackle by cornerback Don McNeal and churned 43 yards for a touchdown. Riggins ran for a record 166 yards.

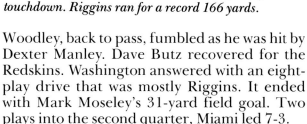

Woodley, back to pass, fumbled as he was hit by Dexter Manley. Dave Butz recovered for the Redskins. Washington answered with an eight-play drive that was mostly Riggins. It ended with Mark Moseley's 31-yard field goal. Two plays into the second quarter, Miami led 7-3.

Fulton Walker's first fine kickoff return (his next one would be even finer) set up Miami at its 47. The Dolphins moved to the Redskins' 3 before settling for Uwe von Schamann's field goal. They should have had a touchdown. On second down at the Redskins' 6, Woodley bootlegged right with blocking in front of him. But safety Mark Murphy came up quickly to make the tackle at the 3.

Theismann then passed and ran the Redskins to their first touchdown, hitting Alvin Garrett on a four-yard pass off the "explode" package. "I could see they were mixed up on him at the snap," Theismann says. "I couldn't wait to get the ball to him."

It was 10-10—but only briefly.

Washington special-teams player Larry Kubin said Theismann almost swallowed his tongue on the next play.

Fulton Walker took the ensuing kickoff and ran 98 yards to a touchdown. "I started left, broke it back on Roy Foster's block, and went straight up the middle," Walker says. "When I saw the kicker [Jeff Hayes] turn his back to run with me, I knew I had it."

That return produced the Dolphins' 17-10 halftime edge.

At halftime, John Riggins had 58 yards on 17 carries. He was 21 carries and 108 yards away from where he would finish his record day: 38 carries for 166 yards.

Riggins had rushed for 553 yards on 177 carries during the abbreviated regular season. In four playoff games including the Super Bowl, he rushed for 610 yards on 136 carries.

"There is this old gentleman I know in Kansas named Glenn Jenkins," Riggins said. "I was telling him that when I'm home on the farm at night, I hear those coyotes howling and it sounds like they're getting closer. I told Glenn that makes me sort of nervous.

"He said, 'I've shot about 200 of those coyotes in my life, so they don't exactly raise the hair on the back of my neck.' I'm sort of like Glenn Jenkins. I've played in about 130 regular-season games and they don't exactly raise the hair on the back of my neck. But the playoffs, they sure are something different."

So was Riggins.

"He was the perfect back to have run behind our line," Starke says.

"Nobody practiced harder, nobody had a better feel for the game," Theismann says. "John's a real intelligent guy. Were we close? No, not at all. John was mostly by himself. What did we have in common? Going out to win."

"He hurt," Miami safety Lyle Blackwood says. "When you hit him, it hurt."

"I couldn't hold him," McNeal says of the 43-yard run that won the game. "I had no idea he was going to be that tough…you can watch a guy on film, but you never really know until you hit him."

"He picks and reads so well, he doesn't need much of a hole," Baumhower said.

Earlier in the week, Gibbs had said Riggins would be the Redskins' key, but the team would need motion, misdirection, and trick plays to keep the pressure off him.

"They had so much movement, sometimes we got confused," Dolphins' linebacker A.J. Duhe says.

"The purpose of all the movement and trick stuff was to get them to stay home and play us straight up," Theismann says. "When they did that, we figured we could win. The Hogs were too strong."

"It must have been totally insulting to play defense against us, because everybody knew what we were going to do," Starke says. "We only had two running plays. Each went left and right, so that's a total of four plays, I guess. But that was all! It was like we just said, 'Here we come… try to stop us.'"

Miami couldn't. Arnsparger's thoughtful defense, built around Duhe and Baumhower, ended up being trampled by Hog hooves.

Miami's offense suffered a worse fate. After a productive first quarter, third-year quarterback Woodley went 0-for-8 in the second half, as Miami made only two first downs and gained 34 yards.

"People talk about Riggo's day and the play I made on Bokamper," Theismann says, "but what won the game was our defense."

After Riggins's run to glory in the fourth quarter put Washington ahead for the first time, 20-17, Theismann hit Charlie Brown on a six-yard scoring pass with two minutes remaining. That was it, 27-17.

"We just couldn't get anything going," Woodley said. "I don't remember that ever happening before, when nothing worked."

Neal Olkewicz, a free agent who ran the Redskins' defense from middle linebacker, says, "So many of us on that team were free agents or castoffs, we just formed this real close bond. We knew we had to be close to be effective…and we knew we had to be effective to be there."

XVIII

L.A. Raiders 38, Washington 9

EAST	10	5
STANDS	GATE	SEC.
100	**A**	**205**
AISLE	ROW	SEAT

 SUNDAY, JANUARY 22, 1984
KICKOFF 4:30 P.M.
GATES OPEN AT 1:45 P.M.
$60.00 • ALL TAXES INCLUDED

AFC-NFC WORLD CHAMPIONSHIP GAME
SUNDAY, JANUARY 22, 1984 • KICKOFF 4:30 P.M.
TAMPA STADIUM • TAMPA, FLORIDA • $60.00

SEAT	ROW	AISLE
205	**A**	**100**
SEC.	GATE	STANDS
5	**10**	**EAST**

Vital Statistics

Starting Lineups

Washington (NFC)	Offense	L.A. Raiders (AFC)
Charlie Brown	WR	Cliff Branch
Joe Jacoby	LT	Bruce Davis
Russ Grimm	LG	Charley Hannah
Jeff Bostic	C	Dave Dalby
Mark May	RG	Mickey Marvin
George Starke	RT	Henry Lawrence
Don Warren	TE	Todd Christensen
Art Monk	WR	Malcolm Barnwell
Joe Theismann	QB	Jim Plunkett
John Riggins	RB	Marcus Allen
Rick Walker	TE-RB	Kenny King
Defense		
Todd Liebenstein	LE	Howie Long
Dave Butz	LT-NT	Reggie Kinlaw
Darryl Grant	RT-RE	Lyle Alzado
Dexter Manley	RE-LOLB	Ted Hendricks
Mel Kaufman	LLB-LILB	Matt Millen
Neal Olkewicz	MLB-RILB	Bob Nelson
Rich Milot	RLB-ROLB	Rod Martin
Darrell Green	LCB	Lester Hayes
Anthony Washington	RCB	Mike Haynes
Ken Coffey	SS	Mike Davis
Mark Murphy	FS	Vann McElroy

Substitutions

Washington-Offense: K-Mark Moseley. P-Jeff Hayes. RB-Reggie Evans, Nick Giaquinto, Joe Washington, Otis Wonsley. TE-Clint Didier, Mike Williams. WR-Alvin Garrett. T/G-Roy Simmons, G-Ken Huff, Bruce Kimball. Defense: E-Charles Mann, Tony McGee. T-Perry Brooks. LB-Stuart Anderson, Monte Coleman, Peter Cronan, Larry Kubin. CB-Brian Carpenter, Vernon Dean. S-Curtis Jordan, Greg Williams. DNP: QB-Bob Holly, Babe Laufenberg. WR-Mark McGrath, Virgil Seay.

Los Angeles Raiders-Offense: K-Chris Bahr. P-Ray Guy. QB-Marc Wilson, David Humm. RB-Frank Hawkins, Greg Pruitt, Chester Willis. TE-Don Hasselback, Derrick Jensen. WR-Cle Montgomery, Calvin Muhammad, Dokie Williams. T-Shelby Jordan, Don Mosebar. G-Steve Sylvester. Defense: E-Johnny Robinson, Greg Townsend. T-Bill Pickel, Dave Stalls. LB-Jeff Barnes, Darryl Byrd, Tony Caldwell, Jeff Squirek. CB-James Davis, Ted Watts. S-Kenny Hill, Odis McKinney.

Officials

Referee-Gene Barth. Umpire-Gordon Wells. Head Linesman-Jerry Bergman. Line Judge-Bob Beeks. Back Judge-Ben Tompkins. Side Judge-Gil Mace. Field Judge-Fritz Graf.

Scoring

Washington	0	3	6	0 —	9
L.A. Raiders	7	14	14	3 —	38

LA-Jensen recovered blocked punt in end zone (Bahr kick)
LA-Branch 12 pass from Plunkett (Bahr kick)
Wash-FG Moseley 24
LA-Squirek 5 interception return (Bahr kick)
Wash-Riggins 1 run (kick blocked)
LA-Allen 5 run (Bahr kick)
LA-Allen 74 run (Bahr kick)
LA-FG Bahr 21
Attendance-72,920

FINAL TEAM STATISTICS

	Redskins	Raiders
TOTAL FIRST DOWNS	19	18
Rushing	7	8
Passing	10	9
Penalty	2	1
TOTAL NET YARDAGE	283	385
Total Offensive Plays	73	60
Average Gain per Offensive Play	3.9	6.4
NET YARDS RUSHING	90	231
Total Rushing Plays	32	33
Average Gain per Rushing Play	2.8	7.0
NET YARDS PASSING	193	154
Pass Att.-Comp.-Int.	35-16-2	25-16-0
Sacks-Yards Lost	6-50	2-18
Gross Yards Passing	243	172
Avg. Gain per Pass (Incl. Sacks)	4.7	5.7
PUNTS-YARDS	8-259	7-299
Average Distance	32.4	42.7
Had Blocked	1	0
TOTAL RETURN YARDAGE	167	30
Kickoff Returns-Yards	7-132	1-17
Punt Returns-Yards	2-35	2-8
Interception Returns-Yards	0-0	2-5
TOTAL TURNOVERS	3	2
Fumbles-Lost	1-1	3-2
Had Intercepted	2	0
PENALTIES-YARDS	4-62	7-56
TOTAL POINTS SCORED	9	38
Touchdowns Rushing	1	2
Touchdowns Passing	0	1
Touchdowns Returns	0	2
Extra Points	0	5
Field Goals-Attempts	1-2	1-1
Safeties	0	0
THIRD DOWN EFFICIENCY	6/17	5/13
FOURTH DOWN EFFICIENCY	0/1	0/0
TIME OF POSSESSION	30:38	29:22

INDIVIDUAL STATISTICS

RUSHING

Washington	No.	Yds.	Avg.	Long	TD
Riggins	26	64	2.5	8	1
Theismann	3	18	6.0	8	0
J. Washington	3	8	2.7	5	0

L.A. Raiders	No.	Yds.	Avg.	Long	TD
Allen	20	191	9.6	74t	2
Pruitt	5	17	3.4	11	0
King	3	12	4.0	10	0
Hawkins	3	6	2.0	3	0
Willis	1	7	7.0	7	0
Plunkett	1	-2	-2.0	-2	0

PASSING

Washington	Att.	Comp.	Yds.	Long	TD	Int.
Theismann	35	16	243	60	0	2

L.A. Raiders	Att.	Comp.	Yds.	Long	TD	Int.
Plunkett	25	16	172	50	1	0

RECEIVING

Washington	No.	Yds.	Long	TD
Didier	5	65	20	0
Brown	3	93	60	0
J. Washington	3	20	10	0
Giaquinto	2	21	14	0
Monk	1	26	26	0
Garrett	1	17	17	0
Riggins	1	1	1	0

L.A. Raiders	No.	Yds.	Long	TD
Branch	6	94	50	1
Christensen	4	32	14	0
Hawkins	2	20	14	0

	No.	Yds.	Long	TD
Allen	2	18	12	0
King	2	8	7	0

INTERCEPTIONS

Washington	No.	Yds.	Long	TD
None				

L.A. Raiders	No.	Yds.	Long	TD
Squirek	1	5	5t	1
Haynes	1	0	0	0

PUNTING

Washington	No.	Yds.	Avg.	TB	Long
Hayes	7	259	37.0	0	48

L.A. Raiders	No.	Yds.	Avg.	TB	Long
Guy	7	299	42.7	1	53

PUNT RETURNS

Washington	No.	FC	Yds.	Long	TD
Green	1	0	34	34	0
Giaquinto	1	2	1	1	0

L.A. Raiders	No.	FC	Yds.	Long	TD
Pruitt	1	3	8	8	0
Watts	1	0	0	0	0

KICKOFF RETURNS

Washington	No.	Yds.	Long	TD
Garrett	5	100	35	0
Grant	1	32	32	0
Kimball	1	0	0	0

L.A. Raiders	No.	Yds.	Long	TD
Pruitt	1	17	17	0

FUMBLES

Washington	No.	Own Rec.	Opp. Rec.
Theismann	1	0	0
G. Williams	0	0	1
A. Washington	0	0	1

L.A. Raiders	No.	Own Rec.	Opp. Rec.
Watts	1	0	0
Allen	1	0	0
Hannah	0	1	0
Branch	1	0	0
Martin	0	0	1

KICKING

Washington	XP-A	FG-A	FG Made	FG Missed
Moseley	0-1	1-2	24	44

L.A. Raiders	XP-A	FG-A	FG Made	FG Missed
Bahr	5-5	1-1	21	--

PLAY-BY-PLAY

Los Angeles won the coin toss and elected to receive.

FIRST QUARTER
Hayes kick into end zone, touchback.

Los Angeles (15:00)
LA 20	1-10	Allen 5 run off left tackle (A.Washington).
LA 25	2-5	Plunkett 6 pass to Allen right flat (Coffey).
LA 31	1-10	Allen 2 run off left tackle (Butz).
LA 33	2-8	Plunkett pass to Christensen broken up (Coffey).
LA 33	3-8	Plunkett 1 pass to King right flat (Green).
LA 34	4-7	Guy 47 punt, Giaquinto fair catch.

Washington (12:02)
W 19	1-10	Riggins 3 run up middle (Long, Kinlaw).
W 22	2-7	Riggins 6 run off right tackle (M.Davis).
W 28	3-1	Riggins 2 run off right tackle (Nelson).
W 30	1-10	Theismann pass to Monk broken up (Haynes).

The odd thing about Raiders football is that it almost never changes, but it always seems to be the inspiration for the NFL's newest evolutionary cycle.

Super Bowl XVIII was widely billed as the matchup of the old and the new—the Washington Redskins' offense of the 1980s against the Los Angeles Raiders' offense of the 1960s. Only after the fact was it apparent the Raiders had whipped the slightly favored Redskins 38-9 by using an attacking defensive style that would become the standard for the rest of the decade.

The Redskins had their one-back offense with two tight ends and 500-odd formations and kaleidoscopic packages of men in motion. The Raiders hadn't changed their playbook much since the West Side Story hairstyles of managing general partner Al Davis and head coach Tom Flores were in vogue. They were so backward, they still let quarterback Jim Plunkett and linebacker Matt Millen call their plays.

Underneath the eyepatch and warpaint, though, the teams weren't all that different. Dan Henning, the assistant head coach who helped head coach Joe Gibbs install the one-back offense in 1981, let slip a few years later that the team he considered most comparable to Washington was the Raiders. The fancy Redskins were just a tank gussied up with a stereo, jazzy wheel covers, and a coat of red paint. "They were a power team, too," Millen says.

Both the Raiders and the Redskins built their offenses around big offensive lines that gave them time either for long passes or for overpowering runs. They both won by passing, but used the run effectively to keep defenses guessing and to finish off their victims. Strip away the bells and whistles of all those formations, and the Redskins didn't use more than four or five running plays and four or five pass plays in any given game.

"We're pretty basic," wide receiver Art Monk said. "We just have so many formations, it looks like we do more than we really do."

The Raiders weren't quite as steeped in tradi-tion as they let on, either. Yes, they threw the long ball well, but not necessarily often. Tight end Todd Christensen led the NFL in 1983 with 92 catches, and Marcus Allen's 68 receptions were the second most by a running back.

The defenses were similar, too. Both teams sent as many pass rushers as it took to make the quarterback run for cover, and they let their cornerbacks cover the outside receivers man-to-man. "Attack football," Flores called it, and one thing set the Raiders' brand apart from everyone else's attacks. As Flores says now, "You can't very well do it without great corners." The Raiders' Mike Haynes and Lester Hayes were considered the best cornerbacks in the league.

"That '83 defense was one of the best defenses the NFL has ever seen," Millen says. "Other teams tried to copy it, but you couldn't because there was too much talent there. And the whole thing was based on our corners. Nobody since then has been able to have two corners of that caliber."

The defense was primarily responsible for the Super Bowl blowout. "Our defense played almost a perfect game," Flores says. "Our defense enabled the offense to have good field position throughout most of the game."

The Raiders scored two of their first three touchdowns—they took a 21-3 halftime lead—on a blocked punt and an interception. The interception at the end of the half was the backbreaker. Once the Raiders were safely ahead, they could turn Marcus Allen loose for his Super Bowl record of 191 rushing yards, including a 74-yard touchdown run that set another record. They broke John Riggins's string of six consecutive 100-yard playoff games for Washington. They held Joe Theismann without a touchdown pass for only the second time all season. And their 38 points and 29-point margin of victory also set Super Bowl records.

"We got after the quarterback pretty good," says Art Shell, who coached the Raiders' offensive line that season. "Greg Townsend and Lyle Alzado and Howie Long were all over him, and Reggie Kinlaw was doing his thing in the running game. We had a lot of big plays that day, on offense and defense."

It was that kind of season throughout the NFL. Scoring peaked in 1983, with a post-

Ageless Jim Plunkett, the most valuable player in Super Bowl XV, directed the Raiders to another victory in XVIII. He completed 16 of 25 passes for 172 yards and threw a touchdown strike to Cliff Branch.

passes by jamming the wide receivers at the line and covering them tight. They also knew Washington would respond to that kind of coverage by throwing the quick up, a long sideline pass for the receiver to run under. "It was kind of automatic for them," Flores says, "so we knew we'd be taking a chance. If they complete one, it's a big play."

When the Raiders had the ball, they knew Washington would be taking the same chance. "We felt we would be able to throw the ball on

Washington's first series ended in disaster. The Raiders' Derrick Jensen (31, left) blocked a punt by Jeff Hayes, and the ball rolled all the way back to the end zone, where Jensen recovered for a touchdown.

merger high of 21.8 points per team per game. But it was defense that brought on the increase. The NFL had 30 interceptions returned for touchdowns in each of its four previous 16-game seasons, 1978-1981, but the figure leaped to 49 in 1983.

It was the year defenses stopped laying back in eight-man zones and started forcing the action. When they didn't actually score, they forced turnovers that set up shorter scoring drives for the offense, or their gambles backfired with quick strikes by the opponent. Either way, scoreboards heated up.

The Raiders' game plan for the Super Bowl reflected the new thinking. On defense, they felt they had to take away Washington's quick

them because they were like us," Flores says. "They used a lot of man coverage. The key was going to be if we could protect [the quarterback] because they put on a good pass rush.

"The running game would just be a solid-type running game. It wasn't anything fancy. They didn't do anything fancy on defense. They were a lot like us. They lined up and they played the game and pressured you."

For the regular season, the result for Washington was pass-defense statistics that seemed to go together like plaids and pinstripes, but typified the NFL in 1983. The Redskins' defense led the league with 34 interceptions and 61 forced turnovers, but it ranked last in passing yards and twenty-sixth in touchdown passes allowed. It was all or nothing.

Washington set an NFL scoring record that year (541 points) that still stands, beating out the second-ranked Cowboys by 62 points. The Redskins averaged 33.8 points per game in a 14-2 regular season. Their only defeats were 31-30 and 48-47. They never scored fewer than 23 points in a game.

They accomplished all that with the fewest offensive turnovers in the league, only 11 interceptions and seven lost fumbles. They led the league in rushing yards allowed and rushing touchdowns allowed. Riggins ran for 1,347 yards and set an NFL record with 24 touchdowns.

The NFC Championship Game was another illustration of the Redskins and 1983. Washington led 21-0 after three quarters, but Joe Montana rallied San Francisco to a 21-21 standoff in the next eight minutes before the Redskins won 24-21. The victory gave them a two-year record of 28-3 and made them the only defending champion from 1980-88 to win a playoff game, let alone go back to the Super Bowl.

The Raiders were hot, too, maybe even hotter. They were 12-4, plus two playoff victories, winning eight of nine after a midseason slump. The streak coincided with Plunkett's return to the lineup after an injury to Marc Wilson. The Raiders tied for second with 31 touchdown passes, two more than Washington, and Plunkett completed a career-high 60.7 percent of his passes. But there was more to their fast finish than passing.

The Raiders avoided a catastrophe early in the second quarter when punter Ray Guy soared to make a one-handed catch of a high snap. After he landed, the athletic Guy managed to get off a 42-yard punt.

Haynes had joined the team in November after holding out at New England, and he fit right into a defense that tied for second with 57 sacks. Allen was improving by the week. He rushed for 154 yards in the Raiders' 30-14 AFC Championship Game victory over Seattle, a team that had beaten the Raiders twice during the season. "Marcus really came on in the playoffs," Millen says. "Once that happened, there was nobody who could touch us."

The Redskins thought they could. "We knew they were the bullies of the AFC and we were the bullies of the NFC," guard Mark May says, "and it was going to be one of those games that, as John Madden says, should be played on grass."

The one big difference between the teams was best summarized by Gibbs's praying and Davis's preying. White hats and black hats were easy to assign. During the week in Tampa, the

Redskins had Theismann changing three-piece suits between TV interviews, and the Raiders had Alzado wearing a cut-off T-shirt and saying he was going to rip off Theismann's head. The Raiders had seven players fined $1,000 each for being late to a Tuesday meeting (however, reports were that the fines never were paid), and the Redskins were growing paranoid about the planes and helicopters that circled their practice field—under Davis's employ, they feared.

"If the Redskins are a family," Flores said, "then we're an orphanage."

Even there, though, the teams had similar philosophies about making room for other teams' rejects.

The difference was the Raiders picked up unwanted veterans and the Redskins went for rookies. Washington had four starters who hadn't been drafted. The Raiders had Plunkett, Christensen, Alzado, Haynes, guard Charley Hannah, fullback Kenny King, and linebacker Ted Hendricks, who had played for other NFL teams.

The Raiders stifled the Redskins' offense most of the game and were particularly hard on John Riggins, holding him to 64 yards in 26 carries. Here cornerback Mike Haynes (22) made a rolling tackle on Riggins.

They had played each other earlier that season, in the fifth week, and Washington's offense drove for 17 points in the last 7:31 to win 37-35. "The most competitive game I ever played in," said Long, who joked he would prepare himself for the rematch by walking around in Tampa's roughest neighborhood. Despite the score of the earlier game, Millen recalled the contest with encouragement before the Super Bowl. The Raiders' offense had lost six turnovers in October. That wouldn't happen again. Allen had missed that game, and Haynes hadn't joined the team yet.

"I just had the feeling from the previous game that no matter what they did, they couldn't do anything to us," Millen says.

The Raiders knew they would have to stop Riggins. "If they can go with Riggins, they'll run him down our throats all day long," Long said. Seattle had presented the same problem in the previous game, with Curt Warner, and the Raiders had solved it with essentially a five-man line. They widened their ends and brought Millen and Bob Nelson, both big inside linebackers, up to take on the Seahawks' guards. Warner, the AFC's leading rusher, gained 26 yards on 11 carries.

"We wanted to make sure Riggins didn't get turned upfield," Shell says. "We plugged all the gaps on him, so he couldn't get turned up."

The tactic went hand-in-hand with man-to-man coverage, which enabled more defenders to stay close to the line, "rather than dropping into zones," Flores says. "By pressuring the wide receivers with the corners, we could pressure the run with the remaining people. The big thing is, their responsibilities in man coverage kept them up on the line of scrimmage.

They were in better position to attack, and that's what we did. You can't do that without great corners."

Los Angeles broke the game open on the last scrimmage play of the first half. Linebacker Jack Squirek intercepted a Joe Theismann pass at the Washington 5, and carried it in for a touchdown and a 21-3 lead.

tablish his territory," Brown says. "If you go out and establish the fact that 'Hey, you're not going to throw anything in my territory all day,' it'll pay off throughout the game. That's what Mike did. Lester, too. Those guys were just on top of their game."

Hayes was built more like a linebacker, and he had the strength to make receivers go where he wanted them to go. Haynes had the speed to stay with receivers. But they both were quick, and, above all, confident. "They challenged guys," says Willie Brown, the Pro Football Hall of Fame cornerback who coached Raiders defensive backs at the time. "That was my style when I played, and it carried on from there. You get up in their face and challenge them."

Before the game, someone asked Haynes if he thought the Redskins would try to play a bombs-away offensive style against him. "I hope so," he said.

They went after Haynes right away, and he might have decided the game on the first three Redskins passes. They were easily forgotten after the game's memorable scoring plays, but Theismann threw sideline passes toward Monk on all three of them, and Haynes had him covered for incompletions every time.

"A defensive back has to go out and es-

Squirek's touchdown set off a Raiders end-zone celebration, which included his teammate at linebacker Matt Millen.

Cliff Branch of the Raiders was the game's leading receiver with six catches. He set up his own 12-yard touchdown reception with this 50-yard, first-half bomb. Branch caught 14 passes in three Super Bowls.

Washington lined up to punt from its 30-yard line after those incompletions. The Raiders didn't send many all-out rushes after punters because they had Greg Pruitt on punt returns. Pruitt had returned one 97 yards for a touchdown in the earlier game against Washington. But Steve Ortmayer, the Raiders' special teams coach, thought he had found a hole in Washington's punt protection that could be pierced with a normal rush. The Redskins tended to overplay the outside, and special teams captain Derrick Jensen was able to break through up the middle. He not only blocked the punt, he also recovered it in the end zone.

"Before the game started, we were in a hole," May says.

The Redskins had

After Washington scored, the Raiders retaliated on Marcus Allen's five-yard scoring run.

two chances to climb out when it was a seven-point game. The first time, Mark Moseley missed a 44-yard field-goal attempt after a 51-yard drive. The second time, Raiders punter Ray Guy snared a high snap that could have set up Washington deep in Raiders' territory.

"The snap was about fifteen feet in the air," Flores says, "but Guy went up and caught it with one hand. He came down and still punted the ball way down the field. He did it so spectacularly, but so effortlessly, that it went unnoticed."

When the Raiders expanded their lead to 14-0, they did it by taking advantage of Washington's vulnerable pass coverage. Immediately after a Redskins punt, Cliff Branch beat two defenders for a 50-yard gain to the 15. Then, two plays later, Plunkett found Branch in the end zone for a 12-yard touchdown.

It was a play, Flores says, that the Raiders had set up specifically to challenge man-to-man coverage inside the 20. Branch had to beat only cornerback Anthony Washington, whom Branch had been saying all game would need help covering him. Branch cut over the middle from the left, faked a cut back outside, and streaked up the middle, with Washington behind him. Branch's six catches in the game gave him 73 in his playoff career, three more than

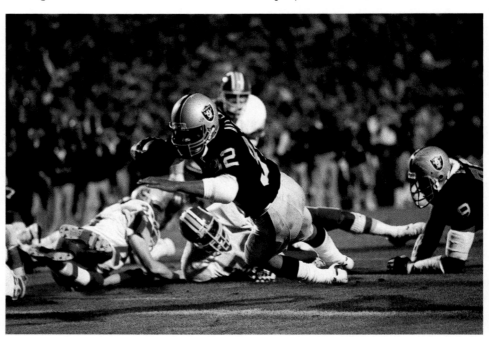

Allen was voted the game's most valuable player after rushing for a Super Bowl-record 191 yards on just 20 carries. Included was this 74-yard touchdown run in the third quarter—another Super Bowl record.

former Raider Fred Biletnikoff's previous NFL record.

Washington came right back with a 73-yard drive, but it stalled on the 7 for a field goal late in the second quarter. Los Angeles's 14-3 lead was within easy range of the Redskins' offense, but Washington got greedy late in the half when it took over at its own 12-yard line with 12 seconds left.

Instead of throwing far downfield, where the Raiders had been breaking up long passes even when they weren't the obvious call, Gibbs ordered a screen pass. The play was called "Rocket Right, Option Right, Screen Left," May

After the Raiders' 38-9 victory—in only their second season in Los Angeles—head coach Tom Flores congratulated his players in the locker room. It was the low-key Flores's second Super Bowl victory in two tries.

says, and it had burned the Raiders for a 67-yard gain to Joe Washington in the regular-season game. When the Redskins started lining up with three receivers on the right and Joe Washington in the backfield, Raiders defensive coordinator Charlie Sumner had a hunch they might try it again.

Just in case, he needed a pass-coverage specialist at linebacker with instructions to call an unusual coverage. "Charlie Sumner put Jack Squirek in specifically for that play," Flores says of the second-year backup linebacker who was faster and taller than Millen. "We were playing not to give up a big play, with everybody playing zone except him. He played man coverage." Squirek would tail Joe Washington.

"That was a great moment," Millen says, laughing, but he didn't think so at the time. This wasn't a situation in which he usually came out of the game, and he didn't like it. "I came out and I said to Sumner, 'What the hell are you taking me out for?' " Millen says. "He said, 'I just have a hunch,' and I said, 'I hope you're right.' "

While the argument was going on, Theismann threw the pass Sumner expected, Squirek cut in front of Washington at the 5, and nobody touched him after his interception until Raiders teammates pounded his back in the end zone. "All of a sudden, it's a touchdown," Millen says. "I picked [Sumner] up, and I was hugging him and yelling, 'Great call!'"

Theismann didn't quibble with Gibbs's call, either. That wasn't the problem. Theismann just threw a bad pass.

"Joe got a little pressure up the middle," May says, "and he turned around and threw it and didn't realize there was a black jersey in front of Joe [Washington]." Theismann told the same story. With everyone else in zone coverage, he hadn't expected Squirek to be man-to-man.

"I was in shock," said Squirek, who hadn't scored since he was a high school wide receiver.

The Redskins were shocked, too, "that we could be behind that far that quickly," May says. It was going to take a great second half to catch up...but they told themselves they could do it. "No matter how far we were down that season, we could always come back," May says.

Their immediate memories were less encouraging. Theismann had a 6-for-18 first half for 78 yards. Riggins had 37 yards on 16 carries. May remembers the Raiders throwing a lot of defensive fronts at them, sometimes even bringing the safeties up and dropping defensive ends back, but that wasn't the problem, he says. The linemen adjusted for everything on the sideline.

Millen agrees. He says the Raiders just outplayed Washington one-on-one as he expected. Kinlaw had a big chore at nose tackle, plugging up the middle against double-team blocking. "But Reggie had a great game," Millen says.

So did Rod Martin at right outside linebacker. The Raiders coaxed Washington into running to that side because it had the advantage of a tight end against a free safety there. The two-tight end offense had to give them that advantage on one side. "We just left it up to Rod Martin to hold the right side down," Millen says, "and he did."

Another thing that helped was Millen's feeling that he could do no wrong calling line stunts. Like many good offenses, the Redskins made predictable play selections depending on their formations. They were used to blocking people even when the defense knew where they were going. But they couldn't block the Raid-

ers, who kept getting in their way. "That was one of the best games I ever called," Millen says. "It seemed like every time I moved somebody, it was right."

As the run grew clearly ineffective, Theismann had more and more black-shirted company when he tried to pass. "They were gambling," May says of the Raiders' blitzes. "It was one of those things, if you got the ball off on time and on the mark, it was six."

The Redskins did that only briefly—going 70 yards on the first drive of the second half. Riggins finished the drive with a one-yard touchdown run. "We felt we were back in the game again," May says, even though the Raiders' Don Hasselbeck blocked the extra point. But the feeling didn't last long. Four minutes later, Allen's five-yard run finished a 70-yard drive that made it 28-9. "When we came right back and scored, the game was over," Millen says.

Late in the third quarter, the Raiders once again slapped the Redskins down just as they were pulling their heads above water. Anthony Washington recovered Branch's fumble on the Raiders' 35, but, on fourth-and-one from the 26, Martin stopped Riggins in his tracks with an open-field tackle. The next play was Allen's 74-yard touchdown run.

"We had at least seven guys touch him and couldn't bring him down," May says.

The play started as a run to left end, but the Redskins had a posse waiting for Allen there. Penned in, he turned 270 degrees to his left as tacklers grabbed at him from all sides. "I just let instinct take over," Allen says. Somehow, he found a crack up the middle and outran all the Redskins to the end zone. "And everybody said he was too slow," Flores says.

"That really snapped our backs," May says.

Like all coaches, Flores wasn't ready to call it a victory. "When we came out in the second half and still were dominating the game, I felt good," Flores says. "But you know how coaches are. We're never happy until it's over. Guys would want to come up and congratulate me with a couple minutes left, and it's pretty obvious it's over, but I'd say, 'No, no, no. It's not over yet.'"

But it was.

XIX

San Francisco 38, Miami 16

6 GATE	**55** STAIR	
4 SECTION	**12** ROW	**10** SEAT

AFC-NFC WORLD CHAMPIONSHIP GAME
SUNDAY, JANUARY 20, 1985   KICKOFF 3:00 P.M.
STANFORD STADIUM $60.00

SUPER XIX BOWL

SUNDAY, JANUARY 20, 1985
KICKOFF 3:00 P.M.   GATES OPEN AT 12:15 P.M.
$60.00 ALL TAXES INCLUDED

NFL

SEAT **10**   ROW **12**   STAIR **55**

SECTION **4**   GATE **6**

Vital Statistics

Starting Lineups

Miami (AFC)	Offense	San Francisco (NFC)
Mark Duper	WR	Dwight Clark
Jon Giesler	LT	Bubba Paris
Roy Foster	LG	John Ayers
Dwight Stephenson	C	Fred Quillan
Ed Newman	RG	Randy Cross
Cleveland Green	RT	Keith Fahnhorst
Bruce Hardy	TE	Russ Francis
Mark Clayton	WR	Freddie Solomon
Dan Marino	QB	Joe Montana
Tony Nathan	RB	Wendell Tyler
Woody Bennett	RB	Roger Craig
	Defense	
Doug Betters	LE	Lawrence Pillers
Bob Baumhower	NT	Manu Tuiasosopo
Kim Bokamper	RE	Dwaine Board
Bob Brudzinski	LOLB	Dan Bunz
Jay Brophy	LILB	Riki Ellison
Mark Brown	RILB	Jack Reynolds
Charles Bowser	ROLB	Keena Turner
Don McNeal	LCB	Ronnie Lott
William Judson	RCB	Eric Wright
Glenn Blackwood	SS	Carlton Williamson
Lyle Blackwood	FS	Dwight Hicks

Substitutions

Miami-Offense: K-Uwe von Schamann. P-Reggie Roby. QB-Don Strock. RB-Joe Carter, Eddie Hill. TE-Dan Johnson, Joe Rose. WR-Jimmy Cefalo, Vince Heflin, Jim Jensen, Nat Moore. KR-Fulton Walker. G-Steve Clark, Ronnie Lee, Jeff Toews. Defense: E-Bill Barnett, Charles Benson. T-Mike Charles. LB-A.J. Duhe, Earnie Rhone, Jackie Shipp, Sanders Shiver. CB-Paul Lankford, Robert Sowell. S-Bud Brown, Mike Kozlowski. DNP: FB-Pete Johnson.

San Francisco-Offense: K-Ray Wersching. P-Max Runager. RB-Derrick Harmon, Carl Monroe, Bill Ring. TE-Earl Cooper. WR-Renaldo Nehemiah, Mike Wilson. KR-Dana McLemore. T-Allan Kennedy, Billy Shields. G-Guy McIntyre. Defense: E-Fred Dean, Jim Stuckey. T-Michael Carter, Gary Johnson, Louie Kelcher, Jeff Stover. LB-Milt McColl, Blanchard Montgomery, Todd Shell, Michael Walter. CB-Tom Holmoe. S-Jeff Fuller. DNP: QB-Matt Cavanaugh. TE-John Frank. CB-Mario Clark.

Officials

Referee-Pat Haggerty. Umpire-Tom Hensley. Head Linesman-Leo Miles. Line Jude-Ray Dodez. Back Judge-Tom Kelleher. Side Judge-Bill Quinby. Field Judge-Bob Lewis.

Scoring

Miami	10	6	0	0 —	16
San Francisco	7	21	10	0 —	38

Mia-FG von Schamann 37
SF-Monroe 33 pass from Montana (Wersching kick)
Mia-Johnson 2 pass from Marino (von Schamann kick)
SF-Craig 8 pass from Montana (Wersching kick)
SF-Montana 6 run (Wersching kick)
SF-Craig 2 run (Wersching kick)
Mia-FG von Schamann 31
Mia-FG von Schamann 30
SF-FG Wersching 27
SF-Craig 16 pass from Montana (Wersching kick)
Attendance-84,059

FINAL TEAM STATISTICS

	Dolphins	49ers
TOTAL FIRST DOWNS	19	31
Rushing	2	16
Passing	17	15
Penalty	0	0
TOTAL NET YARDAGE	314	537
Total Offensive Plays	63	76
Average Gain per Offensive Play	5.0	7.1
NET YARDS RUSHING	25	211
Total Rushing Plays	9	40
Average Gain per Rushing Play	2.8	5.3
NET YARDS PASSING	289	326
Pass Att.-Comp.-Int.	50-29-2	35-24-0
Sacks-Yards Lost	4-29	1-5
Gross Yards Passing	318	331
Avg. Gain per Pass (Incl. Sacks)	5.4	9.1
PUNTS-YARDS	6-236	3-98
Average Distance	39.3	32.7
Had Blocked	0	0
TOTAL RETURN YARDAGE	155	91
Kickoff Returns-Yards	7-140	4-40
Punt Returns-Yards	2-15	5-51
Interception Returns-Yards	0-0	2-0
TOTAL TURNOVERS	2	2
Fumbles-Lost	1-0	2-2
Had Intercepted	2	0
PENALTIES-YARDS	1-10	2-10
TOTAL POINTS SCORED	16	38
Touchdowns Rushing	0	2
Touchdowns Passing	1	3
Touchdowns Returns	0	0
Extra Points	1	5
Field Goals-Attempts	3-3	1-1
Safeties	0	0
THIRD DOWN EFFICIENCY	4/12	6/11
FOURTH DOWN EFFICIENCY	0/0	0/1
TIME OF POSSESSION	22:49	37:11

INDIVIDUAL STATISTICS

RUSHING

Miami	No.	Yds.	Avg.	Long	TD
Nathan	5	18	3.6	16	0
Bennett	3	7	2.3	7	0
Marino	1	0	0.0	0	0

San Francisco	No.	Yds.	Avg.	Long	TD
Craig	15	58	3.9	10	1
Tyler	13	65	5.0	9	0
Montana	5	59	11.8	19	1
Harmon	5	20	4.0	7	0
Solomon	1	5	5.0	5	0
Cooper	1	4	4.0	4	0

PASSING

Miami	Att.	Comp.	Yds.	Long	TD	Int.
Marino	50	29	318	30	1	2

San Francisco	Att.	Comp.	Yds.	Long	TD	Int.
Montana	35	24	331	40	3	0

RECEIVING

Miami	No.	Yds.	Long	TD
Nathan	10	83	25	0
Clayton	6	92	27	0
Rose	6	73	30	0
Johnson	3	28	21	1
Moore	2	17	9	0
Cefalo	1	14	14	0
Duper	1	11	11	0

San Francisco	No.	Yds.	Long	TD
Craig	7	77	20	2
Clark	6	77	33	0
Francis	5	60	19	0
Tyler	4	70	40	0
Monroe	1	33	33t	1
Solomon	1	14	14	0

INTERCEPTIONS

Miami	No.	Yds.	Long	TD
None				

San Francisco	No.	Yds.	Long	TD
Williamson	1	0	0	0
Wright	1	0	0	0

PUNTING

Miami	No.	Yds.	Avg.	TB	Long
Roby	6	236	39.3	0	51

San Francisco	No.	Yds.	Avg.	TB	Long
Runager	3	98	32.7	0	35

PUNT RETURNS

Miami	No.	FC	Yds.	Long	TD
Walker	2	0	15	9	0

San Francisco	No.	FC	Yds.	Long	TD
McLemore	5	0	51	28	0

KICKOFF RETURNS

Miami	No.	Yds.	Long	TD
Walker	4	93	28	0
Hardy	2	31	16	0
Hill	1	16	16	0

San Francisco	No.	Yds.	Long	TD
Harmon	2	24	23	0
Monroe	1	16	16	0
McIntyre	1	0	0	0

FUMBLES

Miami	No.	Own Rec.	Opp. Rec.
Marino	1	1	0
Jensen	0	0	1
Heflin	0	0	1

San Francisco	No.	Own Rec.	Opp. Rec.
McIntyre	1	0	0
McLemore	1	0	0

KICKING

Miami	XP-A	FG-A	FG Made	FG Missed
von Schamann	1-1	3-3	37,31,30	--

San Francisco	XP-A	FG-A	FG Made	FG Missed
Wersching	5-5	1-1	27	--

The San Francisco 49ers were a dominant football team in 1984. They were the first NFL club ever to win 15 games in a regular season, finishing 15-1. They outscored their collective opponents by a two-to-one margin, 475 points to 227. They had 10 players voted to the Pro Bowl, including all four starting defensive backs. In the NFC playoffs, the 49ers brushed aside two rising powers, the New York Giants (21-10) and Chicago Bears (23-0), and made it look easy.

Yet, when Super Bowl XIX rolled into the San Francisco Bay Area, the hometown 49ers found themselves on the bottom half of the marquee.

Top billing went to the AFC champion Miami Dolphins, otherwise known as head coach Don Shula's Flying Circus.

The Dolphins had the league's new glamour boy in quarterback Dan Marino. In just his second pro season, Marino set NFL records for completions (362), passing yardage (5,084), and touchdowns (48). He threw seven more touchdown passes in AFC Divisional Playoff Games against Seattle and Pittsburgh.

That was 55 touchdown passes in just 18 games. By comparison, former Miami quarterback Bob Griese needed his first four full seasons (1967-1970) to reach 55 touchdown passes.

The 1984 Dolphins were a splashy bunch. They had the Marks Brothers (Mark Clayton and Mark Duper) at wide receiver and the Killer B's on defense. They were fast, they were hot, and they were fun to watch. The Super Bowl spotlight accentuated all of that and more.

The 49ers...well, they were just there.

What was their quarterback's name again? Joe Something? Wasn't he considered the best before Dan the Great came along? Poor Joe Montana now was obsolete.

That may sound silly in retrospect, but that's the way it was in January, 1985.

"There was a burning resentment among the players about how we were treated before that game," former 49ers guard and center Randy Cross says. "We were a great team, probably one of the best ever, but we didn't get the credit we felt we deserved.

"We were seventeen-and-one and people were asking us, 'Gee, do you really think you can stay with the Dolphins?' It was like a slap in the face. We talked about it and we agreed we had something to prove in that game. I don't want to say we hated the Dolphins by the end of the week, but...."

He paused. "We didn't like 'em a whole lot, put it that way."

"I never saw a team more focused for a game," says former 49ers defensive end Fred Dean. "A lot was said about how the Miami offense was gonna blow us out of the stadium. We were professionals. We didn't take that kind of talk lightly.

"We went out to show people that we were the better team. It was almost like a grudge thing. We took it personally. I think Joe [Montana] did, too, even though he'd never come right out and say it."

The 49ers wanted a convincing victory in Super Bowl XIX. A knockout, a straight-sets blitz, a no-doubt-about-it landslide. And that's what they achieved with a 38-16 triumph before a wildly partisan crowd of 84,059 in foggy Stanford Stadium.

Most experts had predicted the game would be high scoring but competitive right down to the closing minutes. "Whoever has the ball last will probably win," Chicago head coach Mike Ditka said.

But the 49ers removed most of the suspense by racing to a 28-10 lead midway through the second quarter.

Montana played the finest game of his pro career, at least to that point. He completed 24 of 35 passes for 331 yards and three touchdowns. He also ran for 59 yards and one touchdown. The "other" quarterback walked off with Super Bowl XIX's most valuable player award, his second in four years.

After the game, Montana poked a gentle needle in the direction of the media, saying, "All week it was Miami, Miami, Miami every time we turned around. You people were overlooking us."

On their first series, the Dolphins seized a 3-0 lead on a 37-yard field goal by Uwe von Schamann (5, rear). Miami drove 45 yards to set up the kick, with the big play a 25-yard pass from Dan Marino to Tony Nathan.

In reality, the Dolphins had some explosive weapons and a gifted young quarterback, but they still weren't a complete package. Their running game was ordinary and their defense (twenty-second in the NFL against the run during the season) was softer than pudding.

The 49ers simply had the best of everything. This was a much better San Francisco team than the one that won Super Bowl XVI. This team had two outstanding running backs, Wendell Tyler and Roger Craig, to complement the passing. And the defense had allowed the fewest points in the league during the regular season, an average of just 14.2 per game.

"That was the best team we had as long as I was there," former head coach Bill Walsh says, ranking the 1984 team ahead of his Super Bowl XXIII winner. "It was a solid club with tremendous depth and confidence. The 1981 team was still learning how to win. This team *knew*.

"It was a good blend of young players and older players. Roger Craig [then a second-year pro] was just coming into his own. Bubba Paris [also in his second season] was emerging on the offensive line. We had a sprinkling of veterans like Fred Dean and Gary Johnson who came in and added experience.

"It was a fun team to coach in the sense that every player recognized his role and performed it beautifully. When things happened—such as Joe [Montana] being injured and Ronnie [Lott] going down—other players stepped in and did the job. The bigger the challenge, the better that team responded."

The 49ers answered the challenge of Super Bowl XIX in resounding fashion, rolling up 537 yards in total offense. It was the most yards gained in a Super Bowl to that point and—get this—the most yards gained by a 49ers team in

San Francisco and Joe Montana struck back immediately, driving 78 yards to take a 7-3 lead. From the Dolphins' 33, Montana, who won Super Bowl MVP honors for the second time, rolled right and threw a touchdown pass to running back Carl Monroe.

any game since 1961.

Montana led the offense to scores on five consecutive possessions, turning a 10-7 first-quarter deficit into a 38-16 final. Craig starred in a dual role, rushing 15 times for 58 yards and catching seven passes for 77 yards. The 49ers' fullback scored three touchdowns to set a Super Bowl record.

"We just got into a nice groove," Montana said in a typical understatement. "Once you get going like that you gain confidence and it carries over to the defense and then back to the offense. It's a snowball kind of thing."

They don't see many snowballs in Miami, certainly none that resemble what the 49ers threw at the Dolphins and Marino that day.

The offense that averaged 433 yards and 32 points a game during the regular season started fast, scoring on its first two possessions, but then fell silent. A few mistakes on special teams and a total meltdown by the Miami defense put the game out of reach in a hurry.

"It was a complete turnaround," Shula says. "Everything went the way we hoped in the first quarter. We moved the ball right down the field, kicked a field goal, then got a touchdown [Marino passed to tight end Dan Johnson]. The mood on our bench was very good.

"But we bogged down [offensively] in the second quarter and our punter, Reggie Roby, hit three bad ones in a row. He kicked three line drives, and the 49ers wound up with great field position each time. We couldn't come up with a big play on defense and it was 28-10, just like that.

"In a big game, if one unit has problems, another unit has to rise to the occasion. We didn't

Miami went back in front 10-7 on Marino's two-yard touchdown pass to tight end Dan Johnson.

get that in the Super Bowl. We had a total breakdown. It's unfortunate but that's what happened."

Of course, the 49ers had something to do with the Dolphins' problems. They were alert, aggressive, and opportunistic. The San Francisco coaches came up with excellent game plans on both sides of the ball, and the players carried them out with surgical precision.

Early in the second quarter, the 49ers vaulted ahead 14-10. Montana started the drive with a 19-yard run and ended it with an eight-yard touchdown pass to Roger Craig (33), who was congratulated by Russ Francis (81).

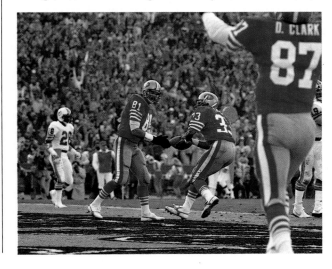

Finding their rhythm, the 49ers jumped ahead 21-10 when Montana ended a 55-yard drive by running six yards up the middle for another touchdown. He passed for 331 yards and ran for 59 more on five carries.

"It was like a boxing match," recalls Dean. "Both teams were throwing punches. The difference was we were getting our punches off first. We were landing, they were taking. We just wore 'em down."

The first thing the 49ers had to do was shut down Marino and the Marks Brothers. It was not an easy assignment, but San Francisco had the personnel for the job. In addition to the four Pro Bowl players in their secondary, the 49ers also had a pass rush that ranked among the NFL's best with a total of 66 sacks through the season.

At 23, Marino was a young player appearing in his first Super Bowl. So was Clayton, 23. Duper, 25, had been on the roster in Super Bowl XVII, but did not play. The 49ers' hope was that with good coverage and a lot of pressure, they could unnerve Marino and company and force mistakes.

Also, San Francisco defensive coordinator George Seifert correctly suspected that Miami would run a no-huddle offense to prevent the 49ers from shuttling their defensive packages on and off the field. The 49ers had nine defensive linemen, eight linebackers, and eight defensive backs, and they all played in various situations.

San Francisco's basic defense was a 3-4, with Lawrence Pillers, Manu Tuiasosopo, and Dwaine Board up front and Dan Bunz, Riki Ellison, Jack Reynolds, and Keena Turner at linebacker. Seifert switched to a 4-3, or sometimes a 4-2 Nickel, in passing situations, with Dean and sometimes Johnson coming in to rush the quarterback.

Shula and the Miami coaches wanted to dictate the day's agenda: They wanted to pass against the 3-4 with the slower linebackers in coverage and Dean on the bench. The best way to do that was with a hurry-up offense. The Dolphins practiced it all week despite Shula's public statements to the contrary.

"To think you'll win this game with some

The 49ers scored on their third successive second-quarter series when the versatile Craig (center) squeezed two yards for a touchdown. Craig, in his second year, scored a Super Bowl-record three touchdowns.

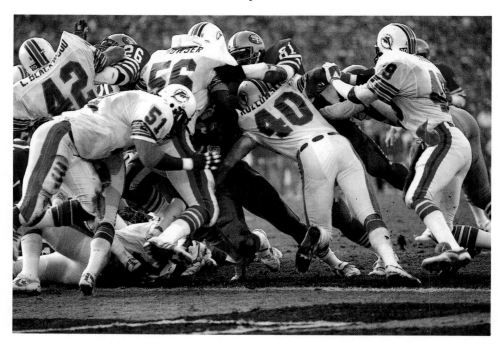

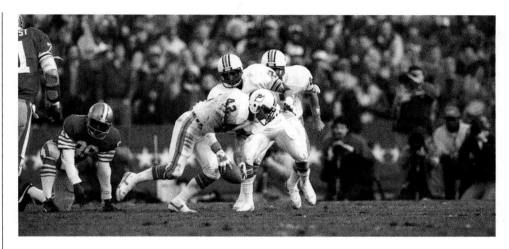

Miami safety Lyle Blackwood scooped up what he thought was a fumble by San Francisco wide receiver Freddie Solomon—but it was ruled an incomplete pass. Both teams had just two turnovers in the game.

gimmick-type thing is unrealistic," Shula said on Wednesday before the game.

Nice try, Don. The only trouble was the 49ers didn't buy it. They knew better.

Despite his quick ball release, Marino was under pressure from the aggressive San Francisco defense most of the day. Ends Dwaine Board (76) and Jeff Stover teamed to sack him on this occasion.

The first time the Dolphins ran the no-huddle offense in the game, they went right downfield—zip, zip, zip—and scored a touchdown. Marino completed five consecutive passes on the drive. It looked as if Miami was on track for another monster game.

But the 49ers adjusted. Seifert went to a four-man line, with Dean, Johnson, and Board playing every snap. Jeff Stover and Michael Carter rotated at the other spot. Turner and Ellison stayed in at linebacker, while safety Jeff Fuller joined a five-man secondary.

The Dolphins tried to counter-punch by running the ball against this Nickel package, but the 49ers stopped them cold.

"When that happened I knew we were in trouble," Shula says. "We had to throw and they really came after us."

The Miami offensive line protected Marino like royalty all season, allowing just 14 sacks in 18 games, but the story was reversed in the Super Bowl. San Francisco's rush sacked Marino four times and knocked him down repeatedly. The constant pressure resulted in several bad throws and two costly interceptions.

"We were always in his face, getting a piece of him, letting him know we were around," Dean says. "After a while, he started flinching when he'd get rid of the ball. He was rushing and trying to force things. Everybody talked about his quick

Craig jubilantly held the ball in the air as he scored his Super Bowl record third touchdown for the 49ers, a 16-yard, third-quarter pass from Montana. Craig caught seven passes in the game.

Trailing 38-16 in the third quarter, the Dolphins tried to come back. But Marino's bid for a touchdown pass to Mark Clayton (83) was thwarted by a brilliant interception by Eric Wright at the San Francisco 1.

release but that was offset by his lack of mobility. Marino doesn't move as well as some other quarterbacks and that makes it easier to put pressure on him. If you get good coverage, it neutralizes his quick release, and he can't buy more time with his feet.

"It takes a team effort to beat him, but you can beat him. We proved that."

Several individuals stood out. The cornerbacks, Lott and Eric Wright, blanketed the Marks Broth-

The frustrated Marino was held to one touchdown, intercepted twice, and sacked four times.

ers. Clayton finished with six catches for 92 yards, Duper had one for 11 yards. The bottom line: Neither receiver made it into the end zone.

Wright made two sensational plays, once leaping to tip a pass away from Duper in the open field, later intercepting a pass in front of Clayton near the San Francisco goal line. Lott got his helmet in the way of another pass intended for Clayton in the end zone.

"I was more nervous before that game than at any time in my whole career," Wright says. "I knew I had to play the game of my life if we were going to win. Those two receivers had torn up the league all year…but Ronnie and I were up to the challenge."

Up front, Board and Dean did a good job pass rushing from the outside. Board got two sacks against Marino, and Dean assisted on another. Johnson, the 31-year-old veteran nicknamed "Big Hands," had a sack and several pressures, collapsing the pocket with his rush up the middle.

"They threw the book at us," Marino said. "They blitzed a lot, they changed up their rushes and coverages. We had seen most of these schemes before—we just never saw them played that well."

Marino finished the game with 29 completions in 50 attempts for 318 yards.

Marino had three straight three-downs-and-out series in the second quarter when the 49ers were on their 21-0 run. He was 1 for 6 on third-down conversions in the first half. That's when the game really fell apart for Miami.

The Dolphins did get a break just before halftime. Uwe von Schamann had kicked a 31-

Montana celebrated the victory with wide receiver Dwight Clark, who caught five passes.

yard field goal, cutting the San Francisco lead to 28-13 with 12 seconds left on the clock.

Von Schamann squibbed the kickoff to a reserve lineman, Guy McIntyre, who first cradled the ball, then decided to run with it. McIntyre was hit and fumbled at his own 18-yard line and the Dolphins recovered at the 12. Von Schamann kicked another field goal, from 30 yards, reducing the 49ers' margin to 28-16.

Head coach Bill Walsh enjoyed a victory ride after the 49ers' second Super Bowl title of the 1980s. Walsh, who won Super Bowls XVI, XIX, and XXIII, retired in 1989 and became a television commentator.

A 12-point cushion was hardly secure given Miami's quick-strike capability. In the AFC Championship Game against Pittsburgh, the Dolphins' three first-half touchdown drives lasted exactly 2:09, 1:22, and 0:33.

But the 49ers never blinked. The defense turned up the heat on Marino in the third quarter, while the offense, led by Montana, did a good job controlling the ball. A field goal by Ray Wersching and Craig's third touchdown put the game away.

"We felt in control all day," wide receiver Dwight Clark said. "We had too many weapons for them."

The San Francisco offense figured to have a big day against Miami, and it went according to form. The Dolphins' defense had been a source of concern for Shula all season. It allowed 119 points in four weeks (November 11 through December 2) and was unable to stop even mediocre running attacks.

"We had some games that were painful to watch on film," defensive end Doug Betters admitted. "The team was winning, but we weren't doing our job."

Part of the problem was inexperience at inside linebacker, where rookie Jay Brophy and second-year man Mark Brown replaced veterans A.J. Duhe and Earnie Rhone. Duhe was nagged by injuries much of the season, while Brown beat out Rhone. But Brophy and Brown often misread fakes and overran plays, leaving the middle of the Miami defense unattended. Montana took full advantage of the situation, using play-action passes to confuse the two inside linebackers and sending his swift receivers criss-crossing through the secondary. Montana's 24 completions went to six different receivers. He threw a 33-yard touchdown pass to Carl Monroe, a reserve halfback, to open the San Francisco scoring. Free safety Lyle Blackwood had Monroe covered but he was a step too slow. Montana exploited mismatches like that all day.

There were mismatches in the trenches as well, notably at left tackle, where the 6-6, 300-pound Paris was blocking Kim Bokamper, a 6-6, 245-pound defensive end. The 49ers rushed for 211 yards.

It was a painful afternoon for the Miami defense, known as the Killer Bees because 9 of the 11 starters had last names that began with the letter 'B.' Unfortunately for Shula, none of his players were named Butkus (as in Dick), Bednarik (as in Chuck), or Blount (as in Mel).

The Miami B's were Betters, Brophy, Brown, Bokamper, nose tackle Bob Baumhower, outside linebackers Bob Brudzinski and Charles Bowser, and safeties Lyle and Glenn Blackwood. They simply were no match for the 49ers, who left them B-fuddled.

"We tried everything we could think of to contain him," Shula says, referring to Montana. "We blitzed, we stunted, we changed our coverages. Nothing worked. He got us off-balance and never let us regroup. That's the mark of a great quarterback."

According to Randy Cross, the toughest challenge the 49ers faced in Super Bowl XIX was not the Miami Dolphins, but surviving what he termed "the home-field disadvantage."

With the Super Bowl scheduled at Stanford Stadium in Palo Alto, just 50 miles south of the Golden Gate Bridge, the 49ers were able to stay home and train all week at their own facility in Redwood City.

The Dolphins, meanwhile, had to move into a Bay Area hotel and practice at the Oakland Coliseum, where they were 0-5 lifetime under Shula, hardly a source of comfort.

All of this would seem to favor the NFC champions, right? Not so, the players claim.

"Too many distractions," Dan Bunz says. "I got more ticket requests than Ticketron. I was getting calls at two in the morning from people saying, 'Remember me? I sat behind you in fourth grade. Can you get me two tickets to the game?'

"We were scheduled to check into a hotel on Friday [before the game] but we had players asking Bill Walsh if they could go in a day or two early just so they could hide out."

"The Super Bowl is a goldfish bowl anyway, but it's ten times worse when it's in your hometown," Cross says. "You can't go out because people recognize you and you can't stay home because the phone never stops ringing. There's no getting away, no letup."

Fred Dean is philosophical.

"That's the price of success," he says. "I'd pay it anytime."

XX

Chicago 46, New England 10

LOGE

GATE	SECTION	ROW	SEAT
K	386	06	20

SUPER BOWL XX

NFL

AFC-NFC WORLD CHAMPIONSHIP GAME

Sunday, January 26, 1986   Kickoff 4:00 P.M.

Louisiana Superdome $75.00

Sunday, January 26, 1986

Kickoff 4:00 P.M.   Gates Open 1:00 P.M.

$75.00   All taxes included

GATE	SECTION	ROW	SEAT
K	386	06	20

LOGE

Vital Statistics

Starting Lineups

Chicago (NFC)	Offense	New England (AFC)
Willie Gault	WR	Stanley Morgan
Jim Covert	LT	Brian Holloway
Mark Bortz	LG	John Hannah
Jay Hilgenberg	C	Pete Brock
Tom Thayer	RG	Ron Wooten
Keith Van Horne	RT	Steve Moore
Emery Moorehead	TE	Lin Dawson
Dennis McKinnon	WR	Stephen Starring
Jim McMahon	QB	Tony Eason
Walter Payton	RB	Tony Collins
Matt Suhey	RB	Craig James
	Defense	
Dan Hampton	LE	Garin Veris
Steve McMichael	LT-NT	Lester Williams
William Perry	RT-RE	Julius Adams
Richard Dent	RE-LOLB	Andre Tippett
Otis Wilson	LLB-LILB	Steve Nelson
Mike Singletary	MLB-RILB	Larry McGrew
Wilber Marshall	RLB-ROLB	Don Blackmon
Mike Richardson	LCB	Ronnie Lippett
Leslie Frazier	RCB	Raymond Clayborn
Dave Duerson	SS	Roland James
Gary Fencik	FS	Fred Marion

Substitutions

Chicago-Offense: K-Kevin Butler. P-Maury Buford. QB-Steve Fuller, Mike Tomczak. RB-Dennis Gentry, Thomas Sanders, Calvin Thomas. TE-Tim Wrightman. WR-Ken Margerum, Keith Ortego. C-Tom Andrews. G-Stefan Humphries. T-Andy Frederick. Defense: E-Mike Hartenstine, Tyrone Keys. T-Henry Waechter. LB-Brian Cabral, Jim Morrissey, Ron Rivera, Cliff Thrift. CB-Reggie Phillips, Ken Taylor. S-Shaun Gayle.
New England-Offense: K-Tony Franklin. P-Rich Camarillo. QB-Steve Grogan. RB-Greg Hawthorne, Mosi Tatupu, Robert Weathers. TE-Derrick Ramsey. WR-Irving Fryar, Cedric Jones. C-Guy Morriss. G-Paul Fairchild. T-Art Plunkett. Defense: E-Smiley Creswell, Ben Thomas. NT-Dennis Owens. LB-Brian Ingram, Johnny Rembert, Ed Reynolds, Ed Williams. CB-Ernest Gibson, Rod McSwain. S-Jim Bowman. DNP: QB-Tom Ramsey.

Officials

Referee-Red Cashion. Umpire-Ron Botchan. Head Linesman-Bama Glass. Line Judge-Dale Williams. Back Judge-Al Jury. Side Judge-Bob Rice. Field Judge-Jack Vaughan.

Scoring

Chicago	13	10	21	2	—	46
New England	3	0	0	7	—	10

NE-FG Franklin 36
Chi-FG Butler 28
Chi-FG Butler 24
Chi-Suhey 11 run (Butler kick)
Chi-McMahon 2 run (Butler kick)
Chi-FG Butler 24
Chi-McMahon 1 run (Butler kick)
Chi-Phillips 28 interception return (Butler kick)
Chi-Perry 1 run (Butler kick)
NE-Fryar 8 pass from Grogan (Franklin kick)
Chi-Safety, Waechter tackled Grogan in end zone
Attendance-73,818

FINAL TEAM STATISTICS

	Bears	Patriots
TOTAL FIRST DOWNS	23	12
Rushing	13	1
Passing	9	10
Penalty	1	1
TOTAL NET YARDAGE	408	123
Total Offensive Plays	76	54
Average Gain per Offensive Play	5.4	2.3
NET YARDS RUSHING	167	7
Total Rushing Plays	49	11
Average Gain per Rushing Play	3.4	0.6
NET YARDS PASSING	241	116
Pass Att.-Comp.-Int.	24-12-0	36-17-2
Sacks-Yards Lost	3-15	7-61
Gross Yards Passing	256	177
Avg. Gain per Pass (Incl. Sacks)	8.9	2.7
PUNTS-YARDS	4-173	6-263
Average Distance	43.3	43.8
Had Blocked	0	0
TOTAL RETURN YARDAGE	144	175
Kickoff Returns-Yards	4-49	7-153
Punt Returns-Yards	2-20	2-22
Interception Returns-Yards	2-75	0-0
TOTAL TURNOVERS	2	6
Fumbles-Lost	3-2	4-4
Had Intercepted	0	2
PENALTIES-YARDS	7-40	5-35
TOTAL POINTS SCORED	46	10
Touchdowns Rushing	4	0
Touchdowns Passing	0	1
Touchdowns Returns	1	0
Extra Points	5	1
Field Goals-Attempts	3-3	1-1
Safeties	1	0
THIRD DOWN EFFICIENCY	7/14	1/10
FOURTH DOWN EFFICIENCY	0/1	1/1
TIME OF POSSESSION	39:15	20:45

INDIVIDUAL STATISTICS

RUSHING

Chicago	No.	Yds.	Avg.	Long	TD
Payton	22	61	2.8	7	0
Suhey	11	52	4.7	11t	1
McMahon	5	14	2.8	7	2
Sanders	4	15	3.8	10	0
Gentry	3	15	5.0	8	0
Thomas	2	8	4.0	7	0
Fuller	1	1	1.0	1	0
Perry	1	1	1.0	1t	1

New England	No.	Yds.	Avg.	Long	TD
C. James	5	1	0.2	3	0
Collins	3	4	1.3	3	0
Grogan	1	3	3.0	3	0
Weathers	1	3	3.0	3	0
Hawthorne	1	-4	-4.0	-4	0

PASSING

Chicago	Att.	Comp.	Yds.	Long	TD	Int.
McMahon	20	12	256	60	0	0
Fuller	4	0	0	0	0	0

New England	Att.	Comp.	Yds.	Long	TD	Int.
Eason	6	0	0	0	0	0
Grogan	30	17	177	24	1	2

RECEIVING

Chicago	No.	Yds.	Long	TD
Gault	4	129	60	0
Gentry	2	41	27	0
Margerum	2	36	29	0
Moorehead	2	22	14	0
Suhey	1	24	24	0
Thomas	1	4	4	0

New England	No.	Yds.	Long	TD
Morgan	6	51	16	0
Starring	2	39	24	0
Fryar	2	24	16	1
Collins	2	19	11	0
Ramsey	2	16	11	0
Jones	1	19	19	0
C. James	1	6	6	0
Weathers	1	3	3	0

INTERCEPTIONS

Chicago	No.	Yds.	Long	TD
Morrissey	1	47	47	0
Phillips	1	28	28t	1

New England	No.	Yds.	Long	TD
None				

PUNTING

Chicago	No.	Yds.	Avg.	TB	Long
Buford	4	173	43.3	1	52

New England	No.	Yds.	Avg.	TB	Long
Camarillo	6	263	43.8	1	62

PUNT RETURNS

Chicago	No.	FC	Yds.	Long	TD
Ortego	2	1	20	12	0

New England	No.	FC	Yds.	Long	TD
Fryar	2	0	22	12	0

KICKOFF RETURNS

Chicago	No.	Yds.	Long	TD
Gault	4	49	18	0

New England	No.	Yds.	Long	TD
Starring	7	153	36	0

FUMBLES

Chicago	No.	Own Rec.	Opp. Rec.
Payton	1	0	0
Suhey	1	0	0
Gentry	1	1	0
Hampton	0	0	1
Singletary	0	0	2
Marshall	0	0	1

New England	No.	Own Rec.	Opp. Rec.
Eason	1	0	0
C. James	1	0	0
Jones	1	0	0
Ramsey	1	0	0
McGrew	0	0	1
Clayborn	0	0	1

KICKING

Chicago	XP-A	FG-A	FG Made	FG Missed
Butler	5-5	3-3	28, 24, 24	--

New England	XP-A	FG-A	FG Made	FG Missed
Franklin	1-1	1-1	36	--

PLAY-BY-PLAY

Chicago won coin toss and elected to receive.
FIRST QUARTER
Franklin kick to C 7, Gault 11 return (Tatupu).
Chicago (15:00)
C 18 1-10 Payton 7 sweep left (Nelson).
C 25 2-3 Payton run right, loss of 5 (Blackmon), fumbled, McGrew recovered for NE at C 19.
New England (14:01)
C 19 1-10 Eason pass to Dawson left sideline incomplete.
C 19 2-10 Eason pass to Morgan dropped at C5.
C 19 3-10 Eason pass to Starring end zone overthrown.
C 19 4-10 Franklin, 36-yard field goal (13:41).
New England scoring drive: 0 yards, 3 plays, :20.
New England 3, Chicago 0

Most of the time, great moments in sports just happen. They aren't accidents, but they aren't planned, either. The scarcity of exceptions is what makes such an enduring legend of Babe Ruth's called shot before his home run in the 1932 World Series. And it's what makes the Chicago Bears' 46-10 victory in Super Bowl XX more remarkable than the lopsided margin.

That whole 1985 season, the Bears were brash enough to dial history's number and make reservations. "How many teams would be cutting a videotape about going to the Super Bowl after the twelfth week of the season?" cornerback Leslie Frazier asks now. That simply isn't done. One does not claim one's place in history. The claiming is history's prerogative.

But the 1985 Bears had no doubt they were choreographing highlight films to be admired in future decades. "We honestly thought we had a team that was capable of doing a lot of things no one had done," defensive tackle Dan Hampton says.

They filled opponents' bulletin boards with insulting predictions before games. They rang opponents' ears with a barking defense during games. Their video, "The Super Bowl Shuffle," was merely the most vivid example of how they stormed to the NFL's throne with a child's ingenuous and presumptuous irreverence, rather like pounding the Buckingham Palace door and asking if Liz and Chuck might want to join the gang for some volleyball in the street.

Somehow, their arrogance made them all the more lovable. Maybe it was because the Bears had been losers long enough to remain underdogs through a 15-1 regular season. Maybe it was because people identified with wide-bodied defensive tackle William (The Refrigerator) Perry's weight struggle, with impetuous head coach Mike Ditka's struggle to control his temper, with eccentric quarterback Jim McMahon's struggle against all forms of convention and authority.

Whatever the reason, the Bears became the leading object of NFL-licensed merchandise sales. Their Super Bowl drew the largest audience of any TV show in history. "The Super Bowl Shuffle" ranked second to Michael Jackson's "Thriller" in all-time video-cassette sales up to that time. Then, at halftime of the Super Bowl, when the Bears led the New England Patriots 23-3, nearly the whole New Orleans crowd of 73,818 stood up and rattled the Superdome's roof by stomping and singing along with the Bears' rap song on the public address system.

The Bears' only disappointment was losing the shutout that linebacker Otis Wilson had predicted publicly and his teammates had expected privately. "I thought we'd shut them out," says Buddy Ryan, the Bears' defensive coordinator that year and the Eagles' head coach since two days after Super Bowl XX. "We had already shut out the Giants and the Rams."

Those consecutive postseason shutouts, 21-0 and 24-0, were the first ever by an NFL playoff team, and New England's only Super Bowl points came on a zero-yard field-goal drive at the Bears' 19-yard line and a so-what touchdown drive that made the score 44-10 in the fourth quarter. "I doubt if any defense will ever play as well as that defense did for those three games," Ditka says.

The compliment is grudging and meaningful. Ditka and Ryan went jaw-to-jaw more often than they saw eye-to-eye. Ditka was not the only Bears executive who was appalled that a mere assistant coach would rate a ride on the players' shoulders after a Super Bowl victory, and he purged the name "46" from the Bears' defensive playbook before Ryan's old office was empty. But it was defense in general and the 46 in particular that made the 1985 Bears so special.

This was a defense that didn't leave the chore of moving the ball to its teammates on offense. In the first half of Super Bowl XX, the Bears moved New England backward—14 yards on pass plays and five yards on runs—for a net halftime yardage of minus-19. The Patriots didn't gain yardage until their tenth play. On their first nine, covering four possessions, they lost 22 yards and two fumbles.

"That's the nature of the way we tried to play all the time," Ryan says. "Take the ball away

Bears defensive end Richard Dent forced two fumbles in the first quarter, including this one by running back Craig James. It was recovered on the Patriots' 13, setting up Matt Suhey's 11-yard touchdown run.

a short road to the end zone. The Bears scored 20 of 44 regular-season touchdowns—and 6 of 8 in the playoffs—on drives of 60 yards or less.

The Bears' style was to break offenses. "If you even gained yardage, they were upset," Patriots defensive end Garin Veris says.

A first down was intolerable. At least it was to middle linebacker Mike Singletary when the Patriots finally made one with 4:06 left in the first half and the Bears ahead 20-3. It was the Patriots' eighteenth play, and only their third that gained yardage, but Singletary jumped up and down in a rage, yelling at his teammates to get their act together.

The Bears' defense set Super Bowl halftime records for the negative rushing, passing, and total yardage, plus the single first down. For the game, their seven sacks and New England's seven yards rushing also were records, as were the

Dent and defensive tackle Steve McMichael (76) teamed to shake quarterback Tony Eason (11) loose from the ball, setting up a Bears field goal. Chicago's defense forced six New England turnovers.

from people. Don't be just three [downs] and out. Take it away on first down. We played defense like it was offense."

When cornerback Reggie Phillips's interception return put the Bears ahead of New England 37-3, he became the eighth Bears defensive player to score that year, not counting Perry's points when he lined up at fullback. In a six-game stretch through week 12, the Bears' *defense* and their opponents' offense each scored 27 points. When it wasn't scoring itself, the defense was giving the offense

two defensive scores (a touchdown and a safety) and New England's 0.64 yards per rushing attempt. The Bears' 46 points, 36-point margin of victory, four rushing touchdowns, and 21 points in the third quarter all were records at the time. "I'm not embarrassed. I'm humiliated," New England guard Ron Wooten said.

The day had only two dark spots for the Bears. There was controversy over Ditka's choice to let Perry score the last, one-yard touchdown instead of Walter Payton, the certain Pro Football Hall of Fame member-to-be in his eleventh season. Payton said only that he was "surprised" and "disappointed," but McMahon was blunter. "I don't think we used Walter as much as we should have or could have," he said. "I felt bad for him."

The other cloud on the horizon was Ryan's impending departure. Several defensive players spent the last moments of the game begging team president Michael McCaskey to do whatever it took to keep him, but they also were pretty sure Ryan was leaving.

"We could tell by the way he was acting," Hampton says. "He was acting a little strange and a little cagey. I could feel it during the week. I told my wife, 'He's leaving after this game. It's over.' " It would be the defense's last time to show what it could do with Ryan's 46.

The 46 started out as a Nickel defense with extra run support, but it turned into a blitzing pass defense that sometimes left only three men in coverage. It began to reach its full potential in 1984, when the Bears could shift into it without substituting so offenses couldn't anticipate it.

There were three linebackers and five linemen, three of them over the guards and center, and two of them outside the tackles. Offenses

The Bears were overwhelming on defense and effective on offense, as Jim McMahon passed for 256 yards and ran for two touchdowns. He gave the Bears a 20-3 second-quarter lead by ramming two yards for a score.

had trouble blocking it because it put players over the guards and not over the tackles, while most defenses covered the tackles and not the guards. The guards weren't free to help the center handle Hampton.

The other problem was that all eight men close to the line were potential pass rushers, and offenses had trouble accounting for them all. Ryan would study an opponent's blocking schemes for blitzes and send whichever of the eight he didn't think the schemes could pick up. Receivers ran free, but quarterbacks didn't have time to find them.

"Nobody knew what to do against it," center Jay Hilgenberg says. "They were confused. We lined up two guys over the tight end, and they didn't know who to block."

With Otis Wilson blitzing from outside the tight end and Richard Dent from the other side, the Bears had an NFL-record 72 sacks in 1984, then 64 in 1985. If an offense blocked Wilson, the Bears could blitz the other outside linebacker, Wilber Marshall, who was inside Wilson and over the tight end. If an offense blocked both Marshall and Wilson, it didn't

have the manpower to handle Hampton, Perry, Steve McMichael, and Singletary between the tackles.

In the game's strangest play, Bears defensive tackle William Perry rolled out to pass—and was sacked.

The 1985 defense led the NFL in points, yards, rushing yards, first downs, pass completion percentage, and was second in third-down efficiency, plus interceptions and turnovers. It was third in passing yards, second in sacks. Dallas head coach Tom Landry called it "more dominant than the Steel Curtain." And it peaked in the playoffs, with 16 sacks, seven fumble recoveries, and three interceptions in three games. Opponents made first downs on only 16 of their 44 possessions and 3 of 36 third-down plays. The three-game averages were 144.7 total yards and 10.3 first downs, but at the ends of the third quarters, when the games were already decided, the Bears' postseason opponents averaged only 70 yards and 3.7 first downs.

"I was disappointed that all eleven of us didn't get into the Pro Bowl," Singletary says.

The success made Ryan a hot head coaching candidate, and the Eagles already had interviewed him. Singletary believes that by Super Bowl week Ryan had told all the defenders except him of his plans to leave. But Hampton says safety Gary Fencik was the only one Ryan told, "and he swore Gary to secrecy. I guess he figured Gary could handle it, but he didn't know if we could play the same game if we knew it would be our last for him."

That became clear at the defense's Saturday night pregame meeting. It started with everyone laughing when Ryan pulled up his sweater and showed the players a T-shirt his son had given him. The shirt said, "I'm Sorry I Can't Remember Your Name, But Is It OK If I Call You [profanity]?" Then he quieted them down. He didn't formally announce his plans, but he said, "Regardless of what happens tomorrow, you'll always be my heroes."

Then he turned over the meeting to the position coaches, but as Ryan says now, "It was a rowdy scene, I guess." McMichael threw a chair into the blackboard, Hampton turned over the

The Bears already led 23-3, but on their first play of the third quarter, they went for more as Willie Gault caught a 60-yard bomb from Jim McMahon. The pass reached the Patriots' 36 and set up a touchdown.

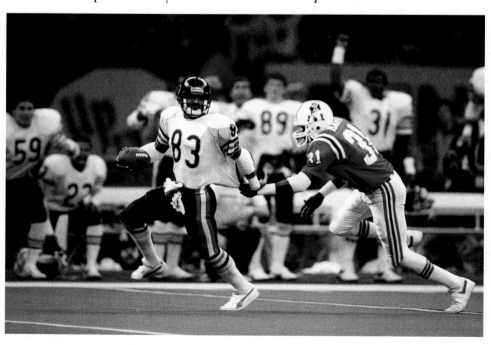

Chicago's Walter Payton ran for 61 yards, but the NFL's all-time leading rusher suffered one major frustration in the game. In his only Super Bowl appearance, he failed to score a touchdown.

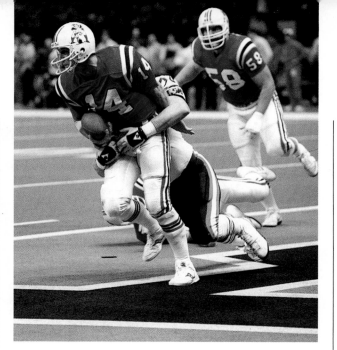

The Bears' defense scored twice—on an interception and this sack of Steve Grogan for a safety by backup defensive tackle Henry Waechter. Grogan replaced starting quarterback Tony Eason in the second quarter.

film projector, and the meeting was adjourned.

The Bears' offense was far more than the defense's ugly stepsister. Early in the year, when the Bears had to overcome deficits of at least a touchdown to win five of their first seven games, the offense carried the team. It finished second to San Diego in scoring, just 11 points back, and it gained 10.7 percent more yards than the NFL average, not far behind the defense's yield of 27.5 percent below the league average.

It had all the elements of great offense. It could control the ball with Payton, still in his prime for a then NFL-record nine consecutive 100-yard games. It could strike quickly with wide receiver Willie Gault, a world-class sprinter who averaged 21.3 yards per catch. Dennis McKinnon was the possession wide receiver. The young offensive line led the Bears to their third of four straight NFL rushing titles.

McMahon was the catalyst at quarterback. He combined inspiration and improvisation to make the Bears think they could score whenever they needed points. "He sees things that others don't see," Ditka said, and it often resulted in big plays to receivers who weren't even in the playbook. In three postseason games, McMahon ran or passed for six of the Bears' eight offensive touchdowns. He didn't throw an interception. And he took pressure off his team-

mates by bringing it upon himself.

Commissioner Pete Rozelle fined McMahon for wearing a shoe company's name on his headband in the first playoff game, so McMa-

William (the Refrigerator) Perry got the Bears' final touchdown when he hurled his 310 pounds into the end zone from the 1. Chicago used the defensive tackle as a short-yardage runner and blocker much of the season.

Richard Dent celebrated when he learned he had been named the game's most valuable player.

doubt on Wednesday that McMahon could play, the team relented, and Ditka later said McMahon "was two-hundred percent better" after treatment from Shiriashi.

McMahon also caused a minor stir by mooning a helicopter at practice—"just showing them where it hurts." And he was thrust into a major flap later in the week when a local TV reporter inaccurately attributed insults of New Orleans men and women to him.

Through it all, the Patriots were all but overlooked. "Even though we had won three big playoff games on the road, everybody was saying Chicago would walk away with it and we had no chance," Veris says. "It does bother you. The main focus was, 'What are you going to do to stop them from blowing you out of the stadium?' Not 'What are you going to do to win?' "

hon's headband said "Rozelle" in the NFC Championship Game. The Bears had just arrived in New Orleans when McMahon started a new controversy. He was furious because he wanted acupuncture treatments for his sore rear-end, and the Bears had banned his acupuncturist, Hiroshi Shiriashi, from the team plane, insisting their medical staff could handle the problem. When Ditka expressed serious

The wild-card Patriots were the first team to reach the Super Bowl by winning three playoff

When the one-sided game ended, the happy Bears carried head coach Mike Ditka (left) and defensive coordinator Buddy Ryan off the field. Ryan quit the Bears shortly afterward to become head coach of the Eagles.

games on the road, beating the Jets, Raiders, and Dolphins. Quarterback Tony Eason hadn't thrown an interception in the playoffs, but he had thrown only 42 passes in the low-risk offense that relied on Craig James's running, field position from the defense, and excellent special teams. "They were hitters," Singletary says of the defense that was led by linebacker Andre Tippett. "They had the same mind-set we had. But offensively, they were unsure."

New England's coaches knew the running game wouldn't be enough against the Bears, who had shut down Joe Morris and Eric Dickerson in earlier playoff games.

"I wanted to come out throwing...to get their attention," Patriots head coach Raymond Berry said. Eason dropped back on the Patriots' first six plays, but the first five were incomplete and the sixth was a sack. If the Bears' running defense offered little hope for New England, the Patriots' passing game was hopeless.

"We tried to change the personality of our team in one week," Wooten said after the game. "If we had it to do again, I'd like to have seen us run right at them. We would have liked to hit them in the chops a few times."

New England had the chance to strike early. On the second play from scrimmage, McMahon called the wrong formation and sent Payton in the wrong direction. With the blocking focused on the other side, Patriots linebacker Don Blackmon was able to knock the ball loose for Larry McGrew to recover at Chicago's 19-yard line.

"It was what we wanted," Singletary says of the early pressure. "They could have gotten it at the one and I think we would have been happy about it. We were excited about getting on the field and letting them know no matter what the situation is, they're not scoring."

After three incompletions, the Patriots settled for Tony Franklin's 36-yard field goal with 1:19 gone. It was the earliest score ever in a Super Bowl, but Ditka had covered that possibility in his pregame talk. "Don't let one bad play ruin it," he had said.

McMahon nearly made it worse moments later, but his errant pass bounced off Blackmon's chest. "I turned and didn't react quick enough," Blackmon said of the potential touch-

Jim McMahon not only was an outstanding quarterback in 1985, he was also a certified flake. The Bears' leader entertained the national television audience during the Super Bowl with a headband fashion show.

down. On the next play, McMahon's 43-yard pass to Gault set up Kevin Butler's first of three field goals, from 28 yards, to make it 3-3.

After an exchange of punts, Chicago's defense set the tone of the game on its next two turns on the field. Both series ended in fumbles, and the Bears recovered both at New England's 13. The first was another pass play. McMichael reached Eason first, so Dent went for the ball. Hampton saw it come loose, "and it was just laying there," he recalls. "It's like one of those stop-action sequences in car-wreck films. It's like I can't get there fast enough and everything slows down, and then finally I took it just before somebody else did."

A few plays later, the Bears began rubbing it in, even though they hadn't actually gone ahead yet. On second-and-goal from the 5, Perry lined up at tailback and took a pitchout as he headed toward the right sideline. In the regular season, he had scored by running and by catching, and now, in the first quarter of a 3-3 Super Bowl, he would try to throw a pass in a game for the first time. But tight end Emery Moorehead was covered. Tippett chased Perry toward the sideline, and nose tackle Dennis Owens became the first player ever to sack a defensive tackle in a Super Bowl. The Bears kicked a field goal.

It didn't matter. Dent forced another fumble on the Patriots' next play. "Certain players have an instinct. They know when to swipe the ball away," Ryan said. As James was losing ground on a run to his left, Dent went for the ball and Singletary recovered it.

It was Dent's eleventh forced fumble, including four in postseason games. In the regular season, when he led the NFL with 17 sacks, Dent also tipped two balls that became interceptions and were returned for touchdowns, hurried the passer to force an interception that resulted in another touchdown, and scored on an interception himself. Dent's plays put the Bears over the hump and eventually made him the game's most valuable player.

Two plays later, fullback Matt Suhey burst through McGrew at the line of scrimmage and safety Fred Marion at the goal line to make it 13-3, with 23 seconds left in the first quarter. It was an 11-yard run, but Suhey says, "I'm sure it'll be fifty yards by the time I turn forty."

"I knew we had it won when Matt Suhey scored," Hilgenberg says.

Hampton thought the Bears had clinched the game even earlier. "On Wednesday," he says. "No kidding. All week long, we had a lot of media coverage and we could see Tony Eason's eyes. That's all we talked about before the game. He was scared to death, and all we had to do was get to him early and the game would be over. That's pretty much how it went."

Eason didn't finish the second quarter. He was in for 15 plays, only one of which gained yardage. He was 0-for-6 passing, the only starting Super Bowl quarterback without a completion, but at least those plays averaged out to zero yards. Altogether, the 15 plays lost 36 yards, minus-8 on six runs and minus-28 on three sacks. The Bears used their 59 blitz, with all three linebackers coming, and the Patriots rarely found a blocker for Wilson from the outside. "I tried to scramble and there was no place to go," Eason said. "They played an almost perfect game."

"We got to him early and I think he got rattled," Singletary says now. "That's when I said,

'Let's go get him.' The look in his eyes said, 'I hope we're not in for another one of these.' " Steve Grogan replaced Eason with 5:08 left in the half.

The Bears already led 20-3. McMahon finished a 59-yard drive 7:24 before halftime with a two-yard touchdown on an option play. He faked a handoff to Perry at fullback, then followed blocks by Perry and tight end Tim Wrightman instead of pitching back to Payton.

The field goal that made it 23-3 at halftime shouldn't have counted. Hilgenberg snapped the ball to kill the clock before referee Red Cashion put it in play, a deliberate penalty that should have cost Chicago the three seconds left and ended the half. But Cashion assessed only the five yards and left Butler time to score.

While the fans were doing the Super Bowl Shuffle at halftime, McMahon was yelling about scoring 60 points. His first play of the second half was a 60-yard pass to Gault that would have been a 96-yard touchdown if Gault hadn't had to slow down for it. McMahon ran the last foot of the 96-yard drive for a 30-3 lead. He left the game with 256 passing yards, two touchdowns, and considerable MVP support.

"There's a certain point where you think, 'This game's over...they're dominating the game,' " Veris says. "You have to keep playing, but it's in your heart. They had a big, physical offensive line that kept pounding....And their defense was just a wild bunch."

With the Patriots safely behind, the Bears' defense could turn its focus to history. Phillips's 28-yard interception return made it 37-3. A fumble recovery and 13-yard return by Marshall to the Patriots' 37 set up a one-yard touchdown run by Perry.

Trailing 44-3, New England scored its only touchdown with 13:14 to play, Grogan's eight-yard pass to Irving Fryar completing a 76-yard drive. With 5:36 left, defensive tackle Henry Waechter sacked Grogan for a safety that finished the scoring and gave the Bears a seemingly appropriate 46 points.

"We're the best of all time," safety Dave Duerson said.

All year, the road to history was lined with laughter. From their headbands to their shuffling feet, the Bears made football fun.

XXI

N.Y. Giants 39, Denver 20

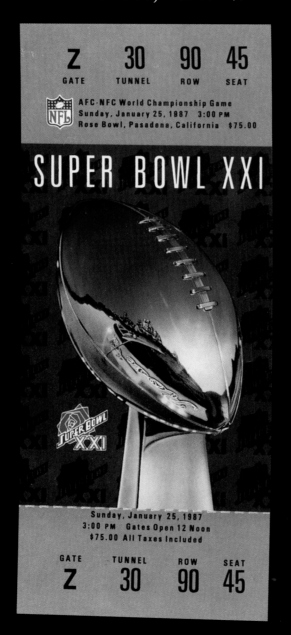

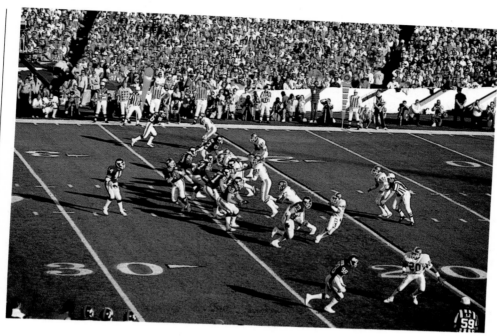

As more than 101,000 fans watched in Pasadena's Rose Bowl, the Giants' offense scored seven points in the first half and exploded for 30 in the second. The victory gave New York its first NFL championship in 30 years.

than Elway ever could have. In a 17-0 NFC Championship Game victory, it held Washington's high-powered offense to 0-for-18 on third and fourth downs. It led the league in stopping the run, allowing just 80 yards a game. In the playoffs, it held the Redskins and 49ers to 34.5 rushing yards a game, or 1.9 yards per carry.

Against the pass, Lawrence Taylor led the league with 20.5 sacks, and any team that overloaded to block him found its quarterback falling beneath Carl Banks, the other outside linebacker. Taylor was the league's most valuable player and the short fuse to the Giants' defense.

"Let's go out there like a bunch of crazed dogs and have some fun," was his typical sideline pep talk. In more quiet reflection, Taylor talked clinically about "kill shots," or said, "When you're yelling and your eyes turn red and you feel like slapping your mother, that's when you know you're ready to play ball."

The Giants' offense was built around power, designed more to help the defense excel than to make a quarterback look good. Joe Morris ran for 1,516 yards and 14 touchdowns, both number two in the NFL. The leading receiver was tight end Mark Bavaro with 66 catches and 1,001 yards. Bavaro's 15.2-yard average gain beat out eight wide receivers that year who made at least 50 catches. The Giants' leading wide receiver, Bobby Johnson (31 catches), was cut the next season.

"He wasn't called upon to put up big numbers all year," center Bart Oates said of Simms. "He was just called upon to produce in critical situations."

That's what Simms did in the Giants' stretch drive. He beat Minnesota with a big pass late on fourth-and-17, then did the same thing to Den-

me that whole week. I'd had a big year myself. Maybe John was more of a marquee name, but I never felt any animosity, like I was getting slighted at all. Not for one second."

Nor did he look forward to the game as a chance to silence his critics. "I wasn't trying to silence anybody or show people or anything like that," he says. "I think motivation to show other people is not very good motivation." This one was for himself and his loved ones.

Yet, he did say, in the rush of victory, "This makes everything worth all the crap I've taken over the years." And why not? New Yorkers had booed Simms since the day he was drafted in 1979, a first-rounder out of Morehead State. Giants fans hadn't heard of Morehead State, but they assumed it must have scheduled Podunk for homecoming.

He went five years without playing a full season, and the Giants were winners just one of those years. Simms was the symbol of their frustration. Even in 1986, the Giants' offense spent much of the year trying mainly not to blow it for the defense.

The defense overshadowed Simms more

ver on third-and-21. He beat San Francisco with three touchdowns in nine minutes after trailing 17-0 at halftime. He beat Washington with two third-and-long touchdown passes. In the playoffs, he led the 49-3 rout of San Francisco.

"Sometimes you get into a groove," Simms said at the time, "and whether it's hitting a tennis ball or golfing or shooting baskets, things start going well."

Nine days before the Super Bowl, on the Friday of the off-week before the Giants went to Los Angeles, Simms was so hot in practice that Parcells told him to save some of it. "We knew all week he was going to have a big game," tight end Zeke Mowatt said.

Simms felt confident not only that he had a big passing game in him, but that the Broncos would give him the opportunity. He remembered the 19-16 victory over Denver in November when the Broncos stacked their defense to stop the run and made their cornerbacks cover the Giants' wide receivers man-to-man. That disrespect for the passing game annoyed him, and he reminded his teammates and coaches of it before the Super Bowl.

He told his receivers, "Look, nobody's giving us any credit. Let's just come out of the gates [fast] and I'll get the ball to you." He lobbied Parcells and offensive coordinator Ron Erhardt to change their tactics so the Giants could come out passing.

New York's Phil Simms shrugged off pressure from Denver rushers such as linebacker Tom Jackson to complete 22 of 25 passes for 268 yards and three touchdowns. His record performance earned him MVP honors.

"I knew the matchups were in our favor," Simms says. "I knew they would have a hard time covering Bavaro. And even though our wideouts weren't well-recognized, I knew [Denver] would have a hard time covering them, the way they play defense with one-on-one outside. It proved to be right. When we wanted to throw outside, we were able to do that."

Before the game, Simms's warm-ups in the Rose Bowl made him feel better than ever. "I've

The Broncos led 10-7 in the second quarter when defensive end George Martin started the Giants' comeback by sacking Elway for a safety. Elway was chased to the end zone from his own 13-yard line.

got it working. I've got the fastball," he told teammates. Oates remembers that Simms told him how the ball felt good and he felt great. "I didn't imagine he would play *that* great, though," Oates says.

By kickoff, the challenge for Simms was to keep from bubbling out of his uniform. His most vivid single memory of the day was the excitement in the air before the game. "You truly could cut the electricity with a knife," he says. "Running onto the field for pregame introductions was the most exciting, thrilling moment of my life emotionally."

He was prepared for it, though. "All I'd heard from players

who'd been in past games was that the emotion carried them away for the first part of the first quarter," Simms says. "I told myself all week I didn't want that to happen. It pumped me up, but I concentrated on being under control from the first play on…on not getting caught up in the emotion and being nervous."

As it turned out, Simms had even more to be nervous about by the time he took the field. On the game's first scrimmage play, Elway did exactly what the Giants' defenders had worried about. He ran from the pass rush and gained 10 yards. "I thought, 'Uh-oh. Wear your track shoes. It could be a long day,' " Banks says. The Broncos' drive stalled, but not before Rich Karlis kicked a 48-yard field goal, the longest in Super Bowl history.

Unfazed, Simms completed his first six passes. The Giants drove 78 yards and scored on a six-yard pass to Mowatt. Simms's wish was coming true. The Giants' coaches were letting him throw. In the first half, they passed on 9 of their 12 first-down opportunities and Simms completed all of the passes. "It surprised us," Den-

In a critical moment early in the game, the Broncos failed to score after having first-and-goal at the New York 1. On third down, linebacker Carl Banks (58) caught Sammy Winder (23) for a four-yard loss.

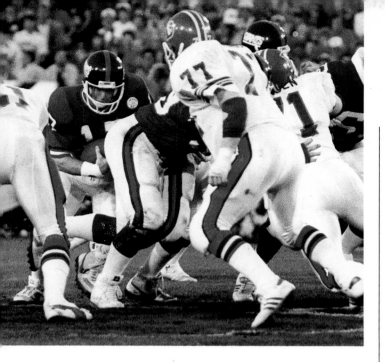

The Giants gambled and won early in the third quarter when backup quarterback Jeff Rutledge (17, left) sneaked two yards on fourth-and-one at his own 46. Five plays later, New York scored the go-ahead touchdown.

ver linebacker Karl Mecklenburg says.

Denver passed, too, of course. The Broncos' leading rusher in the regular season was Sammy Winder, with 789 yards for only a 3.3-yard average. The Broncos had a small offensive line that specialized in pass blocking. It was clear all along that their offense would go only as far as Elway could carry it.

Before long, it was clear that might be far enough. The Broncos came out and drove right back to a 10-7 lead on Elway's four-yard quarterback draw against a defense that was backpedaling into coverage. Then, after a Giants punt, Elway scrambled from Taylor on third-and-12 and completed a 54-yard pass to Vance Johnson that moved the ball to the Giants' 28. Six plays later, the Broncos had first-and-goal at the 1.

This was their chance to prove they could move people off the line, maybe even demoralize the Giants' vaunted defense. The Broncos used three tackles and two

tight ends, matching power with power. "We felt we could run against them," Elway says.

They were wrong. The Giants were a little lucky. They slanted the right direction on all three goal-line plays. But they also were good. There weren't many linebackers who could have caught Elway on his first-down run, headed straight for the right goal-line pylon, but Taylor dropped him at the 2. On second down, inside linebacker Harry Carson, who was bound for his eighth Pro Bowl, met Gerald Willhite in the hole over right guard.

On third-and-two, the Giants still had to guess with Denver, and Banks was remembering the Broncos' only touchdown in the November game, a pitch to Winder around left end. "I expected that play again, and that's what they called," Banks says. It took Winder away from Banks, the left linebacker, but Banks, running across the field, beat him to the corner for a four-yard loss.

"If you're looking for a turning point, that was it," Elway said afterward. "Had we scored there, it really might have turned things around for us."

The Broncos didn't even come away with three points. Karlis, fresh off the longest field goal in Super Bowl history, made his encore the shortest miss. His 23-yard attempt was wide

In a play that helped break the game open, the Giants' Phil McConkey finally was upended at the Denver 1 by cornerback Mark Haynes (36), after catching a 44-yard flea-flicker pass. Joe Morris scored on the next play.

loss, and the Giants didn't argue. "The key was being only one point behind at the half," nose tackle Jim Burt said. Giants players assured each other at halftime they had seen the Broncos' best and stayed within one point of it. They knew their own best would be enough to win. "If he made those two field goals, it could have been Denver sitting here as world champs," Mowatt said.

The Giants surged ahead 33-10 when Phil Simms and Phil McConkey teamed on a deflected six-yard touchdown pass. The ball bounced off Giants tight end Mark Bavaro (89, top) into the hands of the ecstatic McConkey.

right, and the score still was 10-7. But it was starting to look like one of those games when the team that was behind really was the team with the upper hand.

The secret was out on the Broncos' running game. Elway dropped back to pass on their next 24 plays. Denver's backs had gained only 14 yards on 12 carries up to that point and finished with just 52 yards rushing, 27 by Elway. After its early frustrations, the Giants' defense finally had his scent.

The Giants' defense showed its dominance of the other goal line the next time the Broncos had the ball. On third-and-12 from Denver's 13, veteran defensive end George Martin made an inside fake and broke past his blocker toward Elway. Elway saw him, but it didn't help. The inside rush men were chasing him back across the goal line. "I had nowhere to go," Elway said of Martin's safety, 2:46 before halftime. The half ended with Denver ahead 10-9 in a game it should have led 20-7.

Elway led one more first-half drive, but Karlis missed again, this time from 34 yards. After the game, he tearfully blamed himself for the

Probably not, the way Simms was playing. But in the first half, his teammates were suffering the jitters Simms so carefully sidestepped. They were tight, they admitted later. On defense, they did too much thinking. "We were worried about the [Pasadena] heat, about the kind of shoes we were wearing," Taylor says "We were playing finesse defense. In the second half, we just went out and knocked their heads off."

If the Giants left the locker room with any doubt the second half would be theirs, the music playing on the public address system blasted it out of their minds. It was playing "New York, New York" as they took the field to warm up. "I got goose pimples," McConkey says.

With all the big plays Simms made, it's ironic that the one to put the Giants over the hump was a little play by his backup, Jeff Rutledge. The Giants' drive after the second-half kickoff stalled at their own 46, fourth down and two feet. The punting unit replaced the offense.

"That's what it looked like from their sideline," says Oates, the punt snapper. "But instead of the punt team, we ran out a bunch of big backup offensive linemen." And instead of a blocking back, they sent out Rutledge.

The Broncos caught on soon enough. They had kept their regular defense on the field. When Rutledge moved up under center, he had to stay there. "They knew something was up," Parcells says. "But they didn't know what."

Even Oates wasn't sure. "I remember sitting there, and he paused," Oates says. "And I waited, and waited, and waited. I kept looking up at the clock."

One of Rutledge's options was to take a delay-of-game penalty. His other choice was to run a quarterback sneak, but only if he was sure

The Giants won 17 of 19 games, and a postgame "ceremony"—linebacker Harry Carson showered head coach Bill Parcells with Gatorade—followed all the victories. Why should the Super Bowl be an exception?

Denver's Vance Johnson caught a 47-yard touchdown pass from John Elway with 2:06 left, but it failed to lift his spirits. The score was too little, too late, cutting the Giants' final margin to 39-20.

of a first down. The Broncos' problem was they thought he had a third option.

Rutledge lined up the same way in a punt situation in the November game. The Giants made the first down then, too, on "Flow 36," a handoff to the wingback over right tackle. "Their defense kept screaming that we were coming off tackle," Oates says. When the ball was snapped, that's where the defenders went.

"All they had over the middle were a couple of linebackers," Oates says. "We had two guards and a center to block them. We got a big surge." Rutledge gained two yards over Oates's right shoulder.

"That was a big play," Simms says. "It gave us a chance to move down the field and score a touchdown right at the start of the second half, and we played with extreme confidence after that—offensively, of course, but defensively even more so. We really started putting a lot of pressure on their offense, and that's where the game turned. I think they went three straight series without a first down. And we scored after all three of those possessions."

Simms put the Giants ahead 16-10 with 10:08

left in the third quarter, hitting Bavaro for 13 yards on third-and-six. Safety Dennis Smith had Bavaro covered. "I probably shouldn't have thrown it," Simms says, "but I saw this little opening."

The Giants' next two drives made the score 26-10 on Raul Allegre's 21-yard field goal and Morris's one-yard touchdown run. Simms set up the touchdown with a spectacular 44-yard pass to McConkey on a flea-flicker, taking a toss back from Morris. McConkey was sent cartwheeling at the 1 on a great defensive play. "We've run those flea-flickers in practice for I don't know how long, but never in a game," Simms said afterwards. It finished his eight-for-eight third quarter, in which the Giants outgained Denver 163 yards to 2.

Elway battled back. The Broncos scored 10 points in the fourth quarter. "He never gave up," Banks says. "Usually, if you give it to a quarterback, he's worrying about what you're doing. He gets it in his eyes. But he kept his composure and fought all the way."

So did the Giants. "What I liked was we didn't sit on the ball," Oates says. "At times during the season, we had gone conservative when we got ahead, but that day everybody was thinking the same way: Let's carry it through to the end." Simms's third touchdown pass, six yards to McConkey on a deflection off Bavaro, made it 33-10, and Ottis Anderson's two-yard run put the Giants up 39-13 with 3:18 left.

By then, nose tackle Burt had finagled his 5-year-old son, Jim, Jr., onto the sideline, where he would hoist him on his shoulders after the final gun. Carson was about to borrow a security guard's yellow jacket, the disguise he would use for dumping Gatorade on Parcells, just as he did after every Giants victory in the 17-2 season. Back in New York, a conga line was beginning to form on Second Avenue, ready to dance away 30 years of frustration since the Giants' last NFL championship.

Giants fans were quick to remind any and all of the length of their suffering, from Alan Ameche in sudden death in 1958 and Y.A. Tittle on his knees in 1964 to the ticket-burning protest in '78, after the Giants had fumbled away a game against the Eagles trying to run out the clock. Parcells, a Jersey guy himself,

knew the history well. "We buried all the ghosts tonight," he said after the game.

They were put in the ground by the flea-flicker to McConkey. "When we completed the pass and I saw him get tackled, I knew the game was over," Simms says. "I knew we'd get the touchdown, and they weren't going to score three times against our defense."

McConkey symbolized the team that had clawed its way out of a 3-12-1 gutter just three years before. He joined the Giants in 1984, a 27-year-old rookie just out of his five-year commitment to the U.S. Navy. He didn't make the final cut in 1986, but when the Giants realized their mistake, they gave Green Bay a twelfth-round draft choice to get him back four weeks later. And here he was in the Super Bowl, making the play that clinched the game.

"As I caught the ball and turned up, I saw a wide open field," McConkey says. "I thought I was going to get in. I saw the goal line and thought, 'My God, I'm going to get a touchdown in the Super Bowl.'"

Then McConkey saw Denver cornerback Mark Haynes, who went for him low. "I tried to hurdle him, but he got enough of me to send me into a somersault," McConkey says. "When I landed, I knew I was on the one."

He admits now to mixed emotions at the time. "I wanted that score. It was something I had dreamed about since I was a kid. And then, the next time we were down there, I had a gift presented to me."

On a six-yard pass, McConkey saw the ball all the way. He saw the ball go through two defenders in the end zone, and he saw Bavaro go up for it. He saw the ball bounce off Bavaro, back toward the goal line, toward him.

"Things seem so much slower when you're on the field," McConkey says. "Sometimes it's like you're in slow motion. The ball seemed to be just floating down. It reminded me of when I was a kid in Buffalo catching snowflakes in my mouth. I didn't realize until I saw the picture that I caught it just a foot off the ground.

"I had dreamed of scoring a touchdown in a Super Bowl all my life. I've watched it on tape, and sometimes it still seems like a fantasy. I don't know if I'll ever put it in the reality category. Maybe that's the great thing about it."

XXII

Washington 42, Denver 10

P	59	15	07
GATE	SECTION	ROW	SEAT

AFC-NFC World Championship Game
Sunday, January 31, 1988 3:00 P.M.
San Diego Jack Murphy Stadium $100.00

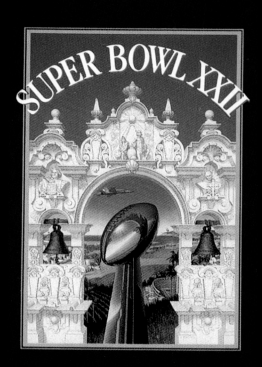

Sunday, January 31, 1988 Gates Open 12 Noon
San Diego Jack Murphy Stadium
$100.00 All Taxes Included

GATE	SECTION	ROW	SEAT
P	59	15	07

Vital Statistics

Starting Lineups

Washington (NFC)	Offense	Denver (AFC)
Gary Clark	WR	Mark Jackson
Joe Jacoby	LT	Dave Studdard
Raleigh McKenzie	LG	Keith Bishop
Jeff Bostic	C	Mike Freeman
R.C. Thielemann	RG	Stefan Humphries
Mark May	RT	Ken Lanier
Clint Didier	TE	Clarence Kay
Don Warren	TE-WR	Ricky Nattiel
Doug Williams	QB	John Elway
Timmy Smith	RB	Sammy Winder
Ricky Sanders	WR-RB	Gene Lang
	Defense	
Charles Mann	LE	Andre Townsend
Dave Butz	LT-NT	Greg Kragen
Darryl Grant	RT-RE	Rulon Jones
Dexter Manley	RE-LOLB	Simon Fletcher
Mel Kaufman	LLB-LILB	Karl Mecklenburg
Neal Olkewicz	MLB-RILB	Ricky Hunley
Monte Coleman	RLB-ROLB	Jim Ryan
Darrell Green	LCB	Mark Haynes
Barry Wilburn	RCB	Steve Wilson
Alvin Walton	SS	Dennis Smith
Todd Bowles	FS	Tony Lilly

Substitutions

Washington-Offense: K-Ali Haji-Sheikh. P-Steve Cox. QB-Jay Schroeder. RB-Reggie Branch, Kelvin Bryant, Keith Griffin, George Rogers. WR-Art Monk, Eric Yarber. TE-Terry Orr, Anthony Jones. G-Rick Kehr. T-Russ Grimm. Defense: E-Markus Koch, Steve Hamilton. T-Dean Hamel. LB-Ravin Caldwell, Kurt Gouveia, Rich Milot. CB-Brian Davis, Clarence Vaughn, Dennis Woodberry. S-Vernon Dean.
Denver-Offense: K-Rich Karlis. P-Mike Horan. QB-Gary Kubiak. RB-Ken Bell, Tony Boddie, Steve Sewell. WR-Vance Johnson, Steve Watson. TE-Bobby Micho, Orson Mobley. T-Keith Kartz. Defense: E-Walt Bowyer, Freddie Gilbert. LB-Mike Brooks, Rick Dennison, Bruce Klostermann, Tim Lucas. CB-Kevin Clark, Bruce Plummer. S-Tyrone Braxton, Jeremiah Castille, Randy Robbins. DNP: C-Larry Lee.

Officials

Referee-Bob McElwee. Umpire-Al Conway. Line Judge-Jack Fette. Head Linesman-Dale Hamer. Back Judge-Al Jury. Field Judge-Johnny Grier. Side Judge-Don Wedge.

Scoring

Washington	0	35	0	7	— 42
Denver	10	0	0	0	— 10

Den-Nattiel 56 pass from Elway (Karlis kick)
Den-FG Karlis 24
Wash-Sanders 80 pass from Williams (Haji-Sheikh kick)
Wash-Clark 27 pass from Williams (Haji-Sheikh kick)
Wash-Smith 58 run (Haji-Sheikh kick)
Wash-Sanders 50 pass from Williams (Haji-Sheikh kick)
Wash-Didier 8 pass from Williams (Haji-Sheikh kick)
Wash-Smith 4 run (Haji-Sheikh kick)
Attendance-73,302

FINAL TEAM STATISTICS

	Redskins	Broncos
TOTAL FIRST DOWNS	25	18
Rushing	13	6
Passing	11	10
Penalty	1	2
TOTAL NET YARDAGE	602	327
Total Offensive Plays	72	61
Average Gain per Offensive Play	8.4	5.4
NET YARDS RUSHING	280	97

Total Rushing Plays	40	17
Average Gain per Rushing Play	7.0	5.7
NET YARDS PASSING	322	230
Pass Att.-Comp.-Int.	30-18-1	39-15-3
Sacks-Yards Lost	2-18	5-50
Gross Yards Passing	340	280
Avg. Gain per Pass (Incl. Sacks)	10.1	5.2
PUNTS-YARDS	4-150	7-253
Average Distance	37.5	36.1
Had Blocked	0	0
TOTAL RETURN YARDAGE	57	106
Kickoff Returns-Yards	3-46	5-88
Punt Returns-Yards	1-0	2-18
Interception Returns-Yards	3-11	1-0
TOTAL TURNOVERS	1	3
Fumbles-Lost	1-0	0-0
Had Intercepted	1	3
PENALTIES-YARDS	6-65	5-26
TOTAL POINTS SCORED	42	10
Touchdowns Rushing	2	0
Touchdowns Passing	4	1
Touchdowns Returns	0	0
Extra Points	6	1
Field Goals-Attempts	0-1	1-2
Safeties	0	0
THIRD DOWN EFFICIENCY	9/15	2/12
FOURTH DOWN EFFICIENCY	0/0	0/0
TIME OF POSSESSION	35:15	24:45

INDIVIDUAL STATISTICS

RUSHING

Washington	No.	Yds.	Avg.	Long	TD
Smith	22	204	9.3	58t	2
Bryant	8	38	4.8	15	0
Rogers	5	17	3.4	5	0
Williams	2	-2	-1.0	-1	0
Clark	1	25	25.0	25	0
Griffin	1	2	2.0	2	0
Sanders	1	-4	-4.0	-4	0

Denver	No.	Yds.	Avg.	Long	TD
Winder	8	30	3.8	13	0
Lang	5	38	7.6	13	0
Elway	3	32	10.7	21	0
Sewell	1	-3	-3.0	-3	0

PASSING

Washington	Att.	Comp.	Yds.	Long	TD	Int.
Williams	29	18	340	80t	4	1
Schroeder	1	0	0	0	0	0

Denver	Att.	Comp.	Yds.	Long	TD	Int.
Elway	38	14	257	56t	1	3
Sewell	1	1	23	23	0	0

RECEIVING

Washington	No.	Yds.	Long	TD
Sanders	9	193	80t	2
Clark	3	55	27t	1
Warren	2	15	9	0
Monk	1	40	40	0
Bryant	1	20	20	0
Smith	1	9	9	0
Didier	1	8	8t	1

Denver	No.	Yds.	Long	TD
Jackson	4	76	32	0
Sewell	4	41	18	0
Nattiel	2	69	56t	1

Kay	2	38	27	0
Winder	1	26	26	0
Elway	1	23	23	0
Lang	1	7	7	0

INTERCEPTIONS

Washington	No.	Yds.	Long	TD
Wilburn	2	11	11	0
Davis	1	0	0	0

Denver	No.	Yds.	Long	TD
Castille	1	0	0	0

PUNTING

Washington	No.	Yds.	Avg.	TB	Long
Cox	4	150	37.5	0	42

Denver	No.	Yds.	Avg.	TB	Long
Horan	7	253	36.1	1	43

PUNT RETURNS

Washington	No.	FC	Yds.	Long	TD
Green	1	1	0	0	0
Yarber	0	1	0	0	0

Denver	No.	FC	Yds.	Long	TD
Clark	2		0	18	9	0

KICKOFF RETURNS

Washington	No.	Yds.	Long	TD
Sanders	3	46	16	0

Denver	No.	Yds.	Long	TD
Bell	5	88	21	0

FUMBLES

Washington	No.	Own Rec.	Opp. Rec.
Sanders	1	0	0
Caldwell	0	1	0

Denver	No.	Own Rec.	Opp. Rec.
None			

KICKING

Washington	XP-A	FG-A	FG Made	FG Missed
Haji-Sheikh	6-6	0-1	-	46

Denver	XP-A	FG-A	FG Made	FG Missed
Karlis	1-1	1-2	24	43

PLAY-BY-PLAY

Washington won the coin toss and elected to receive.
FIRST QUARTER
Karlis kick to W 2, Sanders 16 return (Clark).
Washington (15:00)
W 18 1-10 Smith 4 run right (Ryan).
W 22 2-6 Smith run up middle, no gain (Jones).
W 22 3-6 Williams pass to Clark dropped, incomplete.
W 22 4-6 Cox 34 punt downed at D 44.
Denver (13:11)
D 44 1-10 Elway 56 pass to Nattiel deep right (caught at W 8), touchdown (13:03).
Denver scoring drive: 56 yards, 1 play, :08.
Denver 7, Washington 0
Karlis kick to W 2, Sanders 15 return (Micho).

"It is not the critics who count, not the man who points out how the strong man stumbled or where the doer of deeds could have done them better. The credit belongs to the man who is actually in the arena, whose face is marred by dust and sweat and blood."

—THEODORE ROOSEVELT

His helmet was tilted back on his head. Doug Williams held up the game ball for a moment, his slight concession to triumph. The cameras flashed. Everyone blinked to find perspective for the moment as History's Quarterback stood tall in the pocket of celebrity.

The Washington Redskins had just won Super Bowl XXII, just beaten the Denver Broncos 42-10. Williams had been their quarterback, the first black man ever to start at that position in a Super Bowl. "Redskin, black skin...it all rhymes with win," Williams said and there was pride in his voice.

He limped slightly. The left knee he'd hyperextended in the first quarter was swollen. He slowly led the growing procession of humanity across the field at San Diego Jack Murphy Stadium. Williams walked through the path that parted for him, slowly maneuvering across the big NFL logo painted on the grass at midfield.

Andy Warhol said everyone will be famous for 15 minutes. For Doug Williams, the second quarter of Super Bowl XXII can serve as his quarter-hour of fame. Could Warhol possibly have foreseen such a lightning bolt on the horizon? Could anyone?

Simply by taking the first snap from center, Williams had qualified for pioneer status. But the first black quarterback in a Super Bowl played one of the greatest games of all time.

Williams walked slowly from the field, the ball tucked under his arm, the final score still burning brightly on the scoreboard. Because his knee hurt, each step was increasingly difficult. The three-hour root canal surgery he'd undergone the day before also made talking difficult.

He said he was tired—nervousness had caused him to snap awake at 4 that morning. His nerves were fine now. But still, he was tired.

"When you win, though, everything feels fine," Williams said softly. "This is the best moment I've ever had as a player."

He had been to the mountaintop. But not before spending time in the valley. In the 15 minutes that will define Doug Williams, serve as his statement rather than some sociological flag planted into eternity on his behalf, he threw four touchdown passes. Which shattered more quickly—the stereotypes or the Super Bowl records? In a single quarter, the Redskins turned a 10-0 deficit into a 35-10 bullet train.

Three men led them: the 32-year-old Williams, whose career had seemed at an end not long before; a rookie named Timmy Smith, whose injury problems had threatened to cripple his career before he ever wheeled into motion; and Ricky Sanders, a USFL refugee who slipped into the lineup only because someone else limped out of it. Each set offensive records of some kind. And it took just 15 minutes.

"I just wanted to play and win," Williams says now. "That's all I've been saying all along."

Moral and sociological consequences were for someone else to determine. Williams suddenly may have become the role model for a generation, but that also would be someone else's doing. He had given a gracious answer to the silliest question earlier in the week when he was asked if he had been a black quarterback all his life. When the nervous laughter subsided, Williams had said, "You know, until I got into the NFL, I was always just the quarterback. So I'd have to say I became a black quarterback my rookie year in Tampa."

Williams has to laugh today when he remembers the strange, meandering journey he took before he climbed onto that athletic mountaintop January 31, 1988.

"I've been through some tough times," he says. "The average person might have walked away, been alcoholic, been in a drug center, mouthed off, did something to hurt people. I think I handled my situation better than anyone could have."

Proud talk, tough talk. But most of all, the truth. And as far as being a pioneer, people have tried to pin that label on him ever since he

Because he would be the first black quarterback to start the Super Bowl, Doug Williams was swarmed by members of the media for days before the game. He said he was more interested in trying to beat Denver.

became the first black quarterback ever drafted by the NFL in the first round.

He knew someone inevitably had to be the first one. But that wasn't what he'd been groomed for at Grambling State. He says, "I was just a quarterback. I'd only been a quarterback most of my life. The other stuff was dumped on me from other sources."

But the implications were inevitable. For here was a 6-foot, 4-inch, 215-pound football player too talented to ignore.

Through the first 16 selections of the 1978 NFL draft, Tampa Bay, which had traded the first pick to Houston and watched it become Earl Campbell, squirmed, anxiously waiting out the other teams. Would some other team take the quarterback from the predominantly black Louisiana college?

Commissioner Pete Rozelle announced, "Tampa Bay selects Doug Williams, quarterback, Grambling State," and an invisible fence collapsed all by itself.

The Buccaneers saw the quarterback of their future. Head coach John McKay loved the obvious skills, but he and his offensive coordina-

tor, Joe Gibbs, agreed there also were some intangibles, such as leadership, competitiveness, and poise. Gibbs never forgot them. As Redskins head coach, he welcomed Williams to Washington eight years later, and by the end of the 1987 season, Williams was Washington's starter.

McKay and Gibbs gave Williams the starting job in 1978, too, but it isn't easy being designated savior of a struggling team. Fans booed him unmercifully in his early years. One day after practice, he received a package that contained a watermelon with racial slurs carved into the side. There were other ugly reminders that his progress angered some people.

Although Williams led Tampa Bay to division titles in 1979 and 1981, there were disappointments, too, and he became a villain.

"I heard it all those first couple years," he says. "It's a tough game. Physically, if you don't want contact, better grab your tennis racquet. But things did get a little ridiculous. I gave up my body for that team. Every play, I got hit."

Suddenly, being the first black quarterback to be drafted in the first round didn't mean much. That's the thing with sociological milestones. Once they are reached, they pretty much get wadded up and tossed away.

This was what Williams tried to tell everyone on the eve of Super Bowl XXII. Winning the game was the important thing. He knew society's cancers would not be solved by his simple appearance. He said he would play the game not for black America as much as for the Washington Redskins.

The Broncos were favored to win the game. Many experts thought Williams would be overmatched against John Elway.

It had been a strange season. The players'

strike had caused a terrible rift in pro football. The Redskins had remained together—none crossed the picket lines—and Gibbs and his staff had done a good job collecting replacement players and guiding them through three victories while labor and management bickered. Injuries had taken a terrific toll on the Redskins and the team had sputtered at times, winning seven of its games by a total of 30 points.

But Gibbs liked what he saw before the Super Bowl. His team was active, spirited, extremely exuberant, and aggressive. Maybe the farewell pep talk the team had received before leaving Washington had helped. He would have to remember to write a nice thank-you note to Lt. Col. Oliver North—if the Redskins won.

Gibbs wondered if the Broncos had received any inspirational speeches. He decided Denver's playoff victory over the Cleveland Browns probably accomplished the same thing.

The Broncos, with Elway passing for three touchdowns, had outscored the Browns 38-33 in the AFC Championship Game to earn the trip to San Diego. Denver appeared to be the team with momentum. The Redskins had struggled in the playoffs, and some experts felt the Minnesota Vikings deserved to be the NFC representative more than the Redskins. Oddsmakers agreed, installing the Broncos as four-point favorites for Super Bowl XXII.

Head coach Dan Reeves, however, worried about how his small defense would match up against the Redskins and their huge offensive line, still known as The Hogs. There wasn't much disguise to Washington's attack. The counter-trap, a play in which the Redskins' running back follows the lead of the right guard and tackle pulling around left end, was a staple. Reeves knew that if the Broncos were going to win, they had to stop the counter-trap, or counter-trey, as the Redskins called it.

Former defensive coordinator Joe Collier now says the Broncos overcompensated for the play.

"We overloaded and they kept running away from us all day," Collier says. "They seemed to know what we were doing. Or what we were trying to do. It helped open things up for their passing game."

There never was any question Doug Williams could pass. He had one of the greatest arms ever issued. Whether he still had the legs to support that cannon was another story.

In his second season, Williams led the Tampa Bay Buccaneers to the game before the big game, the 1979 NFC Championship Game. It was close, but the Los Angeles Rams won 9-0.

"I was two-for-thirteen passing," Williams says.

But high completion percentage never has been Williams's thing. He never was sacked a lot, either. He preferred the incompletion to the loss of yardage. But when his initial five-year contract was completed, Williams became involved in a bitter contract dispute with the Buccaneers. The team and the player could not come to an agreement.

However, the infant United States Football League was taking its first steps. Williams now had an option.

Then one day, shortly before Easter, 1983, his world got scrambled irreparably. He and his wife Janice and 10-week-old baby daughter, Ashley, went back to his hometown of Zachary, Louisiana, to take a break from career decisions and other tensions. His wife woke up one day with a crippling headache.

"It was terrible pain she was feeling," Wil-

On Denver's first play, John Elway threw a 56-yard touchdown bomb to Ricky Nattiel, who beat cornerback Barry Wilburn for a fast 7-0 lead. It was the first—and only—touchdown the Broncos would score.

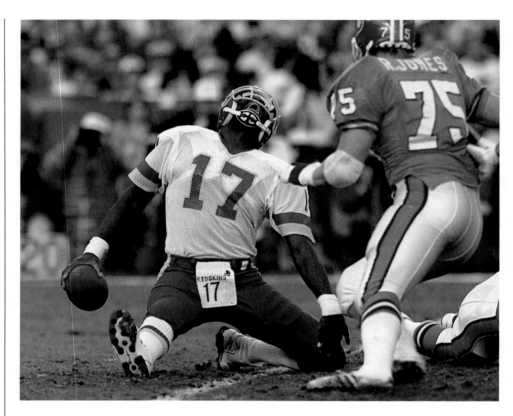

Late in the first quarter, Williams dropped back to pass, slipped, and strained his knee.

of the USFL in 1983, and Tampa Bay went 2-14 without him. Two years later, the USFL went bankrupt. At that point, Williams was over 30, and had gimpy legs and an expensive price tag. Only one NFL team called him: the Redskins. The circle had gone full.

Williams threw only one pass in 1986. He began the 1987 season as Jay Schroeder's backup. If greatness was to come, it was sneaking up and wearing clever disguises.

That's why most of the questions directed at Williams the week before Super Bowl XXII were about the color of his skin. Gibbs announced Williams would be his starter. Because Schroeder had been so inconsistent, the decision was perceived as opting for the lesser of two evils.

After all, the Broncos had John Elway.

It was Tuesday, photo day of the Super Week. Elway was swarmed. Williams was swarmed. The tendency is to seek out the biggest names, the most famous faces.

Timmy Smith looked for someone to talk to. Nobody wants to talk to the reserves during Super Bowl week. The rookie fifth-round running back from Texas Tech didn't seem like much of a story. If someone wanted to do a story on a Redskins running back, then George Rogers or Kelvin Bryant were more logical choices. Timmy Smith was just a guy who gained a total of 126 yards in the regular season.

"I spent most of the week just staring at people," Smith says today. "I was proud just to be

liams says. "Unbearable, really. Doctors took X-rays and found a tumor big as a grapefruit. But it was benign. They operated and things were going fine, we thought. Then one morning, she just died."

Married 11 months and 20 days, a father for 12 weeks...now, suddenly, a widower. Thinking back to those sorrowful times, Williams says, "I was really torn up and I didn't give a damn about football for quite a while."

He unscrambled his feelings later. Time can do that. All the black pioneer stuff, all the contract negotiations that got uglier and uglier. All the adversity, all the glory. Williams had learned how to cope with it.

"I think about James Harris, the quarterback I replaced at Grambling," he says. "Or Joe Gilliam and other people. They should have been the first. They were the real pioneers. Adversity is everywhere. I wasn't the first man to lose a wife to death. I wasn't the first to feel cheated by my employer. You just go on. People always have looked at me and waited for me to fall on my face. I couldn't feel sorry for myself."

Williams bolted for the Oklahoma Outlaws

Trailing 10-0 in the second quarter, the Redskins began their 35-point blitz with Williams's 80-yard touchdown pass to Ricky Sanders. Sanders, who had nine catches, scored on a 50-yard pass 10 minutes later.

there, really. I couldn't blame media people for ignoring me. I hadn't done anything yet."

Gibbs liked the rookie runner, particularly his slashing speed. He had run well in playoff victories over Chicago and Minnesota. Gibbs toyed with an idea.

"We didn't decide until the night before, but I thought about starting Timmy Smith all week," Gibbs says.

Joe Bugel was the Redskins' assistant head coach for offense. He and Gibbs agreed Smith didn't need to know he was about to start in the Super Bowl until the last moment.

"We didn't want to throw a lot of pressure on him," Bugel says. "We told him in the locker room right before we hit the field."

Ricky Sanders knew he was starting. He knew that regular starter Art Monk still was recovering from an injury. Monk would play in the game (and catch a pass for 40 yards) but the bulk of the Redskins' pass-catching duties would fall upon the slender shoulders of a couple of USFL products, Sanders and Gary Clark.

"I knew we'd get lots of action our way," Sanders says. "We practiced all week on lots of different patterns. We knew Elway could put us in a big hole fast. We had to be ready to come back just as fast."

The Broncos' concerns about the Redskins' running attack were compounded by the fact that Denver's defensive secondary was hurting. All of the starters were classified as "walking wounded" by Reeves.

"Looking back," Reeves says, "maybe you could see what was likely to happen. But we sure didn't have any idea what was coming at the time."

As game day approached, Richie Petitbon, the Redskins' assistant head coach for defense,

About four minutes after Sanders's first score, Williams got great protection from his line and lofted a 27-yard touchdown pass to Gary Clark. This score put Washington ahead for the first time, 14-10.

says he could feel a quiet confidence among the Redskins. With Williams at quarterback, they seemed to be a different team. The coaches' biggest concern was that they not put too much of a load on Williams's shoulders.

"We couldn't make him feel like he had to do it all," Petitbon says. "That meant it couldn't come down to a matter of him having to outdo Elway. We had to give him some help defensively."

The Redskins would do very little stunting and not as much blitzing as usual. Petitbon wanted the Washington defensive linemen to rush straight, keep in very strict lanes "so Elway won't be able to scramble like he can."

Free safety Todd Bowles would man the middle, waiting for the Denver quarterback.

In the locker room two hours before the game, Timmy Smith still had no idea he was starting. He told George Rogers he sensed the

The Redskins scored touchdowns on five successive series in the second quarter. Rookie Timmy Smith stretched the lead to 21-10 when he eluded a diving Tony Lilly and ran 58 yards for the first of his two touchdowns.

big fullback was going to run for "about 179 yards." Rogers, who had a recurring groin-pull problem, smiled and said only, "That'd be nice. But the way my groin is, I'm gonna have to do it on about three carries. It doesn't feel real good right now."

Williams was calm. He was wondering how his college coach, the great Eddie Robinson, liked the seats Williams had gotten for him. Williams started thinking about the game.

"Then somebody asked me if I knew it was Jackie Robinson's birthday," Williams says. "I said, 'You're kidding. Oh man, that's just what I needed—another reminder.' "

Elway, meanwhile, was thinking about redemption. The Broncos had been bounced badly the year before in Super Bowl XXI. The New York Giants had won 39-20. Elway had played well, but the Broncos had lost.

"I was thinking, we know how to get here, now let's find a way to win," Elway says.

"Like every other game, I figured if we could score early, we'd be in command."

Redskins defensive end Charles Mann didn't like what he saw in his teammates' faces. He no-ticed the excess squirming while Herb Alpert played the National Anthem.

"Let's calm down; we're tight," he said. "Too ready. Cool it and let's play Redskins football."

The Redskins won the coin toss. Sanders returned the kickoff 16 yards to the Redskins' 18-yard line.

Doug Williams trotted onto the field. Timmy Smith ran by him. The first two plays were runs by Smith, and the Broncos were ready for the play if not the runner. On third down, Williams's pass to Clark was dropped.

After the punt, Denver set up on its own 44-yard line. Elway knew Washington's tendency on first down was to play a lot of man-to-man coverage, to try to bump the wide receivers at the line of scrimmage.

"Ricky Nattiel was isolated on [Washington

The scoring parade continued when Williams and Sanders teamed again, this time on a 50-yard touchdown play. Sanders, who started for the injured Art Monk, set a Super Bowl record with 193 yards receiving.

cornerback Barry] Wilburn," Elway remembers. "I tried not to even look at Nattiel. I knew we had a touchdown unless we really goofed."

Elway's pass to Nattiel was the fastest touchdown in Super Bowl history, 56 yards long and just 1:57 into the game.

On the sideline, Gibbs turned to Petitbon, who offered no excuses.

Washington still suffered from soaring emotion. Another pass was dropped and another punt set up the Broncos' offense again. ˈ

Once more they marched downfield. A 32-yard pass to Mark Jackson and a 23-yard halfback pass from Steve Sewell to Elway—the first time ever a quarterback caught a pass in the Super Bowl—had everyone in the stadium fearing a rout was underway.

"Then I think came one of the three biggest plays in that game," Mann says.

On third-and-three from the Redskins' 6, Elway tried a quarterback draw. Petitbon's pregame strategy paid a huge dividend, and Dave Butz nailed Elway for a one-yard loss.

"If John had gotten the first down and we could have gone on and scored the touchdown," Reeves says, "maybe things would have been different. A 14-0 lead that early in a game sometimes can make a team get desperate."

Instead, the Broncos had to settle for a field goal. Still, being 10 points ahead with almost six minutes left to play in the first quarter has its own degree of comfort.

"Then came big play number two," says Mann.

Sanders stood at the goal line, waiting for the kickoff. We need a big one, he thought to himself. Make something happen.

"Something almost did," Sanders said later. "Something terrible."

At the 15-yard line, Broncos reserve linebacker Bruce Klostermann lunged for Sanders, went under him, and the ball came free when Sanders was hit by Ken Bell at the 16.

"It was probably the biggest pileup in Super Bowl history," says Al Michaels, one of the ABC broadcasters covering the game.

Bell swears to this day he recovered the ball for Denver. Ravin Caldwell and Terry Orr, two Washington reserves, wrestled it away, he claims. At any rate, the turnover was avoided.

"I don't know if we could have overcome 17-0," Gibbs says. "It was a crucial recovery for us."

Gibbs was relieved with the recovery, but he was just as concerned about his team's inability to move the ball. Did he ever consider lifting Williams and going with Schroeder?

"No, my concern was with the dropped passes," Gibbs says. "My real concern was on defense, with Elway so hot. I was afraid he'd keep putting points up on us."

The turf also was causing problems. Several Redskins complained of slipping. Then, in the final minutes of the first quarter, Williams dropped back to pass and his knee caved in.

Schroeder came in for Washington. He got sacked and threw an incompletion...and things looked bleak for the Redskins.

"The knee hurt," Williams says, "but I was familiar with pain. I reminded Joe of our days in Tampa."

An elated Williams celebrated the victory and his big day with Sanders (83) and Gary Clark (84).

"As soon as we got the ball back," Gibbs says, "Doug was going back in."

More than 14 minutes remained until half-time, and Williams and Bugel agreed there was no reason to panic.

"How about Charlie Hitch?" Bugel asked. Williams nodded. It was a conservative call, a seven-yard pass to Sanders.

Sanders lined up and noticed cornerback Mark Haynes moving directly in front of him. Here comes a bump, Sanders correctly figured. It was time to adjust the route and go deep.

They used to say Williams had no touch on his passes, that he could make it sizzle but never simmer. He always hated the accusation. His pass to Sanders, who was behind everyone when the ball arrived about midfield, is the perfect disclaimer. Perfectly delivered. "It hung there for me so pretty, just waiting to be plucked out of the sky," Sanders said later.

The broadcasters in the booth sighed relief. Too many Super Bowls had been one-sided runaways.

"We thought we finally had one that was going to be close," Michaels says.

Gibbs says the 80-yard touchdown was the single most important play.

"You could see us come alive on the sideline," he says. "It was like a fire starting."

"We took a lot of pride in our defense that year," Denver linebacker Karl Mecklenburg says. "We were aggressive, closing to the ball quickly, gang tackling. We were really proud of our defense...and then the second quarter started and everyone got a little dizzy."

Five consecutive possessions by the Redskins produced five touchdowns and 35 points.

"It was the greatest quarter of football I've ever been around," Gibbs says. (He is right—no pro football team ever had scored 35 points in one quarter in the playoffs.)

"We never let down when we fell behind," Williams says. "That was how we were all year. Then we all got hot at the same time."

Clark ran a simple out pattern, got the same man-to-man coverage, and caught a 27-yard touchdown pass.

"Doug was hitting everything," Clark says. "That helped open Timmy up."

Smith followed a crunching block by Raleigh McKenzie, and sped 58 yards to a touchdown.

Sanders took another perfectly thrown pass

for a 50-yard touchdown. Then, 1:04 before halftime, Williams connected again, this time with tight end Clint Didier on an eight-yard touchdown.

Five series, five touchdowns, 357 yards of offense—all in 5:47 of possession time. Smith ran for 122 yards in the quarter, four short of his regular-season total. Williams passed for 228 yards in the quarter, 168 of them going to Sanders.

"I was blessed," Williams says. "I truly feel I was blessed that day."

"It's still an honor to have been associated with that game," Gibbs says.

There was little more to do or say. It took longer to move 88 grand pianos on and off the field at halftime than it did to decide the winner of the game. The second half was of little consequence. Denver had 10 points and 142 yards before the game was 10 minutes old. It scored no more points and accumulated just 185 additional yards the rest of the game.

The day before, Williams and Eddie Robinson talked about Teddy Roosevelt's famous maxim about the doer of deeds. "Just be the best quarterback you can and be so good that nobody can ignore you," Robinson said.

"That's the way I teach," says Robinson, college football's all-time winningest football coach. "I tell 'em to let their play be their statement. Doug was going to show up and he was going to play quarterback and oh how that thrilled me right there. A Grambling player at quarterback in the Super Bowl. I still get smiles when I think of it."

After it was over, Williams spotted his old coach on the field. They smiled and hugged.

The reluctant black hope was on top of the world. Smith ran for 204 yards and Sanders had 193 receiving yards. Williams had passed for 340 yards.

"I know there were a lot of TV sets turned on today," Williams said. "I realize I am a role model whether I like it or not. But I do like it and I feel very proud and very blessed. But the important thing was playing well and winning."

When someone asked Williams if it was the greatest game a quarterback ever had played, he said, "Now you know me better. I don't get into judgment. Somebody else has to do that. I just play quarterback."

XXIII

49ers 20, Bengals 16

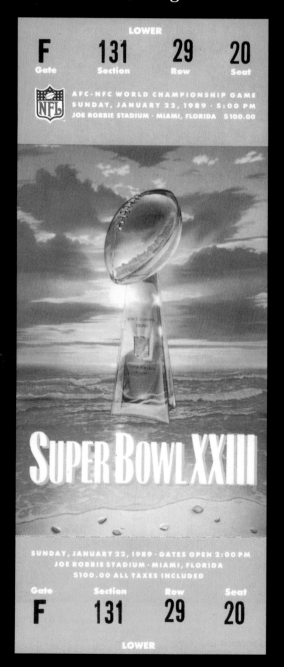

Vital Statistics

Starting Lineups

Cincinnati (AFC)	Offense	San Francisco (NFC)
Tim McGee	WR	John Taylor
Anthony Muñoz	LT	Steve Wallace
Bruce Reimers	LG	Jesse Sapolu
Bruce Kozerski	C	Randy Cross
Max Montoya	RG	Guy McIntyre
Brian Blados	RT	Harris Barton
Rodney Holman	TE	John Frank
Eddie Brown	WR	Jerry Rice
Boomer Esiason	QB	Joe Montana
James Brooks	RB	Roger Craig
Ickey Woods	RB	Tom Rathman
	Defense	
Jim Skow	LE	Larry Roberts
Tim Krumrie	NT	Michael Carter
Jason Buck	RE	Kevin Fagan
Leon White	LOLB	Charles Haley
Carl Zander	LILB	Jim Fahnhorst
Joe Kelly	RILB	Michael Walter
Reggie Williams	ROLB	Keena Turner
Lewis Billups	LCB	Tim McKyer
Eric Thomas	RCB	Don Griffin
David Fulcher	SS	Jeff Fuller
Solomon Wilcots	FS	Ronnie Lott

Substitutions

Cincinnati—Offense: K-Jim Breech. P-Lee Johnson. QB-Turk Schonert. RB-Stanford Jennings, Marc Logan. WR-Cris Collinsworth, Ira Hillary, Carl Parker. TE-Jim Riggs. G-Jim Rourke. T-Dave Smith. Defense: E-Eddie Edwards, Skip McClendon. T-David Grant. LB-Leo Barker, Ed Brady, Emanuel King. CB-Rickey Dixon, Ray Horton, Daryl Smith. S-Barney Bussey. DNP: QB-Mike Norseth.
San Francisco—Offense: K-Mike Cofer. P-Barry Helton. RB-Del Rodgers, Harry Sydney. WR-Terry Greer, Mike Wilson. TE-Ron Heller, Brent Jones. C-Chuck Thomas. G-Bruce Collie. T-Bubba Paris. Defense: E-Pierce Holt, Pete Kugler, Jeff Stover, Danny Stubbs. LB-Riki Ellison, Sam Kennedy, Bill Romanowski. CB-Darryl Pollard, Eric Wright. S-Greg Cox, Tom Holmoe. DNP: QB-Steve Young.

Officials

Referee-Jerry Seeman. Umpire-Gordon Wells. Line Judge-Bob Beeks. Head Linesman-Jerry Bergman. Back Judge-Paul Baetz. Field Judge-Bobby Skelton. Side Judge-Gary Lane.

Scoring

Cincinnati	0	3	10	3	— 16
San Francisco	3	0	3	14	— 20

SF-FG Cofer 41
Cin-FG Breech 34
Cin-FG Breech 43
SF-FG Cofer 32
Cin-Jennings 93 kickoff return (Breech kick)
SF-Rice 14 pass from Montana (Cofer kick)
Cin-FG Breech 40
SF-Taylor 10 pass from Montana (Cofer kick)
Attendance-75,129

FINAL TEAM STATISTICS

	Bengals	49ers
TOTAL FIRST DOWNS	13	23
Rushing	7	6
Passing	6	16
Penalty	0	1
TOTAL NET YARDAGE	229	453
Total Offensive Plays	58	67
Average Gain per Offensive Play	3.9	6.8
NET YARDS RUSHING	106	112
Total Rushing Plays	28	27
Average Gain per Rushing Play	3.8	4.1
NET YARDS PASSING	123	341
Pass Att.-Comp.-Int.	25-11-1	36-23-0
Sacks-Yards Lost	5-21	4-16
Gross Yards Passing	144	357
Avg. Gain per Pass (Incl. Sacks)	4.1	8.5
PUNTS-YARDS	5-221	4-148
Average Distance	44.2	37.0
Had Blocked	0	0
TOTAL RETURN YARDAGE	137	133
Kickoff Returns-Yards	3-132	5-77
Punt Returns-Yards	2-5	3-56
Interception Returns-Yards	0-0	1-0
TOTAL TURNOVERS	1	1
Had Intercepted	1	0
Fumbles-Lost	1-0	4-1
PENALTIES-YARDS	7-65	4-32
TOTAL POINTS SCORED	16	20
Touchdowns Rushing	0	0
Touchdowns Passing	0	2
Touchdowns Returns	1	0
Extra Points	1	2
Field Goals-Attempts	3-3	2-4
Safeties	0	0
THIRD DOWN EFFICIENCY	4/13	4/13
FOURTH DOWN EFFICIENCY	0/1	0/0
TIME OF POSSESSION	32:43	27:17

INDIVIDUAL STATISTICS

RUSHING

Cincinnati	No.	Yds.	Avg.	Long	TD
Woods	20	79	4.0	10	0
Brooks	6	24	4.0	11	0
Jennings	1	3	3.0	3	0
Esiason	1	0	0.0	0	0

San Francisco	No.	Yds.	Avg.	Long	TD
Craig	17	71	4.2	13	0
Rathman	5	23	4.6	11	0
Montana	4	13	3.3	11	0
Rice	1	5	5.0	5	0

PASSING

Cincinnati	Att.	Comp.	Yds.	Long	TD	Int.
Esiason	25	11	144	23	0	1

San Francisco	Att.	Comp.	Yds.	Long	TD	Int.
Montana	36	23	357	44	2	0

RECEIVING

Cincinnati	No.	Yds.	Long	TD
Brown	4	44	17	0
Collinsworth	3	40	23	0
McGee	2	23	18	0
Brooks	1	20	20	0
Hillary	1	17	17	0

San Francisco	No.	Yds.	Long	TD
Rice	11	215	44	1
Craig	8	101	40	0
Frank	2	15	8	0
Rathman	1	16	16	0
Taylor	1	10	10t	1

INTERCEPTIONS

Cincinnati	No.	Yds.	Long	TD
None				

San Francisco	No.	Yds.	Long	TD
Romanowski	1	0	0	0

PUNTING

Cincinnati	No.	Yds.	Avg.	TB	Long
Johnson	5	221	44.2	0	63

San Francisco	No.	Yds.	Avg.	TB	Long
Helton	4	148	37.0	0	55

PUNT RETURNS

Cincinnati	No.	FC	Yds.	Long	TD
Horton	1	0	5	5	0
Hillary	1	0	0	0	0

San Francisco	No.	FC	Yds.	Long	TD
Taylor	3	1	56	45	0

KICKOFF RETURNS

Cincinnati	No.	Yds.	Long	TD
Jennings	2	117	93t	1
Brooks	1	15	15	0

San Francisco	No.	Yds.	Long	TD
Rodgers	3	53	22	0
Taylor	1	13	13	0
Sydney	1	11	11	0

FUMBLES

Cincinnati	No.	Own Rec.	Opp. Rec.
Horton	0	1	0
Skow	0	0	1
Hillary	1	0	0

San Francisco	No.	Own Rec.	Opp. Rec.
Montana	2	1	0
Sydney	0	0	1
Pollard	0	1	0
Craig	1	0	0
Taylor	1	0	0

KICKING

Cincinnati	XP-A	FG-A	FG Made	FG Missed
Breech	1-1	3-3	34,43,40	-

San Francisco	XP-A	FG-A	FG Made	FG Missed
Cofer	2-2	2-4	41,32	19,49

Everyone who played in it—and most of those who watched—agreed that the twenty-third Super Bowl was one for the ages. It was the game the name was created for...the most evenly contested...with few errors (one turnover by each team)...the one with the most electrifying finish.

San Francisco needed a 92-yard drive in the closing minutes, the sorcery of Joe Montana, and a Jerry Rice highlights film to shake off underdog Cincinnati 20-16. In defeat, the Bengals earned more admiration than some Super Bowl teams have garnered in victory.

A crowd of 75,129 filled the National Football League's newest venue, Miami's Joe Robbie Stadium. Robbie, the owner of the Dolphins, had taken a $115 million mortgage on his football team to build it, the only privately funded stadium in the league.

This was the setting for a game that promised maximum fireworks. Not coincidentally, the teams were similar in many ways, featuring creative offenses and cover boy quarterbacks, Joe Montana and Boomer Esiason. The 49ers were seeking a third Super Bowl victory in this decade. The Bengals, who lost 11 games the year before, were trying to make the leap from the outhouse to the penthouse.

Then there was the intriguing sub-plot of the opposing head coaches, Bill Walsh and Sam Wyche, and their almost father-and-son attachment.

Walsh had coached the receivers under Paul Brown in Cincinnati in the late 1960s, when Wyche was their backup quarterback. "I developed Sam," Walsh says, "right to the upper reaches of mediocrity."

Wyche had an undistinguished and well traveled career, but Walsh liked what he saw—"Sam was bright, very expressive, had a great way with people." They stayed in touch after Wyche settled in South Carolina to run a chain of sporting goods stores of which he was co-owner. Walsh tried to hire him after he had become head coach at Stanford, but Wyche declined the offer.

The timing finally was right in 1979. Wyche had been turned down for a high school job, and still was brooding about it when Walsh called again. Walsh now was the head coach with the 49ers, and this time Wyche came running.

His first day on the field as a rookie pro coach in 1979 was Joe Montana's first day as a rookie quarterback. Wyche had his headset on in the coaches' booth in January, 1982, when they beat the Bengals in Super Bowl XVI.

By 1983, Wyche was the new head coach at Indiana. The Hoosiers went 3-8 in his only season, a record that must have impressed the Cincinnati brass, because the next thing you knew Wyche was coaching the Bengals.

In 1987, his job with Cincinnati was in jeopardy down to the final week of a nightmarish season. Everything had gone sour starting with week 2, when the Bengals found a hideous way to lose to—yes, you guessed it—the 49ers.

Cincinnati led 26-20 with six seconds remaining and the ball at its own 30-yard line, facing fourth-and-25. Rather than risk a blocked punt, Wyche ordered an end sweep to run out the clock. But running back James Brooks was stuffed for a five-yard loss, and the ball changed possession with two seconds left. Whereupon Montana threw to Jerry Rice in the end zone for a touchdown. With no time on the clock, the 49ers kicked the extra point for a 27-26 victory. The rest of the season contained similar stories and the Bengals finished 4-11.

A year later, the Bengals were the wonder team of the NFL. They went 12-4 and reached Super Bowl XXIII, where they could fulfill a fairy tale with a twist: Cinderella's younger, dumber brother. Ridiculed and almost fired, Wyche kept his sense of humor. He was back, he said, "on a seven-day renewable contract."

Early in the week before the game, Bill Walsh read the quotes of the Cincinnati veterans, who vowed to get even for the Super Bowl loss in '82. "All they have to do," he said, "is get a pie and hit Sam in the face, because he had as much to do with that win as anyone on the 49ers."

As he approached this encounter with his old friend and mentor, Wyche had what seemed to be two advantages. He knew Montana's tendencies as well as any rival coach could, and he knew how Bill Walsh drew up a game plan. "You can have a generic playbook," he said, "and adjust as you go along. Or you can attack a weakness in the de-

As the sun dimmed, the curtain was raised for a showdown in Miami's Joe Robbie Stadium.

basic 3-4 defensive set most of the game. At times, they even would bring in their safeties, Ronnie Lott and Jeff Fuller, to crowd the line, gambling that the pressure would keep Esiason from going deep to his fleet receivers, Eddie Brown and Tim McGee.

There was uncertainty, however, if not panic, in the 49ers' camp as Rice twisted an ankle during a Monday workout. He didn't practice for three days and limped noticeably all week. With 2,000 members of the media all but cannibalizing each other, Rice's status became a source of daily speculation.

By the time Cincinnati kicked off on Sunday, the miracle of healing had taken place and Rice was at full speed, as the Bengals had predicted he would be.

Still, there would be no shortage of pain or sudden reversals. After 14 plays, the Bengals led the 49ers two broken bones to one. It was the most brutal start in the history of the series, but no indicator of the stressful finish to come.

On the third play of the day, San Francisco's Steve Wallace went down with a fracture just

fense. That is Bill's way and I learned it from him."

The Bengals hoped to confuse the 49ers with their no-huddle, racehorse offense. The coaches thought they could run inside, control the ball, keep Montana off the field, turn loose rookie running sensation Ickey Woods, and soften them up for Boomer to land a few of his left-handed haymakers.

While the media generally pictured the game as a shootout, Walsh expected a low score, with the defensive units controlling the tempo, and the outcome turning on one or two mistakes. The 49ers didn't think the Bengals could cover Rice man for man. Few teams even tried. If they doubled him, Montana would go to Roger Craig, the best receiver among NFC running backs, and the unsung John Taylor, a second-year wide receiver out of Delaware State.

After long nights of studying the Cincinnati game films, Walsh made a key decision. The 49ers would react to the Bengals' no-huddle offense by not reacting. That is, they would stick with their

Super Bowl XXIII matched the wits of Bill Walsh (right, coaching, as it turned out, his last game) and his protégé Sam Wyche, who directed the 49ers' passing game under Walsh from 1979 to 1982.

above the left ankle. Then the Bengals lost their best tackler, nose tackle Tim Krumrie, whose left leg was broken in two places. Bent like the limb of a rag doll, the leg was put in an inflatable cast before they carried him off on a gurney. Krumrie watched the rest of the first half on television in the locker room, before the doctors insisted on taking him to a Miami hospital.

For the first time in the history of the Super Bowl, the teams were tied at halftime, and by the less-than-impressive score of 3-3. It was appropriate that the huge television crowd watched the halftime show through plastic three-dimensional glasses, or two dimensions more than either offense had demonstrated to that point. The defenses were dominating, with Esiason—4 of 12 passes for 48 yards—and Montana both groping for a rhythm.

The 49ers had only a 41-yard field goal by Mike Cofer to show for two long drives. They came up empty after Walsh suffered a lapse of nerve on fourth-and-one at the Bengals' 2-yard line. He decided to play safe and went for three points, and got none, when Randy Cross snapped the ball low, and Cofer missed to the left. Jim Breech's 34-yard field goal, his first of three, tied the score for the Bengals with a little more than a minute left in the second quarter.

In the 49ers' locker room at halftime, a confrontation took place between players that went unreported. One player blurted out, in a tone of pained surprise, "Geez, we've got a real game on our hands."

Roger Craig responded by screaming at him: "I don't want to hear that (bleep). We knew that when we got here. Now we all have to bust our asses."

Meanwhile, Walsh made an adjustment that late in the game would loom large. "The strong safety [Da-

vid Fulcher] was really giving us problems," Walsh said. "We used our tight end to his side of the field and then worked the weakside more. We picked up the blitz better in the second half."

In the first half, Fulcher forced a fumble, sacked Montana on a safety blitz, and made five tackles in the secondary. For the Bengals, this was one of those good news/bad news statistics. The player you least want to lead your defense in tackles is someone from the deep secondary.

To win, the Bengals believed they still needed to establish a running game. Woods carried twice to get a first down to open the third quarter, and an offsides penalty against the 49ers netted five more yards. Suddenly, Esiason found his groove. He completed passes to Cris Collinsworth for 23 yards, to Brooks for 20, to Collinsworth for 11.

They moved inside the San Francisco 20, but a procedure penalty cost them, and Breech kicked a 43-yard field goal for a 6-3 lead. Still, they kept the ball for 12 plays and 9 minutes, 15 seconds. "That," said Esiason, "was the way we wanted to run the offense. Unfortunately, we were only able to do it once or twice."

In the second quarter, San Francisco's John Taylor chased down Lee Johnson's Super Bowl-record 63-yard punt and set a Super Bowl mark of his own as he returned the kick 45 yards into Bengals territory.

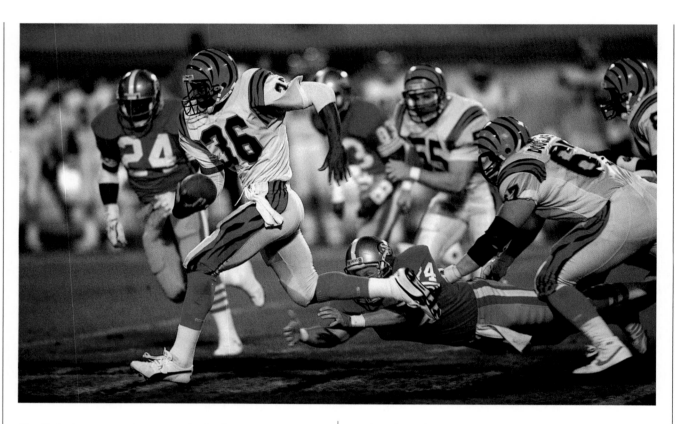

Until the heart-stopping action in the final three minutes, the game's most exciting moment was Stanford Jennings's 93-yard kickoff-return touchdown. Jennings's burst gave Cincinnati a 13-6 lead.

The Bengals would not get a touchdown all day from the most distinctive attack in the NFL. Their no-huddle, quick-snap, hurry-up offense never really kicked in. Nor were they able to unleash Woods and his joyful Ickey Shuffle, the sideline dance Collinsworth described as "so awful it's perfect."

Yet Cincinnati led 6-3, 13-6, and 16-13. Jim Breech, who kicked three field goals, very nearly was the first Super Bowl most valuable player to measure 5 feet, 6 inches and wear a size 5 shoe. And so it went, a tense day in which sad deeds begat glorious ones.

Esiason, who was suffering from a sore left shoulder that plagued him throughout the playoffs, didn't torch the 49ers, but he hadn't made any mistakes, either, until the final two minutes of the third period. A pass intended for McGee was intercepted at the Bengals' 23 by Bill Romanowski, a rookie linebacker off the bench.

On fourth-and-two, the 49ers settled for a 32-yard field goal by Mike Cofer and a 6-6 tie.

Cofer kicked off, and Stanford Jennings returned it 93 yards for the game's first touchdown. This was shock therapy for both teams. Jennings broke it up the middle and suddenly was in the open, overcoming Terry Greer's desperate tackle at the goal line.

As he caught his breath on the bench, Jennings looked into the TV camera and said hello to his wife Kathy and his one-day old daughter Kelsey in Cincinnati.

A backup at four positions, Jennings was seeing added duty in place of the troubled Stanley Wilson, who was suspended on the morning of the game. A terse announcement alluded to an incident at the team's hotel, followed by a failed drug test.

The Bengals led 13-6 going into the final 15 minutes of play, and there were stirrings in the crowd. Fairy tales do come true, some of them... but for the undeniable grace of Joe Montana and Jerry Rice.

On the first of two long fourth-quarter drives, Montana went to the whip, and the 49ers covered

85 yards in 91 seconds to tie the game.

Rice, who seems to have one more gear than most receivers, would not be contained. When the Bengals tried to cover him one-on-one with cornerback Lewis Billups, Montana found him for a 31-yard completion. Then it was Roger Craig in a mismatch with linebacker Joe Kelly for 40, and after Billups dropped a sure interception, back to Rice for 14 yards and the tying touchdown.

This one tested your imagination. On a fade pattern, Rice made the catch at the 5 and stuck the nose of the ball around the flag—and over the plane of the goal line—even as his momentum carried him out of bounds. "I've never made a catch like that one," he said later. "I never dove into the end zone like that before." It is fair to say, nobody else has done so either.

For most of the fourth quarter, the teams reverted to the dance of the dueling legs. Cofer missed a 49-yard field-goal try that would have given San Francisco a lead with less than nine minutes left.

Then the Bengals, with Esiason mixing inside runs and sideline passes, controlled the ball for 10 plays and more than five minutes. Again a false start hurt, and again they grew conservative in field-goal range. They attempted one pass, Boomer overthrowing Brooks at the goal line from the 25.

On fourth down, Breech nailed a 40-yard field goal, and Cincinnati led 16-13.

On his way to the MVP trophy, Jerry Rice caught a pass on a crossing pattern from the Bengals' 14-yard line, outraced the coverage, and dived into the corner of the end zone to produce a 13-13 tie.

The clock showed 3:20 remaining in the game. Night had fallen on a game that had seen the opening kickoff at tea time, under a dazzling Florida sun.

Jim Breech, the smallest player on the field, gave Cincinnati a 16-13 lead with 3:20 left in the game.

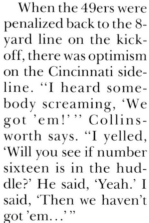

When the 49ers were penalized back to the 8-yard line on the kickoff, there was optimism on the Cincinnati sideline. "I heard somebody screaming, 'We got 'em!'" Collinsworth says. "I yelled, 'Will you see if number sixteen is in the huddle?' He said, 'Yeah.' I said, 'Then we haven't got 'em...'"

The record and story books, of course, are loaded with long and legendary drives— Johnny Unitas against the Giants in the 1958 championship game;

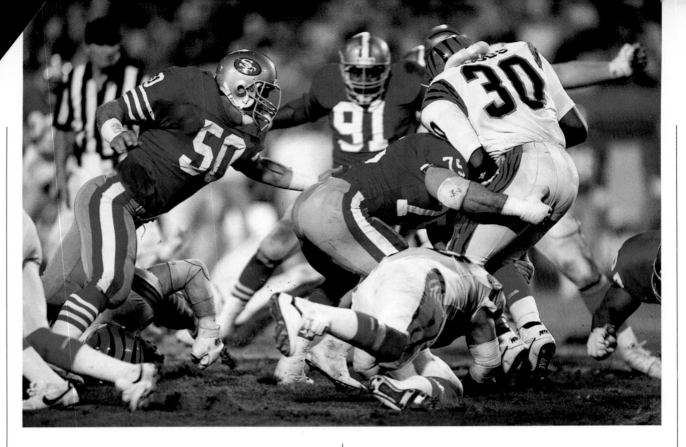

John Elway and the Broncos going coast to coast (98 yards) to tie (and later beat) Cleveland in the AFC playoffs in 1986; and Montana himself, carrying the 49ers to their first Super Bowl in 1981, with a leaping catch by Dwight Clark in the corner of the end zone climaxing an 89-yard advance through Dallas, and signaling the decline of the Cowboys.

But, as late, great, game-winning drives go, this one was the Mona Lisa—because this one happened in the Super Bowl, the largest aquarium in sports.

On San Francisco's side of the stadium, *deja vu* was breaking out all over. Cornerback Don Griffin hugged safety Ronnie Lott. "You gotta believe," he shouted over the noise of the crowd, "we're going to win this one."

"It was eerie," Lott says. "The same thing happened in 1981 against Dallas. [Defensive tackle] Archie Reese came up to me and said the same thing, same words."

In the huddle, Joe Montana also remembered the comeback against Dallas. "Here we go again," he thought to himself.

He started the drive with three safe, short passes to three different receivers for eight, seven, and seven yards. "I was a little cautious down there," Montana says.

Until that drive, the Bengals had stopped the 49ers on 9 of 12 third downs. Now every play, in effect, was third-and-long. "In that situation," says Dick LeBeau, the Cincinnati defensive coordinator, "down and distance don't mean much, so we stayed with the same coverages we used on third down the entire game. We didn't want to be conservative, but we didn't want to sell the farm with a maximum blitz, either."

Says Walsh: "They were dropping the middle linebacker deep to cover the tight end. That let Roger Craig run the curl pattern underneath. But the key was Rice. We just didn't think they could cover him man for man."

The 49ers ran the ball only twice, Craig getting just one yard the first time, then four yards and a first down at the San Francisco 35.

The Bengals lost another starter, defensive end Jim Skow, on the play. He returned after missing two downs, but LeBeau felt his injury hampered their ability to stunt. "The injury may have affected them," Walsh says, "but with the passes we were throwing the pass rush wasn't all that important. If we were going to be stopped, it was going to be with coverage."

The 49ers lined up in a slot formation and got what they wanted; the Bengals showed man-for-man. Rice beat the coverage and stepped out of bounds at the Cincinnati 48.

Billups kept looking for a big play. "We felt like they had to go to the outside of the field," he says, "and that's what the defense we were using does, it shuts off the sideline. We felt like they didn't have enough time to go to the middle. They just did the opposite of what we thought they would do. They started bringing Rice through the middle of the field. It was just great play-calling."

"When the drive started," Randy Cross says, "we were thinking field goal. But once we crossed the fifty we were going for the throat."

The veteran center had announced his retirement before the game, but he had more than a sentimental interest in how it might end. His low snap on the missed field goal in the first half was the difference on the scoreboard.

A pass to Craig underneath was good for a 13-yard gain to the 35, and the 49ers had another first down. Here Montana would have an instant of breathtaking clarity. Other athletes have described such a moment, a feeling, an experience, an almost trance-like state...time suspended... the players moving as if in slow motion.

Joe Montana went beyond that point in Super Bowl XXIII. He almost fainted. "We got the tie," he remembers thinking. But the win was still there in front of him. As he stepped up under center to take the snap, he could feel the adrenalin pumping wildly. He had been changing the plays at the line of scrimmage, repeating his signals, bellowing them, so his teammates could hear over the Niagara of noise in the stadium.

"I was short of breath," he says, "and when I screamed the next play I got dizzy ...like I was blacking out. Then my vision blurred. I figured maybe I was hyperventilating. So I stood there with my hands under center for what seemed like an hour, trying to decide: 'Should I go ahead, or shouldn't I?' My head cleared a little, so I figured, by the time I got the ball back and read the defense, I'd be okay. But the second I stepped back into the pocket, the fuzziness returned. Rice got open breaking outside, but all I saw was the red blur of his shirt. So I threw it away, out of bounds. I couldn't risk an interception because I knew I wasn't all there.

"I looked to the sideline and started pointing in circles to my head to let Bill know I was dizzy on that play. But he wasn't watching me. Then I realized if he thought something was wrong, he might take me out. So I went back to the huddle and I was all right. It was the strangest feeling I've ever had on the field. You can see it on the videotape. I was in another world."

If Montana felt temporarily faint, he was not the sole licensee. The crowd was right there with him. Of course, this is a fellow who came back in two months in 1986 from a back operation that doctors thought might sideline him a year, or the rest of his career.

On the next play, a short pass to Craig was nullified and the 49ers were penalized 10 yards for having an in-

In the postgame chaos, the Team of the Decade celebrated its ascension to the throne.

XXIII

eligible receiver downfield. The guilty party was Cross, who earlier had been flagged for holding.

Then came the most critical play of the drive, on second-and-20 from the 45. Once more Montana went over the middle to Rice, who made the catch as three defenders converged on him. The play gained 27 yards and only a last-man tackle by cornerback Rickey Dixon prevented a touchdown.

"We had three people there," LeBeau says, "but Rice went up for the ball and our three guys knocked one another off."

Reggie Williams, the Cincinnati linebacker, says, "That was the play that broke our backs." Cornerback Ray Horton says, "It was the play of the game. We were in perfect coverage for it. I should have made the interception."

A pass to Craig was good for eight yards, and the 49ers called their second time out with 39 seconds left, facing second-and-2 at the 10.

The play is called "20 halfback curl, X up," and the primary receiver is Craig, who breaks to the outside to split the safeties, then cuts back to the inside. Taylor runs underneath. If the safety goes with Craig, Taylor usually is open.

The Bengals were running out of guesses. "Our last chance," Sam Wyche says, "was to defend against Jerry Rice. I thought when it came down to one play, they would go to Rice."

Taylor lined up at tight end. Horton says, "It didn't pose a problem until they put Rice in motion to that side. When he went, I had to widen out a little bit. It gave Taylor more room to operate. He shot right inside. Before I could react, the ball was in the air."

A cry escaped from the throat of Fulcher: "Nooooo!" He saw what was happening and came hard, but he had too much ground to make up. "Two steps," he says. "That's all. Two steps too late. I've watched the replay dozens of times. If they could rewind the tape, I'd know what to do now."

The winning touchdown pass was caught by Taylor with 34 ticks left on the clock. One would hesitate to suggest that Taylor's moment of fame was a fragile one, but when a panel of analysts wrapped up the game for the television audience, Miami head coach Don Shula kept referring to him as "Turner."

Taylor's catch was his first reception of the game, although he had set a Super Bowl record with a 45-yard punt return earlier. His other claim to fame was that he sold cars in the off-season for a dealership owned by former baseball great Reggie Jackson.

Montana had made it all the way back. He still felt the indignity of being benched in the third quarter of a playoff loss to Minnesota in 1987. "Getting pulled was tough," he says, "but the hardest part was, after the game, people talked as if I couldn't do it anymore. It wasn't like I was being judged on a bad year. I was being judged on half a game."

He would rebound to give as majestic a performance as a quarterback can give when all the goods are on the line. It wasn't just the numbers, the 23 completions in 36 attempts for 357 yards, a Super Bowl record. It was his patience, his coolness, his absolute reveling in the pressure as the clock ticked away. Now we knew why Walsh calls Montana "the most instinctive quarterback ever to play the game."

Montana's best instinct this day, of course, was to throw those long passes to Jerry Rice, who hauled in 11 for a Super-Bowl-record 215 yards. Voted the game's most valuable player, Rice had receptions of 30, 31, 44, and 27 yards. His 11 catches tied the Super Bowl record.

It was a game good enough to retire on, and a few days later, Bill Walsh did. Randy Cross surely thought so, going out a winner in his thirteenth year. "I didn't think about it before the game, to be honest," he says. "I didn't think about it until it was over and everyone was running off the field. I kept turning around and looking at the field and up in the stands. I didn't want to leave."

The Bengals may have lost the best Super Bowl ever played. They lost it hard and late and they lost it honest.

In the end, Montana's drive is guaranteed to grow in memory because the Super Bowl magnifies everything. In the crucible, he was nearly perfect, completing eight of nine passes on the climactic drive. All day he hung tough in the pocket, and he threw almost every pass in the book. He threw them deep and he dumped them off, he threw outs and slants. And, most important, he threw them straight.

"If every game was a Super Bowl," Cross says, "Joe Montana would be undefeated."

XXIV

San Francisco 55, Denver 10

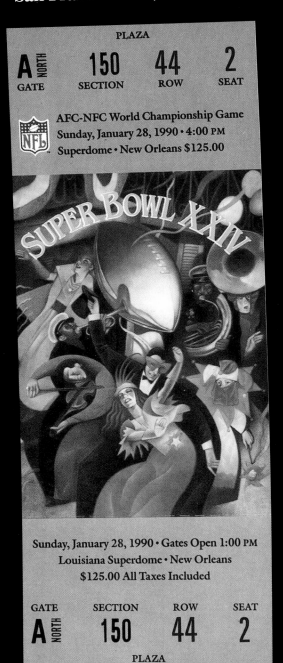

PLAZA

A NORTH	**150**	**44**	**2**
GATE	SECTION	ROW	SEAT

AFC-NFC World Championship Game
Sunday, January 28, 1990 • 4:00 PM
Superdome • New Orleans $125.00

SUPER BOWL XXIV

Sunday, January 28, 1990 • Gates Open 1:00 PM
Louisiana Superdome • New Orleans
$125.00 All Taxes Included

GATE	SECTION	ROW	SEAT
A NORTH	**150**	**44**	**2**

PLAZA

Vital Statistics

Starting Lineups

San Francisco (NFC)	Offense	Denver (AFC)
John Taylor	WR	Vance Johnson
Bubba Paris	LT	Gerald Perry
Guy McIntyre	LG	Jim Juriga
Jesse Sapolu	C	Keith Kartz
Bruce Collie	RG	Doug Widell
Harris Barton	RT	Ken Lanier
Brent Jones	TE	Orson Mobley
Jerry Rice	WR	Mark Jackson
Joe Montana	QB	John Elway
Roger Craig	RB	Steve Sewell
Tom Rathman	RB	Bobby Humphrey
	Defense	
Pierce Holt	LE	Alphonso Carreker
Michael Carter	NT	Greg Kragen
Kevin Fagan	RE	Ron Holmes
Charles Haley	LOLB	Michael Brooks
Matt Millen	LILB	Rick Dennison
Michael Walter	RILB	Karl Mecklenburg
Keena Turner	ROLB	Simon Fletcher
Darryl Pollard	LCB	Tyrone Braxton
Don Griffin	RCB	Wymon Henderson
Chet Brooks	SS	Dennis Smith
Ronnie Lott	FS	Steve Atwater

Substitutions

San Francisco-Offense: K-Mike Cofer. P-Barry Helton. QB-Steve Young. RB-Terrence Flagler, Harry Sydney, Spencer Tillman. WR-Mike Wilson, Mike Sherrard. TE-Wesley Walls, Jamie Williams. C-Chuck Thomas. T-Steve Wallace. G-Terry Tausch. Defense: E-Larry Roberts, Danny Stubbs. NT-Jim Burt, Pete Kugler. LB-Keith DeLong, Steve Hendrickson, Bill Romanowski. CB-Tim McKyer, Eric Wright. S-Johnny Jackson.
Denver-Offense: K-David Treadwell. P-Mike Horan. QB-Gary Kubiak. RB-Ken Bell, Melvin Bratton, Sammy Winder. WR-Ricky Nattiel, Michael Young. TE-Paul Green, Clarence Kay. C-Keith Bishop. G-Monte Smith. Defense: E-Warren Powers, Andre Townsend. NT-Brad Henke. LB-Scott Curtis, Bruce Klostermann, Tim Lucas, Marc Munford. CB-Darren Carrington, Mark Haynes. S-Kip Corrington, Randy Robbins.

Officials

Referee-Dick Jorgensen. Umpire-Hendi Ancich. Line Judge-Ron Blum. Head Linesman-Earnie Frantz. Back Judge-Al Jury. Field Judge-Don Orr. Side Judge-Gerry Austin. Replay Official-Al Sabato.

Scoring

San Francisco	13	14	14	14	—	55
Denver	3	0	7	0	—	10

SF-Rice 20 pass from Montana (Cofer kick)
Den-FG Treadwell 42
SF-Jones 7 pass from Montana (kick failed)
SF-Rathman 1 run (Cofer kick)
SF-Rice 38 pass from Montana (Cofer kick)
SF-Rice 28 pass from Montana (Cofer kick)
SF-Taylor 35 pass from Montana (Cofer kick)
Den-Elway 3 run (Treadwell kick)
SF-Rathman 3 run (Cofer kick)
SF-Craig 1 run (Cofer kick)
Attendance-72,919

FINAL TEAM STATISTICS

	49ers	Broncos
TOTAL FIRST DOWNS	28	12
Rushing	14	5
Passing	14	6
Penalty	0	1
TOTAL NET YARDAGE	461	167
Total Offensive Plays	77	52
Average Gain per Offensive Play	6.0	3.2
NET YARDS RUSHING	144	64
Total Rushing Plays	44	17
Average Gain per Rushing Play	3.3	3.8
NET YARDS PASSING	317	103
Pass Att.-Comp.-Int.	32-24-0	29-11-2
Sacks-Yards Lost	1-0	6-33
Gross Yards Passing	317	136
Avg. Gain per Pass (Incl. Sacks)	9.6	2.9
PUNTS-YARDS	4-158	6-231
Average Distance	39.5	38.5
Had Blocked	0	0
TOTAL RETURN YARDAGE	129	207
Kickoff Returns-Yards	3-49	9-196
Punt Returns-Yards	3-38	2-11
Interception Returns-Yards	2-42	0-0
TOTAL TURNOVERS	0	4
Fumbles-Lost	0-0	3-2
Had Intercepted	0	2
PENALTIES-YARDS	4-38	0-0
TOTAL POINTS SCORED	55	10
Touchdowns Rushing	3	1
Touchdowns Passing	5	0
Touchdowns Returns	0	0
Extra Points	7	1
Field Goals-Attempts	0-0	1-1
Safeties	0	0
THIRD DOWN EFFICIENCY	8/15	3/11
FOURTH DOWN EFFICIENCY	2/2	0/0
TIME OF POSSESSION	39:31	20:29

INDIVIDUAL STATISTICS

RUSHING

San Francisco	No.	Yds.	Avg.	Long	TD
Craig	20	69	3.5	18	1
Rathman	11	38	3.5	18	2
Flagler	6	14	2.3	10	0
Young	4	6	1.5	11	0
Montana	2	15	7.5	10	0
Sydney	1	2	2.0	2	0

Denver	No.	Yds.	Avg.	Long	TD
Humphrey	12	61	5.1	34	0
Elway	4	8	2.0	3t	1
Winder	1	-5	-5.0	-5	0

PASSING

San Francisco	Att.	Comp.	Yds.	Long	TD	Int.
Montana	29	22	297	38t	5	0
Young	3	2	20	13	0	0

Denver	Att.	Comp.	Yds.	Long	TD	Int.
Elway	26	10	108	27	0	2
Kubiak	3	1	28	28	0	0

RECEIVING

San Francisco	No.	Yds.	Long	TD
Rice	7	148	38t	3
Craig	5	34	12	0
Rathman	4	43	18	0
Taylor	3	49	35t	13
Sherrard	1	13	13	0
Walls	1	9	9	0
Jones	1	7	7t	1
Sydney	1	7	7	0
Williams	1	7	7	0

Denver	No.	Yds.	Long	TD
Humphrey	3	38	27	0
Sewell	2	22	12	0
Johnson	2	21	13	0
Nattiel	1	28	28	0
Bratton	1	14	14	0
Winder	1	7	7	0
Kay	1	6	6	0

INTERCEPTIONS

San Francisco	No.	Yds.	Long	TD
Brooks	1	38	38	0
Walter	1	4	4	0

Denver	No.	Yds.	Long	TD
None				

PUNTING

San Francisco	No.	Yds.	Avg.	TB	Long
Helton	4	158	39.5	0	47

Denver	No.	Yds.	Avg.	TB	Long
Horan	6	231	38.5	0	43

PUNT RETURNS

San Francisco	No.	FC	Yds.	Long	TD
Taylor	3	2	38	17	0

Denver	No.	FC	Yds.	Long	TD
Johnson	2	1	11	7	0

KICKOFF RETURNS

San Francisco	No.	Yds.	Long	TD
Flagler	3	49	22	0

Denver	No.	Yds.	Long	TD
Carrington	6	146	39	0
Bell	2	41	24	0
Bratton	1	9	9	0

FUMBLES

San Francisco	No.	Own Rec.	Opp. Rec.
Brooks	0	0	1
Stubbs	0	0	1

Denver	No.	Own Rec.	Opp. Rec.
Humphrey	1	0	0
Elway	2	1	0

KICKING

San Francisco	XP-A	FG-A	FG Made	FG Missed
Cofer	7-8	0-0	--	--

Denver	XP-A	FG-A	FG Made	FG Missed
Treadwell	1-1	1-1	42	--

The San Francisco 49ers and Denver Broncos arrived in New Orleans for Super Bowl XXIV with their roles clearly defined.

The 49ers, still riding the momentum of the 1980s, were the team of destiny, cool and polished, supremely confident, unbeaten in three previous trips to the Super Bowl.

The Broncos, by contrast, never had won the NFL's championship game. Indeed, they never had come close. They lost three earlier Super Bowls by a combined margin of 108-40.

It was hard to take the Broncos seriously, and most people didn't. The 49ers opened as 12-point favorites—the highest for a Super Bowl since Super Bowl XIV—and stayed there all week. A Denver newspaper columnist even wondered if the Broncos should bother showing up at the Louisiana Superdome January 28.

What if this Super Bowl followed the usual pattern and brought out: (a) the best in the 49ers, and (b) the worst in the Broncos? Imagine just how lopsided the game would be.

That's how it turned out.

Worse, maybe.

"I knew we were great," 49ers safety Ronnie Lott said later, "but I didn't think we were that great."

"The 49ers are playing at a level that's incredible," said Dan Reeves, Denver's shell-shocked head coach. "We've got a long way to go to get to that level."

The 49ers set 18 Super Bowl records in crushing the Broncos 55-10, including most points in one game and largest margin of victory. They also became the first team to win back-to-back Super Bowls since the Pittsburgh Steelers in games XIII and XIV. In the locker room after the game, the San Francisco players chanted, "Three-peat, three-peat," meaning they planned to win again in Super Bowl XXV. No NFL team ever has won three Super Bowls in a row, but then no other team had a quarterback playing the way Joe Montana played in 1989, either.

Montana had his greatest year at age 33, playing through an assortment of injuries (elbow, knee, ribs) to compile the highest regular-season passing efficiency rating in NFL history. He was even better in the playoffs, completing 43 of 54 attempts, six for touchdowns, as the 49ers rolled past Minnesota (41-13) and the Los Angeles Rams (30-3) en route to Super Bowl XXIV.

Against Denver, Montana found yet another level. He completed 22 of 29 attempts for 297 yards and five touchdowns, a Super Bowl record. He was voted the game's most valuable player, making the former Notre Dame star the only three-time MVP in Super Bowl history.

It was Montana's finest hour—and one of his easiest.

"I think I might have gotten touched once all day," Montana said, referring to the solid protection he received from the 49ers' offensive line. "I could play until I'm forty if they keep playing like that."

"We tried rushing three men, four men, five men, we tried everything and nothing worked," said Wade Phillips, the Broncos' defensive coordinator. "The way Montana was playing, we could've dropped eleven guys and rushed eleven and it wouldn't have made any difference. He was uncanny."

The same could be said for almost every phase of the San Francisco team.

On offense, the 49ers scored eight touchdowns in their first 11 possessions before mercifully running out the clock in the fourth quarter.

On defense, they swarmed all over Denver quarterback John Elway, sacking him four times and forcing four turnovers, totally dominating the game.

On special teams, placekicker Mike Cofer missed one extra point. Okay, so the 49ers weren't perfect!

In the end, they earned a place alongside the all-time great NFL teams, ranking with the Green Bay Packers of the 1960s, the Steelers of the 1970s, and the legendary clubs of earlier decades.

"We took the attitude that we were a moving train," said offensive tackle Bubba Paris. "We knew that if we could establish our level of play and keep our momentum going, that no matter

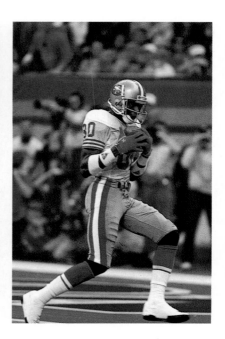

who they put on the tracks in front of us, we'd blow right through them.

Incomparable Jerry Rice caught three of Joe Montana's record five touchdown passes, scoring on throws of 20 (left), 38 (center), and 28 yards (right). Rice led all receivers in the game with seven catches for 148 yards.

little something to try to break the spell.

"It got to a point where, being a Christian and being a person who loves people, I actually felt sorry for the Broncos. I know it must have been a terrible feeling to be sitting there forty or forty-five points behind."

For the Broncos and their legion of fans, it was the latest in a string of heartbreaks dating back to Super Bowl XII. The fact that most people, including those in the Rocky Mountains, saw this one coming a long way off didn't make it any easier to accept.

No matter how many pairs of orange-tinted glasses you wear, 55-10 is still 55-10. And 0-4 in Super Bowls is still 0-4. Hard facts, hard times.

"I'm just trying to figure out how we can win one of these games or at least be in one," Elway said, surveying the wreckage. "The teams we've been playing have manhandled us every time. I don't know why. It's very disappointing, very discouraging."

The Broncos tried to change their luck for Super Bowl XXIV. Reeves brought the team to New Orleans on Sunday, January 21, a full week before the game. For previous Super Bowls, the Broncos arrived on Monday. Just a

Elway also showed up with his blond hair lapping over the collar of his shirt. That, too, was a change. Elway had his hair trimmed and styled before his last two Super Bowl appearances. Each time he went out a well-groomed loser. He figured he

The 49ers started a run of 34 successive points with Montana's seven-yard touchdown pass to tight end Brent Jones at the end of the first quarter. Denver safety Dennis Smith (left) was a step too late.

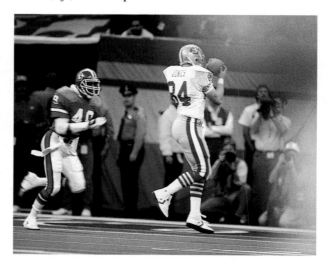

would try something different.

The entire Broncos team reflected a new attitude in the days leading up to the twenty-fourth Super Bowl. No more Mr. Nice Guy. On their first night in New Orleans, a group of Broncos blew off several San Francisco players who offered to buy them a friendly drink in the French Quarter.

"They didn't want anything to do with us," 49ers running back Spencer Tillman said. "I was kind of surprised. I mean, we can at least be cordial to each other."

"To be honest, I think it ticked some of our guys off," Montana said later. "It probably was a good thing for us. It set a tone for the week."

It wasn't just posturing on the part of the Denver players. The Broncos were a much different team in January, 1990, than they had been in previous Super Bowls.

They were bigger and more physical than the teams that had been bullied by the Giants in XXI (39-20) and Washington in XXII (42-10).

Phillips replaced Joe Collier as defensive co-ordinator following the 1988 season, and he scrapped the old system, which had relied on trickery and finesse. Phillips got bigger players and basically turned them loose. The result was that Denver allowed the fewest points in the NFL during the regular season (226) and

Montana had great protection all day, and he took advantage of it, completing 22 of 29 passes for 297 yards and five touchdowns. The performance earned him his third Super Bowl most valuable player award.

forced 43 turnovers, tops in the American Football Conference.

Meanwhile, a rookie halfback, Bobby Humphrey, put new muscle in the Denver offense. Humphrey rushed for 1,151 yards during the

The balanced 49ers not only passed at will, they ran for 144 yards, including this one-yard touchdown blast by powerful Tom Rathman (44) in the second quarter. Rathman also scored from the 4 in the final period.

season, and the Broncos suddenly were able to win games the old-fashioned way. They could grind it out between the tackles, three or four yards a crack.

Owner Pat Bowlen had a term for it: "In-your-face football."

It worked well enough for the Broncos to roll up an 11-5 record in the regular season, then defeat Pittsburgh (24-23) and Cleveland (37-21) in the AFC playoffs. But the 49ers, the defending league champions and coming off a 14-2 regular season, were another dimension.

In Super Bowl XXIV, the Broncos were in over their heads.

Way over their heads.

Some people—media types, mostly—tried to build a case for the underdog. On its pre-game show, CBS-TV used film clips from the Jets' upset of the Colts in Super Bowl III, the U.S. hockey team's miracle win over the Soviets in 1980, and scenes from against-all-odds movies such as *Hoosiers* and *Rocky II*.

Stirring, yes. Convincing, no.

The clear thinkers kept coming back to one simple equation: The Broncos had three inex-

perienced starters in their defensive secondary …and the 49ers had Joe Montana throwing to Jerry Rice and John Taylor. That was a no-win matchup for Denver.

All week, the Broncos insisted they would make up for their lack of experience with hard hitting. Rookie free safety Steve Atwater, a bruising 6-3, 220-pounder, said he would make Rice and Taylor pay when they came across the middle. The idea was to rough up the San Francisco receivers, intimidate them if possible.

Rice's mid-week response proved prophetic: "If they're going to be that aggressive, then they're liable to get themselves caught out of position and we can hit a few big plays."

More than a few, actually.

Rice caught seven passes for 148 yards and three touchdowns, a Super Bowl record. Taylor added a fourth touchdown on a 35-yard reception from Montana. Tight end Brent Jones also scored on a seven-yard pass.

The 49ers made it look easy, and it was.

Phillips's simplified defensive scheme—a traditional 3-4 with two-deep zone coverage—worked fine against the rest of the NFL, but it was made to order for the San Francisco offense with its multiple weapons and peerless triggerman.

Both Denver safeties, Atwater and Dennis Smith, played the run aggressively, which made them vulnerable to the play-action fake. If they froze, even for a second, either Rice or Taylor would streak past them on a deep post pattern. If the safeties stayed back, Montana could lay the ball off to his running backs, Roger Craig and Tom Rathman, underneath.

Montana completed 13 consecutive passes at one point, another Super Bowl record. "Joe gets this sneaky little grin on his face when he's on," Rice said. "It's like he is saying, 'Everything's under control.' He had that smile right from the first series."

The basic blueprint for the San Francisco offense was drawn by former head coach Bill Walsh. There was some question how the 49ers would cope after Walsh retired from his coaching job and eventually joined NBC-TV as a broadcaster in 1989.

How would the defending champions func-

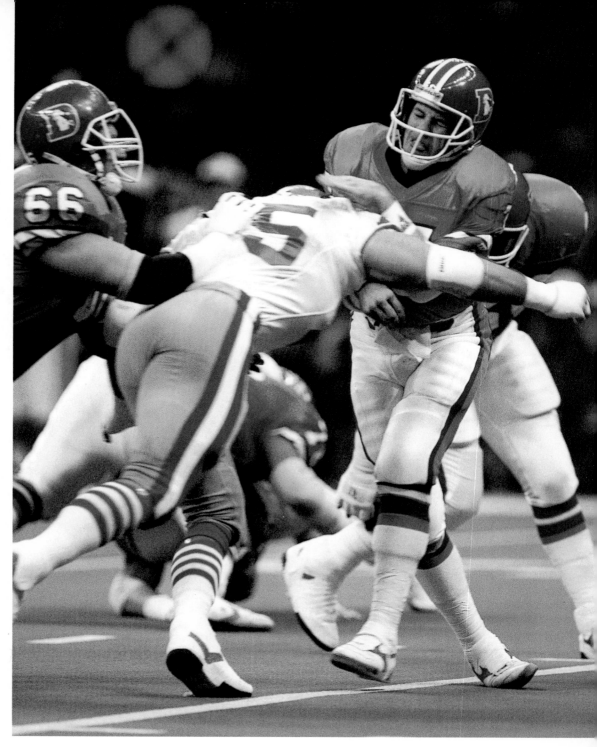

Harassed and hammered by the 49ers all day, Denver's John Elway had a forgettable performance, completing only 10 of 26 passes for 108 yards. He also was intercepted twice, sacked four times, and lost a fumble.

tion without Walsh around to fine-tune things? No one really knew. After all, the 49ers hadn't repeated as NFL champions in two previous tries under Walsh, so some people wondered if the 49ers would slip a few notches.

But George Seifert, the defensive coordinator under Walsh for six years, took over as the 49ers' head coach, and pro football's team of the 1980s rolled into the 1990s without missing a beat.

"We really didn't enter this season with the idea that we were going to change a heckuva lot," said Seifert, who modestly downplayed his own role in the team's success. "We had a very set and sound offense and we felt our defense was established.

"Bill [Walsh] had established something very solid here. All we really sought to do this year was maintain what we had."

Seifert made what he called "subtle" changes, streamlining game plans and platooning players on the offensive and defensive lines to keep everyone fresh. It was no coincidence the 49ers outscored their opponents in the fourth quarter by a whopping 194-71 over the season.

Seifert also eliminated all doubt about who was the team's number-one quarterback. Walsh waffled between Montana and Steve Young in 1988, creating tension all around. Seifert simply told Montana, "You're it." Montana took it from there, winning the Miller Lite/NFL Player of the Year award.

Montana was one of several veterans who said they welcomed the coaching change. They claimed Walsh had been too cold, too autocratic in his later years. Seifert was, in Montana's words, "Like a breath of fresh air. He allowed

On the sideline, Denver head coach Dan Reeves couldn't have been more frustrated. He had guided the Broncos to their third Super Bowl in four years—a superlative record—but once again the dream turned to ashes.

the team to develop its own personality."

More than anything, the players resented the perception that "The System"—*Walsh*, in other words—was what made the 49ers a great team. The players wanted to make their own statement by repeating as Super Bowl champions under Seifert, a rookie head coach.

"The guys have always felt that we're here because of the talent level," said offensive tackle Harris Barton. "We wanted to prove that it wasn't a one-man deal. It's a team deal."

That desire kept the 49ers focused and motivated throughout the 1989 season. Seifert did a good job keeping his players on an even keel, and assistant coach Mike Holmgren took over for Walsh as the offensive play-caller. Everything fell into place. The 49ers posted the NFL's best record (14-2) and walked away with their fourth NFC title in nine years.

When they arrived in New Orleans for Super Bowl XXIV, they felt comfortable and confident. The front office brought along a box of clippings from Super Bowl III—pregame stories predicting the Colts would clobber the Jets —and kept them handy just in case the players showed signs of taking Denver too lightly. They didn't. Practices were crisp. Montana was razor sharp. Four players missed curfew one night but were jarred back to reality in a team meeting the next day. Safety Ronnie Lott, who called the meeting, said, "Everyone needs a kick in the butt once in a while. It's no big deal."

When Montana got to the Superdome for the game on Sunday, he found two surprises waiting in the dressing room.

Equipment manager Frank Hinek (ironically nicknamed "Bronco") had hung a white number 87 jersey in the locker next to Montana. That was the number worn by Dwight Clark, Montana's favorite receiver and best friend, before his retirement after the 1987 season.

"I smiled when I saw it," Montana said later. "It was like a ghost from the past. It brought back some pleasant memories."

The second surprise was a framed photograph of Montana's three children: Alexandra, 4; Elizabeth, 3; and Nathaniel, three months. The photo, taken by Montana's wife Jennifer, showed each of the children wearing one of their father's Super Bowl rings. The girls had the rings on their thumbs; Nathaniel had his pinned to his 49ers T-shirt.

Underneath the photo was an engraved plaque that read: "OK, Daddy. The next ring is yours."

Jennifer gave her husband the photograph in November, shortly after Nathaniel's birth. Joe liked it so much he kept it in his locker at the 49ers' practice facility in Santa Clara. "My inspiration," he called it.

As NFL Commissioner Paul Tagliabue (top, left) prepared to present the Vince Lombardi Trophy to 49ers owner Edward DeBartolo, Jr., and head coach George Seifert (far right), he was interrupted by cornerback Eric Wright, who gave DeBartolo a postgame shower.

When the team left for New Orleans, Hinek quietly tucked the photo in with the rest of Montana's gear. The equipment manager didn't put it out until game day, however.

"I wanted Joe to just show up today and find it," Hinek said. "You know, a little touch of home."

"Do you think it helped?" someone asked.

"It didn't hurt," Hinek replied with a smile.

Montana was superb in the big game: cool, precise, and deadly. He missed on his first two pass attempts, then settled into a groove. He converted two third downs on the opening drive — one on a 10-yard scramble — then hit Rice over the middle for a 20-yard touchdown. Elapsed time: four minutes, 54 seconds.

Denver cut the lead to 7-3 on David Treadwell's 42-yard field goal, but it was apparent the Broncos were in trouble. Elway completed just one of his first seven pass attempts. His first throw, a hook to wide receiver Mark Jackson, bounced yards short of its intended target.

"When I saw that, I knew something wasn't right with him [Elway]," said Lott. "He never bounces that pass. He just looked out of sync all day. Maybe he was trying too hard."

If Elway was pressing, he had his reasons. On Wednesday before the game, former Steelers quarterback Terry Bradshaw offered a stinging analysis of Elway, saying he lacked the mental toughness to be a great quarterback.

"John's problem is he has been babied by the city, he has been babied by the coach [Reeves]," Bradshaw told reporters. "He's got to get better emotionally. He's too...too inconsistent."

Elway bristled when he saw Bradshaw's comments in print. "He [Bradshaw] has been bashing me since I came into the league," Elway said. "He doesn't like the money I make. He can stick it in his ear."

Earlier in the week, Elway had talked about how important it was for him to win a Super Bowl game so he could be mentioned in that elite class of big-game quarterbacks with Montana, Bart Starr, Roger Staubach, Joe Namath, and, yes, Bradshaw. "This is my third chance," Elway said. "Who knows if I'll ever get another one?"

So Elway didn't need any extra pressure going into Super Bowl XXIV, but Bradshaw tossed another ton on his shoulders, anyway. It showed. He came out skittish. Elway was 6 for 20 passing in the first half as the 49ers mixed up their coverages expertly.

"He has a problem reading zone," cornerback Tim McKyer said. "We kept showing him man [coverage], but playing zone. We really confused the guy."

The 49ers capitalized on every Denver mistake. Humphrey, who was playing despite cracked ribs suffered in the Broncos' AFC Championship Game victory, fumbled in the first quarter, and safety Chet Brooks recovered near midfield. The 49ers scored in 10 plays, with Montana passing to Jones to extend their lead to 13-3.

The 49ers stretched their lead to 27-3 at halftime, but the real crusher came early in the third quarter when Elway was intercepted twice within three minutes by linebacker Michael Walter and Brooks. Montana quickly cashed in with touchdown passes to Rice and Taylor. Suddenly, it was 41-3 and the Denver fans began evacuating the building.

The two teams played out the remaining quarter and a half with the 49ers pulling their punches. Montana was replaced by Young for the last 11 minutes.

At one point, San Francisco linebacker Matt Millen helped Elway to his feet and whispered in the quarterback's ear.

"He just said, 'Hang in there. It's a tough one,'" Elway recalled. "I said, 'You got that right.'"

When it was over, Montana stood alone as the most prolific passer in Super Bowl history. He held eight records, including most career passes (122), completions (83), touchdown passes (11), and yards (1,142). He also had the Super Bowl record for fewest interceptions (none).

As he accepted another MVP award, Montana shrugged off questions about whether he might be the greatest quarterback ever. Seifert had given Montana his vote a few moments earlier.

"Those [judgments] are reserved for the guys who are no longer in the game," Montana said. "I'm still very much a part of the game. I'm looking ahead."

APPENDIX

Team Records

SCORING

Most Points, Game
55	San Francisco vs. Denver, XXIV
46	Chicago vs. New England, XX
42	Washington vs. Denver, XXII
39	New York Giants vs. Denver, XXI
38	Los Angeles Raiders vs. Washington, XVIII
	San Francisco vs. Miami, XIX

Fewest Points, Game
3	Miami vs. Dallas, VI
6	Minnesota vs. Pittsburgh, IX
7	Baltimore vs. New York Jets, III
	Minnesota vs. Kansas City, IV
	Washington vs. Miami, VII
	Minnesota vs. Miami, VIII

Most Points, Both Teams, Game
66	Pittsburgh (35) vs. Dallas (31), XIII
65	San Francisco (55) vs. Denver (10), XXIV
59	New York Giants (39) vs. Denver (20), XXI
56	Chicago (46) vs. New England (10), XX
54	San Francisco (38) vs. Miami (16), XIX

Fewest Points, Both Teams, Game
21	Washington (7) vs. Miami (14), VII
22	Minnesota (6) vs. Pittsburgh (16), IX
23	Baltimore (7) vs. New York Jets (16), III
27	Miami (3) vs. Dallas (24), VI
29	Dallas (13) vs. Baltimore (16), V

Largest Margin of Victory, Game
45	San Francisco vs. Denver, XXIV (55-10)
36	Chicago vs. New England, XX (46-10)
32	Washington vs. Denver, XXII (42-10)
29	Los Angeles Raiders vs. Washington, XVIII (38-9)
25	Green Bay vs. Kansas City, I (35-10)

Most Points, Each Half
1st:	35	Washington vs. Denver, XXII
2nd:	30	New York Giants vs. Denver, XXI

Most Points, Each Quarter
1st:	14	Miami vs. Minnesota, VIII
		Oakland vs. Philadelphia, XV
2nd:	35	Washington vs. Denver, XXII
3rd:	21	Chicago vs. New England, XX
4th:	14	Pittsburgh vs. Dallas, X
		Dallas vs. Pittsburgh, XIII
		Pittsburgh vs. Dallas, XIII
		Pittsburgh vs. Los Angeles, XIV
		Cincinnati vs. San Francisco, XVI
		Washington vs. Miami, XVII
		San Francisco vs. Cincinnati, XXIII
		San Francisco vs. Denver, XXIV

Most Points, Both Teams, Each Half
1st:	45	Washington (35) vs. Denver (10), XXII
2nd:	40	New York Giants (30) vs. Denver (10), XXI

Fewest Points, Both Teams, Each Half
1st:	2	Minnesota (0) vs. Pittsburgh (2), IX
2nd:	7	Miami (0) vs. Washington (7), VII
		Denver (0) vs. Washington (7), XXII

Most Points, Both Teams, Each Quarter
1st:	17	Miami (10) vs. San Francisco (7), XIX
		Denver (10) vs. New York Giants (7), XXI
2nd:	35	Washington (35) vs. Denver (0), XXII
3rd:	21	Chicago (21) vs. New England (0), XX
		San Francisco (14) vs. Denver (7), XXIV
4th:	28	Pittsburgh (14) vs. Dallas (14), XIII

FIRST DOWNS

Most First Downs, Game
31	San Francisco vs. Miami, XIX
28	San Francisco vs. Denver, XXIV
25	Washington vs. Denver, XXII
24	Cincinnati vs. San Francisco, XVI
	Washington vs. Miami, XVII
	New York Giants vs. Denver, XXI

Fewest First Downs, Game
9	Minnesota vs. Pittsburgh, IX
	Miami vs. Washington, XVII
10	Dallas vs. Baltimore, V
	Miami vs. Dallas, VII
11	Denver vs. Dallas, XII

Most First Downs, Both Teams, Game
50	San Francisco (31) vs. Miami (19), XIX
47	New York Giants (24) vs. Denver (23), XXI
44	Cincinnati (24) vs. San Francisco (20), XVI

Fewest First Downs, Both Teams, Game
24	Dallas (10) vs. Baltimore (14), V
26	Minnesota (9) vs. Pittsburgh (17), IX
27	Pittsburgh (13) vs. Dallas (14), X

TOTAL YARDS

Most Yards Gained, Game
602	Washington vs. Denver, XXII
537	San Francisco vs. Miami, XIX
461	San Francisco vs. Denver, XXIV
453	San Francisco vs. Cincinnati, XXIII
429	Oakland vs. Minnesota, XI

Fewest Yards Gained, Game
119	Minnesota vs. Pittsburgh, IX
123	New England vs. Chicago, XX
156	Denver vs. Dallas, XII

Most Yards Gained, Both Teams, Game
929	Washington (602) vs. Denver (327), XXII
851	San Francisco (537) vs. Miami (314), XIX
782	Oakland (429) vs. Minnesota (353), XI

Fewest Yards Gained, Both Teams, Game
452	Minnesota (119) vs. Pittsburgh (333), IX
481	Washington (228) vs. Miami (253), VII
	Denver (156) vs. Dallas (325), XII
497	Minnesota (238) vs. Miami (259), VIII

RUSHING

Most Attempts, Game
57	Pittsburgh vs. Minnesota, IX
53	Miami vs. Minnesota, VIII

52	Oakland vs. Minnesota, XI
	Washington vs. Miami, XVII

Fewest Attempts, Game
9	Miami vs. San Francisco, XIX
11	New England vs. Chicago, XX
17	Denver vs. Washington, XXII
	Denver vs. San Francisco, XXIV

Most Attempts, Both Teams, Game
81	Washington (52) vs. Miami (29), XVII
78	Pittsburgh (57) vs. Minnesota (21), IX
	Oakland (52) vs. Minnesota (26), XI
77	Miami (53) vs. Minnesota (24), VIII
	Pittsburgh (46) vs. Dallas (31), X

Fewest Attempts, Both Teams, Game
49	Miami (9) vs. San Francisco (40), XIX
53	Kansas City (19) vs. Green Bay (34), I
55	San Francisco (27) vs. Cincinnati (28), XXIII

Most Yards Gained, Game
280	Washington vs. Denver, XXII
276	Washington vs. Miami, XVII
266	Oakland vs. Minnesota, XI

Fewest Yards Gained, Game
7	New England vs. Chicago, XX
17	Minnesota vs. Pittsburgh, IX
25	Miami vs. San Francisco, XIX

Most Yards Gained, Both Teams, Game
377	Washington (280) vs. Denver (97), XXII
372	Washington (276) vs. Miami (96), XVII
337	Oakland (266) vs. Minnesota (71), XI

Fewest Yards Gained, Both Teams, Game
171	Baltimore (69) vs. Dallas (102), V
174	New England (7) vs. Chicago (117), XX
186	Philadelphia (69) vs. Oakland (117), XV

PASSING

Most Passes Attempted, Game
50	Miami vs. San Francisco, XIX
44	Minnesota vs. Oakland, XI
41	Baltimore vs. New York Jets, III
	Denver vs. New York Giants, XXI

Fewest Passes Attempted, Game
7	Miami vs. Minnesota, VIII
11	Miami vs. Washington, VII
14	Pittsburgh vs. Minnesota, IX

Most Passes Attempted, Both Teams, Game
85	Miami (50) vs. San Francisco (35), XIX
70	Baltimore (41) vs. New York Jets (29), III
69	Denver (39) vs. Washington (30), XXII

Fewest Passes Attempted, Both Teams, Game
35	Miami (7) vs. Minnesota (28), VIII
39	Miami (11) vs. Washington (28), VII
40	Pittsburgh (14) vs. Minnesota (26), IX
	Miami (17) vs. Washington (23), XVII

Appendix

Most Passes Completed, Game

29	Miami vs. San Francisco, XIX
26	Denver vs. New York Giants, XXI
25	Cincinnati vs. San Francisco, XVI

Fewest Passes Completed, Game

4	Miami vs. Washington, XVII
6	Miami vs. Minnesota, VIII
8	Miami vs. Washington, VII
	Denver vs. Dallas, XII

Most Passes Completed, Both Teams, Game

53	Miami (29) vs. San Francisco (24), XIX
48	Denver (26) vs. New York Giants (22), XXI
39	Cincinnati (25) vs. San Francisco (14), XVI

Fewest Passes Completed, Both Teams, Game

19	Miami (4) vs. Washington (15), XVII
20	Pittsburgh (9) vs. Minnesota (11), IX
22	Miami (8) vs. Washington (14), VII

Most Yards Gained, Game

341	San Francisco vs. Cincinnati, XXIII
326	San Francisco vs. Miami, XIX
322	Washington vs. Denver, XXII

Fewest Yards Gained, Game

35	Denver vs. Dallas, XII
63	Miami vs. Minnesota, VIII
69	Miami vs. Washington, VII

Most Yards Gained, Both Teams, Game

615	San Francisco (326) vs. Miami (289), XIX
583	Denver (320) vs. New York Giants (263), XXI
552	Washington (322) vs. Denver (230), XXII

Fewest Yards Gained, Both Teams, Game

156	Miami (69) vs. Washington (87), VII
186	Pittsburgh (84) vs. Minnesota (102), IX
205	Dallas (100) vs. Miami (105), VI

Most Times Sacked, Game

7	Dallas vs. Pittsburgh, X
	New England vs. Chicago, XX
6	Kansas City vs. Green Bay, I
	Washington vs. Los Angeles Raiders, XVIII
	Denver vs. San Francisco, XXIV

Fewest Times Sacked, Game

0	Baltimore vs. New York Jets, III
	Baltimore vs. Dallas, V
	Minnesota vs. Pittsburgh, IX
	Pittsburgh vs. Los Angeles, XIV
	Philadelphia vs. Oakland, XV

PENALTIES

Most Penalties, Game

12	Dallas vs. Denver, XII
10	Dallas vs. Baltimore, V
9	Dallas vs. Pittsburgh, XIII

Fewest Penalties, Game

0	Miami vs. Dallas, VI
	Pittsburgh vs. Dallas, X
	Denver vs. San Francisco, XXIV

Most Yards Penalized, Game

133	Dallas vs. Baltimore, V
122	Pittsburgh vs. Minnesota, IX
94	Dallas vs. Denver, XII

Fewest Yards Penalized, Game

0	Miami vs. Dallas, VI
	Pittsburgh vs. Dallas, X
	Denver vs. San Francisco, XXIV

FOR THE RECORD

	Date	Site	Attendance	Winner	Loser	Most Valuable Player
XXIV	1-28-90	New Orleans	72,919	San Francisco (NFC) 55	Denver (AFC) 10	Joe Montana
XXIII	1-22-89	Miami	75,129	San Francisco (NFC) 20	Cincinnati (AFC) 16	Jerry Rice
XXII	1-31-88	San Diego	73,302	Washington (NFC) 42	Denver (AFC) 10	Doug Williams
XXI	1-25-87	Pasadena	101,063	New York Giants (NFC) 39	Denver (AFC) 20	Phil Simms
XX	1-26-86	New Orleans	73,818	Chicago (NFC) 46	New England (AFC) 10	Richard Dent
XIX	1-20-85	Palo Alto	84,059	San Francisco (NFC) 38	Miami (AFC) 16	Joe Montana
XVIII	1-22-84	Tampa	72,920	Los Angeles Raiders (AFC) 38	Washington (NFC) 9	Marcus Allen
XVII	1-30-83	Pasadena	103,667	Washington (NFC) 27	Miami (AFC) 17	John Riggins
XVI	1-24-82	Pontiac	81,270	San Francisco (NFC) 26	Cincinnati (AFC) 21	Joe Montana
XV	1-25-81	New Orleans	75,500	Oakland (AFC) 27	Philadelphia (NFC) 10	Jim Plunkett
XIV	1-20-80	Pasadena	103,985	Pittsburgh (AFC) 31	Los Angeles (NFC) 19	Terry Bradshaw
XIII	1-21-79	Miami	79,484	Pittsburgh (AFC) 35	Dallas (NFC) 31	Terry Bradshaw
XII	1-15-78	New Orleans	75,804	Dallas (NFC) 27	Denver (AFC) 10	Harvey Martin/Randy White
XI	1- 9-77	Pasadena	103,438	Oakland (AFC) 32	Minnesota (NFC) 14	Fred Biletnikoff
X	1-18-76	Miami	80,187	Pittsburgh (AFC) 21	Dallas (NFC) 17	Lynn Swann
IX	1-12-75	New Orleans	80,997	Pittsburgh (AFC) 16	Minnesota (NFC) 6	Franco Harris
VIII	1-13-74	Houston	71,882	Miami (AFC) 24	Minnesota (NFC) 7	Larry Csonka
VII	1-14-73	Los Angeles	90,192	Miami (AFC) 14	Washington (NFC) 7	Jake Scott
VI	1-16-72	New Orleans	81,023	Dallas (NFC) 24	Miami (AFC) 3	Roger Staubach
V	1-17-71	Miami	79,204	Baltimore (AFC) 16	Dallas (NFC) 13	Chuck Howley
IV	1-11-70	New Orleans	80,562	Kansas City (AFL) 23	Minnesota (NFL) 7	Len Dawson
III	1-12-69	Miami	75,377	New York Jets (AFL) 16	Baltimore (NFL) 7	Joe Namath
II	1-14-68	Miami	75,546	Green Bay (NFL) 33	Oakland (AFL) 14	Bart Starr
I	1-15-67	Los Angeles	61,946	Green Bay (NFL) 35	Kansas City (AFL) 10	Bart Starr

COMPOSITE STANDINGS

	W	L	Pct.	Pts.	Opp.
Pittsburgh Steelers	4	0	1.000	103	73
San Francisco 49ers	4	0	1.000	139	63
Green Bay Packers	2	0	1.000	68	24
Chicago Bears	1	0	1.000	46	10
New York Giants	1	0	1.000	39	20
New York Jets	1	0	1.000	16	7
Oakland-Los Angeles Raiders	3	1	.750	111	66
Baltimore Colts	1	1	.500	23	29
Kansas City Chiefs	1	1	.500	33	42
Washington Redskins	2	2	.500	85	79
Dallas Cowboys	2	3	.400	112	85
Miami Dolphins	2	3	.400	74	103
Los Angeles Rams	0	1	.000	19	31
New England Patriots	0	1	.000	10	46
Philadelphia Eagles	0	1	.000	10	27
Cincinnati Bengals	0	2	.000	37	46
Denver Broncos	0	4	.000	50	163
Minnesota Vikings	0	4	.000	34	95

376

XXV

Individual Records

RUSHING

Most Yards Gained, Game

204	Timmy Smith, Washington vs. Denver, XXII
191	Marcus Allen, Los Angeles Raiders vs. Washington, XVIII
166	John Riggins, Washington vs. Miami, XVII
158	Franco Harris, Pittsburgh vs. Minnesota, IX
145	Larry Csonka, Miami vs. Minnesota, VIII
137	Clarence Davis, Oakland vs. Minnesota, XI
121	Matt Snell, New York Jets vs. Baltimore, III
116	Tom Matte, Baltimore vs. New York Jets, III
112	Larry Csonka, Miami vs. Washington, VII

Most Attempts, Game

38	John Riggins, Washington vs. Miami, XVII
34	Franco Harris, Pittsburgh vs. Minnesota, IX
33	Larry Csonka, Miami vs. Minnesota, VIII
30	Matt Snell, New York Jets vs. Baltimore, III
27	Franco Harris, Pittsburgh vs. Dallas, X

Most Touchdowns, Game

2	Elijah Pitts, Green Bay vs. Kansas City, I
	Larry Csonka, Miami vs. Minnesota, VIII
	Pete Banaszak, Oakland vs. Minnesota, XI
	Franco Harris, Pittsburgh vs. Los Angeles, XIV
	Marcus Allen, L.A. Raiders vs. Washington, XVIII
	Jim McMahon, Chicago vs. New England, XX
	Timmy Smith, Washington vs. Denver, XXII
	Tom Rathman, San Francisco vs. Denver, XXIV

Longest Run

74	Marcus Allen, L.A. Raiders vs. Washington, XVIII (TD)
58	Tom Matte, Baltimore vs. New York Jets, III
	Timmy Smith, Washington vs. Denver, XXII (TD)
49	Larry Csonka, Miami vs. Washington, VII
43	John Riggins, Washington vs. Miami, XVII (TD)

PASSING

Most Yards Gained, Game

357	Joe Montana, San Francisco vs. Cincinnati, XXIII
340	Doug Williams, Washington vs. Denver, XXII
331	Joe Montana, San Francisco vs. Miami, XIX
318	Terry Bradshaw, Pittsburgh vs. Dallas, XIII
	Dan Marino, Miami vs. San Francisco, XIX
309	Terry Bradshaw, Pittsburgh vs. Los Angeles, XIV
304	John Elway, Denver vs. New York Giants, XXI
300	Ken Anderson, Cincinnati vs. San Francisco, XVI

Most Attempts, Game

50	Dan Marino, Miami vs. San Francisco, XIX
38	Ron Jaworski, Philadelphia vs. Oakland, XV
	John Elway, Denver vs. Washington, XXII
37	John Elway, Denver vs. New York Giants, XXI
36	Joe Montana, San Francisco vs. Cincinnati, XXIII

Most Completions, Game

29	Dan Marino, Miami vs. San Francisco, XIX
25	Ken Anderson, Cincinnati vs. San Francisco, XVI
24	Joe Montana, San Francisco vs. Miami, XIX
23	Joe Montana, San Francisco vs. Cincinnati, XXIII
22	Phil Simms, New York Giants vs. Denver, XXI
	John Elway, Denver vs. New York Giants, XXI
	Joe Montana, San Francisco vs. Denver, XXIV

Most Touchdowns, Game

5	Joe Montana, San Francisco vs. Denver, XXIV
4	Terry Bradshaw, Pittsburgh vs. Dallas, XIII
	Doug Williams, Washington vs. Denver, XXII
3	Roger Staubach, Dallas vs. Pittsburgh, XIII
	Jim Plunkett, Oakland vs. Philadelphia, XV
	Joe Montana, San Francisco vs. Miami, XIX
	Phil Simms, New York Giants vs. Denver, XXI
2	By many players

RECEIVING

Most Yards Gained, Game

215	Jerry Rice, San Francisco vs. Cincinnati, XXIII
193	Ricky Sanders, Washington vs. Denver, XXII
161	Lynn Swann, Pittsburgh vs. Dallas, X
148	Jerry Rice, San Francisco vs. Denver, XXIV
138	Max McGee, Green Bay vs. Kansas City, I
133	George Sauer, New York Jets vs. Baltimore, III
129	Willie Gault, Chicago vs. New England, XX

124	Lynn Swann, Pittsburgh vs. Dallas, XIII
121	John Stallworth, Pittsburgh vs. Los Angeles, XIV
	Vance Johnson, Denver vs. New York Giants, XXI

Most Receptions, Game

11	Dan Ross, Cincinnati vs. San Francisco, XVI
	Jerry Rice, San Francisco vs. Cincinnati, XXIII
10	Tony Nathan, Miami vs. San Francisco, XIX
9	Ricky Sanders, Washington vs. Denver, XXII
8	George Sauer, New York Jets vs. Baltimore, III
	Roger Craig, San Francisco vs. Cincinnati, XXIII
7	Max McGee, Green Bay vs. Kansas City, I
	John Henderson, Minnesota vs. Kansas City, IV
	Lynn Swann, Pittsburgh vs. Dallas, XIII
	Roger Craig, San Francisco vs. Miami, XIX
	Jerry Rice, San Francisco vs. Denver, XXIV

Most Touchdowns, Game

3	Jerry Rice, San Francisco vs. Denver, XXIV
2	Max McGee, Green Bay vs. Kansas City, I
	Bill Miller, Oakland vs. Green Bay, II
	John Stallworth, Pittsburgh vs. Dallas, XIII
	Cliff Branch, Oakland vs. Philadelphia, XV
	Dan Ross, Cincinnati vs. San Francisco, XVI
	Roger Craig, San Francisco vs. Miami, XIX
	Ricky Sanders, Washington vs. Denver, XXII

Longest Reception

80	Kenny King (from Plunkett), Oakland vs. Philadelphia, XV (TD)

	Ricky Sanders (from Williams), Washington vs. Denver, XXII (TD)
76	Jimmy Cefalo (from Woodley), Miami vs. Washington, XVII (TD)
75	John Mackey (from Unitas), Baltimore vs. Dallas, V (TD)
	John Stallworth (from Bradshaw), Pittsburgh vs. Dallas, XIII (TD)
73	John Stallworth (from Bradshaw), Pittsburgh vs. Los Angeles, XIV (TD)
64	Lynn Swann (from Bradshaw), Pittsburgh vs. Dallas, X (TD)

SCORING

Most Points, Game

18	Roger Craig, San Francisco vs. Miami, XIX (1-r, 2-p)
	Jerry Rice, San Francisco vs. Denver, XXIV (3-p)
15	Don Chandler, Green Bay vs. Oakland, II (3-pat, 4-fg)
14	Ray Wersching, San Francisco vs. Cincinnati, XVI (2-pat, 4-fg)
	Kevin Butler, Chicago vs. New England, XX (5-pat, 3-fg)

Most Points, Career

24	Franco Harris, Pittsburgh, 4 games (4-td)
	Roger Craig, San Francisco, 3 games (4-td)
	Jerry Rice, San Francisco, 2 games (4-td)
22	Ray Wersching, San Francisco, 2 games (7-pat, 5-fg)
20	Don Chandler, Green Bay, 2 games (8-pat, 4-fg)

CAREER PASSING LEADERS
(minimum 40 attempts)

Player, Team	Games	Att.	Comp.	Pct. Comp.	Yds.	Avg. Gain	TD	Pct. TD	Long	Int.	Pct. Int.	Rating Points
Joe Montana, San Francisco	4	122	83	68.0	1142	9.36	11	9.0	44	0	0.0	127.8
Jim Plunkett, Oakland-L.A. Raiders	2	46	29	63.0	433	9.41	4	8.7	80t	0	0.0	122.8
Terry Bradshaw, Pittsburgh	4	84	49	58.3	932	11.10	9	10.7	75t	4	4.8	112.8
Bart Starr, Green Bay	2	47	29	61.7	452	9.62	3	6.4	62t	1	2.1	106.0
Roger Staubach, Dallas	4	98	61	62.2	734	7.49	8	8.2	45t	4	4.1	95.4
Len Dawson, Kansas City	2	44	28	63.6	353	8.02	2	4.5	46t	2	4.5	84.8
Bob Griese, Miami	3	41	26	63.4	295	7.20	1	2.4	28t	2	4.9	72.7
Dan Marino, Miami	1	50	29	58.0	318	6.36	1	2.0	30	2	4.0	66.9
Joe Theismann, Washington	2	58	31	53.4	386	6.66	2	3.4	60	4	6.9	57.1
John Elway, Denver	3	101	46	45.5	669	6.62	2	1.9	56t	6	5.9	49.5
Fran Tarkenton, Minnesota	3	89	46	51.7	489	5.49	1	1.1	30	6	6.7	43.7

CAREER RUSHING LEADERS

Player, Team	Games	Yards	Attempts	Avg.	Long	TD
Franco Harris, Pittsburgh	4	354	101	3.5	25	4
Larry Csonka, Miami	3	297	57	5.2	49	2
John Riggins, Washington	2	230	64	3.6	43t	2
Timmy Smith, Washington	1	204	22	9.3	58t	2
Roger Craig, San Francisco	3	198	52	3.8	18	2
Marcus Allen, L.A. Raiders	1	191	20	9.6	74t	2
Tony Dorsett, Dallas	2	162	31	5.2	29	1
Mark van Eeghen, Oakland	2	148	36	4.1	11	0
Rocky Bleier, Pittsburgh	4	144	44	3.3	18	0
Walt Garrison, Dallas	2	139	26	5.3	19	0

CAREER RECEIVING LEADERS

Player, Team	Games	No.	Yards	Avg.	Long	TD
Roger Craig, San Francisco	3	20	212	10.6	40	2
Jerry Rice, San Francisco	2	18	363	20.2	44	4
Lynn Swann, Pittsburgh	4	16	364	22.8	64t	3
Chuck Foreman, Minnesota	3	15	139	9.3	26	0
Cliff Branch, Oakland-L.A. Raiders	3	14	181	12.9	50	3
Preston Pearson, Balt.-Pitt.-Dall.	5	12	105	8.8	14	0
John Stallworth, Pittsburgh	4	11	268	24.4	75t	3
Dan Ross, Cincinnati	1	11	104	9.5	16	2
Otis Taylor, Kansas City	2	10	138	13.8	46t	1
Dwight Clark, San Francisco	2	10	122	12.2	33	0
Tony Nathan, Miami	1	10	83	8.3	25	0

Super Bowl All-Time Roster

A

Abell, Harry (Bud), LB, ... KC, I
Adams, Julius, DE ... NE, XX
Adderley, Herb, CB ... GB, I, II; DAL, V, VI
Alderman, Grady, T ... MIN, IV, VIII, IX
Aldridge, Lionel, DE ... GB, I, II
Alexander, Charles, RB ... CIN, XVI
Allegre, Raul, K ... NYG, XXI
Allen, Jim, CB ... PITT, IX, X
Allen, Marcus, RB ... L.A. RAI, XVIII
Allen, Nate, CB ... MIN, XI
Allison, Henry, T ... DEN, XII
Alston, Mack, TE ... WAS, VII
Alworth, Lance, WR ... DAL, VI
Alzado, Lyle, DE ... DEN, XII; L.A. RAI, XVIII
Anderson, Anthony, RB ... PIT, XIV
Anderson, Bill, WR ... GB, I
Anderson, Dick, S ... MIA, VI, VII, VIII
Anderson, Donny, RB-P ... GB, I, II
Anderson, Fred, DE ... PIT, XIII
Anderson, Ken, QB ... CIN, XVI
Anderson, Larry, CB ... PIT, XIII, XIV
Anderson, Ottis, RB ... NYG, XXI
Anderson, Scott, C ... MIN, IX
Anderson, Stuart, LB ... WAS, XVIII
Andrews, George, LB ... LA, XIV
Andrews, Tom, C ... CHI, XX
Andrie, George, DE ... DAL, V, VI
Arbanas, Fred, TE ... KC, I, IV
Archer, Dan, T ... OAK, II
Ard, Billy, G ... NYG, XXI
Armstrong, Otis, RB ... DEN, XII
Asher, Bob, C ... DAL, V
Atkinson, Al, LB ... NYJ, III
Atkinson, George, S ... OAK, XI
Atwater, Steve, S ... DEN, XXIV
Audick, Dan, T ... SF, XVI
Austin, Ocie, CB ... BAL, III
Ayers, John, G ... SF, XVI, XIX

B

Babb, Charley, S ... MIA, VII, VIII
Bahr, Chris, K ... OAK, XV; L.A. RAI, XVII
Bahr, Matt, K ... PIT, XIV
Bain, Bill, G ... LA, XIV
Baird, Bill, S ... NYJ, III
Baker, Ralph, LB ... NYJ, III
Baker, Ron, G ... PHI, XV
Ball, Larry, LB ... MIA, VII, VIII
Ball, Sam, T ... BAL, III, V
Ballman, Gary, TE ... MIN, VIII*
Banaszak, John, DE ... PIT, X, XIII, XIV
Banaszak, Pete, RB ... OAK, II, XI
Banks, Carl, LB ... NYG, XXI
Bankston, Warren, TE ... OAK, XI
Bannon, Bruce, LB ... MIA, VIII
Barker, Leo, LB ... CIN, XXIII
Barnes, Benny, CB ... DAL, X, XII, XIII
Barnes, Jeff, LB ... OAK, XV; L.A. RAI, XVIII
Barnes, Rodrigo, LB ... OAK, XI
Barnett, Bill, DE ... MIA, XIX
Barnwell, Malcolm, WR ... L.A. RAI, XVIII
Barton, Harris, T ... SF, XXIII, XXIV
Bass, Don, WR ... CIN, XVI
Bass, Mike, CB ... WAS, VII
Baumhower, Bob, NT ... MIA, XVII, XIX
Bavaro, Mark, TE ... NYG, XXI
Beamon, Autry, S ... MIN, XI
Beasley, John, TE ... MIN, IV
Beasley, Tom, DT ... PIT, XIII, XIV
Beathard, Pete, QB ... KC, I
Bell, Bobby, LB ... KC, I, IV
Bell, Ken, RB-KR ... DEN, XXI, XXII, XXIV
Bell, Theo, WR ... PIT, XIII, XIV
Belser, Caesar, S ... KC, IV
Benjamin, Guy, QB ... SF, XVI*
Bennett, Woody, RB ... MIA, XVII, XIX
Benson, Brad, T ... NYG, XXI
Benson, Charles, DE ... MIA, XIX
Benson, Duane, LB ... OAK, II
Bergey, Bill, LB ... PHI, XV
Berry, Bob, QB ... MIN, VIII*, IX*, XI*
Bethea, Larry, DT ... DAL, XIII
Betters, Doug, DE ... MIA, XVII, XIX
Beverly, Randy, CB ... NYJ, III
Biggs, Verlon, DE ... NYJ, III; WAS, VII
Biletnikoff, Fred, WR ... OAK, II, XI
Billups, Lewis, CB ... CIN, XXIII
Biodrowski, Dennis, G ... KC, I
Bird, Rodger, S ... OAK, II
Birdwell, Dan, DT ... OAK, II
Bishop, Keith, G ... DEN, XXI, XXII, XXIV
Bishop, Richard, NT ... MIA, XVII*
Blackmon, Don, LB ... NE, XX
Blackmore, Richard, CB ... PHI, XV
Blackwell, Alois, RB ... DAL, XIII
Blackwood, Glenn, S ... MIA, XVII, XIX
Blackwood, Lyle, S ... MIA, XVII, XIX
Blados, Brian, T ... CIN, XXIII
Blahak, Joe, CB ... MIN, IX*
Blair, Matt, LB ... MIN, IX, XI
Blanda, George, K ... OAK, II
Bleier, Rocky, RB ... PIT, IX, X, XIII, XIV
Blount, Mel, CB ... PIT, IX, X, XIII, XIV
Board, Dwaine, DE ... SF, XVI, XIX
Boddie, Tony, RB ... DEN, XXII
Bokamper, Kim, DE ... MIA, XVII, XIX
Bonness, Erik, LB ... OAK, XI
Boone, David, DE ... MIN, IX*
Boozer, Emerson, RB ... NYJ, III
Bortz, Mark, G ... CHI, XX
Bostic, Jeff, C ... WAS, XVII, XVIII, XXII
Bowles, Todd, S ... WAS, XXII
Bowman, Jim, S ... NE, XX
Bowman, Ken, C ... GB, I, II
Bowser, Charles, LB ... MIA, XVII, XIX
Bowyer, Walter, DE ... DEN, XXII
Boyd, Bob, CB ... BAL, III
Braase, Ordell, DE ... BAL, III
Bradley, Ed, LB ... PIT, IX, X
Bradshaw, Morris, WR ... OAK, XI, XV
Bradshaw, Terry, QB ... PIT, IX, X, XIII, XIV
Brady, Ed, LB ... CIN, XXIII
Bragg, Mike, P ... WAS, VII
Branch, Cliff, WR ... OAK, XI, XV; L.A. RAI, XVIII
Branch, Reggie, RB ... WAS, XXII
Bratkowski, Zeke, QB ... GB, I, II
Bratton, Melvin, RB ... DEN, XXIV
Braxton, Tyrone, S-CB ... DEN, XXII, XXIV
Breech, Jim, K ... CIN, XVI, XXIII
Breeden, Louis, CB ... CIN, XVI
Breunig, Bob, LB ... DAL, X, XII, XIII
Brinson, Larry, RB ... DAL, XII, XIII
Briscoe, Marlin, WR ... MIA, VII, VIII
Brock, Pete, C ... NE, XX
Brooks, Chet, S ... SF, XXIV
Brooks, James, RB ... CIN, XXIII
Brooks, Larry, DT ... LA, XIV
Brooks, Michael, LB ... DEN, XXII, XXIV
Brooks, Perry, DT ... WAS, XVII, XVIII
Brophy, Jay, LB ... MIA, XIX
Brown, Aaron, DE ... KC, I, IV
Brown, Bill, RB ... MIN, IV, VIII, IX
Brown, Bob, DE ... GB, I, II
Brown, Bud, S ... MIA, XIX
Brown, Charlie, WR ... WAS, XVII, XVIII
Brown, Dave, S ... PIT, X
Brown, Eddie, S ... LA, XIV
Brown, Eddie L., WR ... CIN, XXIII
Brown, Guy, LB ... DAL, XII, XIII
Brown, Larry, TE-T ... PIT, IX, X, XIII, XIV
Brown, Larry, RB ... WAS, VII
Brown, Mark, LB ... MIA, XIX
Brown, Terry, S ... MIN, VIII, IX
Brown, Thomas, DE ... PHI, XV
Brown, Tim, RB ... BAL, III
Brown, Tom, S ... GB, I, II
Brown, Willie, CB ... OAK, II, XI
Browner, Ross, DE ... CIN, XVI
Browning, Dave, DE ... OAK, XV
Brudzinski, Bob, LB ... LA, XIV; MIA, XVII, XIX
Brundige, Bill, DT ... WAS, VII
Brunet, Bob, RB ... WAS, VII
Bryan, Bill, C ... DEN, XXI
Bryant, Bobby, CB ... MIN, VIII, XI
Bryant, Cullen, RB ... LA, XIV
Bryant, Kelvin, RB ... WAS, XXII
Buchanan, Buck, DT ... KC, I, IV
Buck, Jason, DE ... CIN, XXIII
Budde, Ed, G ... KC, I, IV
Budness, Bill, G ... OAK, II
Buehler, George, G ... OAK, XI
Buetow, Bart, DT ... MIN, XI*
Buford, Maury, P ... CHI, XX
Bujnoch, Glenn, G ... CIN, XVI*
Bulaich, Norm, RB ... BAL, V
Bunting, John, LB ... PHI, XV
Bunz, Dan, LB ... SF, XVI, XIX
Buoniconti, Nick, LB ... MIA, VI, VII, VIII
Burford, Chris, WR ... KC, I
Burley, Gary, DE ... CIN, XVI
Burman, George, C ... WAS, VII
Burt, Jim, NT ... NYG, XXI; SF, XXIV
Bush, Blair, C ... CIN, XVI
Bussey, Barney, S ... CIN, XXIII
Butler, Kevin, K ... CHI, XX
Butz, Dave, DT ... WAS, XVII, XVIII, XXII
Byrd, Darryl, LB ... L.A. RAI, XVIII

C

Cabral, Brian, LB ... CHI, XX
Caffey, Lee Roy, LB ... GB, I, II
Caldwell, Ravin, LB ... WAS, XXII
Caldwell, Tony, LB ... L.A. RAI, XVIII
Camarillo, Rich, P ... NE, XX
Cameron, Glenn, LB ... CIN, XVI
Campbell, Joe, DE ... OAK, XV
Campfield, Billy, RB ... PHI, XV
Cannon, Billy, TE ... OAK, II
Capone, Warren, LB ... DAL, X
Capp, Dick, WR ... GB, II
Carano, Glenn, QB ... DAL, XIII*
Carmichael, Harold, WR ... PHI, XV
Carolan, Reg, TE ... KC, I
Carpenter, Brian, CB ... WAS, XVIII
Carreker, Alphonso, DE ... DEN, XXIV
Carrington, Darren, CB ... DEN, XXIV
Carson, Harry, LB ... NYG, XXI
Carter, Joe, RB ... MIA, XIX
Carter, Michael, NT ... SF, XIX, XXIII, XXIV
Carter, Rubin, DT ... DEN, XII
Carthon, Maurice, RB ... NYG, XXI
Casper, Dave, TE ... OAK, XI
Caster, Rich, TE ... WAS, XVII*
Castille, Jeremiah, S ... DEN, XXII
Cavanaugh, Matt, QB ... SF, XIX*
Cefalo, Jimmy, WR ... MIA, XVII, XIX
Celotto, Mario, LB ... OAK, XV
Chandler, Bob, WR ... OAK, XV
Chandler, Don, K ... GB, I, II
Charles, Mike, DT ... MIA, XIX
Chavous, Barney, DE ... DEN, XII
Chesley, Al, LB ... PHI, XV
Chester, Raymond, TE ... OAK, XV
Choma, John, C-G ... SF, XVI
Christensen, Todd, RB-TE ... OAK, XV; L.A. RAI, XVIII
Christy, Earl, CB ... NYJ, III
Clabo, Neil, P ... MIN, XI
Clack, Jim, G ... PIT, IX, X
Clark, Dwight, WR ... SF, XVI, XIX
Clark, Gary, WR ... WAS, XXII
Clark, Ken, P ... LA, XIV
Clark, Kevin, CB ... DEN, XXII
Clark, Mario, CB ... SF, XIX*
Clark, Mike, K ... DAL, V, VI
Clark, Steve, T ... MIA, XVII*, XIX
Clarke, Ken, NT ... PHI, XV
Clayborn, Raymond, CB ... NE, XX
Clayton, Mark, WR ... MIA, XIX
Coan, Bert, RB ... KC, I
Cofer, Mike, K ... SF, XXIII, XXIV
Coffey, Ken, S ... WAS, XVII
Cole, Larry, DT ... DAL, V, VI, X, XII, XIII
Cole, Robin, LB ... PIT, XIII, XIV
Cole, Terry, RB ... BAL, III; MIA, VI
Coleman, Monte, LB ... WAS, XVII, XVIII, XXII
Collie, Bruce, G ... SF, XXIII, XXIV
Collier, Mike, RB ... PIT, X
Collins, Mark, CB ... NYG, XXI
Collins, Tony, RB ... NE, XX
Collinsworth, Cris, WR ... CIN, XVI, XXIII
Colorito, Tony, NT ... DEN, XXI
Colquitt, Craig, P ... PIT, XIII, XIV
Colzie, Neal, S-KR ... OAK, XI
Comeaux, Darren, LB ... DEN, XXI
Conn, Richard, S ... PIT, IX
Conners, Dan, LB ... OAK, II
Cooper, Earl, RB-TE ... SF, XVI, XIX
Cooper, Jim, G-T ... DAL, XII, XIII
Cooper, Mark, G ... DEN, XXI
Corey, Walt, LB ... KC, I
Cornish, Frank, DT ... MIA, VI
Corral, Frank, K ... LA, XIV
Corrington, Kip, S ... DEN, XXIV
Courson, Steve, G ... PIT, XIII, XIV
Covert, Jim, T ... CHI, XX
Cox, Fred, K ... MIN, IV, VIII, IX, XI
Cox, Greg, S ... SF, XXIII
Cox, Steve, P ... WAS, XXII
Craig, Roger, RB ... SF, XIX, XXIII, XXIV
Craig, Steve, TE ... MIN, IX, XI
Crane, Paul, LB ... NYJ, III
Creswell, Smiley, DE ... NE, XX
Cromwell, Nolan, S ... LA, XIV
Cronan, Pete, LB ... WAS, XVII, XVIII
Cross, Randy, G-C ... SF, XVI, XIX, XXIII
Crusan, Doug, T ... MIA, VI, VII, VIII
Crutcher, Tommy, LB ... GB, I, II
Csonka, Larry, RB ... MIA, VI, VII, VIII
Culp, Curley, DT ... KC, IV
Cunningham, Bennie, TE ... PIT, XIII*, XIV
Cuozzo, Gary, P ... MIN, IV
Curry, Bill, C ... GB, I; BAL, III, V
Curtis, Isaac, WR ... CIN, XVI
Curtis, Mike, LB ... BAL, III, V
Curtis, Scott, LB ... DEN, XXIV

D

Dalby, Dave, C ... OAK, XI, XV; L.A. RAI, XVIII
Dale, Carroll, WR ... GB, I, II; MIN, VIII
D'Amato, Mike, S ... NYJ, III
Daney, George, G ... KC, IV
Davidson, Ben, DE ... OAK, II
Davis, Brian, CB ... WAS, XXII
Davis, Bruce, T ... OAK, XV; L.A. RAI XVIII
Davis, Charlie, DT ... PIT, IX

Reynolds, Ed, LB .... NE, XX
Reynolds, Jack, LB .... LA, XIV; SF, XVI, XIX
Rhone, Earnest, LB .... MIA, XVII, XIX
Rice, Andy, DT .... KC, I
Rice, Floyd, LB .... OAK, XI
Rice, Jerry, WR .... SF, XXIII, XXIV
Rich, Randy, DB .... DEN, XII
Richards, Golden, WR .... DAL, X, XII
Richards, Jim, S .... NYJ, III
Richardson, Gloster, WR .... KC, IV; DAL, VI*
Richardson, Jeff, G .... NYJ, III
Richardson, John, DT .... MIA, VI*
Richardson, Mike, CB .... CHI, XX
Richardson, Willie, WR .... BAL, III
Riggins, John, RB .... WAS, XVII, XVIII
Riggs, Jim, TE .... CIN, XXIII
Riley, Jim, DE .... MIA, VI
Riley, Ken, CB .... CIN, XVI
Riley, Steve, T .... MIN, IX*, XI
Ring, Bill, RB .... SF, XVI, XIX
Rivera, Ron, LB .... CHI, XX
Rizzo, Joe, LB .... DEN, XII
Robbins, Randy, S .... DEN, XXI, XXII, XXIV
Roberts, Larry, DE .... SF, XXIII, XXIV
Roberts, William, T .... NYG, XXI
Robinson, Dave, LB .... GB, I, II
Robinson, Jerry, LB .... PHI, XV
Robinson, Johnny D., NT .... L.A. RAI, XVIII
Robinson, Johnny N., S .... KC, I, IV
Robinson, Stacy, WR .... NYG, XXI
Roby, Reggie, P .... MIA, XIX
Rochester, Paul, DT .... NYJ, III
Rock, Walter, T .... WAS, VII
Rodgers, Del, RB .... SF, XXIII
Rogers, George, RB .... WAS, XXII
Romanowski, Bill, LB .... SF, XXIII, XXIV
Rose, Joe, TE .... MIA, XVII, XIX
Rourke, Jim, G-T .... CIN, XXIII
Rouson, Lee, RB .... NYJ, XXI
Rowe, Dave, DT .... OAK, XI
Rowser, John, CB .... GB, II
Rucker, Reggie, WR .... DAL, V
Runager, Max, P .... PHI, XV; SF, XIX
Russell, Andy, LB .... PIT, IX, X
Rutledge, Jeff, QB .... LA, XIV*; NYG, XXI
Ryan, Jim, LB .... DEN, XXI, XXII
Ryczek, Dan, C .... LA, XIV

S

Sally, Jerome, NT .... NYG, XXI
Sample, Johnny, CB .... NYJ, III
Sampson, Clint, WR .... DEN, XXI
Sanders, Ricky, WR .... WAS, XXII
Sanders, Thomas, RB .... CHI, XX
Sapolu, Jesse, G-C .... SF, XXIII, XXIV
Sauer, George, WR .... NYJ, III
Saul, Rich, C .... LA, XIV
Schmitt, John, C .... NYJ, III
Schoenke, Ray, G .... WAS, VII*
Schonert, Turk, QB .... CIN, XVI*, XXIII
Schroeder, Jay, QB .... WAS, XXII
Schuh, Harry, T .... OAK, II
Schultz, John, WR .... DEN, XII
Sciarra, John, S .... PHI, XV
Scott, Herbert, G .... DAL, X, XII, XIII
Scott, Jake, S .... MIA, VI, VII, VIII
Seiple, Larry, P .... MIA, VI, VII, VIII
Sellers, Goldie, CB .... KC, IV
Sellers, Ron, WR .... MIA, VIII*
Septien, Rafael, K .... DAL, XIII
Severson, Jeff, S .... WAS, VII
Sewell, Steve, RB .... DEN, XXI, XXII, XXIV
Shanklin, Ron, WR .... PIT, IX
Sharockman, Ed, CB .... MIN, IV
Shell, Art, T .... OAK, XI, XV
Shell, Donnie, S .... PIT, IX, X, XIII, XIV
Shell, Todd, LB .... SF, XIX
Sherman, Rod, WR .... OAK, II*
Sherrard, Mike, WR .... SF, XXIV
Shields, Billy, T .... SF, XIX
Shinnick, Don, LB .... BAL, III
Shipp, Jackie, LB .... MIA, XIX
Shiver, Sanders, LB .... MIA, XIX
Shull, Steve, LB .... MIA, XVII
Shumann, Mike, WR .... SF, XVI
Siani, Mike, WR .... OAK, XI
Siemon, Jeff, LB .... MIN, VIII, IX, XI
Simmons, John, CB .... CIN, XVI
Simmons, Roy, G .... WAS, XVIII
Simms, Phil, QB .... NYG, XXI
Singletary, Mike, LB .... CHI, XX
Sisemore, Jerry, T .... PHI, XV
Sistrunk, Manuel, DT .... WAS, VII
Sistrunk, Otis, DT .... OAK, XI
Skoronski, Bob, T .... GB, I, II
Skow, Jim, DE .... CIN, XXIII
Slater, Jackie, T .... LA, XIV
Slater, Mark, C .... PHI, XV
Sligh, Richard, DT .... OAK, II
Small, Gerald, CB .... MIA, XVII
Smith, Billy Ray, DT .... BAL, III, V
Smith, Charles (Bubba), DE .... BAL, III, V
Smith, Charlie, WR .... PHI, XV
Smith, Daryl, CB .... CIN, XXIII
Smith, Dave, G-T .... CIN, XXIII
Smith, Dennis, S .... DEN, XXI, XXII, XXIV
Smith, Fletcher, DB .... KC, I
Smith, Jackie, TE .... DAL, XIII
Smith, Jerry, TE .... WAS, VII
Smith, Jim, WR .... PIT, XIII, XIV
Smith, Monte, G .... DEN, XXIV
Smith, Paul, DT .... DEN, XII
Smith, Ron, WR .... LA, XIV
Smith, Steve, DE .... MIN, IV
Smith, Timmy, RB .... WAS, XXII
Smith, Tody, DE .... DAL, VI
Smolinski, Mark, TE .... NYJ, III
Snell, Matt, RB .... NYJ, III
Solomon, Freddie, WR .... SF, XVI, XIX
Sowell, Robert, CB .... MIA, XIX
Spagnola, John, TE .... PHI, XV
Squirek, Jack, LB .... L.A. RAI, XVIII
Stabler, Ken, QB .... OAK, XI
Stalls, Dave, DE-T .... DAL, XII, XIII; L.A. RAI, XVIII
Stallworth, John, WR .... PIT, IX, X, XIII, XIV
Stanfill, Bill, DE .... MIA, VI, VII, VIII
Starke, George, T .... WAS, XVII, XVIII
Starr, Bart, QB .... GB, I, II
Starring, Stephen, WR .... NE, XX
Staubach, Roger, QB .... DAL, V*, VI, X, XII, XIII
St. Clair, Mike, DE .... CIN, XVI
Steele, Robert, WR .... DAL, XIII
Stein, Bob, LB .... KC, IV
Stenerud, Jan, K .... KC, IV
Stephenson, Dwight, C .... MIA, XVII, XIX
Stincic, Tom, LB .... DAL, V, VI
Stoudt, Cliff, QB .... PIT, XIII*, XIV*
Stover, Jeff, NT .... SF, XIX, XXIII
Stover, Stewart, LB .... KC, I
Stowe, Otto, WR .... MIA, VI, VII*
Strock, Don, QB .... MIA, XVII, XIX
Stubbs, Danny, DE .... SF, XXIII, XXIV
Stuckey, Henry, CB .... MIA, VII, VIII
Stuckey, Jim, DE .... SF, XVI, XIX
Studdard, Dave, T .... DEN, XXI, XXII
Stukes, Charles, CB .... BAL, III, V
Suhey, Matt, RB .... CHI, XX
Sullivan, Dan, G-T .... BAL, III, V
Sully, Ivory, CB .... LA, XIV
Sunde, Milt, G .... MIA, IV, IX
Sutherland, Doug, DT .... MIN, VIII, IX, XI
Svihus, Bob, T .... OAK, II
Swann, Lynn, WR .... PIT, IX, X, XIII, XIV
Swenson, Bob, LB .... DEN, XII
Swift, Doug, LB .... MIA, VI, VII, VIII
Sydney, Harry, RB .... SF, XXIII, XXIV
Sylvester, Steve, G .... OAK, XI, XV; L.A. RAI, XVIII
Szymanski, Dick, C .... BAL, III

T

Talamini, Bob, G .... NYJ, III
Talbert, Diron, DT .... WAS, VII
Tarkenton, Fran, QB .... MIN, VIII, IX, XI
Tatum, Jack, S .... OAK, XI
Tatupu, Mosi, RB .... NE, XX
Tausch, Terry, G .... SF, XXIV
Taylor, Charley, WR .... WAS, VII
Taylor, Jim, RB .... GB, I
Taylor, John, WR .... SF, XXIII, XXIV
Taylor, Ken, CB .... CHI, XX
Taylor, Lawrence, LB .... NYG, XXI
Taylor, Otis, WR .... KC, I, IV
Taylor, Roosevelt, S .... WAS, VII
Thayer, Tom, G .... CHI, XX
Theismann, Joe, QB .... WAS, XVII, XVIII
Thielemann, R.C., G .... WAS, XXII
Thomas, Ben, CE .... NE, XX
Thomas, Calvin, RB .... CHI, XX
Thomas, Chuck, C .... XV, XXIII, XXIV
Thomas, Duane, RB .... DAL, V, VI
Thomas, Emmitt, CB .... KC, I, IV
Thomas, Eric, CB .... CIN, XXIII
Thomas, Gene, RB .... KC, I
Thomas, Isaac, CB .... DAL, VI
Thomas, James (J.T.), CB .... PIT, IX, X, XIV
Thomas, Lynn, CB .... SF, XVI
Thomas, Pat, CB .... LA, XIV
Thomas, Skip, CB .... OAK, XI
Thompson, Bill, S .... DEN, XII
Thompson, Jack, QB .... CIN, XVI*
Thompson, Steve, DE .... NYJ, III
Thornton, Sidney, RB .... PIT, XIII, XIV
Thrift, Cliff, LB .... CHI, XX
Thurman, Dennis, CB .... DAL, XIII
Thurston, Fred (Fuzzy), G .... GB, I, II
Tillman, Rusty, LB .... WAS, VII
Tillman, Spencer, RB .... SF, XXIV
Tingelhoff, Mick, C .... MIN, IV, VII, IX, XI
Tippett, Andre, LB .... NE, XX
Todd, Larry, RB .... OAK, II
Toews, Jeff, G .... MIA, XVII, XIX
Toews, Loren, LB .... PIT, IX, X, XIII, XIV
Tomczak, Mike, QB .... CHI, XX
Toomay, Pat, DE .... DAL, V, VI
Torrey, Bob, RB .... PHI, XV*
Townsend, Andre, DE-NT .... DEN, XXI, XXII, XXIV
Townsend, Greg, DE .... L.A. RAI, XVIII
Treadwell, David, K .... DEN, XXIV
Trosch, Gene, DE .... KC, IV
Truax, Billy, TE .... DAL, VI
Tuiasosopo, Manu, NT .... SF, XIX
Turk, Godwin, LB .... DEN, XII
Turner, Bake, WR .... NYJ, III
Turner, Jim, K .... NYJ, III; DEN, XII
Turner, Keena, LB .... SF, XVI, XIX, XXIII, XXIV
Twilley, Howard, WR .... MIA, VI, VII, VIII
Tyler, Wendell, RB .... LA, XIV; SF, XIX
Tyrer, Jim, LT .... KC, I, IV

U

Unitas, Johnny, QB .... BAL, III, V
Upchurch, Rick, WR .... DEN, XII
Upshaw, Gene, G .... OAK, II, XI, XV

V

Vactor, Ted, CB .... WAS, VII
Valentine, Zack, LB .... PIT, XIV
Vandersea, Phil, LB .... GB, I
Van Eeghen, Mark, RB .... OAK, XI, XV
Van Horne, Keith, T .... CHI, XX
Vaughn, Clarence, CB .... WAS, XXII
Vella, John, T .... OAK, XI
Vellone, Jim, G .... MIN, IV
Veris, Garin, DE .... NE, XX
Verser, David, WR .... CIN, XVI
Vigorito, Tommy, RB .... MIA, XVII
Villapiano, Phil, LB .... OAK, XI
Vogel, Bob, T .... BAL, III, V
Voigt, Stu, TE .... MIN, VIII, IX, XI
Volk, Rick, S .... BAL, III, V
von Schamann, Uwe, K .... MIA, XVII, XIX

W

Waddy, Billy, WR .... LA, XIV
Waechter, Henry, DT .... CHI, XX
Wagner, Mike, S .... PIT, IX, X, XIII
Walden, Bobby, P .... PIT, IX, X
Walker, Fulton, CB .... MIA, XVII, XIX
Walker, Rick, TE .... WAS, XVII, XVIII
Wallace, Jackie, CB .... MIN, IX; LA, XIV
Wallace, Steve, T .... SF, XXIII, XXIV
Walls, Wesley, TE .... SF, XXIV
Walter, Michael, LB .... SF, XIX, XXIII, XXIV
Walters, Stan, T .... PHI, XV
Walton, Alvin, S .... WAS, XXII
Walton, Bruce, T .... DAL, X*
Walton, Sam, T .... NYJ, III
Ward, Jim, QB .... BAL, III*
Warfield, Paul, WR .... MIA, VI, VII, VIII
Warren, Don, TE .... WAS, XVII, XVIII, XXII
Warwick, Lonnie, LB .... MIN, IV
Washington, Anthony, CB .... WAS, XVIII
Washington, Gene, WR .... MIN, IV
Washington, Joe, RB .... WAS, XVII*, XVIII
Washington, Mark, CB .... DAL, V, X, XII, XIII*
Waters, Charlie, S .... DAL, V, VI, X, XII, XIII
Watson, Steve, WR .... DEN, XXI, XXII
Watts, Ted, CB .... L.A. RAI, XVIII
Weathers, Robert, RB .... NE, XX
Weatherwax, Jim, DT .... GB, I, II
Webster, Mike, C .... PIT, IX, X, XIII, XIV
Weese, Norris, QB .... DEN, XII
Welch, Claxton, RB .... DAL, V, VI
Welch, Herb, S .... NYG, XXI
Wells, Warren, WR .... OAK, II
Wersching, Ray, K .... SF, XVI, XIX
West, Charlie, S .... MIN, IV, VIII
Westbrooks, Greg, LB .... LA, XIV
White, Danny, QB-P .... DAL, XII, XIII
White, Dwight, DE .... PIT, IX, X, XIII, XIV
White, Ed, G .... MIN, IV, VIII, IX, XI
White, James, DT .... MIN, XI
White, Jeris, CB .... WAS, XVII
White, Leon, LB .... CIN, XXIII
White, Randy, DT-LB .... DAL, X, XII, XIII
White, Sammy, WR .... MIN, XI
Whitley, Wilson, NT .... CIN, XVI
Whittington, Arthur, RB .... OAK, XV
Widby, Ron, P .... DAL, V, VI
Widell, Dave, G .... DEN, XXIV
Wilbur, John, G .... WAS, VII
Wilburn, Barry, CB .... WAS, XXII
Wilcots, Solomon, S .... CIN, XXIII
Wilkes, Reggie, LB .... PHI, XV
Wilkinson, Jerry, DE .... LA, XIV
Willhite, Gerald, RB .... DEN, XXI
Williams, Dokie, WR .... L.A. RAI, XVIII
Williams, Doug, QB .... WAS, XXII
Williams, Ed, LB .... NE, XX
Williams, Greg, S .... WAS, XVII, XVIII
Williams, Howie, S .... OAK, II
Williams, Jamie, TE .... SF, XXIV
Williams, Joe, RB .... DAL, VI
Williams, John, G .... BAL, III, V
Williams, Lester, NT .... NE, XX
Williams, Mike, TE .... WAS, XVIII
Williams, Perry, CB .... NYG, XXI
Williams, Reggie, LB .... CIN, XVI, XXIII
Williams, Sidney, LB .... BAL, III
Williams, Travis, RB .... GB, II
Williamson, Carlton, S .... SF, XVI, XIX
Williamson, Fred, CB .... KC, I
Williamson, John, LB .... OAK, II
Willis, Chester, RB .... L.A. RAI, XVIII
Willis, Leonard, WR .... MIN, XI
Wilson, Ben, RB .... GB, II
Wilson, Brenard, S .... PHI, XV
Wilson, Jerrel, P .... KC, I, IV
Wilson, Marc, QB .... OAK, XV*; L.A. RAI, XVIII
Wilson, Mike R., WR .... SF, XVI, XIX, XXIII, XXIV
Wilson, Mike W., T .... CIN, XVI
Wilson, Otis, LB .... CHI, XX
Wilson, Steve, CB .... DEN, XXI, XXII
Winder, Sammy, RB .... DEN, XXI, XXII, XXIV
Winston, Dennis, LB .... PIT, XIII, XIV
Winston, Roy, LB .... MIN, IV, VIII, IX, XI
Wolf, Jim, DE .... PIT, IX*
Wonsley, Otis, RB .... WAS, XVII, XVIII
Wood, Willie, S .... GB, I, II
Woodard, Ken, LB .... DEN, XXI
Woodberry, Dennis, CB .... WAS, XXII
Woodley, David, QB .... MIA, XVII
Woodruff, Dwayne, CB .... PIT, XIV
Woods, Ickey, RB .... CIN, XXIII
Woolsey, Rolly, CB .... DAL, X
Wooten, Ron, G .... NE, XX
Wright, Eric, CB .... SF, XVI, XIX, XXIII, XXIV
Wright, George, DT .... BAL, V*
Wright, Jeff, S .... MIN, VIII, IX, XI
Wright, Louis, CB .... DEN, XII, XXI
Wright, Nate, CB .... MIN, VIII, IX, XI
Wright, Rayfield, T .... DAL, V, VI, X, XII, XIII
Wright, Steve, T .... GB, I, II*
Wrightman, Tim, TE .... CHI, XX
Wyche, Sam, QB .... WAS, VII

Y

Yarber, Eric, WR .... WAS, XXII
Yary, Ron, T .... MIN, IV, VIII, IX, XI
Yepremian, Garo, K .... MIA, VI, VII, VIII
Young, Charle, TE .... LA, XIV; SF, XVI
Young, Charles L., RB .... DAL, X
Young, Michael, WR .... DEN, XXIV
Young, Roynell, CB .... PHI, XV
Young, Steve, QB .... SF, XXIII*, XXIV
Youngblood, Jack, DE .... LA, XIV
Youngblood, Jim, LB .... LA, XIV

Z

Zander, Carl, LB .... CIN, XXIII
Zaunbrecher, Godfrey, C .... MIN, VIII*

*Did not play

Credits

The Game Stories

Ray Didinger wrote the stories for Super Bowls XV, XVI, XIX, and XXIV; *Mickey Herskowitz* wrote I, II, VIII, and XXIII; *Kevin Lamb* wrote XI, XVIII, XX, and XXI; *Bill McGrane* wrote V, VI, XII, and XVII; *Phil Musick* wrote IX, X, XIII, and XIV; *Shelby Strother* wrote III, IV, VII, and XXII.

The Theme Illustrations

Super Bowl I—Sculpture by *Jean Isaacson*; Super Bowl II—Design by *Jean Isaacson*, wood carving by *Ron Wolin*; Super Bowl III—Illustration by *Merv Corning*; Super Bowl IV—By *Don Weller*; Super Bowl V—Sculpture by *Howard Rogers*; Super Bowl VI—Designed by *Mike Gaines*; Super Bowl VII—Constructed by *Don Weller*, photographed by *Stan Caplan*; Super Bowl VIII—By *Peter Palombi*; Super Bowl IX—By *Bart Forbes*; Super Bowl X—Designed by *Amy Yutani*, photographed by *Stan Caplan*; Super Bowl XI—By *Peter Palombi*; Super Bowl XII—By *Donald Moss*; Super Bowl XIII—By *Peter Lloyd*; Super Bowl XIV—By *Chuck Ren*; Super Bowl XV—Designed by *David Boss*, photographed by *Stan Caplan*; Super Bowl XVI—By *Andy Zito*; Super Bowl XVII—By *Charles White, III*; Super Bowl XVIII—By *James Endicott*; Super Bowl XIX—Photographed by *Baron Wolman*; Super Bowl XX—Designed by *Glen Iwasaki*, illustration by *Chris Hopkins*, logo by *Tom Nikosey*; Super Bowl XXI—By *Jayme Odgers* and *Chris Hopkins*; Super Bowl XXII—By *Lisa French*; Super Bowl XXIII—By *Chris Hopkins*; Super Bowl XXIV—By *Gary Kelley*; Super Bowl XXV—By *Merv Corning*.

The Foldout Illustrations

Super Bowl I—*Bryan Robley*; Super Bowl II—*R. Kenton Nelson*; Super Bowl III—*Bart Forbes;* Super Bowl IV—*Don Weller*; Super Bowl V—*Marv Rubin*; Super Bowl VI—*Chris Hopkins*; Super Bowl VII—*Allen Garns*; Super Bowl VIII—*Dick Oden*; Super Bowl IX—*Dick Lubey*; Super Bowl X—*Wayne Watford*; Super Bowl XI—*George Gaadt*; Super Bowl XII—*F. Bruce Dean*; Super Bowl XIII—*Rick Farrell*; Super Bowl XIV—*Chuck Ren*; Super Bowl XV—*Jim Auckland*; Super Bowl XVI—*Paul Kratter*; Super Bowl XVII—*Kirk Caldwell*; Super Bowl XVIII—*Rick Brown*; Super Bowl XIX—*Cliff Spohn*; Super Bowl XX—*Gary Kelley*; Super Bowl XXI—*Tom Nikosey*; Super Bowl XXII—*George Bartell*; Super Bowl XXIII—*Merv Corning*; Super Bowl XIV—*Greg Spalenka*.

The Photographs

Legend: T-top, M-middle, B-bottom, TL-top left, TM-top middle, TR-top right, ML-middle left, MR-middle right, BL-bottom left, BR-bottom right.

The Allens—161, 163T, 202B, 205T, 243T, 284B. *Tom Alexander*—312T. *John Biever*—106TR, 118B, 145, 175TR, 214TR, 215T-B, 229T-B, 230TR, 275T, 288T, 314B, 316B. *Vernon Biever*—14, 22T, 25T, 31, 62, 76, 88T, 175TL, 191T, 200MR, 201, 256B, 261BL-BR. *David Boss*—25B, 46T, 47, 48B, 50T, 61T-B, 63B, 64T-B, 88B, 116T, 117B, 329T, 368TR, 370. *Rob Brown*—37, 298BR, 303T, 345, 356. *Bill Cummings*—327, 328T. *Scott Cunningham*—342. *Gin Ellis*—343MR. *Malcolm Emmons*—23, 24, 60, 74B, 78T-B, 90T, 116B, 119T-B, 120T-B, 131, 147TR-BL, 159B, 163B, 177, 203TL, 204B, 205B, 216B, 228TL, 258T. *Nate Fine*—27, 186T, 187, 189T, 217T, 217TR, 218TR, 243B, 244T, 245B. *James F. Flores*—20, 49T, 51T, 132B, 133B. *Richard Gentile*—231T, 233B. *George Gojkovich*—302B. *Rod Hanna*—22B, 26, 149. *John Iacono for Sports Illustrated*—176. *Walter Iooss, Jr.*—107 (2nd in sequence). *Fred Kaplan*—21, 102T, 130B, 134B. *Ross Lewis*—219B, 242T, 246T. *Long Photography*—134, 135TL, 341. *Amos Love*—29TR, 233T, 247TR. *Richard Mackson*—19, 32B, 33B, 257BL, 270B, 272T, 326, 358, 368B. *Tak Makita*—146. *John McDonough*—274B, 299T, 301B. *Al Messerschmidt*—35B, 217B, 218B, 219T, 256T, 259, 270T, 273, 275B, 284T, 289T, 298TL, 300T, 316T, 317TR, 330MR, 331T-B, 340, 344T, 368TL, 372, 373M-B. *Peter Read Miller*—33T, 200TL-BL, 202T, 203TR, 204T, 272B, 274T, 275M, 285, 287T-B, 289B. *NFL Photos*—79T, 118T, 186B, 216T. *Darryl Norenberg*—38, 48T, 92B, 105B, 130T, 132T, 230BL. *Jack O'Grady*—103M, 106TL. *Dick Raphael*—74T, 75, 92T, 93B, 102B, 103T, 106B, 107 (1st and 3rd in sequence), 135TR, 159, 160B, 162, 172T, 173T, 174B, 260, 300B, 302TL, 344B. *Russ Reed*—51B. *Chuck Ren*—10 (illustration). *Fred Roe*—50B, 105T. *Bob Rosato*—357T. *George Rose*—303B, 371. *Manny Rubio*—28-29L, 30T, 34T, 36T, 91, 104B, 107 (4th in sequence), 214TL, 232BL-BR, 257T-BR, 261TL, 314T, 317BL-BR, 329B; 357B. *Alan Schwartz*—34B. *Carl Skalak, Jr.*—148B. *Paul Spinelli*—315TL-TR. *Paul Spinelli/NFLP*—35T. *Hitoshi Suzumuri*—158T-B. *Tony Tomsic*—32TL, 46B, 49B, 63T, 65, 79B, 89, 90B, 93T, 121T-B, 133T, 135B, 148T, 160T, 172-73B, 174T, 175B, 188, 189B, 190T-B, 191B, 214B, 218TL, 261TR, 286, 299B, 302TR, 312B, 369. *Corky Trewin*—301T, 317TL, 328B. *Jim Turner*—368TM. *Herb Weitman*—144T, 313, 315B, 330TL, 343TL, 355. *Lou Witt*—144B. *Baron Wolman*—354T. *Michael Zagaris*—36B, 228BR, 231B, 232T, 244B, 247BL, 258B, 271T-B, 288B, 354B, 359. *John Zimmerman*—30B.